THE MATERIAL IMAGE

Cultural Memory
in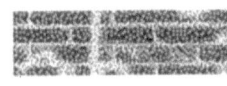
the
Present

Mieke Bal and Hent de Vries, Editors

THE MATERIAL IMAGE
Art and the Real in Film

Brigitte Peucker

STANFORD UNIVERSITY PRESS

STANFORD, CALIFORNIA

2007

Stanford University Press
Stanford, California

© 2007 by the Board of Trustees of the Leland Stanford Junior University.
All rights reserved.

No part of this book may be reproduced or transmitted in any form or by any means, electronic or mechanical, including photocopying and recording, or in any information storage or retrieval system without the prior written permission of Stanford University Press.

The following essays have been republished here in whole or part, revised or unrevised:

For Chapter One: "The Moment of Portraiture: Scorsese Reads Wharton," *Beyond Fidelity: The Dialogics of Adaptation*, ed. Robert Stam (London: Blackwell, September 2004), 358–67. (Other versions of this material have appeared in *Edith Wharton's The Age of Innocence: The Norton Critical Edition*, ed. Candace Waid (New York: W. W. Norton, 2002), 504–14, and in *The Edith Wharton Review*, XII:1 (Fall 1996), 19–22.

For Chapter Two: "Filmic Tableau Vivant: Vermeer, Intermediality, and the Real," *Rites of Realism*, ed. Ivone Margulies (Durham, NC: Duke University Press, 2003), 314–24.

For Chapter Three: "The Fascist Choreography: Riefenstahl's Tableaux, *Modernism/Modernity* 11:2 (April 2004), 279–97.

For Chapter Four: "The Cut of Representation: Painting and Sculpture in Hitchcock," *Hitchcock: Centennial Essays*, ed. Richard Allen and S. Ishii-Gonzales (London: BFI, 1999), 141–158.

For Chapter Six: "Kubrick and Kafka: The Corporeal Uncanny," *Modernism/Modernity* 8:4 (Nov. 2001), 663–74.

For Chapter Seven: "The Castrato's Voices: Fassbinder's *Year of Thirteen Moons*," *Sound Matters: Essays on the Acoustics of German Culture* eds. Nora Alter and Lutz Koepnick (Providence: Berghahn Press, 2004), 104–114.

For Chapter Eight, Part I: "Fragmentation and the Real: Michael Haneke's Family Trilogy," *After Postmodernism: Austrian Literature and Film in Transition*, ed. Willy Riemer (Riverside, CA: Ariadne, 2000), 176–88.

Library of Congress Cataloging-in-Publication Data

Peucker, Brigitte.
 The material image : art and the real in film / Brigitte Peucker.
  p. cm.
 Includes bibliographical references and index.
 ISBN-13: 978-0-8047-5430-9 (cloth : alk. paper)
 ISBN-13: 978-0-8047-5431-6 (pbk. : alk. paper)
 1. Art and motion pictures. 2. Realism in motion pictures. I. Title.

PN1995.25.P46 2007
791.43'657--dc22

2006017976

Typeset by Thompson Type in 11/13.5 Adobe Garamond

To my students

Contents

Acknowledgments	xi
Introduction: Art and the Real in Film	1
I. Art and Embodiment	
1 The Moment of Portraiture: Scorsese Reads Wharton	19
2 Dutch Realism: Vermeer, Greenaway, Wenders	30
3 The Fascist Choreography: Riefenstahl's Tableaux	49
4 The Scene of Art in Hitchcock, I	68
II. Illusions of the Real	
5 The Scene of Art in Hitchcock, II	87
6 Kubrick and Kafka: The Corporeal Uncanny	104
7 The Castrato's Voices: Fassbinder's *In a Year of Thirteen Moons*	116
III. Art and Embodied Spectatorship	
8 Violence and Affect: Haneke's Modernist Melodramas	129
9 Images of Horror: Taste, Cannibalism, and Visual Display	159
Notes	*193*
Index	*235*

Acknowledgments

My thanks, first of all, to those who spurred me on by soliciting parts of the following chapters as articles in books and journals: Richard Allen, Nora Alter, S. Ishii-Gonzales, Lutz Koepnick, Ivone Margulies, Lawrence Rainey, Willy Riemer, Robert Stam, and Candace Waid. I owe a debt of gratitude to the following friends and colleagues who've listened to and commented on my work in a variety of venues: Jane and Marshall Brown, Angela Dalle Vacche, Maria DiBattista, my husband and colleague Paul H. Fry, Leo Lensing, Susan Felleman, Catriona MacLeod, David Marshall, Charlie Musser, Noa Steimatsky, Henry Sussman, and Candace Waid. Warm thanks to Carol Jacobs for her collegial support. Special thanks, once again, to Anthony J. Niesz for his invaluable technical assistance, and to Michael Kerbel of the Yale Film Study Center and Susan Hart of the Film Studies Program for help with the acquisition of materials. I am much indebted to Norris Pope, who has been an especially supportive and sensitive editor, and to Angie Michaelis of the Stanford University Press for her assistance. Yale University has supported my work in the form of faculty leaves.

THE MATERIAL IMAGE

Introduction: Art and the Real in Film

For the moment, let's put to one side the idea of the real as that which is inherently unrepresentable to explore the ways in which it is gestured toward in art, particularly in film art. What is meant by figuring the real or gesturing toward it? Here are some of the questions raised by the chapters that follow: How is the "real" suggested by visual metaphors? What is its relation to illusion? How does it manifest itself in the literalist gesture? Is the boundary between art and the real permeable, and what is the "reality bleed"? How is the spectator figured as entering the text, and how does the image enter our world? In cinematic experience, what promotes the impression of reality, and when does medium awareness come into play? Another—integrally related and complementary—aspect of our concern is anchored in the (real) body of the spectator. Cognitive and phenomenological approaches to perception alike tell us that spectatorial affect is "real" even when it is film and not reality that produces it. Thus, the emotional and bodily response of the spectator can be said to extend textuality into the real world. As will already be clear, it is not the spectrum of historically and culturally shaped "realisms" that is the focus of this study,[1] and only on occasion will we take up the documentary image, with its unique claim to the representation of reality. André Bazin's and Siegfried Kracauer's beliefs in film's mission to show the real, in film's ontological connection to reality, are central to the larger issue of realism, of course. But here it is primarily the assertion of film's indexicality that enters the discussion. Insofar as photographic registration is seen as natural, the film image itself is both material and referential, a fusion of art and the real. Further, the imprint of the real in the photograph intersects with moments that play on filmic illusion or in other ways concern the interface of the image with the material world. It is only seemingly a paradox that the real and its relation to representation are centrally at issue in the trompe l'oeil and tableau vivant moments that occur in film—in the visual games, that is, that film plays with reality. Aesthetic practices such as these serve as occasions for staging the real in its relation to representation. The means by which the real is suggested range from the metaphorical to attempts to represent more literally.

This introduction serves, then, to contextualize the issues addressed more specifically in the chapters that follow by locating them among related problems of visual and literary representation. In this it resembles the introduction to the final chapter, which also takes up questions of visuality and spectatorship. We will begin by sketching out a few of Kracauer's views on the material aspects of film and film experience, views that intersect with several central ideas concerning the real in relation to images. Kracauer's realism will be approached first with respect to the materiality of the medium itself—including indexicality—and second, with regard to the embodied spectator and his (*sic*) relation to the "things of the world" as they appear in the images of film. Finally, a parable of realism alluded to by Kracauer will serve as a transition to other kinds of permeability between images and the real that will concern us in subsequent sections.

Material Effects

As is well known, Kracauer's *Theory of Film: The Redemption of Physical Reality* (1960) asserts film's unique capacity to "picture transient material life," claiming that its task is to preserve the existence of things.[2] Kracauer's film theory is a realist—and, as he points out—a *materialist* project: in *Theory of Film*, the relation of the photographic image to its referent is repeatedly expressed in the metaphor of the umbilical cord. Although the affinities in their thinking have not been emphasized, there is much to connect Bazin's ideas of realism with Kracauer's.[3] Bazin's almost mystical devotion to realism is also a "heightened search for the eclectic materiality of film . . . for visceral signifiers of the real."[4] But it is the shared belief in the indexicality of the photographic image that comes as something of a surprise. Like Bazin, Kracauer suggests that the images of film are indexical, as the anecdote in which Kracauer identifies his interest in film makes clear. Here Kracauer recounts his first experience as a spectator, of a film entitled—rather prophetically for his work—"Film as the Discoverer of the Marvels of Everyday Life": "What thrilled me so deeply," writes Kracauer, "was an ordinary suburban street, filled with lights and shadows which transfigured it. Several trees stood about, and there was in the foreground a puddle reflecting invisible house facades and a piece of the sky. Then a breeze moved the shadows, and the facades with the sky below began to waver. The trembling upper world in the dirty puddle—this image has never left me."[5] From this poignant description of a childhood experience, tinged with melancholy, we can derive a number of the salient features that for the Kracauer of *Theory of Film*, at least, make the filmic medium significant. In the sequence described by Kracauer, the film camera has recorded a moment of everyday life, its location a street. The experience is ephemeral, spanning the brief moments in which a breeze passes over a puddle. Along with the sky, the facades of houses are mimetically reflected in the mirror of the puddle. From the point of view of their spectator, they are upside down. A breeze then sets the reflected scene in motion. Until the moment when the breeze begins to blow, the image conjured up by Kracauer's description is purely photographic. But with the introduction of movement the images become filmic: nature and culture—the sky, the houses—begin to move and "take on life," they "waver" and "tremble." Both are reflected together on the muddy surface of the puddle; both are aspects of the physical reality that film is capable of "redeeming." Insofar as ideology enters this image, it is invested in the animism—the movement—that makes things take on life. It resides as well in the act of desublimation involved in the reflection of the heavens—the "upper world"—in the dirty puddle below.

Echoing the work of Bazin as well as his own earlier writings, Kracauer's *Theory of Film* claims that films are proportionately more cinematic the more they cling to the surface of things, their relation to reality seeming mystically to extend beyond the merely mimetic.[6] The relation of art to nature here described contains the residue of romantic theories of art: the dirty puddle with its "wavering" and "trembling" motion provoked by a breeze resembles nothing so much as an aeolian harp—a stringed instrument played, as it were, by the wind. It is an instrument in which sensory and aesthetic effects are produced by the natural world itself, an instrument that serves as a model for the romantic imagination. In Kracauer's revision, however, this model is given a new valuation. Here, Kracauer would have us realize, images of physical reality produce the visual effects, the moving images, that constitute film. The puddle assumes the role of film stock, of celluloid whose surface receives the image of the real. The "pattern of light and shadows" is produced by the referent itself. Not only does this surface function as a mirror that reflects the image but, more importantly, it acts as a surface that receives the physical impression of the wind. On the one hand, the focus of interest here is the material support of film, its optical and photochemical processes.[7] But there is also something more, for Kracauer's description points in the direction of the idea Bazin had already developed into a doctrine of realism: that the unique value of the photographic image—the film image—resides in its indexicality. Like the veil of Veronica mentioned by Bazin—the *vera icon*, the true image[8]—film receives the imprint of the real. The photographic image, like the image of Christ on the veil of Veronica, is an image "not made by human hands," and it is similarly invested with an iconic (and quasi-religious) significance. As Joseph Koerner writes by way of the topic of portraiture, the veil of Veronica "brings forth a theology of the sign . . . as a perfect match between image and model, *signum* and *res*."[9]

Kracauer's anecdote of the reflecting puddle recounts a filmic memory formative for his theoretical work in a number of ways. Kracauer describes a similar scene later on in *Theory of Film*, where it occurs in his discussion of the "found story," the story discoverable in "the material of actual physical reality." In this passage, too, the impression on the surface of the water is pivotal: "After you have watched long enough the surface of a river or lake," he writes, "you will detect certain patterns in the water which may have been produced by a breeze or some eddy. Found stories are in the nature of such patterns. Being discovered rather than contrived, they are inseparable from films animated by documentary intentions."[10] Movement and narrative are launched together: essential to Kracauer's metaphor for the found story is a spectator who perceives the movement that introduces temporality, hence discovers the narrative embedded in the material of the scene. But, as we shall see later, movement also has another significance for him.

It is Adorno who refers to his teacher Kracauer admiringly as a tourist, as a spectator whose mode of seeing is like that of a man on a journey, transforming the everyday into an object of wonder.[11] Kracauer himself elevates this attitude into a principle of cinematic representation: "Film ought to proceed like a tourist who, in strolling through the landscape, lets his eyes wander about."[12] It is not that the camera must shun the formative impulse altogether. For Kracauer, the photographer resembles the spectator—and hence interpreter—of the text of physical reality itself. He is "most of all the imaginative reader intent on studying and deciphering an elusive text."[13] His role as reader and spectator does not, however, necessarily imply a distance. Like the spectator of the film, "the photographer summons up his being . . . to dissolve it into the substances of the objects that close in on him."[14] In *Theory of Film,* the filmic medium is not the place for discursive reasoning: dialectical materialism and its expression through montage are rejected in favor of a phenomenological interest in the material world. Kracauer's approach to cinema is grounded in the material body, both in the sensory perceptions of the photographer/cinematographer and in those of the film's spectator.

Repeatedly, Kracauer privileges what he calls the "psychophysical" response of the spectator, the affective response to sensory stimuli, in other words,[15] and the movement of film's images has a major role to play here. Movement evokes the "flow of life," setting up a "resonance effect" between spectator and image: moving images provoke visceral responses in the "deep bodily layers" of the sense organs, producing "organic tensions, nameless excitements."[16] Thus film experience has the immediacy of lived experience; it produces somatic responses in its spectator, responses that promote continuity between the moving image and the embodied observer. Yet there is also a metaphysical strain in Kracauer's relation to the things of the world. The spectator who contemplates the things of the world in the images of film perceives that "he [*sic*] is listening, with all his senses strained, to a confused murmur." Images begin to sound and sounds are again images. "When this indeterminate murmur—the murmur of existence—reaches him," Kracauer continues, "he may be nearest to the unattainable goal."[17] This synesthetic experience—seeing becomes listening, listening becomes seeing—is a sensory experience: "[objects] must be experienced sensually," writes Kracauer to Panofsky.[18] Does the synesthesia described here—seeing becomes listening, listening becomes seeing—take spectatorial experience beyond the world of the senses, into the phenomenology of Edmund Husserl or Maurice Merleau-Ponty?[19] For Merleau-Ponty, as Vivian Sobchack puts it, signification is born concretely, "from the surface contact, the fleshly dialogue, of human beings and the world together, making sense sensible."[20]

For Kracauer, too, objects resonate, and the spectator dissolves into the substance of the objects. The things of the world that appear in film resonate "multiple meanings and psychological correspondences," creating a "maze" through which the spectator wanders towards the thing as if in a dream.[21] Interestingly, in what constitutes a parable concerning a certain kind of realism, Kracauer suggests that the spectator drifts into the things recorded by filmic images "much like the Chinese painter who, longing for the peace of a landscape he had created, moved into it, walked toward the faraway mountains suggested by his brushstrokes and disappeared in them never to be seen again."[22] Alluding to but not citing Walter Benjamin's

"Work of Art in the Age of Its Technological Reproducibility" by way of the Chinese legend, Kracauer redirects the force of Benjamin's reference to it. For Benjamin, the legend illustrates the concentrated attention elicited by painting, an attention that results in its spectator's metaphorical absorption by the work—while in Benjamin's account the spectators of the mass medium of film, conversely, absorb its tactile images materially.[23] For Kracauer, in contradistinction to Benjamin, the relation between the "things of the world" in the images of film and their spectator is one of *mutual* permeability, a "dialogue" of the senses—and absorption is a response to the images of film. If the Chinese painter's entry into the painting functions as a parable of realism here, what kind of realism is it? It is certainly not descriptive of the range of Kracauer's aims as realist: the Chinese painter's realist drive is for fusion with the images of his painting, which—no matter how abstract they may be—are nevertheless represented as "real" enough to enter.[24] Much in the same way, Michael Fried will read the central expression of Courbet's realist drive in the spectator/painter's figured corporeal entry into his own paintings.[25] Fried's interest in corporeality—may we not call it materiality?—extends, like Kracauer's, to the materiality of his medium. Further, Fried acknowledges his debt to Merleau-Ponty in several ways: in (1) his focus on Courbet's embodiedness, (2) in his interest in the corporeality of painting, and finally, (3) in his emphasis on the relation of painting and beholder.[26] It is the latter concern—expanded to include a spectrum of relations between images and the real—that will be developed here.

Reality Effects/Games with Illusion

The spectators in Plato's cave are fettered, able to see only the movement of shadows on the wall before them. Because they have been in this condition from childhood, this is all that they know. And yet, were they to be freed, they would still remain in the cave; such is the power of the images to enchain them. The moving shadows on the wall that pass before the prisoners, Plato would have us know, are at several removes from truth; they are illusions; they are copies of the copy. It is Jean-Louis Baudry who famously elaborated the analogy between the fettered spectators in Plato's cave and the spectators entranced by the moving images of cinema. For Baudry, cinema, too, is an apparatus that promotes simulation. In both of these scenes of looking, Baudry suggests, the spectators are victims of an illusion of reality, they are the "prey of an impression, of *an impression of reality.*"[27] What promotes this bondage to the image? What is the nature of the images that spectators see? Projected on the wall of the cave, the images are flat, two-dimensional, although Baudry speculates that a sense of depth is suggested by the movement of the images on the wall, by "their crossings-over, superimpositions, and displacements."[28] Sound exists in Plato's cave, but like the images, it is secondary, because it occurs as an echo of voices, reverberating from the walls of the cave. It is self-evident that Plato's description of a situation—or, as Baudry puts it, apparatus—that demonstrates the illusoriness of reality is an idealist project. For Plato, what is known through the senses—here the eyes and ears—rather than understood by the mind, must always be insufficient, secondary, and illusory. Truth resides in the idea.

In cinema, Baudry suggests, the impression of reality is a subject effect, one that allows the perception of the image to pass for the perception of reality. Yet even for Baudry cinema, although conducive to the suspension of the reality principle, does not suspend it completely. Whereas Baudry anchors the confusion between representation and perception in Freud's concept of primary process—"the basic condition for the satisfaction produced by hallucination"[29]—and in the relation of film experience both to dream and to the oral phase in infant development, this is not our focus here. Indirectly, however—by way of examples—we will take up a question entertained by Baudry in passing: "what desire was aroused . . . what urge in need of fulfillment would be satisfied" by a montage whose goal is to create the impression of reality?[30] The desire for cinema, of course, is what Baudry has in mind. No doubt Bazin's canonical essay "The Ontology of the Photographic Image" prompted this question, with its insistence that the history of the plastic arts is primarily a matter of psychology. Bazin understands "the story of resemblance, or, if you will, realism" as a "mental" need, not an aesthetic one.[31] For Bazin, at the center of the controversy over realism in the arts—beyond the struggle for resemblance in mimesis—there is confusion between the aesthetic and the psychological aims of mimesis. Perhaps he had been reading—and disagreeing with—the early work of Rudolf Arnheim and E. H. Gombrich.

We can no doubt agree that the reading of illusion, anchored in the spectator, has both a perceptual and a psychological component. To what extent is the spectator complicit with the illusions contained in so many kinds of visual experience? Cinema is only one of many representational practices that promote illusionistic effects. As Richard Allen points out, illusion is "central to our experience of diverse forms of cultural practice."[32] Illusion may be sensory without being epistemic—we need not be deceived into taking what we see for reality. The spectator of a film is aware that what she is viewing is not real but, in Allen's convincing reading, she voluntarily participates in the experience of illusion. We should keep in mind that there is, after all, aesthetic pleasure to be derived from illusion. Attempts to categorize the varieties and degrees of illusion—both from an aesthetic point of view and from the perspective of cognitive science—sometimes overlook the pleasure lurking in the both/and of ambiguity.

Like cinema, trompe l'oeil painting involves the suspension of medium awareness. Or at least this is the effect it seeks to promote in its spectator, who derives satisfaction both when medium awareness is relinquished and again when illusion reveals itself as such. In visual as well as literary practices, there is often a deliberate blurring between the—aesthetic? psychological?—goals of figuring the real and a satisfaction in the awareness of illusion's role in its figuration. As spectators, we are placed alternately in the position of belief and disbelief. Our pleasure in these effects derives from their oscillation, much as we experience in the famous figure/ground effect, in which one perception recedes as the other comes to the fore. Our pleasure in such effects is the pleasure we take in aesthetic play, but it is also something more. Groping for terms with which to address the incursion on the real by illusion and vice versa, we resort to formulations such as "the invasion of semiotic systems by the real," "the illusion of the natural sign," and "visceral signifiers for the real."[33] With respect to trompe l'oeil painting, yet also more generally concerning the visual arts, Jacques Aumont among others has noted that it is the goal of certain representations to be confused with what they represent.[34] It is in this sense that the metaphor of the "material image" is a suggestive one for the present study, pointing beyond the indexicality of film's photographic images to the games with illusion and the pursuit of the real that I have been describing.

Illusion and Mimetic Drive

Aesthetic practices that rely on the oscillation between illusion and reality have a history, of course, and flourish especially in certain periods of cultural history. One of these practices is trompe l'oeil: Pliny's foundational tale of Zeuxis and Parrhasios has been cited through the ages, its theoretical interest recently revivified for art historians, theoreticians of the gaze, and cultural historians alike by Lacan and Baudrillard.³⁵ In particular, the Baroque period is noted for its interest in illusion, known for the trompe l'oeils in which the images of painting are extended into and concretized by sculptural effects. And the art of the Dutch seventeenth century especially thrives on the intertwining of realism with illusionism, its obsession with representation approached from multiple points of view, including the economic.³⁶ Can we speculate about "the mysteries of temperament" that lead to such interests in painting? asks Simon Schama, only to conclude that images we make of a culture are of necessity "fugitive and ghostly."³⁷ In point of fact, the ambiguities surrounding Dutch Realism are pursued as well in the eighteenth century, another era fascinated with the borderland between reality and illusion. In England, France, and Germany, aesthetic practices that embrace these ambiguities seem to have generated a particular *frisson* in their spectator, whether they involve the transformation of the real landscape into a painting by way of a traveler's Claude glass, or a walk through a candlelit sculpture galley, its flickering light animating the statues on display.

Indeed, the concept of the movement between representation and the real that interests me here owes a great deal to Fried's work on French eighteenth-century painting, with its various forms of figured permeability between the place of the (real) spectator and the painted image, a line of thinking that Fried pursues as well in his later work on Courbet.³⁸ Games with representation and the real were much the vogue in the eighteenth century, as Diderot's *Salons* make especially clear—as when, for instance, Diderot as spectator describes a walk through the countryside he is taking with his friend the Abbé, only to reveal at the end of his lengthy description that it has not been a natural scene, after all, but rather a landscape painting he has been describing. It is the realism of the depicted scene that promotes Diderot's figurative entry into the painting, of course, and he uses his description to make that point. But Diderot's conceit also implies more than that. In Diderot's *Salons* the figured movement into the image world is often accompanied by a countermovement: the (figured) movement out of painted surface into the world of the spectator, a movement such as we see in trompe l'oeil painting.

Preoccupations such as these are not peculiar to Diderot. They abound in the eighteenth century. The examples that follow are taken from Germany, the United States, and England, and they are not isolated examples. (In mentioning Diderot, we have, of course, barely touched the surface of this interest in France.)³⁹ A key text in this discussion is Goethe's epistolary novelette, "The Collector and His Circle" (1798), in which Goethe—a staunch opponent of strict mimesis for whom it is nevertheless a source of fascination—elaborates on the aesthetic proclivities of a collector whom he refers to as an "imitator."[40] The imitator's collection of paintings begins with still-lifes of objects from nature, is expanded to include realistic portraits of family members, moves to full-body paintings of family members, then embraces paintings of human subjects surrounded by their favorite objects. Next, the collector's obsession with illusion leads to the commission of trompe l'oeil portraits of himself and his wife, located behind a false door (the architectural form of trompe l'oeil is a false door or window). Finally, his "blind drive" leads to the commission of a life-size wax figure whose head is based on a plaster cast of his own face. It is not known whether Goethe modeled his imitator on an historical person, but the American painter Charles Willson Peale would certainly have served him well.

Peale was an "imitator" in the sense that Goethe means it, as well as a collector and the owner of a museum. His life-size portrait of his two sons ("Staircase Group: Raphaelle and Titian Ramsay Peale," 1795) was hung in a doorway, drawing on architecture to extend its illusion in the manner of the trompe l'oeil commissioned by Goethe's collector. From Peale's painting an actual step protruded—Baroque fashion—extending in three dimensions the painted image of the stairway on which the figures were positioned. A sculptural piece by Peale recalls the final stage of the imitator's drive: a life-size wax figure of Peale presided over his museum. Further, in a perfect amalgam of illusion and reality that typifies eighteenth-century predilections, Peale was said to have ridden in a carriage harnessed to both living and *stuffed* animals.[41] Susan Stewart reads Peale's aesthetic obsessions as derealizations, as defenses against death—thus suggesting another point of connection with Goethe's imitator/collector, whose efforts likewise seem aimed at arresting time.

It was Goethe's novel concerning the representational practices of the eighteenth century (*Elective Affinities*, 1808) that established the fashion for tableaux vivants as the embodiment of painting by human actors. But this novel catalogues a number of other eighteenth-century representational obsessions as well, including a death mask, which, as a contact icon, shares its indexical status with the photograph.[42] Similarly, Charles Willson Peale's interest in taxidermy supplemented his collector's drive: both taxidermy and collecting have been read in connection with the desire for preservation that also finds expression in photography. Interestingly, Peale's museum also featured a physiognotrace (1802), an apparatus that created images—silhouettes—through direct bodily contact.[43] No doubt the various practices conflating representation with the real in which Peale indulged and which fascinated Goethe did have a psychological significance beyond the mere indulgence in aesthetic play. Does the highly developed "attachment to representation, the taste for simulacra" such as we find in Peale take his aesthetic practices in the direction of obsessional neurosis? Perhaps, suggests Serge Daney. For Daney, tastes such as these point to "a certain love for the cinema."[44]

Pleasure in the movement between the image and the real is not an amusement specific to the 18th century. Does not the mimetic drive—in both its aesthetic and psychological manifestations—simply take on different guises and degrees of importance, mushrooming in one era, and receding from view in another? There is no doubt, however, that the eighteenth century was a focal point for such interests, whether or not we can account for them historically. It is perhaps no accident that it was in 1750 that Alexander Baumgarten took a term that had always been applied to sensory experience—*aesthetica*—and gave it an intellectual dimension. This blurring parallels the deliberate blurring between art and the real or art and nature in so many of the aesthetic practices of the period. If the senses, as in Plato, can only produce illusions, why not then affirm illusion by way of the aesthetic games played with reality? Or perhaps the increased stress on the objectivity of science—of seeing at a distance—during this period resulted in an offsetting need for immediacy, for the dissolution of objectivity involved in the practices that featured the interpenetration of art and reality. But one thing that *is* clear is that similar tastes are taken up again with gusto in postmodernism, which has many affinities with the non-Kantian eighteenth century. In the postmodern cultural moment, in which the experience of reality is said to be undermined already by the emptied-out, commercialized images that surround us, the indulgence in aesthetic play has been famously read as a symptom of the loss of reality, of inauthenticity, and of the waning of affect.[45] Already clichéd in our twenty-first century, Fred Jameson's descriptions of the postmodern subject refer more to what he calls a "new type of emotional groundtone" than to the salient characteristics of images and art objects themselves, characteristics he acknowledges as having already been visible "in this or that" modernism.[46] Simulacra have a negative implication for Plato's idealist project, it is true, and for Jameson and Baudrillard they are further tarred with the brush of late capitalism, a materialism of yet another kind.

This book does not address the postmodern loss of connection with the real as such. Where the postmodern has a role to play, it is concerned instead with the ways in which the real is illusion's necessary complement. In order, perhaps, to demonstrate postmodernism's connection to eighteenth-century games with illusion, Wim Wenders's film *Until the End of the World*

(1991) may very well have taken its title from a German eighteenth-century garden of that name, a garden that notably contained a landscape painting at the center of its natural clearing.[47] Compelling examples abound in Susan Sontag's *The Volcano Lover* (1992), a novel about yet another eighteenth-century collector. Postmodern in its relentless intertextuality, heavily indebted to Goethe's *Elective Affinities*, Sontag's novel offers its reader a full array of eighteenth-century practices that conjoin the real with representation and adds some new ones of its own. Here Goethe as picturesque tourist appears as a refuser of festivities in the midst of pleasure seekers who include Lord Hamilton, the collector. Sontag's account of Goethe's visit to Lord Hamilton in Naples is followed by a party in the here and now that is similarly interrupted. Sontag's novel takes on the features of a parable as none other than the "stony guest," a statue come to life in the eighteenth-century mode, appears on the scene: "In comes this guest, this alien presence, who is not here to have fun at all. He comes to break up the party and haul the chief reveler down to hell. You saw him at the graveyard, atop a marble mausoleum."[48] Mediated by Aristotle, Molière, and Mozart, intertextual to the bitter end, the poet as statue come to life turns out to be none other than a "huge, granite, forbidding father." Goethe is featured as literary precursor. This father as cultural monument—the formulation is Sontag's—brings the modern-day revelers up short: "he's pretentious, overbearing, humorless, aggressive, condescending. A monster of egotism," writes Sontag, "Alas: he's also the real thing."[49]

Sontag's "stony guest" is not just a monument, he's also a "work of art collected by his admirers," she adds, in all probability alluding to Tischbein's famous portrait of Goethe, a cultural icon appropriated by Andy Warhol for his silkscreen prints in the manner of a Duchampian ready-made (1982). Like Warhol's, Sontag's images are multiple and play on the relation of the original to the copy. Perhaps in imitation of Warhol, too, whose images manage to be at once simulacral and referential, Sontag creates a portrait of Goethe that is the sum of various textualities, and yet lays claim to something more. Like Warhol's "Coca Cola Bottles"—the commodity turned icon—for Sontag Goethe—the icon turned commodity—nevertheless remains, as she puts it, "the real thing." What does she mean? There is yet another allusion embedded here, and it is to Slavoj Zizek's "answer of the real." In response to the question of why the symbolic has to be hooked into a "thing," into some "piece of the real," as he puts it, Zizek responds that the function of the "piece of the real" is to fill the void that gapes in the very heart of the symbolic."[50] As his example, Zizek refers to the coincidence that takes us by surprise and produces a vertiginous shock, such as in the case of the politician whose platform collapses after he proclaims: "may God strike me down if I have spoken a single lie!" Behind such situations, Zizek suggests, "the fear *persists* that if we lie and deceive too much, the real itself will intervene to stop us—like the statue of the Commandatore, who responds to the insolent dinner invitation from Don Giovanni by nodding its assent."[51] At the heart of our fictions, Zizek implies, it is the threat of the real that produces the uncanny effect. This statue come to life is not the fulfillment of Pygmalion's erotic dreams: when the stony guest arrives, it is our death that is signalled. Sontag's stony guest wields a scythe.

A congenial model for thinking about the relation of images to the real and its attendant issues can be found in Hal Foster's "Return of the Real," a seminal essay that takes on the critical models that govern the visual arts and art theory from the 1960s to the 1990s. Foster suggests that readings of art based on either one of the two basic models of representation alone—the "simulacral" and the "referential"—necessarily result in a "reductive either/or."[52] Instead, Foster would stress the interdependence of these attitudes in the art under discussion, as when, for instance, he reads Warhol's pop images as both *screening* the real (simulacral) and letting the real "poke through" (referential), so that the spectator seems nearly to be able to touch it.[53] The spectrum of possible relations among simulation, illusionism, and realism that Foster applies to the visual arts of this period maps out a series of interconnections that are operative in film, as well. A central concern is a shift from the idea of reality as an effect of representation to the real experienced as shock or trauma—from an emphasis on representation, that is, to the body. Here the work of Cindy Sherman is Foster's example. When Foster writes about artists who use illusionism not to hide or cover over with representation, but to "push illusionism to the point of the real," he has the work of Duane Hanson in mind.[54] In an opposite but related gesture, yet another group of artists rejects illusionism in order to lay bare the abject body. Foster suggests a new term to define the art that is made by rejecting the symbolic order, by rendering the body abject: the "mimesis of regression." But how far removed is this from the literalism that makes the corpse itself a sculpture from Jeremy Bentham's wish that his embalmed corpse be exhibited as a statue in the University of London, dressed and seated on a chair as an "auto-icon"?[55] When Adorno wrote that one model for art would be the corpse in its arrested, undecaying (embalmed) form, did he have Goethe's *Elective Affinities* in mind?[56] For Goethe himself, the corpse featured in his novel as work of art was precisely that—he called it a symptom of "mimetic regression." Work of the imitative imagination at its most relentlessly literal, this form of sculpture resembles the "art" of the cannibal horror film. Striving for absolute literalism, the artwork of cannibal horror suggests the collapse between representation and the real that characterizes psychosis. That will be the endpoint of this study.

Art Effects

The Material Image represents a contribution to the burgeoning scholarship that seeks to elaborate the relation of film to the visual arts.[57] Sometimes taking up the representation of works of art directly, it more often probes the theoretical and interpretative boundaries of the disciplines. Intertextuality provides a mode of access to the problem of boundary crossings in the arts, and I refer here both to the intertextuality of the films under discussion, deliberately drawing, as many of them do, on other forms of aesthetic and cultural expression. But I refer as well to the methods employed in their analysis, to approaches derived from art historians and theorists of visuality. I have learned a great deal from Michael Fried, in particular, but also from Richard Wollheim, Louis Marin, E. H. Gombrich, Marina Warner, Norman Bryson, Svetlana Alpers, and Hal Foster. The work of cultural theorists as diverse as Roland Barthes, Slavoj Zizek, Susan Stewart, and Mary Douglas informs this study. Although psychoanalytic issues sometimes have a role to play in the readings to follow, they are rarely the focus of attention. And, since spectatorship is a pivotal concern of this book, cognitive and perceptual theory also finds a place. I owe special debts to Steven Shaviro's fine study, *The Cinematic Body*; to Gaylyn Studlar's *In the Realm of Pleasure: Von Sternberg, Dietrich, and the Masochistic Aesthetic*; to Kaja Silverman's *Male Subjectivity at the Margins*; to Linda Williams's *Hard Core*; and also to Vivian Sobchack's *Address of the Eye*.

Although they do not always occupy center stage in the chapters that follow, the implication of tableaux vivants for film is one sustained concern of this book. Needless to say, such moments crucially address the relation of film to painting, but also to the photograph, to sculpture, to theater and dance, as well as to literature. Tableau vivant is central to the staging of intermediality in film. Tableaux in their different permutations exemplify the merger of representation with reality with which we are concerned here insofar as they present the "real" body as an arrested image in a variety of scenarios. Chapter 1 takes up the intermedial layering of images—literary, painterly, filmic—to produce an accumulation of textualities that aspires to the status of thing. Chapter 2 features one film in which the tableau vivant staging of Vermeer paintings is the culmination of the mimetic drive gone awry and another film in which one such moment serves to anchor a discussion of filmic and electronic images that record optical effects, much in the way that Dutch painting does. Here again the focus of attention is the layering of heterogeneous representational systems that characterizes tableau vivant. Chapter 3 reverses this procedure and reveals the tableau's stasis—and the arrested, sculptural body—as intrinsic to a particular array of aesthetic and cultural practices. In this chapter, the presence of theater, sculpture, dance, and photography in film are read with respect to their implications for a fascist aesthetic. Chapter 4 connects tableaux with painting and with death. Chapter 5 examines the juxtaposition of modernist with realist effects in painting. While Chapter 7 includes tableaux of the body in pain and connects them with voice, Chapter 8 recurs to the tableaux of bourgeois melodrama in order to discuss the tension between violence and affect, on the one hand, and a modernist aesthetics, on the other. Chapter 9, the chapter on cannibalistic horror, examines the literalism of psychopathic tableaux that use the body as material or that provide the setting for fantasy exchanges. Several chapters, including the last one, take up masochistic erotic tableaux.

From the first chapter to the last, there is an increasing emphasis on the real in its various permutations. Not surprisingly, this takes the form of an increasing focus on the body, including that of the spectator. If the real is at issue, the body cannot be far behind. Although this study privileges looking and the eye, it returns to the pre-Kantian notion of aesthetic experience as the product of *all* the senses, hence the ear and especially the mouth also appear on the scene. In this regard, too, my approach is materialist. I should add almost by way of a postscript that each chapter takes up a different film or set of films. From chapter to chapter, the issues addressed are intimately entwined, but each chapter also reads the particular texts at hand. Whether the films in question are by Fassbinder or by Kubrick, whether they are horror films, propaganda films, or melodramas, the readings that follow address their specificity as well as the representational and cultural questions through which they cohere. The chapters on Riefenstahl, Hitchcock, and Haneke are based on a wide selection of their work, while others examine one or two films in close-up. In all of them, art and the body—images and the real—are juxtaposed and entwined in an oscillating set of relations that remains in play.

PART I   ART AND EMBODIMENT

The Moment of Portraiture: Scorsese Reads Wharton

Although she approved of the adaptations of her fiction to the theater, Edith Wharton, we are told, had little or no use for the cinema. Wharton's experience of the movies was probably limited to one visit in Bilbao, Spain, in 1914, a visit that may have given rise to the brief rendering of cinematic spectatorship we find in Wharton's novella *Summer*, published three years later. Insofar as *Summer*'s evocation of cinematic experience emphasizes visual sensations such as "swimming circles of heat and blinding alternations of light and darkness," it participates in an attitude of the times that sees the moving images of cinema as waging an assault on the human sensorium.[1] From this point of view, cinema constitutes one aspect of the "chaos" of urban experience, of which the crowds constitute another. In *Summer*, interestingly, Charity Royall's act of spectatorship merges the images on the screen with those of the crowd around her, whose faces "became part of the spectacle, and danced on the screen with the rest."[2] Wharton may have absorbed this contemporary perspective on cinematic images, but it is also likely that the traumatic merging of screen images with those of real-world experience has its origins in Wharton's personal abhorrence for a "spectacle shared by a throng of people."[3] In any case, in 1917 Wharton shared the American attitude toward cinema that stressed its entertainment rather than its artistic values. It would not be until D. W. Griffith released *Broken Blossoms* as a "European art film" in 1919 that the expectations of the public would begin to change.

But Wharton's attitude appears to have remained constant. Although not averse to the income derived from cinema—proceeds from film and stage adaptations of her work were substantial, her primary source of support during the Depression—Wharton had no interest in what Hollywood now calls "the product" and did not see either of the two movie versions of *The Age of*

Innocence that were released during her lifetime.[4] Had Wharton been able to see Martin Scorsese's 1993 adaptation of her novel, however, she might have experienced a conversion. Shot with the most minute attention to visual surface, Scorsese's film is suffused with "high art" values and subtleties: it is, as he has put it, shot and composed for "the purists."[5] Scorsese seems intuitively to grasp that the intriguing issue of cinematic adaptation is most appropriately viewed against the backdrop of a broader approach to the interrelation of the arts in cinema, as it is that interrelation that determines film as a medium. Scorsese's *Age of Innocence* substantiates the claim that, as a latecomer among the arts, film alludes to, absorbs, and undermines the language of the other arts in order to create its own idiom.[6] Borrowing from literature and painting equally, the medium of film is an amalgam of image and narrative that renders film heterogeneous, a hybrid that emerges out of traditionally sanctioned cultural forms. Seen in this light, as the convergence of literary and painterly concerns, film as a medium might very well have appealed to Edith Wharton, for the conjoining of language and image is figured in Wharton's fiction: a preoccupation with the visual is central to her writing.

Indeed, this interest in the visual is central even to the plot of *The Age of Innocence*, which it may be useful briefly to recall here. When the beautiful and nonconformist Countess Ellen Olenska—a woman around whom scandalous rumors circulate—returns from Europe to her proper and socially prominent New York family, the family rallies around her to safeguard her reputation. In a gesture of solidarity, Newland Archer, scion of another such family, hastily announces his engagement to Ellen's cousin, May Welland. From this point on, the die is cast. Archer, one of Wharton's "collectors" and a man of sensibility, customarily escapes from the strict decorum and from what he takes to be the stifling lack of imagination of New York society into a world of literature and painting. A reader of Ruskin and Walter Pater, Archer reads in Ellen an "incarnation of the life of art"[7] and falls deeply in love with her, but society impedes their union at every turn. The conflict between social codes and the yearning to break free plays itself out both in the arena of the erotic and in the desire to lead a more unconventional—read "artistic"—life, but emotional turmoil remains contained beneath the surface of manners and mores. Wharton's world is a world represented by the objects that populate it, a world in which bringing out the Sèvres and the George II plate are significant acts. As Wharton's narrator puts it, "in reality they all lived in a kind of hieroglyphic world, where the real thing was never said or done or even thought, but only represented by a set of arbitrary signs" (44).

Not surprisingly, then, in this novel as elsewhere Wharton makes use of painting in order to delineate her characters. It tells us a great deal about the dashing Julius Beaufort that he "ha[s] the audacity to hang 'Love Victorious'"—a painting that Wharton calls "the much-discussed nude of Bouguereau"—in his drawing room (23). It is telling, too, that the portrait of Mrs. Henry van der Luyden painted twenty years ago is still "a perfect likeness" of this lady who, as Wharton puts it "has been gruesomely preserved in the airless atmosphere of a perfectly irreproachable existence," entombed like the image of the portrait in a kind of "life-in-death" (52). Somewhat predictably, Newland falls in love with the Countess Olenska in part because she represents the "decadent" European world of culture and also because, as her grandmother notes, she is a woman whose portrait has been painted nine times. Because, for Newland, art is both the suppressed realm of the imagination and the erotic, it is not surprising that he chooses the art museum as the location of their tryst.

In keeping with these concerns, Scorsese frames Wharton's characters in painterly effects: in the profilmic, of course, the actors are arranged in painterly compositions, but Scorsese goes far beyond these arrangements. Using color in film as though it were paint, Scorsese tells us in a compelling interview that "the camera moves in on the back of Newland's head, music comes up, and the wall goes red, like a blush."[8] The film's syntax, in paying homage to the syntax of silent cinema with its irises, masking, and fades, was also designed to reinforce Scorsese's painterly aesthetic: instead of fading to black at the end of scenes, he chose to fade to red and yellow because, as he says, he "was interested in the use of color like brushstrokes throughout the film."[9] Editing procedures also contribute to the painterly look of this film, Scorsese tells us, as when he chose to shorten many of its shots in order to suggest "a brush coming through and painting bits and pieces of color, swishing by."[10] Sometimes camera movement, too, is used to suggest the sweep of the artist's paintbrush, as when a slow tracking shot from left to right gradually reveals—to Newland's eye and to ours—the long landscape painting that hangs in the Countess's drawing room.[11]

Literary concerns also suffuse this film. Its visual surface, its minute attention to detail, have been termed fetishistic by critics,[12] and Scorsese's style does indeed mirror and emphasize the attention to objects and ceremonies that function emblematically in Wharton's novel. But Scorsese's attention to the world of things is also an attempt to render Wharton's language which—to borrow a phrase from Walter Benjamin—is a language "heavy with material display."[13] Likewise, Scorsese's almost slavish attention to detail is not simply a bow to realism and period style, or a recognition of the importance of mise-en-scène in Wharton, be its function fetishistic or not. It is also a means of transposing novelistic description into the imagistic terms of film, an attempt to bridge what Scorsese calls the "schism" between novelistic and filmic description.[14] Further, the use of Joanne Woodward's third-person voice-over is designed to give the impression of the narrator's voice—or actually of Wharton's voice, Scorsese tells us—and therefore to simulate the experience of reading the novel.[15] Thus the voice of a woman is superimposed upon our experience of the film, constituting an aural dimension that both distances and draws the spectator in,[16] reinforcing the spectatorial position that Scorsese strove to create. The emotional power of melodrama to entangle the spectator is to be tempered, according to the director, by the distance achieved through the conscious aestheticization of the film's surface.[17] Scorsese's critics have tended primarily to fix their gaze upon the impression of distance that the film conveys,[18] but Amy Taubin puts it aptly in suggesting that "Scorsese's desire was somehow 'to present' Wharton's novel."[19]

Film understood as a medium in which different representational systems—specifically those of painting and writing—supplement one another make film a medium particularly congenial to the artistic concerns of Wharton, whose fiction not only manifests a pronounced interest in the visual, but whose mode of allusion is so frequently intermedial—so frequently involves the multiple layering of painterly and writerly references. As Cynthia Griffin Wolff has pointed out, *The Age of Innocence* derives its title from a Joshua Reynolds portrait of the same title and is connected by this means—"a private pun"—to Henry James's *Portrait of a Lady*, thus making Newland Archer the subject of Wharton's "portrait of a gentleman."[20] And Candace Waid has allowed us to see that Wharton's *The House of Mirth*, which features a Reynolds portrait in a tableau vivant, alludes via Reynolds's painting both to the Ariosto story of Angelica and Medora and to the many artists—Tiepolo among them—who have chosen to depict it.[21] Both of these instances of intertextuality—and there are many similar moments in Wharton's writing—are intermedial: they draw simultaneously upon painting and literature, creating a textual overlay, a palimpsest of sorts, that is at once imagistic and verbal.

Any filmmaker who, in adapting Wharton's text to film, had done his or her homework—and Martin Scorsese has—would certainly have noticed this method of layering representational systems in Wharton's work. It is precisely this stylistic feature that makes adapting Wharton's work to film cinematically challenging—a working out of what it means to transpose one medium into another—for this layering of allusions necessitates a conscious working through of the relation of film to writing and painting. Scorsese mentions other filmic influences on his work,[22] but the manner in which Scorsese addresses these concerns makes it quite evident that, in preparation for shooting *The Age of Innocence*, Scorsese had not only seen Philip Moeller's 1934 adaptation, but also Eric Rohmer's *The Marquise of O.*, another film that is notable for the manner in which it approaches a literary text suffused with references to the visual arts, the novella of that title by Heinrich von Kleist. The relation of the visual to the literary and their transumption by film is the central preoccupation of Rohmer's *Marquise*. And Rohmer, like other French New Wave directors a writer on film as well as a filmmaker, in his turn learned a great deal from the films of F. W. Murnau, the German art historian turned filmmaker of the 1920s from whose work the French New Wave directors developed their theory of the filmmaker as auteur. Indeed, Rohmer himself wrote a book about Murnau's *Faust* that remains one of the most sustained meditations on the relation of painting and literature to cinema.[23]

Intermedial Layering: The Tableau Moment

What do these relationships have to do with Scorsese's adaptation of Wharton? By my next example, I'd like to suggest that they have a great deal to do with it. If they suggest a complex genealogy, they also suggest the essential forces that shaped Scorsese's adaptation. At one decisive moment in Wharton's novel—in Newport, after the honeymoon that marks his marriage to May Welland—Newland is sent down to the water to fetch Ellen, the Countess Olenska, who is standing near a "pagoda-like summerhouse" facing the bay (215). Newland pauses at a distance, contemplating Ellen as a spectator might view a sculpture, and decides that he will go to her only if she turns before a certain sailboat reaches Lime Rock. He will go to her only, that is, if her inanimate figure—her body as sculpture—will, like Pygmalion's Galatea, come magically to life.[24] But this crucial moment in which Newland watches Ellen by the bay takes on an additional significance in Scorsese's film. In imitation of Wharton, Scorsese uses painting to evoke social position, taste, and the historical moment that he is representing. But he uses it also to say something about his chosen medium of film as when, for instance, the camera sweeps across the long canvas that hangs in Ellen's house as though in imitation of a brushstroke, emphasizing by this means that film has the diegetic flexibility and the temporal dimension that painting lacks. Predictably, then, when Scorsese approaches Newland's decisive moment in Newport, he makes it decisively and complexly cinematic.

Whereas Wharton tells the reader that the immobile Ellen is "gazing at a bay furrowed with the coming and going of sailboats, yacht-launches, fishing-craft and trailing black coal barges hauled by noisy tugs" (215), Scorsese radically reduces this scene to the movement of a single sailboat—not out to sea, as in Wharton—but very slowly from right to left across the cinematic frame. In this scene, Scorsese's film is very pointedly quoting *Nosferatu*, Murnau's 1922 classic, a film known among film directors, scholars, and fans alike for its painterly beauty. A hallmark of Murnau's visual style—pointed out by Alexandre Astruc, one of the contributors to the *Cahiers du Cinéma*—is what Astruc termed the "invasion of the frame," a moment in which a moving object is represented slowly and deliberately entering an otherwise static cinematic frame. Imagine a large nineteenth-century sailboat as it enters the frame from right to left, a frame devoid of anything but a seemingly motionless sea and sky: the effect of this "invasion" is to call attention to the introduction of movement—and therefore narrative, story—into the stasis of painting, thus creating the narrative of moving images that is film.

As I mentioned earlier, Murnau was trained as an art historian and derived many of his images from painting. The image of the sailboat, for instance, is based on the coastal paintings of Caspar David Friedrich, one of Murnau's favorite sources. More pointedly than other filmmakers, Murnau calls attention to the manner in which film subsumes pictorial moments within the flow of its narrative. Although his carefully composed frames must of necessity give way to one another—as that is the nature of the medium—the tension between the static images of painting and film's capacity for animating those images is one of the motivating forces of Murnau's film. In *The Age of Innocence*, Scorsese's allusion to Murnau—no doubt mediated by Rohmer—is not only an homage to a filmmaker of the silent period, but comments on film's indebtedness to the compositional practices of painting while nevertheless flaunting film's capacity for movement and hence for storytelling. Very often in film, such moments present the filmic medium as triumphing over the other static visual arts.

In Scorsese's *Age of Innocence*, however, this scene in Newport takes on an additional significance. Not only does the image of the sailboat recall the paintings of Caspar David Friedrich, but the motionless figure of Ellen, her back to her spectators—both to Newland and to the spectator of the film as well—is an example of Friedrich's famous *Rückenfigur*, a human figure in the act of looking, viewed from behind. At this moment in Scorsese's film, then, the figure of the woman is multiply encoded as a figure of art. At once (1) an enactment of a scene from a novel; (2) a reference to Ovid's *Metamorphoses*, notably to a story that is itself a parable of art, in which the sculpted female figure comes to life; (3) a quotation of another scene in *Nosferatu* in which a woman sits motionless in a seaside graveyard, gazing out at the sea; and hence (4) a cinematic allusion already a quotation of another Friedrich painting. Finally, all of these layered allusions, so much in the mode of Wharton's textual layering, are suddenly intensified as we realize that in this scene from Scorsese's film Michelle Pfeiffer performing the role of Ellen Olenska is herself enacting a tableau vivant—a point to which I will return.

In this scene at the bay and elsewhere in his film, Scorsese consciously adapts Wharton's technique of layering one representational mode with another: he alludes to his precursors in the art of "painterly" film—to Murnau and to Rohmer—via the painting of Caspar David Friedrich. At this point it will be useful to recall the manner in which, as Cynthia Griffin Wolff puts it, Wharton uses a "private pun" in order to allude to Henry James's novel by way of Reynolds's painting. The pun, or what we might call, in allusion to *The House of Mirth*, "the word which made all clear" is, of course, "portrait." Indeed, *The Age of Innocence* retains in its title a residual trace of the tableaux vivants so central to Wharton's earlier novel, *The House of Mirth* (1905). (Wharton's readers will recall that in this novel an entire evening is devoted to this form of entertainment, a parlor game in which costumed participants pose in stillness to enact well-known paintings.)[25] Once again the key to the solution is through another text: this time it is *Vanity Fair*, in which a series of what Thackeray calls "charade-tableau" are performed in a picture gallery. In Thackeray's novel the charade-tableau is a form of visual representation—helped along by music—that uses the human body as a vehicle to spell out syllables of words. Here images, as one might put it, serve as riddles whose solution is verbal. This is precisely the nature of Lily Bart's tableau in *The House of Mirth*, a tableau vivant that, as Candace Waid has pointed out, dramatizes a painting whose subject is writing.[26]

But Michelle Pfeiffer's tableau vivant in Scorsese's film is not only yet another sign of this director's involvement with Wharton's writing and its complicated conjunction of literature with painting. Film, too, has an abiding interest in tableau vivant, for tableau vivant moments in film—moments of arrested motion, by and large—remind us by contrast that the "motion picture" is the first medium able to animate visual representation, to make painting "come to life." From the point of view of the human perceptual apparatus, it is motion that confers the impression of three-dimensionality upon the image. Tableau vivant moments in film set up a tension between the two- and three-dimensional, between stasis and movement, between the "death" of the human body in painting and its "life" in cinema. Further, because tableau vivant exists at the nodal point that joins painting, sculpture, and theater, its evocation in film is a moment of intensified intermediality. The film's evocation of multiple textualities and modes is analogous to Wharton's, too, in the attempt to suggest that their resonance—seen as an intermedial layering—in some sense gestures toward materiality, toward a "thingness" that both written word and filmic image can only metaphorically suggest.

Picture Writing

Siegfried Kracauer has contended that there are no films on the subject of art in which the camera is not featured.[27] And, indeed, flashy camera work is everywhere apparent in Scorsese's film. Interestingly, it is Michael Ballhaus, Rainer Werner Fassbinder's erstwhile cameraman, who is Scorsese's cinematographer here. Fassbinder, also very much concerned with the conjunction of literature, painting, and theater, is a director in whose films artifice and formal arrangements can be understood as erotic display. The ostentatious movement of the camera in *The Age of Innocence*, so typical of films Ballhaus shot for Fassbinder, calls attention to itself, underlining the way in which the camera virtually generates space and gestures toward the three-dimensionality of that space in the process. Camera motion also affects our perception of the human body in film: in *The Age of Innocence*, the camera's striking mobility forms a pronounced contrast to the relative immobility of the characters, as when, for instance, the members of New York society are seated in formally scripted places at table in shots that suggest arranged displays. At such times the camera zooms in and moves in circles, tracking around the actors as though to expose the painterly stasis that emblematizes the fixed social hierarchy in which they are entrapped. Interestingly, Scorsese cast himself as the still photographer in his film.

But Ballhaus's camerawork has yet another point of connection to Wharton. Designed by Saul and Elaine Bass (best known for their work for Hitchcock, to whom we'll return), the film's opening credits superimpose a text being written in cursive over the image of a flower, thus aptly figuring the conjunction of the literary—the flow of writing—with the imagistic. With its operatic sound track and the repeated erotic image of an unfolding flower shot in stop-action photography first opening, then finally going to seed, this credit sequence is followed by the first diegetic shot of the film, a close-up of a chrysanthemum. The camera then tracks back to reveal a bunch of chrysanthemums, part of the stage set of Gounod's *Faust*. One of these flowers is plucked, and the camera pulls back to reveal the garden scene with Marguerite holding the flower by means of which she will symbolically deflower and dismember herself. After this operatic "defloration," the camera, in what we discover to be an extreme close-up of Newland Archer's evening attire—the frame is black—pans to the left to focus on his boutonniere, on the white gardenia in his lapel. A few shots later, Newland's gaze through opera glasses (another citation of spectatorship with antecedents in film and painting),[28] followed by shots from his point of view, establishes Newland's gaze and the sensibility of the connoisseur and spectator as the determining sensibility of the camera. The shots that follow, of several men looking through opera glasses—Larry Lefferts, arbiter of style in Wharton's novel, is the most prominent among them—confirm the conjunction of camera and opera glass in joint connoisseurship. Under their gaze the woman as flower must ever be aestheticized and, like Goethe's and Gounod's Marguerite and her model, Ophelia, consigned to death—if not to an actual death, then to death in art.

A brief look at the other extant film version of *Age of Innocence*, a film to which Scorsese referred while planning his own, provides additional insight into the trope of the woman dying into art. Like Scorsese's film, Philip Moeller's 1934 adaptation simultaneously addresses concerns of Wharton's writing and filmmaking, perhaps most clearly in the scene in the Metropolitan Museum. Moeller's version of this scene—in marked distinction from the novel—begins in a room that contains a few classical sculptures of male and female nudes, among which the Countess Olenska and Newland Archer wander: in this film, too, there's a suggestion of Pygmalion and Galatea. Soon the couple enters the room containing the Egyptian collection, where they converse among Egyptian sculptures and encounter a mummy, labeled "A Woman Who Lived in Egypt."[29] This label functions as an interesting diversion from the factuality of the female corpse and its "mummification," its preservation in art. In Egyptian culture, of course, art and the preservation of the body go hand in hand: Egyptian art at once defies and is in complicity with death, expressing, as André Bazin has put it, "the mummy complex," or what Bazin has called the "psychological ambition" of all art to "embalm time"[30] By means of this Egyptian Room setting, the film version of 1934 addresses the issues implicit in Scorsese's summer-house sequence in which Ellen stands immobile—the issues posed by the Galatea story and in tableau vivant: the "bringing to life" of painting or the "killing off" of the living body into the stasis of sculpture. Again the fate of Lily Bart in *The House of Mirth* looms large. Displayed in death, her corpse is a still life or rather, as the French put it, a *tableau mort*.[31]

But in what sense may this scene in the Egyptian collection be understood as self-consciously cinematic? On the one hand, it may very well allude to an early Hitchcock film, *Blackmail*, released in 1929, which includes an astonishing chase sequence through the Egyptian collection of the British Museum. *Blackmail* contains the first of several museum sequences in Hitchcock's films, many of which are concerned with precisely the issues we have been discussing, with the conjunction of film, narrative, and painting, and with the "killing off" of the female body into the aesthetic: *Vertigo* is a prime instance of this obsession.[32] On the other hand, we recall that for early writers on film such as Vachel Lindsay, film images are best understood as "hieroglyphics": Lindsay develops his notion of "photoplay hieroglyphics" as analogous to Egyptian picture writing.[33] Moeller's scene in the Egyptian collection, then, additionally serves as a reminder that film is indeed a "mixed medium," a form of picture writing.[34] As the term *picture writing* could reasonably serve as another metaphor for the simultaneously verbal and imagistic allusions in Wharton, as a metaphor for the multiple layering of visual and verbal allusion, it seems a particularly resonant choice. Paradoxically, perhaps, in this scene "hieroglyph" is "the word which makes all clear."

In conclusion, I'll briefly call to mind the scene at the end of Scorsese's film, the moment at which the golden light shining on the Countess's Paris window recalls Newland Archer's "decisive moment" at Newport to his memory. Wharton tells her readers that for Newland "by some queer process of association, that golden light became for him the pervading illumination in which she lived" (359). Wharton's readers recognize that light as the auratic glow of the aesthetic: this moment in Paris serves as Wharton's private tribute to Henry James.[35] But in his film Scorsese elaborates on this moment to play once again on the painterly quality of his earlier, multivalent scene. When, this time, in Pygmalion-like fashion, Newland Archer succeeds in making his Galatea come to life—she turns, if only briefly, in his imagination—we realize that at this moment, for Scorsese, film has triumphed over painting's entombment of the human figure by its capacity for rendering movement, for its representation of *life*.

2

Dutch Realism: Vermeer, Greenaway, Wenders

Tableau Vivant and Hybridity

Promoted by the fashionable novels of their day, tableaux vivants as a parlor game—the static embodiment of well-known paintings by human actors—came into vogue in the first decade of the nineteenth century. Yet their origins are earlier and twofold, both high and low cultural. One of these is the tableau of Diderot's bourgeois tragedies, a paradigmatic moment of dramatic intensification during which the actors hold their pose and all motion on the stage ceases, a temporally circumscribed and "out-of-time" moment within the flow of dramatic action (see Chapter 8). There is little doubt that this form of tableau, in turn, as theorized and practiced by Diderot, is the ancestor of the tableau moment or *apothéose* in the staged melodrama and French variety shows on which Méliès was to rely so heavily in his films.[1] The other origin of tableau vivant is pornographic: the best known tableaux of this genre may be those staged by an eighteenth-century London sex therapist in which Emma Hart posed scantily clad as a "nymph of health," tableaux designed to inspire the performance of clients in a so-called "Celestial Bed."[2] Pornographic tableaux vivants, apparently, have not gone out of fashion, nor has their relevance to cinema gone unremarked, as evidenced in Lyotard's essay "Acinéma."[3] It is in its manifestation as an embodiment of painting that the tableau vivant as visual spectacle is most suggestive for an analysis of representational hybridity. As we shall see, this does not preclude its erotic lure.

Tableau vivant is a meeting point of several modes of representation, constituting a palimpsest or textual overlay simultaneously evocative of painting, drama, and sculpture. As the staging of well-known paintings by human performers who hold a pose, it involves the "embodiment" of the inanimate image. Tableau vivant, in other words, translates painting's flatness, its two-dimensionality, into the three-dimensional. By this means it figures the introduction of the real into the image—the living body into painting—thus attempting to collapse the distance between signifier and signified. Film is a medium in which different representational systems may collide, may replace, but generally supplement one another, suggesting that those moments in films that evoke tableaux vivants are moments especially focused on film's heterogeneity. It is interesting to note that in his discussion of the related tableaux scenes of early cinema, Noël Burch focuses on what he calls "the unexpected cohabitation in a transition period of two modes of representation,"[4] a "tension between surface and depth."[5] Burch reads this "cohabitation" as evidence of a collage principle that suggests "a certain reflexivity"[6] in those films in which collage techniques appear. Implicit in Burch's analysis is a concern with the way in which scenes that juxtapose conceptions of space appropriate to several visual modes suggest a deliberate attempt at collage effects.[7] Broadening the discussion to include more recent films, Pascal Bonitzer reads tableau vivant in cinema as a "composite monster, a sphinx" that poses an "enigma."[8] One aspect of the enigma that is posed, I'd like to suggest, pertains to the hybrid nature of the cinematic medium—itself a kind of "sphinx"—of which tableau vivant is a deliberate troping.

Elaborating, then, on the idea of tableau vivant as a lens that focuses hybridity, this chapter explores tableau vivant in its expanded sense. Our discussion is not confined to the stricter definition of tableau vivant as a moment of arrested action that interrupts the flow of images in cinema.[9] Rather, it concentrates on the cinematic reenactment of painting treated as the nodal point of several representational modes, as a means of textual layering that produces a suggestive semantic resonance. In this chapter I draw upon two films, *A Zed and Two Noughts* (1985) by Peter Greenaway and Wim Wenders's *Until the End of the World* (1991), films that take a postmodern stance toward the cinematic medium. Although Greenaway and Wenders embrace a variety of signifying practices and a multivalent approach to signification—and precisely for this reason, perhaps—both directors are intent upon locating the place of the real within signification. Although the search for the real and authentic is staged differently by each director, both of their films "take up" well-known paintings by Vermeer, a painter who worked within an artistic milieu notable for its realism—an added irony being that Vermeer's work is the target of one of the twentieth century's most famous cases of forgery.[10] I will argue that these films exemplify somewhat different attitudes toward the accumulation of textual systems typical of tableau vivant moments. *A Zed and Two Noughts* examines tableau vivant at the level of the narrative, and its excess of textuality serves as a foil to the simulation of the real. In a perverse troping of tableau vivant, in this film van Meegeren, artist and surgeon, carries his fetishization of the real body within representation to a violent extreme. In Wenders's film, on the other hand, the layering of representational systems within the filmic text itself leads virtually to the point of epistemic collapse, to a near breakdown of representation within which the real is figured as a physiological act of perception. Interestingly—and here a potentially pornographic moment of tableau vivant is signaled—both films use Vermeer's paintings primarily to situate women within textuality. In each instance, the real enters the text primarily as or through the female body.

"The Flesh of a Human Presence"

Poised between *The Draughtsman's Contract* (1982) and *The Cook, the Thief, His Wife and Her Lover* (1989), *A Zed and Two Noughts* has in common with Greenaway's other films an obsession with the relation of representation to the real. As I have argued elsewhere,[11] Greenaway's draughtsman is a "realist" whose wish to bring the real into the space of his frames is displaced onto and enacted upon the body of the woman with whom he has entered into a dubious contract. Both the draughtsman's mimetic drive, acknowledged by the grid imposed upon the image by his viewfinder, and his desire for visual mastery over space that its central perspective implies, find their counterparts in *Zed and Two Noughts*. The interest in the realist project of Dutch painting that the still-life compositions of *The Cook, the Thief, His Wife and Her Lover* express is already present in the preoccupation with Vermeer's women that is the idée fixe of van Meegeren, the surgeon in *Zed and Two Noughts*, who is fixated on the artist's ability to render "the flesh of a human presence." Vermeer's work, Greenaway admits in a recent interview, has served as a "treasure chest" for his own production of images since[12] the 1960s, guiding him in "project after project."[13] Following Godard's lead, Greenaway agrees that Vermeer is the prototype of the filmmaker, because his paintings represent a "world of light," while his rendering of temporality "pins the world down," at once arresting and eternalizing the moment. In this same interview, Greenaway mentions another project, "Writing to Vermeer," which takes up the relation of writing and image—one of his recurrent preoccupations—within the context of Vermeer's letter paintings.

It is obviously not their thematic content alone that makes Vermeer's paintings so interesting to Greenaway, a filmmaker/painter with a pronounced interest in and knowledge of art theory. We will look to Svetlana Alpers' pivotal study of Dutch art of the seventeenth century, *The Art of Describing*, for an analysis of representational issues that shed further light on Greenaway's engagement with Vermeer's painting. Written in the wake of Foucault's *Order of Things*, *The Art of Describing* locates in Northern Dutch painting of the seventeenth century a system of representation antithetical to that of the Albertian (narrative) model, through which painting had hitherto been read. The Northern descriptive mode, as Alpers reads it, lacks a fixed point of view, and substitutes the model of the painting as mirrored image for that of the painting as Albertian "window on the world." With its mimetic emphasis, the Dutch mode of painting thus emphasizes "seeing" the world, rather than narrativizing and "reading" it; in Alpers' view, its mode is decidedly not allegorical.[14] Indeed, Alpers claims that the term *descriptive* as she uses it—can be substituted for *realistic*, and that the realism of this kind of painting can be likened to the "pictorial mode of photographs."[15] This is not to say that Dutch art of this period shares the impulses of nineteenth-century realism, or that it is as accessible to verbalization: Dutch art shows instead that the "realistic" image can serve as a lure for the eye, and that "meaning by its very nature is lodged in what the eye can take in—however deceptive that might be."[16] In its most extreme form, approaching trompe l'oeil illusionism, "Dutch art is notoriously subject to confusion with life."[17] Greenaway's van Meegeren—who bears the name of Vermeer's famous forger—is prey to just such confusion.

It is clear that one reason for Vermeer's centrality to the art of filmmaking lies with the enigmatic image of the woman, an image that is voyeuristically explored by artist and filmmaker alike. A surgeon who fancies himself a painter, Greenaway's van Meegeren is obsessed with Vermeer's women: they are said to be his "specialty," both in the medical and in the aesthetic realms. We might well ask whether van Meegeren's goal is to bring Vermeer's women to life or whether, a Pygmalion in reverse, his aim is to kill off the living body into art. As a character he embodies the voyeuristic attitude toward women that Vermeer's paintings record, both in the earlier work in which, as Lawrence Gowing puts it, "man's attention to women"[18] is depicted in represented acts of spectatorship, or in the later paintings, in which the voyeuristic attention and sexual investment of the artist himself are understood to permeate the scene.[19] In Greenaway's film, van Meegeren's mistress, Catherina Bolnes, bears the name of Vermeer's wife, but she, too, is not the genuine article: unlike Vermeer's wife, who bore him fourteen children, van Meegeren's mistress aborts rather than gives birth, thus paralleling the failed "creative" efforts of van Meegeren. Van Meegeren himself is an inauthentic Vermeer who takes realism to an unprecedented extreme and grotesquely sculpts in human flesh: having amputated one of Alba's legs, van Meegeren is prompted by the lack of symmetry this produces in her body to remove the other.

Vision spells entrapment for van Meegeren, whose desire for the image of Vermeer's women motivates his desire for their transposition into real flesh. To this end, Catherina assists van Meegeren in his efforts to "stitch and suture" the unfortunate Alba into the space of representation—to use her, that is, in various attempts at tableau vivant embodiments of Vermeer paintings. In one tableau vivant sequence, van Meegeren's recreation of "Couple Standing at a Virginal" is loosely construed, and the narrative of Greenaway's film is by no means arrested. Yet van Meegeren evokes Vermeer's painting cinematically in several crucial respects, including the mirrored image of the woman, a spatial trick that reveals what would ordinarily be hidden from the spectator's eye. Indeed, the act of spectatorship is foregrounded in this scene in a number of ways. Consulting a reproduction of the painting, as though to check on the authenticity of their representation, Catharina and van Meegeren glance repeatedly from a print to the embodied scene. Meanwhile, in the background, the twins Oswald and Oliver view another erotic painting, van Baburen's "Procuress," to which we'll recur in a moment.

But vision is not the only sense that is brought into play here: van Meegeren forces Alba to play the piano/virginal, thus bringing the painting "to life" by the introduction of sound. Greenaway claims to see the origin of cinema in Vermeer's oeuvre, and we know that their suggestion of sound is one of the sources of fascination that Vermeer's paintings hold for him.[20] Yet here Greenaway ironically undermines the efforts of van Meegeren to recreate Vermeer's erotic scenario in the "real": the only tune that Alba can play is "The Teddy Bear's Picnic," its infantility no doubt underscoring the regressive sexuality expressed in van Meegeren's compulsive "making real" of these paintings. In Greenaway's film—although not in the painting on which this tableau vivant is most closely based—the scene at the virginal also contains the van Baburen "Procuress" that hangs on the wall in two other Vermeers—in "The Concert" and in "A Lady Seated at a Virginal"—thus underscoring in both painting and film the erotic barters transacted through the seductive medium of music.

This tableau vivant scene is initiated by a montage of close-ups of Vermeer women, details of a series of paintings quickly passed in review that underscore van Meegeren's obsession with a characteristic yellow bodice worn by women in four of Vermeer's paintings.[21] Dressed in the yellow bodice, "stitched and sewn to the music stool," as she puts it, Alba complains that she has become "an excuse for medical experiments and art theory." As a realist "artist" constantly torn between the "truth of the real and the knowledge that representation is only representation,"[22] van Meegeren is trapped within the structure that is operative in fetishism, torn between the belief in the fetish and the knowledge of the "real" wound that it is designed to cover over. Indeed, van Meegeren stands literally revealed as a fetishist, caught between his need to operate upon the female body and to cover the wound—a function fulfilled by the yellow bodice as fetish, as an icon that obscures the "view."

It should be noted that the van Baburen "Procuress," represented twice within Vermeer's paintings, is a notable example of Northern Caravaggism, and that its use within this scene therefore alludes to van Meegeren's obsession with illusionism and the real.[23] If his mistress Catherina accedes to his will regarding the transformation of Alba into a Vermeer woman, van Meegeren tells her, Catharina is guaranteed a place in his "operating theater" and his bed. With this (not unusual) formulation, Greenaway signals another set of multiple allusions of an art historical and theoretical nature, allusions that likewise layer the real and the representational. Within the context of Dutch painting, surgery as performance calls to mind the foregrounding of spectatorship in Rembrandt's "Anatomy Lesson of Dr. Tulp" (1632). And, within the context of "art theory," as Alba puts it—specifically within the context of shocking realism—we are reminded of Michael Fried's reading of the Thomas Eakins's "The Gross Clinic" (1875). Within the context of realism, Fried convincingly argues that the portrait of Dr. Gross in the medical amphitheater is a representation of Eakins's personal relation to writing and painting. Within the context of this reading, the bloody scalpel in Gross's hand stands in for the paintbrush in that of Eakins. The "nearly overwhelming realism of effect,"[24] produced by Eakins's work is parodied in Greenaway's van Meegeren, who operates with an open book of Vermeer reproductions as his guide.

Along with his mistress, Catharina Bolnes, van Meegeren himself enacts a tableau vivant: tellingly, it is "The Artist in His Studio" with van Meegeren, arrayed in a striped black and white doublet, playing the part of Vermeer. Wearing a red hat and nothing else but earrings, Catharina takes the place of the sedate young woman who embodies Clio, the muse of History enacting an allegory of Fame in Vermeer's actual painting. The laurel wreath that adorns Clio's head is rejected in favor of the red hat of another erotically charged Vermeer woman, "The Girl with the Red Hat," Catharina's headgear intensifying the effect of her nakedness and giving it a pornographic cast. Thus van Meegeren—and Greenaway—definitively put aside the allegorical significance of the female figure in this painting (whose allegorical significance is currently in dispute among art historians, anyway)[25] in favor of the shock value produced by the woman's naked flesh. The film intensifies the realistic effect that the presence of the human figure already has in Vermeer's painting.[26]

In this scene, van Meegeren, like Vermeer, is positioned with his back to the spectator. The sequence begins as the film camera pulls back slowly and steadily from an extreme close-up of the black and white stripes of the doublet to reveal the entirety of the scene, camera movement and an accompanying voice-over clearly marking this tableau vivant sequence as cinematic. Periodically, we see the flash of a time-lapse camera imposed upon the scene, reminding the spectator of the lights of the two other significant deployments of the photographic medium in *A Zed and Two Noughts* that must be brought to bear upon our reading of tableau vivant here. One of these is an experiment with time-lapse photography in which a series of dead animals is photographed in the various stages of decomposition. The other example—in some sense equal but opposite to this one—is a teleological film within the film about evolution, whose projection within the diegesis is marked by the streaming light of the projector. Motivated by the deaths of their wives, the twin zoologists Oswald and Oliver are engaged upon a study of death and decay. Increasing formlessness, which is the object of their scientific scrutiny now, exists in an inverse relation to their previous object of study, evolution with its ever-increasing complexity of form. But vision has not been left out of the picture. The grids upon which the decay of various animal bodies in their experiment is charted evoke the grid through which Dürer's draftsman famously apprehends his female nude.[27] And although the flashing of the time-lapse cameras marks the isolated moment of each photograph, these moments occur in sequence. By way of this tableau vivant of "The Artist in His Studio," then, the distinct temporalities of three modes of visual representation are juxtaposed: the celebrated "phenomenon of temporal stasis" implied in Vermeer's paintings[28] is marked by the *punctum* of photography, and subverted by the devolution of narrative in cinema and theater. With death as its temporal limitation, the body remains at the center of Greenaway's concern.

Further, in this re-creation of Vermeer's "Artist in His Studio," the notion of van Meegeren's operating theater, the *enactment* of this painting in cinema—its sheer theatricality—and the movie theater are fused, suggesting an allegory of Greenaway's filmmaking as postmodern and hybrid. But the semantic resonance produced by these overlapping representational systems stresses simulation rather than making real, as the spectator's awareness of these textualities produces a shock of awareness—the suspension of belief—that realism in art cannot tolerate. Van Meegeren's realist project, with the naked female body at its center, is enclosed within Greenaway's multiple representational brackets that enhance, but also expose, its simulations.

One more example of the juxtaposition of body with painting in this film—only a tableau vivant in a very expanded sense of the term—needs mentioning. In this scene, which also takes place in Van Meegeren's "studio," the naked twins, Oswald and Oliver, sit on chairs positioned under Vermeer's "The Astronomer" and "The Geographer." But these are not exactly the pendant portraits as painted by Vermeer: Greenaway has turned the astronomer around, although, as he is doubtless aware, there's a precedent for this composition in an engraving of 1672 by Louis Garreau.[29] In both the Garreau engraving and in Greenaway's film, the portraits face one another, creating a symmetrical arrangement around a central axis. The stripped, exposed bodies of Greenaway's twins creates an ironic counterpoint to the complexity of Vermeer's rendering of *his* scientists, surrounded by the tools of their trade. In Greenaway's scene, it is suggested that the (here falsified) symmetries of art bear a relation to those of the body. The twins—once Siamese twins, their bodies joined at birth—have decided to reassume their original body symmetry, thus capitulating, it would seem, to a central preoccupation of this film that locates the origin of representational strategies in the body. Van Meegeren, who has amputated Alba's legs, is now asked to stitch the twins together. But the price for this procedure is high: in yet another attempt at "creativity," van Meegeren demands that Oswald and Oliver allow him to stand as father to their own twin sons. In a last effort to grasp the enigma of life and death, form and formlessness, Oswald and Oliver embark upon a joint suicide, having made arrangements to have their own decaying bodies fixed periodically by the lens of the camera. Here we have come full circle to Vermeer's "twin" portraits of "The Geographer" and "The Astronomer." It is clear that the same young man served as a model for both of Vermeer's scientists: interestingly, scholars suggest that this young man was probably Anthony van Leeuwenhoek, the Delft microscopist.[30] Greenaway's twin scientists—microscopists too—are finally themselves objects of scrutiny under a lens.

At this point it will be useful to return briefly to the tableau vivant of "The Artist in His Studio," and to the black-and-white-striped "doublet" worn by van Meegeren/Vermeer. As we recall, the scene begins as the camera pulls back from an extreme close-up of the painter's striped doublet: this image of the black-and-white stripes doubles the black-and-white stripes of the zebra in the previous scene, to which the tableau vivant is connected by way of a sound bridge. What is the link, then, between the zebra and the doublet? Black and white dominate Greenaway's film not only as binarisms to be reconciled, even if the spectator does take note of the fact that Oswald is at first associated with black and with image making (photography), while Oliver is associated with white and with writing, specifically with the newspaper stories from which he clips phrases and paragraphs. As the twins become increasingly similar and their identities begin to merge, a reconciliation of these representational systems—of written narratives and images—is effected. This is a reconciliation that Greenaway reads in Vermeer's paintings and on which film also necessarily relies. Yet the cut from zebra to artist's doublet has another significance, as well: black and white stand in for the rigid structures that guide our vision and perception, that allow us to read images and to compose them: in Greenaway's view, it is fortuitous that Vermeer wears a black-and-white doublet in his self-portrait.[31] But the artist's task, that of forming and composing, has its counterpart in the twins's preoccupation with the decomposition of bodies—that of the zebra, among others—and with the formlessness promoted by decay. At what point, Greenaway appears to be asking, is the structure of the real no longer readable, despite the fact that it is no less real? Perhaps this is one sense in which the van Leeuwenhoek portraits, portraits of a microscopist and lensmaker, have something further to say about the representational practices upon which Greenaway is meditating.

    The van Leeuwenhoek portraits also point toward another concern of the film. If we agree with Stephen Heath that the camera itself is bound to the Albertian perspectival system, a system that postulates a spectator prior to and external to the scene viewed, then this system is not easily subverted.[32] In *A Zed and Two Noughts*, Greenaway chooses to expose the Albertian model by working within it, intensifying the effect of central perspective produced by the camera by exaggerating symmetries in the arrangement of the profilmic in his frames, thus making his spectator constantly aware of the way in which the scene is laid out before the eye. In scene after scene, for instance, Alba recumbent on her bed is represented at the very center of a symmetrical mise-en-scène, functioning as an ironic cinematic pendant to van Meegeren's attempts to bring her into the space of representation via tableaux vivants. Insofar as Greenaway accentuates Alba's entrapment within central perspective, his mise-en-scène calls the project of Dürer's draftsman to mind, suggesting the camera's difficulty in avoiding a similar appropriation of the female body. There can be little doubt that Greenaway is aware of the restriction that the camera imposes on the representational possibilities of film: his filmmaking is of the "staged" variety precisely because he believes that by juxtaposing a variety of representational modes—hence troping the very idea of representation—this representational excess will expand the boundaries of his medium.

The Keplerian Mode and the Operation of the Eye

As I have argued elsewhere, Wim Wenders's interest in the real, and its entry, figured or otherwise, into the space of the text is mediated by a strong commitment to the photographic basis of film, a commitment that is well documented in his films and essays.[33] For Wenders, photographs, as "monuments of moments," are privileged objects that link the problem of identity to that of perception and memory.[34] Polaroids hold a particular fascination for Wenders, because their status is ambiguous: as photographs without negatives, they are unprintable, unique, and thus assume something of the status of paintings. But like other photographs, polaroids, too, arrest the flow of time, "embalming" it, as André Bazin would have it.[35] The representation of time in its cessation is one significance that photographs hold for Wenders, whose early short films were shot without cuts, recording the passage of time by means of what he terms his phenomenological approach.[36] Wenders's narrative films have their visual origins in the photographs he takes in preparation for their shooting, but even recent films are shot in continuity, shot "in the present tense."[37] The very title of *Until the End of the World* evokes the collapse of time and space into one another that Wenders's phenomenological approach suggests.

The camera's relation to the real, as we are aware, has been variously and complexly read. Like Walter Benjamin, Wenders is fascinated with the physiognomic and topographical aspects of people, places, and things that the camera in the early period of photography—in the photographs of August Sander, for example—is capable of revealing to the eye.[38] A materialist aesthetics similar to that of Benjamin is also promoted by Siegfried Kracauer, from whose *Theory of Film: The Redemption of Physical Reality* Wenders derives many aspects of his approach, an approach by which he, too, asserts film's unique capacity to "picture transient material life."[39] For Wenders, as for Kracauer, one of film's unique tasks is to preserve "the existence of things."⁴⁰ With both Kracauer and Walter Benjamin, Wenders shares an interest in the traces that photographic images bear of that "tiny spark of contingency, of the here and now, with which reality has, so to speak, seared the subject."⁴¹ For Wenders, its relation to the real is the utopian—albeit nostalgic—aspect of film. Echoing the work of Bazin as well as his own earlier writings,⁴² Kracauer's *Theory of Film* claims that films are proportionately more cinematic the more they cling to the surface of things, their relation to reality seeming mystically to extend beyond the merely mimetic.

In conjunction with Bazin's writings, Kracaeur's *Theory of Film* provides a source for Roland Barthes's contention, in "The Photographic Message," that the photograph transmits "the scene itself, the literal reality."⁴³ For Barthes, the very nature of the photograph is at once cultural and natural, both susceptible and insusceptible to being read. The "filmic" itself, Barthes contends, is paradoxically most accessible in the still, by means of which film is closest to the photograph and hence most capable of revealing its "uncoded" or natural dimension.⁴⁴ This belief in a residual uncodedness also underlies Wenders's fascination with the photographic medium, suggesting the question of whether the real is most readily available for scrutiny when the stillness of the photograph intersects the filmic flow. Moreover, like Bazin and Roland Barthes, Wenders takes an interest in the indexicality of the photographic image, in the photographic image as an "emanation of the referent."⁴⁵ It is Bazin's idea that the photographic image and the object "share a common being, after the nature of a fingerprint," and his comparison of the photograph with the death mask⁴⁶ that provide us with a key at once to a fascinating sequence in Wenders's *Tokyo-Ga* (1985), and to the indexical relation that it draws between the image and the real.

In this essay film, Wenders lingers over a visit to a factory that produces the realistic waxen replicas of the foods by means of which Japanese restaurants advertise their dishes. As Wenders says in voice-over: "It all starts with real food. Then gelatine is poured over it and allowed to set. The moulds thus created are filled with wax, and these wax shapes are then trimmed, painted, and refined."⁴⁷ It is not the simulacral quality of the "fake food" that is a source of interest here, as has been suggested,⁴⁸ but rather the molds' ability to carry the imprint of the real. Wenders's sequence speaks to Bazin's assertion that the photograph is "a mould in light"⁴⁹ and refers as well to the death masks and other imprints of the body to which Bazin has likened the photographic image, metaphors that resonate in Baudrillard's description of the Polaroid as "a sort of ecstatic membrane that has come away from the real object... enabling us to hold the image and object almost simultaneously."[50] What is figured by the careful attention to food replicas in *Tokyo-Ga*, then, is a complex relation among (1) the *real* in the form of real food items; (2) the mold poured around these real items, a metaphor for the indexical photograph; and (3) the *copy*—the "fake food" that serves a commercial purpose, that of advertising. Here the real lingers within postmodern inauthenticity, just as it resides in modernity's photographic traces, the *Tokyo Story* of Ozu, for example, to which Wenders's film pays homage.

Video and digital images, of course, lack the indexical quality of the photograph. Wenders's *Notebook on Cities and Clothes* (1993) takes up the status of these "new" images alongside the photographic image, juxtaposing them with one another, sometimes in split-screen format—and with fashion and the making of clothes. Fashion as a metaphor for "the transient, the fleeting, the contingent" is familiar to us from Baudelaire's *Painter of Modern Life*, where it is connected to the protocinematic through the figure of the modern artist, M. Guy, whose kaleidoscopic acts of perception resemble those of a camera.[51] In *Notebook*, Wenders represents himself in voice-over as a "tourist from another art form" who variously discusses the fashioning of clothes as a form of image making, including as an indigenous art, based on the cultural language of Japan. But Wenders's interest is also more narrowly representational: the cutting and reassembling of fabric by the designer Yoji Yamamoto is likened to the montage procedures of filmmaking. Central to Wenders's concern is Yamamoto's practice of cutting clothes upon the body, which imparts its shape to his materials. As "moulds for the body," clothes function in Wenders's meditations as images for the indexical photograph: Yamamoto's clothes are imprinted with the body, as we might put it, in the manner of the death mask. As Wenders's voice-over asserts: "the issue is to wear not clothing, but reality itself." My intention here, then, is to look at the other side of the question asked by some critics[52] concerning Wenders's postmodern concern with simulation and to examine simulation with respect to the position occupied by the real in his filmmaking.

In turning now to *Until the End of the World* and to the way in which the real intersects here with simulation and the painting of Vermeer, it will be useful to recur briefly to *The Art of Describing* and to the expanded notion of realism that we find there. Realism in Alpers's sense refers not only to the mimetic mirror—whose perverse troping we can locate in the activities of van Meegeren—but to representational practices that record the artist's awareness of the effects of the perceptual apparatus on the image. The Northern system is not Albertian, she asserts, it is Keplerian, concerned with optics and perception. Alpers is not the first interpreter of Dutch art to notice this involvement with optics; Gowing's work on Vermeer also gestures in this direction when it refers to a "mathematical net" in which Vermeer's figures seem caught and to a style that "relies entirely on the retina for its guide."[53] Gowing locates an "optical impartiality," "optical abstraction," and "photographic tonality" in Vermeer, concurring with Godard and Greenaway about the role of light in his painting when he claims that Vermeer's world seems to "wear to the last the garment of a retinal impression, to claim no greater depth than the play of light."[54] For Gowing, Vermeer's paintings record the apparent deformation of the retinal image, distorted in the manner of images in a convex mirror. Further, Vermeer is thought by David Hockney and others to have made use of a camera obscura and his paintings are believed to contain optical traces of this device.[55]

In the interview with Greenaway cited above, he seems to have been echoing not only Godard, but also Wenders's earlier remarks that "Vermeer is the only painter there is. He's really the only one who gives you the idea that his paintings could start moving. He'd be the ultimate cameraman, the ultimate top-notch cameraman."[56] It comes as no surprise, then, that Wenders makes use of Vermeer paintings in composing an image that, as the narrative has it, is being viewed through a special kind of sci-fi camera that enables "the blind to see" by literally recording the act of perception—the "brain waves," or neurological activity—of the person who views the image through the lens of the camera. With somewhat different intentions from those of Greenaway, in *Until the End of the World*, Wenders sets up a tableau vivant loosely based upon two Vermeer paintings in recognition, I would argue, of the optical concerns of Dutch art and of today's debates concerning simulation and the real. One of the tensions governing tableau vivant issues has its origin in an uncertainty about the boundaries that divide the representational from the real. In keeping with these concerns, Wenders may very well have based the title of his film on an eighteenth century German garden that contained a painted landscape at the end of a clearing in the natural scene: the garden is called "The End of the World."[57]

The sci-fi apparatus created by the scientist Farber (a name meaning "he who colors or dyes"—or, in this case, paints) has been called a "machine of vision"[58] and a "sight simulator."[59] It consists of a digital camera that supposedly records the neurological activity of the viewer and cameraperson and a computer that translates the images recorded first into electronic images, and then into impulses that trigger neurological activity in the brain. To transmit the recorded impulses, the viewer/cameraperson must see them again, so that the impulses triggered by a re-viewing may serve as a corrective on the first set. As the narrative would have it, Farber's blind wife, the object of the experiment, is thus enabled to see the images previously recorded and transmitted. Not unpredictably if we consider that Wenders's filmmaking is governed by an oedipal trajectory,[60] the images recorded by the camera are images of absent family members. Of these, the most central to this discussion is a sequence containing the daughter, who is dressed like Vermeer's "Girl With a Pearl Earring" in a setting that recalls "Young Woman with a Water Pitcher."

One thing that Wenders shares with Greenaway's false artist, van Meegeren, is his fascination with the image of the Vermeer woman. This may be because Wenders resembles Vermeer in his interest in the "ungraspable nature of the world seen," as Alpers puts it, and so chooses to pose "the basic problem of a descriptive art in the form of repeated images of women."[61] Although, as Thomas Elsaesser has put it, the mother is "wired up to a machine serviced simultaneously by father and son,"[62] the person best able both to record and to transmit the images (the most empathic medium?) is another woman, Claire. Given that Wenders has repeatedly been criticized for his reluctance or inability to represent women as central to his narratives, it seems somewhat heavy-handed—though not surprising—that he chooses to portray the images and story of a daughter as being recorded and transmitted for a mother through the medium of a would-be daughter-in-law. It should nevertheless be noted that Wenders situates women on both sides of the camera. By various means, then, Wenders's tableau vivant sequence is divested of its pornographic potential.[63]

But what end does Wenders's allusion to Vermeer serve? The sequence is not anachronistic, and it does not particularly call attention to itself. Unlike a Vermeer woman, the daughter faces the camera, telling her story while her brother and daughter look on as the sole spectators of the scene. She gives voice, that is, to the contained silence of Vermeer's women. Subsequently she is joined by her young daughter, who also faces and addresses the camera and, by extension, the grandmother for whom these images are recorded. Not only does Wenders animate Vermeer's woman, but he violates her isolation by introducing a child into her domestic space, by confirming her ties to the patriarchal family by way of her narrative, and finally by causing her to look into and acknowledge the camera. During this sequence, the spectator of Wenders's film sees the image of the woman first through Robby Müller's camera and finally through the eye of the sci-fi digital camera within the diegesis. When seen through the digital camera—constructed by a man though used by a woman—a grid resembling that of Dürer's draftsman is superimposed upon the daughter's image. But this grid refers not only to the draftsman's grid—it is also that of the computer. In the sequence prior to the successful visual experiment, we see images on a large monitor in which the actors' bodies appear trapped behind a grid that resembles a fence. In the case of Dürer, of Vermeer, *and* of Wenders, the question remains the same: how is the body, in particular the body of a woman, appropriated by and for representation? Although the daughter moves about in Wenders's sequence, she appears to be no less "pinned to the drawing board" than the draftsman's image of the nude.

Dressed as the "Girl With Pearl Earrings," the daughter is seated near a window with leaded panes. It is a Vermeer composition par excellence, complete with light streaming through the window, a map hanging on the wall, and a table with Persian rug and jug. The subject of the daughter's monologue is her amazement that her mother will soon "see her face." By way of a dream that she relates to the camera and to her mother, it is made clear that the mother's recognition would serve to confirm the daughter in her identity. But in this dream, as she puts it, there is "something wrong with my face" that prevents the mother's recognition, causing the young woman to protest "but I *am* your daughter." Later, when the blind mother is made to see, she will first see colors, then the image of her daughter. Asking her husband if the young woman could be their daughter, the mother enjoins Farber to "look at her face." What has been "missing" from the Vermeer composition, one might say—the *mirror*—is present after all: it is implied in the two sequences that, taken together, comprise the mirror stage experience that the daughter has hitherto lacked. The mirror is metaphorically present in the composition as well when the granddaughter and her mother face the camera that will "mirror" their joint image. Another lack is supplied by the blind woman, as well: by way of superimposed images of the Vermeer-like daughter and her blind mother, the mother's pearl ring notably appears in the place of the daughter's absent pearl earring. Somewhat sentimentally, perhaps, mother and daughter are united through the image of the pearl, or tear.

In the initial shot of this tableau vivant sequence we see Claire, wearing the sci-fi camera that resembles glasses, from behind. Shot from behind, wearing the camera that records images, Claire is in the position of the painter in Vermeer's "Artist in His Studio," and appears to be, to use Alba's phrase in *Zed and Two Noughts,* "an excuse for art theory." We know that the daughter, object of Claire's look as artist and cameraperson, is to be transformed into a digital image and, as a gloss on this image, a passage from Norman Bryson's well-known essay, "The Gaze and the Glance," seems particularly apt. Arguing that Vermeer's paintings are examples of the "painting of the Gaze," Bryson uses a pertinent analogy to distinguish such painting from the Albertian model with its embodied viewer, a passage that may even have inspired Wenders in making this film: "An analogy from computer-based video display may help to clarify this difficult spatial transformation. When sectional drawings are 'rotated' on a television screen, the space through which the image turns is purely virtual—perhaps the purest virtual space so far devised: no one has actually seen this space in the real world; ultimately its only 'real' location is within the distribution data in the computer program."[64]

Using "The Artist in His Studio" as his example, Bryson goes on to claim that, in Vermeer's work, "the viewer [of the painting] and painter no longer inhabit the same continuum, and so far from entering into the perceptual inner field of the painter's body, the viewer sees that body from the outside, from behind."[65] In this painting, Bryson argues, the "bodily address" of the Albertian model is dissolved into a "computative space," in which "unique, discontinuous, disincarnate bodies, move in spatial apartness."[66] Certainly Wenders's sequence, with its layering of several mediums—painting, film, video, and digital images—creates a palimpsest of textualities under which the body might be said to "vanish . . . in the play of signs."[67] It would initially appear, then, that those who point to Wenders's postmodern emphasis on the simulacrum rather than on the real may be right, as Wenders chooses to suggest that the representational determinants of Vermeer's painting are not very different from those that produce the digital image. The "perceptual incoherence" of Vermeer's paintings, as Bryson reads it, is not simply a product of recording acts of perception, but an aspect of Vermeer's deliberate exaggeration of the "conflicting grids of transcriptive fidelity."[68] For Bryson, then, Vermeer's work does not participate in any kind of "realism," even in Alpers's expanded sense of "realistic" painting as an art form whose images bear the stamp of the artist's optical awareness.

But what, we must ask again, happens to the digital image in *Until the End of the World* after it is recorded? In Wenders's fiction, the recorded electronic impulses must first reenter the body of the artist/cameraperson, so that neurological activity extraneous to that produced by the desired image may be excluded; they are then introduced into the body of the blind woman who will be their "spectator." Because the electronic impulses produce "biochemical" images, as Farber puts it, the image is grounded in the body once more, producing both a spectator and an image that are "embodied." Although these images originate in a "machine of vision," Wenders ultimately uses this sci-fi camera to undo the "damage" done by representation: the camera is firmly tied to the physiological aspect of vision. Although triggered by electronic images, the nerve impulses that produce the mother's vision are real.

But what of the visual qualities of the images that she sees? In the sequence described above, images seen by the mother are either cut with or superimposed upon her eyes, hence deliberately coded as her vision. They are beautiful, flickering images awash with colors that exceed the contours of bodies, colors that keep changing. In these images, bodies in outline are covered with a gridlike design that here resembles the weave of a canvas support. Initially blurred, they come to look like moving versions of Andy Warhol's silk screen photo portraits, with each image in a series variously colored; the work of Chuck Close and Gerhard Richter[69] also comes to mind. At one point during this sequence, the spectator of the film sees a chain of serial images, each in different tints. As images, they share with Warhol's silk screens and Richter's paintings with their photographic origin an ambiguous status between the photographic and the painterly. Moreover, Warhol's silk screens are at once photographic in origin, mass-produced, and hand tinted.[70] If Wenders deliberately alludes to Warhol in these transformations of Vermeer-like tableaux, then he may do so to further reinforce the simulacral quality of these images by connecting them with pop art. Yet, as in a Dutch realism understood to be produced by the recording of optical effects within representation, the visual qualities manifested by these images are decidedly realistic. They are marked as neurological, anchored in the real. For the spectator of the film, however, like Warhol's silk screens these manipulated images come precariously close to being "art." Wenders chooses, it would seem, to create painterly images that compete with Vermeer on his own territory.

Why Tableau Vivant?

In their filmmaking, both Greenaway and Wenders openly experiment with the variety of representational systems—photographic, electronic, digital—available to film. Sequences that focus images of writing and print are as common as painterly compositions and allusions in Greenaway's work, and they are evident in Wenders's films as well. Moments that seek figuratively to *split* the image from acts of narration coexist with what I have called tableau vivant here, with moments of representational layering in which painting is brought into the picture. As he has implied, Greenaway reads Vermeer as a realist who addresses senses beyond that of sight, whose paintings depict moments of arrested action, and hence closely resemble film stills. In the figure of the surgeon, van Meegeren, Greenaway has created a horribly literal version of the realist, a false Vermeer who does not create in paint, but uses the flesh itself as his material. Wenders, too, reads Vermeer as a realist painter, one whose paintings share the properties of the photographic image. It's interesting, then, that both of the films under discussion animate the paintings to which they allude; at no time do they draw upon the possibilities of tableau vivant to halt the action of film. Instead, they "make real": they introduce the body (of the actor) into representation.

Embodiment is the theoretical focus of attention and, in the case of both films, the questions that it generates are taken to an extreme: the decomposing bodies of *A Zed and Two Noughts* will finally exist only at the microscopic level; the neurological activity that allows the blind to see in *Until the End of the World* is submicroscopic. What concerns Greenaway is a dialectic between composition (which has an analogue in the harnessing of representational systems that produce a scene) and decomposition, the real taken to its extreme end point (with its analogue in the separation of representational systems that produce a scene). By means of the "technologically advanced" sci-fi camera of *Until the End of the World*, Wenders reduces vision to its material determinants, and vision becomes wholly internalized. This process can be reversed: a further sci-fi development allows Wenders's characters to record the neurological activity produced in dreaming. Their neurological impulses are converted into electronic images, allowing them to externalize and watch their dreams on a monitor. Thus dreams are rendered material and portable.

In a talk about high definition television given in Tokyo in 1990, Wenders interrogates the applicability of terms such as "the original" and "reality" to the images produced by contemporary technology.[71] Wenders confesses that the High Vision dream images of *Until the End of the World* are based upon photographs taken in Wenders's and Solveig Dommartin's childhood,[72] highly personal images. The images that we see on the screen, comprised of up to 100 layers, with image superimposed over image, have the look of animated watercolors. But this layering of different types of images—what I have referred to above—as representational layering—can be said to produce a "spatialization of the moving image," an "image cluster" that lends the image a kind of material density.[73] Here sci-fi's world of the future mirrors the beliefs of the aborigines of the film, who hold that a man's "bad dreams" can be "taken away" by sleeping next to him. When science fiction, primitive magic, and the cutting edge of technology meet, the final irony may be that these "material images" look painterly. In more than one sense, then, the "new images" produced by today's technology are evocative of tableau vivant.

3

The Fascist Choreography: Riefenstahl's Tableaux

"Leni! Pity she's dead," Helmut Newton says in response to the news that Leni Reifenstahl has just died at the age of 101. "She once made me promise never to call her an old Nazi, you know."[1] Newton, the photographer who notoriously created scenarios of sadomasochism and perversion for the display of high fashion escaped from Berlin in 1938, having already begun his apprenticeship as a photographer there. Although Riefenstahl's photographs are not as overtly erotic as Newton's and don't appear to play to perversions, there is nevertheless a continuity between their work. It was looking at the posed, arrested bodies in Riefenstahl's *Last of the Nuba* that prompted Susan Sontag's famous meditation on Riefenstahl's films and on fascist aesthetics in general.[2] The fascist choreography that governs movement and stasis in Riefenstahl's work, Sontag writes in "Fascinating Fascism," "flow[s] from (and justif[ies] a preoccupation with situations of control, submissive behavior, and extravagant effort),"[3] suggesting—though not making—a connection between such behaviors and psychosexual dispositions. Yet the implication is there.

Drawing in all likelihood on Wilhelm Reich's *Mass Psychology of Fascism* (written in Germany in 1933; banned by the Nazis in 1935) as well as on Adorno's "Freudian Theory and the Pattern of Fascist Propaganda," Sontag's essay points both to the sublimation of sexuality, the transformation of libidinal energies into a "spiritual" force in fascism, as well as to its expression in an "orgiastic transaction" between leader and masses.[4] It is Reich who famously claims that fascism converts the "orgasm anxiety" of the "man subjected to authority" into an eternalized purity,[5] while Adorno draws on Freud in asserting that the source of Hitler's libidinal power over the masses is linked to infantile orality and promotes an "archaic regression."[6] "Nazi art is both prurient and idealizing," Sontag points out, its aesthetics "exalt two seemingly opposite states: egomania and servitude."[7]

In Sontag's scattered remarks concerning the psychosexual dimension of fascist art there are lingering echoes that connect the fascist aesthetic to masochism, an aggressive, oral stage perversion that indefinitely defers orgasmic satisfaction, and that, like fascism in Saul Friedlander's reading, "aestheticizes the erotic plane."[8] Sontag's description of a fascist choreography as one that "alternates between ceaseless motion and a congealed, static, 'virile' posing,"[9] calls to mind that masochism "reveals the stillness in movement, the edge of Thanatos in Eros that aestheticizes the erotic into cold suspense and diverts sexuality from orgasm to an erotic contemplation at once frustrating and pleasurable."[10] By way of its tableaux moments and its dialectic of stasis and motion, I would suggest, the fascist choreography has a great deal to do with the theatrical scenarios of masochism. In these scenarios, eros is desexualized, death is sexualized, and repetition and control are of central importance.

Although we will return to this subject later, the psychosexuality of Riefenstahl's choreography is not my central concern. Sontag's essay has notably pointed the way to some of the rhetorical structures that govern Riefenstahl's work, a few of which I pursue, choosing to look to one feature in particular that suggests a boundary crossing between mediums. In Riefenstahl's filmmaking, this is the recurrent presence of tableau vivant moments—or, more loosely, staged tableaux. Kracauer was the first to call attention to the tableau arrangements in Riefenstahl's films, but the term is invoked repeatedly in conjunction with her style.[11] Sontag's description of the fascist choreography as the alternation of motion with static posing likewise draws on an understanding of tableau moments and of their subsequent subsumption by the ongoing flux of film's images. In the course of examining tableaux in Riefenstahl's films and the rhythm of movement and stasis in which they participate, this chapter positions aspects of Riefenstahl's visual style within a matrix of related cultural and aesthetic phenomena. With a "thicker" description of these formal features as its object, this chapter places them within other artistic practices, including the baroque tragic drama, sculpture and dance, and finally, photography. By isolating moments in Riefenstahl's work that feature the posed, static body, I seek to contextualize these moments artistically and historically and to ask questions concerning the aesthetic and ideological freight they are made to carry.

Triumph of the Will: Tableaux and Trionfi

In a self-described turn away from *Ideologiekritik*, Russell Berman's 1989 essay "Written Right Across Their Faces: Leni Riefenstahl, Ernst Jünger, and Fascist Modernism" initially locates its interest in "the rhetorical grounding of Riefenstahl's *énoniciation*" and, more broadly, in a rhetorical politics of fascist representation per se.[12] Understanding rhetoric as expressive of a "politics prior to ideological contents," Berman clusters his brief remarks on Riefenstahl's *Triumph of the Will* around the notion of a fascist practice as one that prioritizes visual in favor of verbal representation. Using Riefenstahl as a lead-in to his essay proper—a nuanced and evocative reading of Jünger's work within the context of competing types of modernism—Berman's gaze, though soon averted from Riefenstahl, continues to linger on matters of rhetorical politics. Drawing on the ekphrastic impulse in Jünger's writing and ringing changes on the relations of language and image that reside in ekphrasis, Berman joins his voice to others who claim that the status of writing occupies a position inferior to that of the image in fascist textual practice. Betraying a general "antipathy toward the symbolic order,"[13] fascist textuality as read by Berman corporealizes writing, hence reduces "the distance between body and text."[14] Further, fascist artistic practice favors the respatialization that occurs when the temporality of language is abandoned in favor of the image—in this case of the ideologically inflected *Gestalt*. Along with this reference to Rosenberg, Susan Sontag, Lessing, and even Thomas Mann are not far to seek in Berman's observations. "Fascism as the aestheticization of politics transforms the world into a visual object:"[15] Appropriately, Walter Benjamin is also pressed into service.

Simultaneously evocative of painting, drama, and sculpture, tableau vivant generally features the immobile, held pose of human actors. Tableau vivant is most familiar from the fashionable novels of the nineteenth century— preeminently Goethe's *Elective Affinities* (1809)—where they function as a diversion, a parlor game involving the static embodiment of well-known paintings. Their origins include the tableau moment in the bourgeois tragedy of the eighteenth century and the staged melodrama of the nineteenth century, but earlier still the term occurs in descriptions of processions and open-air festivals held during the Italian Renaissance. A widely practiced public art form during this period, tableaux vivants were often staged on portable platforms carrying first relics or devotional statues and eventually supporting performances of scenes by live actors.[16] Although early instances were religious in nature, mythological allegory later became their favored subject: the fetishized body part that is the relic is replaced first by the statue, then by the living, posed, and emblematic body of allegory. On this subject, too, Walter Benjamin is well-informed: as we recall from *The Origins of German Tragic Drama* (published in 1928), the triumphal procession involving tableaux was favored in Italy where "the *trionfi* were the dominant mode of the processions,"[17] inspiring similar formal structures in German tragic drama. Here, too, language is subordinate to image, and the political function of tableaux is apparent: they enact the authority of the ruler and elicit public support. Predictably, such tableaux occurred frequently in celebrations of cultural dominance, so it is hardly surprising, as Benjamin tells us, that they flourished in Florence under the Medici.[18] During the Nazi period, workers participated in tableaux vivants for similar reasons.[19]

Surely the infamous Nuremberg party rally is such a pageant, an occasion for the public display of power, a *Triumph of the Will*, indeed. In the motorcade sequence of Riefenstahl's film, Hitler's triumphal procession features his body—primarily stationary—in the rigid pose of a devotional statue or mythological figure, this rigidity playing a vital role in the film's myth-making program. Although the motorcade and traveling camera contribute to the illusion of a moving body, the camera also favors shots of Hitler erect in an open car, gliding immobile through the cheering crowd. In *Triumph of the Will*, Hitler as icon signifies politically— propagandistically—just as the statuary and tableaux of Venetian trionfi did. Here Benjamin's observation on the rhythm of the German tragic drama (the *Trauerspiel*, or "mourning-play")—derived from these trionfi—is of interest. His description of its "irregular rhythm of constant pause, the sudden change of direction, and consolidation into new rigidity"[20] is noticeably echoed in Sontag's comment on movement and stasis in the fascist choreography, specifically in the alternation "between ceaseless motion and a congealed, static, 'virile' posing" mentioned above. Riefenstahl's film establishes its irregular rhythm as fast tracking shots of the crowd are cut with Hitler as icon and effigy, both the fixed point around which the action revolves and the eroticized object of the look.[21] This quality of an effigy that Riefenstahl's film imparts to the figure of Hitler is something that Hans-Jürgen Syberberg must have noticed.

Steve Neale, too, has commented on this film's relation to baroque drama and its particular form of display. As he remarks of *Triumph of the Will*, "theatricality—in all its artifice—is crucial to the particular mode of spectacle to which I am referring here, a mode whose traditions stem from, and are exemplified by, Baroque painting, theatre and opera."[22] In triumphal processions as described by Benjamin, language is reduced to a "caption, conjured up from the allegorical constellations in which the figures are related to one another."[23] Language as caption is emblematic and "entire speeches sound as if they properly belong beneath an allegorical engraving."[24] Following the work of an earlier scholar, Carl Horst, Benjamin suggests that language in the German tragic drama of the baroque period is similarly ornamental, its dramatic structure "hidden" beneath ornamentation, specifically tableaux vivants in the form of the "staged *exemplum*, staged antithesis, and staged metaphor."[25] Here, too, language is respatialized and multiply eclipsed by the image, an image whose constituent parts include human bodies whose purpose is nevertheless significatory, if opaque.

With reference to *Triumph of the Will*, Berman points out that the priority of the image is asserted in this film even when it features a series of political speeches, claiming that "the verbal character of speech in the film is always secondary to the visual spectacle and the image of the present speaker."[26] Once again language is subsumed within the greater pattern of spectacle. Given the propagandistic character of the speeches, however, what strategies reduce language to a role of secondary importance? Granted, the speakers are but one aspect of the overall design of the frame—"beneath an allegorical engraving," as it were, beneath the emblematic Reich's eagle— but as they are political figures, well known, even controversial, how can their individual characters be suppressed? Riefenstahl manages this in a variety of ways. Rudolf Hess's speech, for example, is heard in voice-over with reaction shots of listeners as varied as Goebbels, a young child, and Hitler himself. Presented from a variety of angles that heighten visual interest, these faces register Hess's words visually, affectively, as their impact on his listeners. In the montage of diatribes that follows, each speaker is preceded by a title engraved with the glowing ornamental script of his own handwriting: here, too, writing is rendered as image. Repetition likewise has its effect, de-emphasizing duration and thus spatializing language as one by one, similarly framed by the camera, the speakers deliver their speeches at the podium. By various means, then, formal procedures produce what Benjamin, quoting Horst on baroque tragic drama, has called an "advance of the plastic arts into the territory of the rhetorical arts."[27]

Although Riefenstahl's use of repetition and accumulation are fascist aesthetic strategies shared in common with the German baroque tragic drama, repetition is also one of the linchpins of masochistic scenarios, where repetition produces the "aesthetic coherence" of a fantasy that expresses infantile fixation, and promotes the behaviors that defer (orgasmic) resolution. What, then, of the image of the body in this articulation? In Sacher-Masoch's *Venus in Furs*, (female) characters assume tableau postures, freezing—as Deleuze notes in his study of masochism—into postures that connect them with statues, paintings, or photographs.[28] Riefenstahl's film similarly has recourse to tableau arrangements that feature the posed body, the body in arrested motion. It is not only Hitler whose "virile posing" is suggestive of a sculpture or icon: another notable instance involves the close-up of faces in the workers' brigade, arranged in sculptural bas-relief, a frieze over which the tracking camera passes. Here is the fascist merger of body and artwork that Arno Breker's and Josef Thorak's sculptures unwittingly pursue to the point of self-parody.[29] It will not be necessary to rehearse the many instances in this film in which the mass ornament submits human bodies to its geometry—Kracauer's famous essay as well as his references to the "living ornaments" of *Triumph of the Will* have provoked much observation on this topic.[30]

But relentless movement propels Riefenstahl's film forward. Within the containment provided by the "set" of Speer's monumental architecture, Riefenstahl's orchestrated, ornamental phalanxes seem to have lives of their own, their movement throwing immobility into relief and subsuming it within its flow. As Sontag suggests, movement in the "fascist dramaturgy" traces "grandiose and rigid patterns" that sweep up the static figure into its "choreography."[31] Interestingly, nearly fifty years earlier Benjamin had used similar language to suggest to his reader that the dramaturgy of the German tragic drama, the *Trauerspiel*, unfolds "in a spatial continuum which one might describe as choreographic."[32] What are we to make of these multiple echoes of Benjamin's analysis of the *Trauerspiel* in Sontag's description of fascist aesthetics? Could it be that Sontag—an avid reader of Benjamin who imitated Benjamin's art of quotation[33]— had recourse to his descriptions of tragic drama's formal characteristics and inverted their significance? Whether or not this is the case, in both the *Trauerspiel* and in *Triumph of the Will*, bodies posed and contained in arrangements function as images even when they are subjected to motion.

As I have suggested, Benjaminian allegory can be said to hold sway in the tableau insofar as it is a mixed mode, a boundary crossing of several arts: alluding once again to Horst, Benjamin reads allegory as revealing a "crossing of the borders into a different mode."[34] Tableau vivant as a layering of mediums implies a transgression of organic unity in the manner of German tragic drama. In the tableaux scenes of tragic drama, the actor's body is arrested in motion and rendered sculptural; the allusion to, if not direct imitation of, paintings or iconographic scenes from mythology or the Bible render narrative by means of the image. Ultimately plastic, because enacted by human figures, the tableau reduces narrative to a spectacle supported by the body. Conversely, tableau scenes also render the body as text, a tendency that Berman reads in the ekphrastic cast of fascist textuality.

For the German reader in particular, Lessing's preference for writing over the image[35] is not far to seek in Berman's discussion. For Benjamin, however, the baroque tragic drama's allegorical tendency makes it a productively mixed mode: it is at one and the same time linguistic and imagistic, both corporeal—tied to bodies—and rooted in history. The Christian origins of German tragic drama allow corporeality—Christ as man—to guarantee both its immanence and its reflection of temporality as transitoriness. In contradistinction, Riefenstahl's *Triumph of the Will* is engaged in staging history and rendering it myth. It will come as no surprise that what distinguishes the German tragic drama irrefutably from fascist art is its mode of structuration, its reliance on the fragment as the producer of meaning. If scenes of violence, cruelty, and death are so frequently represented in these plays, Benjamin suggests, it is because "the human body could be no exception to the commandment which ordered the destruction of the organic so that true meaning, as it was written and ordained, might be picked up from its fragments."[36]

As remarked above, bodies in *Triumph of the Will* are often subsumed within the ornamental patterns that characterize its style. By promoting the part only in relation to the whole, Riefenstahl's film contains and neutralizes the heterogeneity of tableaux moments. As Steve Neale suggests, the film's markers of theatricality do not subvert its unity; they do not contribute to a self-consciousness that disrupts and critiques. They are—on the contrary—contained by this unity.[37] Needless to say, the generative principle, the anti-Eisensteinian principle of accretion that governs Riefenstahl's editing style has as its model an organic theory of art whose governing structure is wholeness. As in a kaleidoscope, patterns within this film change yet in some sense remain constant: in substituting for narrative, movement and editing merely replace one form of spectacle with another. It is the film's dynamism, then, that promotes wholeness, and the inexorability of its motion suggests that it is a libidinal energy that propels the film forward.

If it can be said of *Triumph of the Will* that it has a choreography as well as a dramaturgy, that it plays off stasis against motion, then Nietzsche's *Birth of Tragedy* (1872) may not be far to seek. One of the texts that serves as a foil for Benjamin's treatise on the German tragic drama, Nietzsche's reading of Greek tragedy supplements the "noble simplicity and serene grandeur" that the German tradition had predominantly read in Greek antiquity from the time of Winckelmann's writings on sculpture with its opposite: a Dionysian (erotic) energy. As is well known, Nietzsche locates the Dionysian aspect of Greek tragedy—the affective urges and the dynamic principle of art—in the chorus, in music, whereas the Apollonian principle of form is allied with sculpture. Their dialectical relation opposes the (Apollonian) containment of form in composed, static images with the dynamic, ecstatic (Dionysian) energy of dance. In some sense, it may be the "amorous struggle" between these two principles—to use Lacoue-Labarthe and Nancy's phrase[38]—that *Triumph of the Will* and, indeed, Riefenstahl's choreography more generally, expresses.

Body Art: Sculpture and Dance

The paradigm for German thinking concerning both sculpture and Classical antiquity famously emerges with J. J. Winckelmann's *Thoughts on the Imitation of Greek Art in Painting and Sculpture*, published shortly before he left Dresden for Rome (1755). In Dresden, Winckelmann's viewing of classical sculpture, although confined to plaster casts, nevertheless produced very vivid experiences in their spectator. The most famous of Winckelmann's meditations is centered on the Laocoön sculptural group that evoked the often-cited "noble simplicity and serene grandeur" that would eventually propel much of Europe into neoclassicism. Here Winckelmann focuses on the way in which the smooth contours and the restrained pose of Laocoön's sculptural body contain his pain, reading this containment as expressive of the noble Greek soul.[39] Winckelmann's attitude towards the physical body notably changes after his arrival in Rome, however, where his encounter with the Belvedere Apollo results in enraptured, homoerotically tinged ekphrasis in which the spectator describes himself as transported, possessed by the beauty of the god. Despite all claims to the contrary, Winckelmann's description seems not to transcend a physical fixation on the beautiful male body. When Winckelmann is moved affectively at the sight, his experience prompts an ecstatic prose that animates and corporealizes the sculpture. Between them, Winckelmann's seminal texts suggest a spectrum of reactions to the sculptural body in which the spiritual attitude is favored, but physical response is incompletely sublimated.

Riefenstahl's first appearance in film is as Diotima in Arnold Fanck's *The Holy Mountain* (1926), a clichéd amalgam of Winckelmannian neoclassicism and romantic motifs.[40] In Fanck's film, Diotima's dwelling place is the space where mountain cliffs drop down to meet the ocean's waves, conjuring up the Diotima of Hölderlin's *Hyperion* (1777–79) as well as her model, the priestess in Plato's *Symposium* whose role is to explain both the nature of love as well as the connection between the beautiful body and the ideal. In *The Holy Mountain*, Riefenstahl as Diotima expresses herself through dance as editing links her movements to the sea, the (female) element to which her pantheistic dance is dedicated. Like Venus, Diotima is seemingly born of this element and expresses its natural rhythms by way of her own. At once idealized and eroticized, Riefenstahl's body participates in a narrative that moves toward—but fails to achieve—the formation of an ideal couple. Desire for the character played by Luis Trenker, conflated with the (male) space of the sublime mountain peak, motivates Diotima's second dance. At times, the film fixes both characters in sculptural poses, backlit against the landscapes with which they are identified. Following the tradition that emerges from Winckelmann's thinking, the beautiful body is the posed body, its contours in harmonious balance, while dance and a graceful athleticism define the movement that Fanck's film demands of its characters. Expressive bodily movement and the sculptural pose continue to be central to Riefenstahl's acting in the feature films of her own directing.[41]

Even more prominently, Winckelmann's ideas form a backdrop for the prologue of Riefenstahl's *Olympia, Part I: Festival of the People* (1938), where attitudes toward classical antiquity are reshaped to conform to Nazi ideology, and the dialectic of movement and stasis finds an overtly political expression. In this astonishing sequence, movement develops out of stillness as classical statues are brought, Pygmalion-like, to life. Shot on location by Willy Zielke at the Poseidon Temple, the Parthenon and Ereichtheion on the Acropolis, at Cape Sunion and Corinth, and at the National Museum in Athens,[42] it features the authentic statuary of Greek antiquity, not the plaster casts or Roman copies with which Winckelmann was familiar. As usual, the choice of images and the editing were Riefenstahl's own: Zielke complained bitterly that "she did only what she had thought out at the editing table, [it was] theoretical,"[43] and that her editing style had ruined his material. Out of material shot on location, the prologue creates the feeling that Zielke refers to as "something imaginary, it has no tempo, it is hundreds of years long, Greece, soul, mythology."[44] It is precisely this dreamlike, out-of-time representation of Greece as origin that makes this prologue an ideal illustration of Lacoue-Labarthe and Nancy's "The Nazi Myth."

Appearing as engraved inscriptions on stone tablets, the opening credits of *Olympia, Part I*, including the director's name, hubristically link the art of film to the most notable achievements of Greek architecture and sculpture, providing an even more convincing example of the subsumption of writing by the image than the subverted script in the prologue to *Triumph of the Will*. What is presented here is filmic ekphrasis, with the camera visually rendering inscription for the spectator. Lyric poetry per se is thought to have originated in the ekphrastic epigrams and inscriptions collected in the Greek Anthology, poetic forms which have resonance in German writing through and beyond Rilke. Riefenstahl's film thus proclaims itself a participant in the tradition of ekphrastic writing and in the *paragones*—or battle of the arts—within which this genre situates itself. Although writing—it should be noted in qualification of Berman—usually triumphs over the image in ekphrastic poetry,[45] here the camera's writing renders the archaicized letters as embedded in the scene. Film as the art of technology emerges triumphant. From the start, then, it is suggested that premodern and modern modes of representation are continuous, reconciled.[46]

The camera's insistent and progressive motion as it generates a space around and through the ruins of classical antiquity serves symbolically to reassemble them, creating wholeness out of fragmented ruin. Larger fragments are superimposed upon smaller, and the camera's power is revealed to be formative as it progresses from a single column to the Parthenon in its entirety. The camera's constitutive function is similarly revealed as the (fascist) devices of repetition and expansion include the shooting of one object from multiple perspectives, as though to give the object shape, to present it in its three-dimensional plasticity. By means of shot transitions in the form of dissolves, some as long as eight or ten seconds,[47] the film suggests that it proceeds by way of a layering of images, by accretion rather than by means of the cuts that stress fragmentation.

If the epilogue of Benjamin's "Work of Art in the Age of Mechanical Reproduction," published in 1935, responds to the aestheticized politics of *Triumph of the Will*, the prologue to *Olympia, Part I* seems conceived to refute Benjamin's analysis and to substantiate its epilogue. Contradicting Benjamin's understanding of the cinematic medium as necessarily fragmentary, Riefenstahl's prologue deliberately serves to ally film with idealist artistic practice. Fragmentation is scorned, and the evocatory power of the ruin elaborated in Benjamin's *Trauerspiel* treatise is rejected in favor of reconstruction. Both the camera's powers and the mode of editing are regenerative,[48] bringing to life a culture that lies in ruins. Because the bridge to that culture is created via the body, its images serve to substantiate Rosenberg's contention that the Aryan race originated with the Greeks. Later in the prologue, the collapsing of time and space is rendered imagistically when the Olympic torch is passed from runner to runner, its path traced on a schematic map of Europe by way of the camera, cut with paradigmatic documentary shots of cities. Finally, the camera descends through clouds to alight in Hitler's Olympic Stadium.[49] In moving from the Parthenon to the Olympic stadium in Berlin, Riefenstahl's film enacts an ellipsis that transports the spectator into a temporality it represents first as mythological, then as historical. Thus Riefenstahl's prologue closely illustrates Lacoue-Labarthe and Nancy's elaboration of "the Nazi myth" as promoting a spatial and temporal bridge from ancient Greece—via Winckelmann's eighteenth century—to Nazi Germany.[50]

Sculpture has an important role to play in the myth-making program of the prologue: myth is a plastic fiction, a "fictioning" whose role is to propose types to be imitated, as Lacoue-Labarthe and Nancy put it.[51] After entering the Parthenon at the beginning of the prologue, the camera focuses on statues of Greek gods from multiple perspectives, its movement producing the illusion of their movement. The arrangement of the statues creates a striking depth of field, and the orchestration of the dissolves contributes to the illusion that the statues themselves are animated, seeming to move around freely as the camera tracks around the figures. Enhanced by the liberal use of Vaseline and smoke,[52] the impression of movement in this sequence is nonetheless an allusion to Pygmalion, whose sculpture of the beautiful Galatea Venus brought to life. While filming against a dark background with a strong key light highlighting faces, Zielke created an auratic glow by means of the softer and more dispersed light emanating from behind the sculptural figures. Giving the impression of candlelight, this flickering lends a suggestion of motion to the statuary, calling to mind a late-eighteenth-century protocinematic practice: the fashion for nocturnal visits to sculpture galleries that allowed spectators to enjoy the impression of "living sculptures," on whom candlelight conferred an uncanny sensation of movement.[53] By this means, too, Riefenstahl's prologue situates itself within a spectrum of received artistic tradition: it is precisely by participating in the Greek production of myth as art that Riefenstahl mimetically allies her work with Greek tradition. Here the (film) art that rehearses myth's embodiment as sculpture clearly functions as a means of identification.

The staged rebirth of myth and perfect beauty continues as a series of shots of the perfect male form—a statue of Apollo—is interspersed with shots of Aphrodite, the perfect female form. Images overlap and fade quickly as the two appear to move across the screen toward one another, soon to be replaced by a life-size sculpture of Discobulus, the ideal *human* form as athlete, metaphorically rendered as the offspring of the gods. But the apotheosis of Riefenstahl's regenerative strategies occurs as, with a nearly perfect match on the dissolve, a human athlete in an identical posture and against a natural setting takes its place.[54] Here art produces life: having enlivened the stasis of sculpture by means of its own motion, the camera now records the movements of a living human figure superimposed upon the statue. As the static sculpture is released from the tableau, exploding into life and movement, it is suggested that the mythical past has come alive as well. By formal means, then, the prologue suggests the German claim that the experience of Greek art is that of the *Formwillen*, the will to form, and claims Rosenberg's goal of "an organic art that produces life" as the guiding principle of Riefenstahl's work.[55]

In her memoirs, Riefenstahl represents her experience of the visual arts and dance as continuous with one another,[56] and both are continuous with film in her artistic practice. Indeed, the next sequence that concerns us here[57]—figure studies of male athletes—derives from a series of paintings of male nudes by the American painter Stowitts, paintings much admired by Riefenstahl, who had hoped to incorporate them directly into the prologue by means of filters and out-of-focus effects.[58] Although these paintings themselves did not find their way into the film, their look influenced the rendering of live male athletes throwing javelins and shot put, figures characteristically shot from below. In the next sequence—the dance sequence—dance is not simply the female counterpart to male athleticism, but continues the meditation on movement and stasis begun earlier by the juxtaposition of camera movement with sculpture. Their arms swaying rhythmically, the women's movements are mythologically inflected as well as "organic," in unison with the rhythms of nature, the rolling waves and the swaying grasses. This, too, is body art: at one and the same time their ornamentally arranged bodies allude to the many-armed Aryan god Shiva and to similar patterns formed by the Tiller Girls. Once again Riefenstahl conflates premodern and modern references.

Choreographed by Riefenstahl herself, the women's dances harken back to her acting debut as Diotima in Fanck's *The Holy Mountain*,[59] where her performance is likewise cut with waves breaking on the shore. Yet this sequence, too, may have been inspired by Stowitts, who was himself a dancer in the mode of Isadora Duncan.[60] In the sequence under discussion, the women's dances are in the expressive style promoted by Duncan, who often performed in Greek chitons and claimed to have been schooled by "wind and wave and winged flight of bird and bee."[61] Because Duncan reflected her era in believing that the harmony of body and soul produce movement as the soul's "natural language," her views were compatible with the dominant German understanding of Greek antiquity, as well as with Riefenstahl's own ideas of dance.[62] Although its erotic element is not wholly repressed, dance in *Olympia*'s prologue is a far cry from its origins in dionysian rites as envisioned by Nietzsche—yet here, too, it is connected with the natural, communal, and religious.

But Riefenstahl's choreography doesn't harken back to Isadora Duncan alone: it is synthetic, incorporating Duncan's style, yet even more indebted to that of Mary Wigman, Riefenstahl's erstwhile teacher. Wigman for her part had for years been a student of Rudolf von Laban at Monte Verita in Ascona, Switzerland, where she and others performed ritualistic dances naked—in harmony with nature—at sunrise and sunset. It was also at Ascona that Wigman developed the ecstatic, dionysian rhythms that forged her Witch Dance (*Hexentanz*), said to have been the origin of modern dance as we know it. Further, as Riefenstahl suggests in her memoirs, Wigman's dance performances were also influenced by rhythmical gymnastics,[63] a form of exercise closely linked to the art of sculpture—and likewise promoted by the Nazis. Indeed, both Laban and Wigman had roles to play in the dance performances originally planned around the Olympics themselves—Laban as head of Goebbel's organization for German dance performance (the *Tanzbühne*, or dance stage) was to orchestrate the planned Dance Olympics (*Tanz Olympiade*), in which Wigman and her troupe were to perform. Quite appropriately, one might say, Laban choreographed the planned program around themes from Nietzsche texts, including *Thus Spoke Zarathustra*.[64] After watching the performance, however, Goebbels cancelled the program: denounced as "hostile to the state," perhaps its ideology was too explicit.[65]

Interestingly, the dancers who performed in Riefenstahl's prologue were chosen by Willy Zielke from among students at the Laban and Wigman schools of dance in Berlin.[66] Read as originating in sculpture, as moving sculpture, or as a series of sculptures, dance in Riefenstahl's prologue has a relation to rhythmical gymnastics (*rhythmische Gymnastik*) that must have derived from Wigman. A form of open-air exercise much promoted in Germany during this period, rhythmical gymnastics involved the creation of dancelike exercise movements in which participants modeled their poses on

Greek statuary. Originally progressive in spirit, rhythmical gymnastics was promoted during the Nazi period as an aspect of body culture (*Körperkultur*): the implications of Körperkultur and naturism for the pursuit of racial hygiene need no documentation here.[67] Suffice it to say that the ideology of rhythmical gymnastics is consonant with that of the "Strength Through Joy" (*Kraft durch Freude*) movement, and with the Nazi emphasis on physical strength and health more generally.[68]

Imitating sculptural poses is seen as an act of mimetic identification that promotes the beautiful spirit and body espoused by the neoclassical tradition. Mimetic identification is effected through the body's pose, by means of which it physically enacts myth as embodied in sculpture.[69] Transitional dance movements link these poses, producing a rhythm of movement and stasis. In miming sculptural poses, the body is at once aestheticized and trained, subjected to a "theory of dressage" that also has its origins in the eighteenth century.[70] Sculpture is brought to life and the living body rendered periodically immobile. Not surprisingly, given the late-eighteenth-century interest in protocinematic spectacles, another artistic practice of this period serves as a model for rhythmical gymnastics: Emma Hart's tableau performances of classical statues and figures from mythology, with their erratic rhythm of bursts of motion contrasted with moments of prolonged stillness. Witnessed by Goethe during his stay in Naples, Hart's performances are described in his memoirs no doubt served to inspire the famous tableaux vivants in *Elective Affinities*.[71] Absent from Hart's tableaux, of course, is the discourse of physical self-improvement: her performances are perceived as theatrical spectacles whose impact was to be spiritual—although there is little doubt that Hart's performances also produced a pornographic effect upon her audiences.[72] Both Hart's "living pictures" and rhythmical gymnastics resemble the children's game of "statues," which requires the moving player to "freeze" suddenly and hold her pose. Rhythmical gymnastics, too, rehearses the choreography of stasis and movement even as it recalls tableau vivant and the staged tableau. The flow of temporality that is motion is arrested and held in the static pose, only to be released again into temporality. In this alternation it, too, serves as a model for Riefenstahl's filmic choreography.

Of course dance itself suggests the complementary nature of movement and stasis; it defines motion as emerging from and returning to the "stillness of an ideal pose."[73] Alternatively, we might say that the Dionysian aspect of dance—its expressive movement—is tempered in dance by the poses that derive from Apollonian—sculptural—form. For Nietzsche, famously, Wagnerian musical theater represents the ideal artistic compromise between the Dionysian and Apollonian principles. Similarly, perhaps, tableau moments within the flux of filmic images—the "ceaseless motion" mentioned by Sontag and by Kracauer before her—may be their particular form of compromise in Riefenstahl's filmmaking. Understood as a programmed series of images—hence both spatial and temporal—the body art that is dance has marked similarities to the series of images that is film. At one level, Riefenstahl's fascist, filmic choreography as read by Sontag expresses the struggle between erotic energy and formal control articulated by the body in dance.

Tableau and Photograph

"Photography is a kind of primitive theater, a kind of *Tableau Vivant*," Roland Barthes writes in *Camera Lucida*, "a figuration of the motionless and made-up face beneath which we see the dead."[74] Here is another form of visual representation to be placed alongside the tableau moment. The many collections of photographs published by Riefenstahl[75] confirm the view that the photograph relates to an interest in posed bodies and stasis in her work more generally: As we recall, Sontag's "Fascinating Fascism" begins as a review of *Land of the Nuba*. Decorated with scars and with ceremonial paint, the beautiful bodies of the Sudanese Nuba are perfect subjects not only for Riefenstahl's photographic aesthetic, but also for photography per se as read by Barthes. "She interprets the Nuba as a mystical people with an extraordinarily developed artistic sense . . . she insists that their principal activity is ceremonial," writes Sontag.[76] At the center of this ceremonial and artistic activity is death, thus doubly rendering the Nuba photography's ideal subjects. Of course Barthes is not the first theorist of photography to link the photograph with death.[77] What is distinctive in Barthes' formulation, however, is the link with death through theater, through the *cult* of the dead. "To make oneself up," Barthes writes, "is to designate oneself as a body simultaneously living and dead: the whitened bust of the totemic theater, the man with the painted face in Chinese theater, the rice-paste makeup of the Indian Katha-Kali, the Japanese No mask."[78] Barthes, waxing anthropological here, might well have expanded his catalogue to include the Sudanese Nuba who, for purposes of ceremony, paint their bodies with a grayish-white ash, a substance that "unmistakably suggests death."[79]

This is not the place to reexamine the centrality and nauseating glamorization of death in fascist ideology, or its connection with pornography and kitsch so compellingly sketched out by Saul Friedlander.[80] We will not linger over the ideology that Riefenstahl brings to her photographic work on the Nuba, her interest in their funeral rites as a "ballet of ghosts,"[81] or her easy acceptance of the trope of the "noble savage," determined by a specifically German form of primitivism that has been variously linked to fascism.[82] Our subject continues to be the significance of tableau moments in Riefenstahl's artistic practice, and we take up here its specifically photographic element, suggesting that we must also read the tableau moment in Riefenstahl's work in light of a tendency to play off a specifically photographic arrestation against film's flow of images. Thomas Elsaesser has made the connection between "a certain photographic aesthetic" in Riefenstahl's work and the film practices of Arnold Fanck, the director who enabled Riefenstahl's career as filmmaker.[83] If Fanck, as Elsaesser puts it, was "essentially a still photographer . . . primarily interested in the tonalities of the photographic print," can we not also, Elsaesser asks, read the failures as well as the success of *Triumph of the Will* as deriving from "a box of photographers' tricks"?[84] In lieu of such tricks, we will examine the staging of the photographic in Riefenstahl's *The Blue Light*, first released in 1932.

In this film—her first feature film as a director—a few instances of the arrested and aestheticized human body are of particular interest. The first of these is a sculptural group, a monument representing young men lured to their deaths by Junta, the Riefenstahl character, and a mystical blue light. In the context of the film's romanticizing narrative and by virtue of its auratic lighting, this sculptural group has the uncanny look not of a monument, but of bodies themselves, mummified, perhaps, or otherwise preserved. In keeping with the film's suggestion that the men are martyrs, this monument has the look of a religious icon.[85] Further, these sculptural figures bear a marked resemblance to the tableau of Mexican mummies with which—years later—*Nosferatu* (1978), Werner Herzog's "Symphony of Death " will open. As in the case of the actual mummies in Herzog's film, the sculptural bodies of *The Blue Light* appear to be "real" bodies (of actors) taken up into representation. This is not a freeze-frame, not actually a photograph—but the uncanny "real," yet arrested, quality of the bodies in this sculpture, their tableau vivant quality, calls to mind Bazin's insight concerning the photograph's ability to embalm time. It suggests as well Bazin's insistence on its indexical quality, on the manner in which, in registering the body's imprint, the photograph records something of its materiality.[86] The arrested bodies of the monument suggest an interrogation of the photograph.

These frozen bodies are visually continuous with the static poses and immobile expressions of the villagers in this film, repeatedly shot as tableaux, especially of heads arranged friezelike and in close-up that foreshadow similar configurations in *Triumph of the Will*. In these arrangements, bodies are doubly aestheticized, at once sculptural and photographic, held up to the scrutiny of a meditative camera.[87] Such images exist in striking contrast to the nimbleness of Junta's movements: her sinuous motion from cliff to peak is expressive of the natural eroticism that has lead the young men to their deaths—for if they are martyrs, it can only be to their libidinal drives. In pitting expressive dynamism against formal containments and stasis, Riefenstahl pits eros against thanatos even in this early film.

We turn now to our final object of scrutiny, to the actual photograph of Junta that frames *The Blue Light*. Throughout the film's narrative, the painter Vigo's struggle to arrest the mobile image of Junta on his canvas has also been the film's struggle. In the final shot of the narrative—those of the version still available to us, without the frame story—Junta is found by Vigo as she lies dead amid flowers. Death, especially female death, is predictably aestheticized, predictably floral—recall the dead Ophelia—and Junta's face is surrounded by an auratic halo of light that alludes to Pre-Raphaelite portraits. Found first by eye of the painter Vigo, Junta is only then discovered by the film camera that frames her face: the filmic image is held, becomes a still—and is finally revealed to the film's spectators as a framed photograph. Located first in the eye of the painter, in other words, Junta's image is appropriated by the film camera, then passed along to the medium to which, in death, it properly belongs: photography. Underscoring its photographic basis, the film's narrative ends in the image that has motivated it from the start.

Of course Junta has occupied the space of representation from the film's beginning: as a creature with a dancer's agility, Junta is linked as firmly to the rhythms of the natural world as is Diotima in *The Holy Mountain*. Notably, Fanck's 1926 film, which appeared five years before *The Blue Light*, opens with a shot of Diotima's inanimate face in extreme close-up. "Her eyes are shut," writes Eric Rentschler, "we seem to be looking at a death mask."[88] Soon this photographic shot of Diotima's face will be animated, enveloped by the film's movement, and incorporated into its narrative.[89] These complementary instances—the photograph in *The Blue Light* and the photographic "death mask" of *The Holy Mountain*—both bracket narrative in their respective films, suggesting an approach to film that insists on its photographic origin.[90]

Although a tableau moment in film is itself bracketed by the succession of images that precedes and follows it, its essential stasis and "out-of-time" feel suggest an affinity between tableau vivant and the photograph. As in the case of the still photograph when it occurs in film, tableau vivant introduces a pause into the film's narrative. Here time is converted into space and the temporal flow of images takes on the aspect of a spatial object. We are reminded of Raymond Bellour's contention in "The Film Stilled" that those photographic instants that "suspend the time of movement and open it up" seem to introduce "a kind of paralysis—comparable to one that strikes painting into film."[91] With Bellour, then, we can agree that tableau vivant also "makes cinema lean in the direction of photography, towards its power to inscribe death."[92]

By way of conclusion, let us make a brief detour to an earlier moment in the history of photography—to staged photography in England in the 1850s and 1860s, which rekindled an interest in tableau vivant among the English bourgeoisie. During this period, there is a fashion especially for staged photographs of dead women, such as Henry Peach Robinson's rendering of "The Lady of Shalott."[93] For the spectators of staged photographic images, their *frisson* seems to have consisted precisely in the juxtaposition of the living actress with the dead character she portrays, now rendered doubly "dead" via the photographic medium. Of course the dead woman is in any case a Pre-Raphaelite subject: Elizabeth Siddal, for instance, was often painted as dead or dying by her husband Rossetti and his fellow artists.[94] There is something necrophilic in this interest, of course—it has been claimed that Rossetti was "obsessed with the relation of art to necrophilia."[95] But Riefenstahl goes farther. In *The Blue Light*, Riefenstahl's Junta is herself martyred and rendered icon, becoming in the process masochism's ideal figure. In the masochistic regime, as we recall, the erotic object is immobilized and identified with a "statue, a painting, a photograph."[96] In its extreme form, the object becomes indistinguishable from the representation. Now, perhaps, we are in a position to suggest how the psychosexual dynamic of fascist art—its masochistic choreography of movement and stasis—is imbricated in the several mediums within which we have situated Riefenstahl's work. For in Riefenstahl's aesthetic, I would suggest, a libidinal charge is actually transferred from the erotic object to the statue, painting, or photograph—in other words, to art itself. "Art"—which has more than once motivated Riefenstahl's denial, served as her excuse—therefore becomes the object of an all-consuming, erotically charged fixation. Whereas Winckelmann's poetic prose lets slip just how much he is moved by male beauty—sculpture becomes warm flesh—in the case of Riefenstahl we find precisely the opposite movement: aesthetic pleasure is generated by those forms of art into which the body has been absorbed, rendered corpse—and work of art.

4

The Scene of Art in Hitchcock I

In 1944, while at work on *Spellbound*, Alfred Hitchcock and his wife Alma Reville began to collect art. The first paintings they acquired were by Salvador Dali, who was then designing the famous dream sequence for Hitchcock's film. Both paintings they bought derived from Dali's work on *Spellbound*: one is notably titled "L'oeil" ("The Eye"), the second is dedicated to Hitchcock as the "Chevalier of Death."[1] As it turns out, these two acquisitions are paradigmatic for the relation of Hitchcock's films to painting: it comes as no surprise, of course, that the visual arts play a central role in delineating Hitchcock's governing metaphor of vision. Or that Hitchcock's films, so narrative oriented, so intent on the twists and turns of plot, mask a continuous preoccupation with the stasis of sculpture and painting, suggestive of and displaced by the death around which every Hitchcock plot inevitably turns. Indeed, the centrality of art to Hitchcock's films was recently marked by two exhibitions planned around centenary celebrations of Hitchcock. The first opened at the Museum of Modern Art in 1999, and the second took place at the Musée des Beaux-Arts in Montreal in 2000. The catalogues for these exhibitions suggest a variety of painterly influences on Hitchcock's images: they record the famous collaboration with Dali in *Spellbound*, they mention the prevalence of portraits in Hitchcock's films, and the images in the exhibit suggest a variety of visual influences on the filmmaker's style. Photographs of the frame-by-frame drawings executed by Hitchcock for his storyboards demonstrate the master's painstaking control over his images. Nevertheless, the essays in these catalogues rarely go beyond the suggestion of painterly influence to examine it. Pursuing the nature of Hitchcock's fascination with the visual arts, my own approach draws both on art historical and filmic interpretive strategies.

The following two chapters focus on sculpture and painting in their relation to representational issues in Hitchcock's films. Drawing on Louis Marin's reading of a self-portrait by Caravaggio, Part One illustrates that several important formal strategies in Hitchcock's films have their origin in the compositional codes familiar to us from painting. Fleshing out and deepening these findings, Part Two examines the modernist frontal look out of the frame familiar from Michael Fried's work on Manet, the "portrait shot" that so shockingly penetrates the fourth wall in Hitchcock's films. Here the direct look out of the frame—famously read as the "returned gaze" of the image by Slavoj Zizek—is analyzed against other strategies which, with Fried on Courbet, I term "realist" strategies. Such strategies seek to collapse the space of the film with that of the spectator. I analyze as well the alternation between the two- and three-dimensional that signals the blurring of ontological registers so central to illusion. Repeatedly figuring the uncanny movement between the real and representation that is the lure of tableau vivant, such moments ritualistically rehearse a (desired) mastery over death. More centrally, perhaps, such moments achieve the intensity of their spectatorial effect by emblematizing the breakdown of the subject/object opposition, even in its specularized, Lacanian form. Although from a psychoanalytic perspective the figured coextensiveness of the real with the film may indeed figure the dissolution of boundaries typical of the oral stage, I suggest as well that such figurations function at the level of perception and affect to break down the oppositions inherent in the gaze.

Part One: The Cut of Representation

We will begin with the relation between bodies and their conversion into works of art, both still lifes and sculpture—that is, by considering the most straightforward aspect of the figured movement between the real and representation. Moving beyond these strategies, which take place on both the linguistic and imagistic levels in Hitchcock's films, we will consider moments of painterly doubling, linking them to the Janus-face and specularity, as well as to instances of "decapitation" figured through portraits and portrait busts.[2] The practice and figuration of dismemberment in Hitchcock's films is the first thematic—and cinematic—preoccupation to be examined from this perspective. In many instances, it is the body of the woman that is fragmented or dismembered, conflated with the "dead" space of the pictorial or with the sculptural fragment, and most intimately bound up with the capacity of cinema to fragment the body and animate it. Often, the body of the fragmented woman is mirrored in that of a male counterpart. Suffice it to add, for the moment, that in 1927 Hitchcock chose to send a Christmas card to friends depicting the famous caricature of himself in profile: the card was a jigsaw puzzle, meant to be taken to pieces and then reassembled.[3]

Vision, cutting or fragmentation, and specularity: this constellation of concerns in Hitchcock is contextualized and aptly brought into relief by Louis Marin's work on Caravaggio's "Head of Medusa," setting the scene for a more direct application of Marin's reading to an analysis of painting and sculpture in Hitchcock's filmmaking.[4] Not surprisingly, Ovid's narrative of Medusa resonates thematically with his films, with issues of fragmentation (Perseus severed Medusa's head from her body), the death-bringing power of the gaze and castration (Medusa's gaze turned men to stone), and of mirroring (Medusa's head is reflected in Perseus's shield).[5] More particularly, however, Caravaggio's *painting* of Medusa's head has representational strategies in common with Hitchcock's films—a reliance on doubling and on contradiction, such as the both/and of ambiguous gendering. Caravaggio's painting does not simply represent Medusa's decapitated head, as Marin points out, but is a "decapitation" of another kind.[6] As I will show, the metaphysics of representation that Marin locates in Caravaggio's painting is centrally operative in Hitchcock's films and provides a schema within which to locate his compulsive recycling of the images, themes, and strategies to which it is linked.

Natures mortes, Trophies, Mummies

Still-life paintings in Hitchcock's films seem incidental, remote from the action, and their connection to the body—fragmented or whole—may initially appear oblique. But Hitchcock's detectives look at still lifes in puzzlement, as though the solution of a mystery lies there. If Detective Benson is fascinated by a cubist still life for a brief "out of action" moment in *Suspicion* (1941), this is, as Stephen Heath has suggested, a fleeting escape from a scene dominated by the portrait of General MacLaidlaw.[7] But the alternative space that Benson's diegetic excursion creates is a fragmented female space of fruits and flowers. A cubist rendering in the manner of Picasso, this still life embodies a "fractured" image, produced by the multiple planar surfaces by means of which its objects are rendered.[8] Speaking more generally, we can say that in Hitchcock's films character and spectator attention is drawn to still lifes not only as the space of the feminine, but also because these paintings embody an uncanny contradiction. No matter that their subject is organic, was once living: still lifes are *natures mortes* (dead nature), their flowers and fruits killed off into and fixed within the space of representation. Nevertheless, like other paintings in this regard, still lifes also function to preserve their subject in the atemporal present of art.

In *Rear Window* (1954), for instance, we find a still life of fruits and flowers over Jeffries's fireplace, occupying the place where a portrait so often hangs in Hitchcock's films. This painting, in front of which another detective pauses as though it contained a clue, features the natural as food, thus gesturing toward the nourishing maternal body. In a telling instance of *Rear Window*'s black humor, Stella's fascinated musings about cutting up a woman's body take place just as Jeffries is cutting up his breakfast. This is not the only Hitchcock film to link the female corpse with food, creating the distinct suggestion of cannibalism that *Frenzy* (1972) will repeatedly reinforce, a topic I pursue in my final chapter.[9] If Jeffries's voyeuristic eroticism is eventually to be superseded by an adult sexuality that involves a rapprochement with Grace Kelly's Lisa Freemont—and the film suggests that it is—we can expect that this still life will be replaced by "Mona Lisa," by the representation of the woman whom Jeffries will not want to call "my Lisa" until the end of the film. In fact, "Lisa" is the title of a song in the process of composition by a neighbor of Jeffries, a song that functions as the equivalent of a musical portrait, a low-cultural version of Da Vinci's masterpiece. In *Rear Window*, the musical portrait performs recuperative strategies, reversing those operations performed by Mr. Thorwaldson on the body of his wife. A work in progress, the song is completed with the film's completion, just as Lisa Freemont is finally "fashioned," rendered symbolic in the erotic imagination of Jeffries.

Sometimes in Hitchcock's films, bodies remain too relentlessly within the material world, and the real of the corpse is inadequately subsumed by the symbolic.[10] In these scenes, they are often featured as material representations, as sculpture rather than painting. *The Man Who Knew Too Much* (1956) presents representational issues in a comic light, diverting the spectator from the awareness that, in this film, body parts are preserved to become sculptural and fetishistic objects of display. The fragmented body is introduced in a joke by the James Stewart character, a surgeon who recites a catalog of the body parts that have financed the vacation upon which he and his family have embarked: one patient's appendix, another's gall bladder, the triplets produced in the womb of yet another. The film suggests that someone who thinks about fragmented body parts in terms of profit deserves the experience that Stewart has in this film.

During the film's course, Stewart mistakenly enters a taxidermist's establishment that has the look of an artist's studio and the atmosphere of a mortuary. As he wanders about in search of his son's kidnappers, the surgeon is terrorized by fierce-looking stuffed animals and animal heads on display—a fitting punishment for one so inured to dismemberment as to think of gall bladders and appendixes primarily as separable from their owners. Displaced from the human onto the animal, the body's fragmentation is countered by the preservation of its parts and corpses, the taxidermist's stuffed and mounted trophy heads. And it is supplemented by the action of the camera as a "chasseur d'images"[11] that stalks and "shoots" its prey, as though it were the rifle that had killed them off. If the camera is hunter and gun, its aim—like that of the taxidermist—is to preserve the fragmented body.

Taxidermy is Norman Bates's hobby, too; he likes "stuffing things," as the spectator of *Psycho* (1960) is only too well aware.[12] Beaks open, wings arrested in flight, the stuffed birds that decorate Norman's parlor are now objects of display. Stuffed birds on perches can be found among arrangements of dried or artificial flowers as well, constituting three-dimensional still lifes, more natures mortes whose lighting emphasizes their sculptural status. Still other images in *Psycho* underline its preoccupation with death, art, and objecthood: when Lila enters the mother's bedroom, her eyes stray to a bronze sculpture of a woman's hands, at once image and object.[13] But it is the preserved corpse of the mother that has the most in common with the stuffed birds. As André Bazin has famously said with regard to the photographic image: "if the plastic arts were put under psychoanalysis, embalming the dead might turn out to be the fundamental factor in their creation. The process might reveal that at the origin of painting and sculpture there lies a mummy complex."[14] Norman's macabre "mummy," both body and image, gruesomely tropes the camera's capacity to "embalm time."[15]

Near the sarcophagus, Bazin goes on to report concerning Egyptian burial practices, terra-cotta statuettes were placed to stand in for mummies, lest they after all suffer the depradations of time.[16] It is our awareness of the vulnerable interior of the body, placed within its all too penetrable shell, that must be magically denied by the "idealized carapace" of the statue, a protective shell that also functions as a crypt or a tomb.[17] We can bring this sense of the sculpture as a figured "container" for the body—like the anthropomorphic Egyptian sarcophagus that contains the body[18]—to bear on two different yet related images in and around Hitchcock's work: one of these is an anecdote involving the making of *Spellbound*, the other occurs in *North by Northwest* (1959). Famous for its dream sequence based on drawings by Salvador Dali, *Spellbound* contains only an attenuated form of the sequence originally planned; its best-known image is that of a man using scissors to cut drapes covered with huge eyes, an image obviously inspired by Bunuel's Dali-designed *Un Chien Andalou* (1929) and combining images of castration with images of theater. Interestingly, Hitchcock claims that other images in the dream sequence as conceived by the surrealist were too excessive even for him, complaining to Truffaut that "Dali had some strange ideas: he wanted a statue to crack like a shell falling apart, with ants crawling all over it, and underneath, there would be Ingrid Bergman, covered by ants! It just wasn't possible."[19]

When, in *North by Northwest*, Eva Marie Saint is called a "little piece of sculpture" for which the villain "must have paid plenty" at an art auction, the implication of the remark is rather different. But when, at the end of the film, a statue with which Eva's character has become identified is dropped, breaks into pieces, and reveals hidden microfilm—pointing, as Stanley Cavell also supposes, to "the present film,"[20] something more is at stake. If, in one sense, the statue in *North by Northwest* can be said to generate the film, then the fate of this statue demonstrates that the female body must be shattered—fragmented—in order to produce it. In both instances—in the case of the "impossible" image in *Spellbound* that Hitchcock, in the kind of evasive conversational move typical of him, attributes to Dali—and in the case of *North by Northwest*, the statue functions as carapace. Somewhat shockingly, the cracked statue of *Spellbound* would have opened to reveal Ingrid Bergman as a corpse, already covered with ants, thus exposing the real of the body after the shell of representation cracks open. It is an image of the cadaver. In *North by Northwest*, the statue connected with Eva Marie Saint is opened in order to give birth to the film. But the contradiction governing these two examples is only a seeming contradiction. At some level, the film and the female corpse function simultaneously as opposites and equivalents—as mirror images, in fact.

The Janus-Face

In conversation with Truffaut, Hitchcock speaks of making the same film over and over, comparing himself to the painter Rouault in the bargain.

"Not that I'm comparing myself to him," Hitchcock says in a typical disclaimer, "but old Rouault was content with judges, clowns, a few women, and Christ on the Cross. . . . That constituted his life's work."[21] It is in Rouault's work, interestingly, that the paintings of Bruno Anthony's mother (*Strangers on a Train*, 1951) find their inspiration. Bruno claims that his mother has long been unwell, and gives as her reason for painting that it soothes her: notwithstanding that Bruno's remark parodies Freud's connection of neurosis with the production of art, it is meant to be taken seriously. Mrs. Anthony's portrait of her husband is one with which her son has sympathy, as it represents his father as a king who exerts despotic control over wife and son—the double allusion to *Oedipus* and to *Hamlet* is not lost on us here. Another portrait of a father as a representative of the patriarchal order, this painting resembles those of General MacLaidlaw and Mr. Brenner, the dead father in *The Birds* (1963). But in this instance, too, visual representation is coterminous with the space of death, for his mother's portrait of his father places him under the sign of death in Bruno's eyes.

The space of painting can be occupied by male figures in Hitchcock's films, especially the sexually ambiguous males in whom a murderous psychosis often resides.[22] Although as plotmaker Bruno is tied to the principle of narrative, he, too, is connected with representational issues that engage painting and sculpture. One sequence in *Strangers on a Train* presents Bruno in a stunning long shot as a tiny figure within the Jefferson Memorial, his still body a statue trapped within this architectural space of monument and tomb. As Bruno's placement within the monument suggests, once again the space of noncinematic visual representation is coterminous with the place of death, much as the portrait of Bruno's father painted by his mother places him under the sign of death in the eyes of his son. Another sequence in particular is notable for the way this film evokes a painterly space: it occurs during the tennis championship as Bruno sits staring directly into the camera, in marked contrast to the other spectators, whose heads follow the ball back and forth in synchronized engrossment in the action. It is one of the moments that famously exemplifies the blot or stain for Zizek, and it will be discussed further below.[23] For the moment, we should note that its significance turns on Bruno's stillness: accentuated by the other heads turning in unison, Bruno's pronounced lack of movement reinforces his placement within a different kind of space, a painterly space within the cinematic one. More important, Bruno's intent gaze similarly draws our own gaze into the cinematic frame. Hitchcock's adaptation of what Fried describes as a self-conscious, painterly theatricality[24] reinforces themes of mirroring and doubling, because the situation of character gaze *at* the camera and out of the film[25] engages both camera and spectator with the direct gaze of the character. This relation is the focus of Chapter 5.

The issue of male and female doubling within the context of painterly representation takes a suggestive form in *Blackmail* (1929). This film tells the story of the near-seduction of a young woman, Alice, who is lured into the apartment of an artist to "see his etchings." Playfully and under the artist's direction, Alice picks up his palette and brush, and accidentally places a mark upon an empty canvas. She is then encouraged by the artist to "draw something," as if in order to recuperate the transgressive mark, and paints a female head around it, transforming the mark into its mouth. Taking up the brush himself, the artist and would-be seducer hastily sketches the outline of a naked female body under this head, a body complete with breasts, but lacking genitalia. Thus both man and woman create a composite portrait, a work that is genuinely heterogeneous. Soon, stabbing and killing the artist in defense of her virtue, Alice brandishes the knife as she has brandished the paintbrush and becomes the prey of a blackmailer. In an ironic reversal typical of Hitchcock, the blackmailer meets his end in a chase sequence that begins in the sculpture gallery of the British Museum, and Alice goes free.

Punctuating the narrative of this film is yet another portrait, that of a jester who points an accusing finger at his beholder. The first of these beholders is Alice herself, once before and once after the stabbing, when she slashes the painting as though to enact at the level of representation what she has done in the domain of the real. Its second beholder is her fiancé, a policeman whose image in the form of a photograph exerts its authority on the wall of Alice's bedroom. While investigating the crime, her fiancé is mocked by the portrait in the apartment that is both the scene of a murder and of a more personal transgression. The fiancé also looks twice at the portrait of the jester (once while fetishistically holding something that will prove to be Alice's glove), another instance in which a detective examines a painting in search of knowledge or understanding. Not surprisingly, the portrait of the mocking jester has been read as a self-representation of Hitchcock,[26] the jester/filmmaker as both prankster and truth teller. Interestingly, we see the portrait again at the end of the film, in Scotland Yard, when its mocking laugh will function as yet another commentary on the ironies of the plot. This time, it is being carried by someone whose shape suggests that he may be Hitchcock himself. The painting of the jester is being carried back to back with the composite figure of the woman, created jointly by Alice and the artist.

The surprising doubling that we see in the two paintings, back to back, plays on the two-headed Janus-face.[27] In *Blackmail,* the significance of this relation is underscored by being revealed in the moment that suggests a Hitchcock cameo, as though in humorous acknowledgment of the fact that the Janus-face[28] was most often represented in the profile and relief typical of actual cameos. The painting of the woman on one side is created around a circular mark that will be naturalized as a mouth, around a vacancy that marks the site of castration. This act of recuperation—an act that turns the wound of castration into the organ of speech and therefore marks it as phallic—is performed by Alice. The artist, on the other hand, avoids the problem by resorting to a convention of representation that simply eliminates all genitalia from his drawing of the nude. But both man and woman are complicit in a rendering that makes ambiguous the supposed castration of the female body and the binarism of male and female. Alice's conversion of the mark of absence into a mouth allows us to read the mouth both as the organ of speech and as vagina dentata, just as the absence of genitalia on the male artist's nude can be read both as a representation of castration and as an avoidance of the issue.

But what is the relation of the back-to-back images? Their position suggests a Janus-face whose two heads gaze in opposing directions, at once opposites and doubles: in this case, the male and female aspects of an ambiguous gendering that is both and neither. Does the gaze of the jester as artist, in an ironic echo of Medusa's, have the power to fix the female body in the death that is painting, much as the Medusa's gaze renders men statues? In some sense, the position of the two paintings suggests that the gaze and the laughter of the jester are connected with the female body whose "castration" is simultaneously covered over and manifest. I will return to their relation below. For now let it be noted that the spaces of the two paintings are made permeable by means of the slash in the canvas that Alice has made with the knife, creating an opening in the canvas reminiscent of the eye-shaped hole we see in *Psycho*.

In this later film, Norman Bates lifts a painting representing the familiar subject matter of "Susannah and the Elders" in order similarly to spy on the naked Marion in her shower bath. This painting of the bathing female body with its male voyeurs both doubles the events of the narrative and serves as a screen of sorts that covers Norman's peephole. Modeled upon the eye, the peephole has jagged edges that suggest a torn canvas as well as the organ of sight. In a sense, then, we can say that this painting, when "slashed," provides Norman's deadly gaze access to the naked Marion. As Bellour has suggested, the "pressure of the doubling process that underlies all of [Hitchcock's] films" is operative in a doubling that links Norman (already doubled, as both Norman and Mother) to Marion.[29] We can surely say, then, that the slashed painting of the jester in *Blackmail* opens up a space for the merger of jester and female figure, as well. In *Blackmail*, the female portrait—product of a man and a woman—is a self-portrait that represents the two sides of the composite body.

An earlier film, *The Thirty-nine Steps* (1935), contains a mirror portrait that is illuminating with respect to this relation. Here, in a bitterly ironic inversion of the bourgeois domestic scene—or, perhaps, its ultimate exposure—the camera lingers on a mirror over a fireplace in a deserted apartment, a mirror that reflects the image of a desperate woman facing it, a woman involved in espionage, whose life is threatened, and about whom the worst is suspected. This woman is soon to die, punished for the ambiguity that surrounds her, although after her death the film will rehabilitate her as a patriot. As an image in the mirror—desirable but under the sign of death—for the man who looks at her reflection, she functions not only as a negative and threatening image, a Medusa, but as an image of a feminine self. In *Vertigo*, a similar doubling takes place in a mirror shot in the flower shop, where the images of Scottie and Madeleine are joined within the "mirror of representation," just as Roger and Eve are so joined in the dining car in *North by Northwest*.

We can read the figure of the Janus-face, with its two heads in profile emerging from one neck, as a variant of the specular relation—the mirror portrait—that links Caravaggio to his representation of Medusa. Not surprisingly, the Janus-face is a figure for dialectic. Like "Head of Medusa," the Janus-face is a decapitation and is rarely, if ever, represented on a body. The gazes that look outward from its two heads are the inverse of the opposing gazes of a figure and its mirror reflection and of the opposing gazes of doubles looking at one another. These seemingly opposite—but essentially equivalent—doublings relate to the way in which the female figure, when read as castrated and powerless, is an image the male thus fears may reflect his own condition. It is in this instance an image of the castrated self, a mirroring based upon equivalence. But when the woman is read as castrating and powerful—as Medusa—the defensive strategy such a reading engenders turns the castrating and murderous gaze against itself.

Herein lies one aspect of the appropriateness of Marin's reading of Medusa as a paradigm for specular relations in Hitchcock. Just as the castrating gaze of Medusa is defended against and mirrored by Perseus's bronze shield that turns the deadly gaze upon its reflection, thus leading to Medusa's death and decapitation, so in Hitchcock's films the camera is trained upon the castrating woman, at once absorbing her power and fragmenting—even destroying—her by means of it. As Marin points out, Caravaggio's portrait of Medusa is, interestingly, also a self-portrait: "the painter, after all, not only disguises himself as Medusa; he also cross-dresses as a Gorgon, a woman, or at least the head of a woman."[30] In the case of this painting, the female portrait is also the image that the male artist sees in the mirror. In Hitchcock's films this form of specularity is of central significance: when the man looks at female portraits and still lifes, he hopes that he will not find himself mirrored there.

Decapitations: Cut-outs and Busts

Blackmail's best-known image does not include either of the portraits I have discussed. Most frequently cited is the image of the mammoth Egyptian-style stone head next to which the blackmailer, a tiny figure by contrast, slithers down a rope in the British Museum. This is not a serious decapitation: the stone head is smiling even though—like justice itself in this film—it is blind. Likewise in ironic jest, the Mount Rushmore sequence in *North by Northwest* juxtaposes the gigantic, impassive presidential heads of stone with specks of human figures moving across them, figures for whom this is the setting of a life-and-death struggle. These heads, representations of power and authority though they may be, are nevertheless portrait busts, heads separated from the bodies to which they belong. Where, we ask, is the Medusa who has turned these men to stone? And why, like Medusa herself, have they been beheaded?

The nameless heroine of *Rebecca* (1940), the second Mrs. de Winter, is tricked by the housekeeper into dressing as the woman in white from one of the full-length family portraits that hang in the gallery. Appearing at a fancy-dress ball in this costume, however, it is not the woman of the portrait whom this second wife evokes for her spectators, but Rebecca, the first wife, whose gothic presence haunts this film with a deadly power. It is not the ancestral portrait that is brought to life, in other words, but the dead Rebecca who had worn this same costume to an earlier ball. We never see Rebecca: her body is only conjured up for the spectator by the fetishistic garments that hid—or did not quite hide—it. Yet the lady of the portrait and Maxim De Winter's two wives, enclosed in the folds of identical dresses, faces framed by identical hats, are virtually indistinguishable. Or perhaps we should say that they *would* be indistinguishable were it not for their faces: in some sense, then, their heads are cutouts, separable from their bodies in separable, paper-doll dresses,[31] the result of some ghastly decapitation. These women's heads also function as portrait busts. Recalling that the head in the hybrid female portrait in *Blackmail* was "executed" by Alice, while the body was sketched by the male artist, we realize that this head, too, is not of a piece with the body.[32]

In *Vertigo*, another painting made by a woman has the uncanny look of a composite figure, a monstrous hybrid. Midge, the artist, has copied the body of a woman, Carlotta Valdes, from a painting that hangs in the Legion of Honor museum. But on Carlotta's body, Midge has painted her own head, perhaps in an effort to suggest to Scottie, the James Stewart character with whom she is in love, that she herself would be an adequate substitute for the inaccessible woman linked in his imagination with the woman in the painting. The shock value of Midge's painting for the spectator of the film is difficult to account for when one considers how accustomed we are now to similar effects created in modernist painting. In fact, Midge is a fashion designer who works in a studio full of examples of abstract painting and sculpture, among them a brassière mounted on a free-standing wire bust, that she describes as working on the principle of the cantilever bridge. When Midge tells Scottie that she has "gone back to her first love, painting" (it was Hitchcock's, too),[33] Scottie asks whether she is painting a still life. "Not exactly," she replies, and in the irony of her reply lies a partial explanation for the shock that her painting occasions in us, as the unnatural conjunction of body and head has rendered her painting a decapitation. It is transgressive and uncanny in part because it violates an order whose linchpin is the wholeness of the body. Notwithstanding the presence of the brassière-bust nearby (the breast as a partial object recalling other still lifes to mind), this portrait may be morte, but it is no still life.

This scene, with its flaunting of fragmented and modernist works of art, figures the hesitation created in *Vertigo* by its multiplicity of perspectives, the splitting of point of view that finds its visual analogue in the fragmentation of the female body. This fragmented body is displayed not only in the doubled portrait, with its "portrait bust" head, but in the sculptural model of the brassière, which is in some sense the breast's carapace. Like the breast for which the brassière stands in—and as in the portrait "bust" that it ironically figures—the head is separated from the body on which it belongs. The fact that this portrait is the work of a female artist and that she has superimposed upon the portrait her own head complete with the spectacles that signify her access to the gaze, contributes to the sense of unnaturalness that we perceive in the painting. It renders her as Medusa, thus more emphatically separating the body from the head and displacing it a second time in that it looks back at itself knowingly. Midge claims to have made the painting for Scottie: "I thought I might give it to you," she says, but the extreme reaction of *this* detective tells her that she has been foolish indeed to confront him with what is a mirror image of his own fears.[34] Subsequently, this painting, like the one in *Blackmail*, is "wounded": when Midge defaces her portrait with a paintbrush, she is at once committing self-mutilation and striking out at an other.

Tableaux vivants; femmes mortes

Vertigo echoes the story of Pygmalion, the sculptor who fell in love with his own creation, Galatea. Because Pygmalion is at once father and husband to Galatea, Ovid's story narrativizes incest, "the relation in which same mates with same,"[35] and inverts the narrative of *Psycho* in which a son fashions his mother into a sculpture. A film about a female portrait "brought to life," *Vertigo* also tells the tale of a body rigidified into a statue. The Galatea with whom Scottie becomes obsessed is first presented to the spectator as a sculpture: at Ernie's restaurant, Madeleine is briefly framed by the tracking camera in a composition that has a painting at its center. Moving in on her from behind, the camera lingers on her motionless body, surrounded by the draperies of stole and dress, and focuses on the marmoreal whiteness of her naked back and neck. When, from the point of view of Scottie, the camera centers Madeleine within the frame of a doorway, she begins to move, creating the effect of a sculpture not quite fully brought to life, her movements interspersed with static shots that present her face in profile, in cameolike relief.[36] (This is one half of the Janus-face: later in the film, Scottie's dream will also feature the separable head in profile.) Later, for the benefit of Scottie's gaze, Madeleine performs a series of silent tableaux in spaces that further promote the connection of her living body with painting and sculpture—and with death. One of these spaces is the flower shop, where Madeleine is first connected with the flowers that she will throw into the

San Francisco Bay just before she hurls herself into its waters in imitation of the mad Ophelia. Another is the graveyard, where we see her in a gray suit among the tombstones, posed in long shot and resembling graveyard statuary. These arranged scenes suggest that Madeleine has "died into art," her unmoving body suggesting funerary sculpture next to the grave and headstone of Carlotta Valdes. The museum, of course, is the cultural edifice in which the exchange between real body and image is finalized. From his vantage point in an antechamber, Scottie surveys Madeleine seated still as a statue before Carlotta's portrait, her trancelike look at Carlotta simulating a mystical communication effected through the gaze. The backdrop against which these tableaux take place is the Pre-Raphaelite interest in the drowned female corpse—witness the many Ophelias of that canon—as well as the animation fantasy recorded, for instance, in Edward Burne-Jones's "Pygmalion" series.[37] Like the Pre-Raphaelites, Scottie is fascinated with the aestheticized and ever-remote Madeleine rather than with the flesh-and-blood Judy.

In the museum scene as elsewhere, Scottie is an apt interpreter of Madeleine's tableau: twice the camera's motion, standing in for Scottie's glance, traces a connection between the real and the represented, focusing first on the bouquet lying next to Madeleine, and then on an identical one in the portrait of Carlotta at which she gazes. Next it fixes on the whorl into which Madeleine's hair is sculpted in order to point to that same figure in the painting. This whorl—a visual analogue for the snakes that replace Medusa's hair—is also the figure for vertigo. Although Madeleine is seated before the painting as its beholder, the scene implies that for Scottie, at least, her space is continuous with that of the painting. If Madeleine can be said to collapse into the portrait of Carlotta, a moment refigured by her "death," then Judy under Scottie's direction later brings the painting to life again. After Madeleine's "death," she is figured in Scottie's dream as Carlotta's animated portrait, an animation fantasy that paradoxically stresses her death rather than the portrait's coming to life. Repeatedly in this film, the experience of vertigo is connected to the perceptual shift that accompanies the collapse into the two-dimensionality of the image, as well as the reverse movement from flatness into the three-dimensional. I will return to this movement below.

It has always been the "art effect"—not the reality effect—that has enchanted Scottie. Between the death of Judy's "Madeleine" and her re-creation by Scottie in the role of Pygmalion, Scottie suffers from extreme melancholia, from an intense unwillingness to separate from the loved object. Scottie's dream during his illness suggests that he has not withdrawn his libido from Madeleine, but has withdrawn her into his ego instead. He sees himself in the graveyard where Madeleine had once posed, and substitutes his body for hers in the dream's final image, the corpse that has landed on the roof. For the head of Madeleine that fixes his attention when he first sees her, the dream substitutes Scottie's own head in yet another instance of doubling, of same figured as same. Like Medusa's, Scottie's head, too, is a decapitation: it exists in the dream as a fragment, detached from his body, a fetish that is at once a sign of castration and a defense against it. Like the head of Medusa on the shield of Perseus, the function of this fetishistic head is apotropaic: it wards off what it conjures up.

Perseus, we are told, captures Medusa's image as a reflection in the mirror of his shield. Like Hitchcock, Perseus uses a "ruse of representation,"[38] the mirror. At work on his "Head of Medusa," Caravaggio gazing into the mirror sees his own reflection, a reflection that provides the features for the portrait of Medusa's severed head. It is, then, the "head of a transvestite" that he is painting directly on the actual shield that functions as the painting's support. Here ambiguities of other kinds are produced. As Marin points out, the support of Caravaggio's painting, the shield, is convex, but the painting itself looks concave.[39] The movement of the eye from background to foreground and back again that these antithetical optical effects invite has its analogue in the visual effect of vertigo engendered by the approach and retreat—the simultaneous tracking out and zooming in—of Hitchcock's camera. We see it more graphically in the dream sequence, where the diagonal lines that radiate from Scottie's head seem to move backward as the camera brings his head ever closer. The problem of vertigo—of what Marin refers to as the problem of the convex mirror and its effects—is the problem of the both/and—of male and female, life and death—transposed to the field of vision. The motif of decapitation in painting—the use of self-portraits of painters for heads of mythological figures, say, in history painting—suggests acts of artistic self-disguise.[40] The decapitation that Midge performs in her portrait, therefore, is deeply self-revelatory for Hitchcock. We might look to the photograph of Hitchcock holding a wax model of his own head at Madame Tussaud's wax museum for an ironic commentary on this reading.[41]

The Shield of Perseus

There is yet another kind of doubling that warrants investigation in Hitchcock's films, a doubling that can also be explored by means of Caravaggio's painting. Earlier, I mentioned the painterly space within *Strangers on a Train*, a space that announces the self-consciousness of the filmic text by means of a painterly theatricality revealed through a direct gaze into the camera by a character in the film. In addition to Midge's portrait that looks straight out at us through her glasses—perhaps the most obvious example of Medusa's reifying gaze—there are two related moments in *Vertigo*. One occurs after Scottie, who has pursued Judy into her apartment and persuaded her to have dinner with him, leaves Judy alone, initiating the flashback that reveals the events surrounding Madeleine's death to have been duplicitous. Marian Keane has read Judy's direct look into the camera here as a turning point of *Vertigo*, as a direct declaration of the camera's presence, a look that "acknowledges Hitchcock and us."[42] Keane draws on the work of William Rothman (and ultimately of Stanley Cavell), for whom the direct gaze into the camera, restricted to a few characters in Hitchcock, "confronts" the camera.[43] The characters to whom it is permitted, claims Rothman, "seem to have access to the views that make up the film itself, as if they shared Hitchcock's position as author or our position as viewers," although he goes on to declare these characters "signifiers of Hitchcock's authorship and our own acts of viewing."[44] What Judy sees when she first looks into the camera, Keane does not say, although she speculates that "what she views there will be, in part, a figure for Hitchcock's camera, an embodiment of its gaze."[45] What Keane doesn't mention is that Judy's somewhat oblique gaze into the camera is also a gaze at the spectator who has in effect become her mirror image.

With Caravaggio's painting in mind, Marin writes that representation is "a cutting blade," a cut that "severs the story from the subject who tells it while also severing the scene from those who look at it and produce it as a scene,"[46] severing it from author and spectator alike. If, in the context especially of Hitchcock's interest in cutting, we are tempted to say the same of his films, then it is must be pointed out that the mirroring relation such as we find in Hitchcock's work does not allow the blade to cut completely. In the sequence of *Vertigo* under discussion, spectator and character are face to face, engaged in a specular relation. Later on, in the bell tower, Judy will look briefly out of the frame again. At the moment of her glance—it is not a sustained gaze—it can only be the spectator who is its object. Judy's look out of the frame fleetingly brings the spectator into the space of representation. Almost immediately, editing procedures replace us with the ghostly nun, now become the object of Judy's look. But that ghostly figure is only retrospectively the object of her gaze. In the shadowy moment before the nun materializes, perhaps it is ourselves we fear to see within the frame. This is the moment of the "cut" in a Hitchcock film: a hesitation, a gap, is introduced between the one object of the gaze—the spectator—and its diegetic replacement. Rather than separating us from the scene, Hitchcock's camera fleetingly brings the spectator into the space of representation. If for that instant Medusa's gaze renders us statues, this act of petrification forms a shield between ourselves and our death.[47]

PART II ILLUSIONS OF THE REAL

5

The Scene of Art in Hitchcock II

The Picture Looks Back

Scholarly work on the semiotics of the image typically suggests that the frontal view is perceived as addressing the spectator, engaged in an I-you relationship with the character whom she or he faces. This, as Louis Marin says in his analysis of Caravaggio's *Head of Medusa*, is the "iconic dialogue." It is a dialogue into which the spectator is necessarily and irresistibly drawn: the portrait "seizes my viewing and receptive eye by means of her gaze," Marin writes. "But as a viewer I do the same to her. I seize her gaze with my viewing and emitting eye."[1] With respect to film, Francesco Casetti in particular illuminates the questions surrounding the look out of the frame and the discursive situation that generates it.[2] For Casetti, too, what is at issue in this look is "an interpellation of the spectator that functions as if the character wants to involve the spectator in the action on the screen," a situation that posits the permeability of the on-screen space with that of the movie theater.[3] More broadly, such looks suggest the continuity of representation with the real, a relation that is central to the Hitchcock film.

Needless to say, the gaze out of the frame is not an unexplored problem in Hitchcock's films. As noted earlier, Rothman and Cavell notably read the direct gaze out of the frame as an acknowledgment of the camera's presence, as well as of the author's agency.[4] Cavell was the first to note that there is a "look back" in Hitchcock's films, an observation also made later by Jean-Luc Godard.[5] But it is in his reading of the look out of the frame in Hitchcock's films that Slavoj Zizek famously suggested with Lacan what it means for the picture to look back at us. "It is by means of the 'phallic' spot that the observed picture is subjectivized: this paradoxical point undermines our position as 'neutral,' 'objective' observer, pinning us to the observed object itself," writes Zizek. "This is the point at which the observer is already included, inscribed in the observed scene—in a way, it is the point from which the picture itself looks back at us."[6] The phallic spot of which Zizek writes is also the "blot that denatures the picture," the "meaningless stain," and, as the point of anamorphosis (the famous image of the death's head in Holbein's *The Ambassadors* as read by Lacan), it is the point at which the search for meaning begins. With respect to *Rear Window* (1954), for instance, for Zizek the Hitchcockian blot is also the gaze of the other. As a rupture of the filmic enunciation, the direct look out of the frame at the spectator—or at the camera—is often experienced as uncanny. "What is seen in the look at the camera," Marc Vernet writes, "is the Invisible, Elsewhere, Death."[7] Following Vernet, Tom Gunning invokes the uncanny in his analysis of the frontal look as a modernist strategy in the films of Fritz Lang.[8]

Against the backdrop of structuralist and psychoanalytic approaches, I will proceed from the compositional strategies and codes in painting in which these cinematic moments originate, reading the direct gaze out of the frame in pictorial as well as filmic terms. Drawing on the work of Michael Fried, I will show that such moments in Hitchcock's films typically figure a hesitation between the self-conscious frontality of a modernist stance and a "realist" attempt to merge with the space of the frame. In his writings, Fried distinguishes between compositional strategies in figural painting designed to convey the idea of "absorption," an attitude that promotes the exclusion of the spectator from the canvas, from those designed to effect "theatricality," or a direct address of the beholder. Although an "absorptive" painting makes use of strategies that promote the fiction of the spectator's nonexistence before the canvas, a "theatrical" painting confronts its spectator boldly, refusing to erect the metaphorical fourth wall that separates the spectator from the space of the painting.[9] In French painting of 1750 to 1840, Fried suggests, the absorptive mode predominates: artists of this period deliberately sought ways of neutralizing the convention that paintings are made to be beheld. During the eighteenth century, this end was achieved primarily by means of pictorial drama—by representing a moment or situation in which the figures would appear to be sealed off in the world of the painting as though by means of a fourth wall. It will be clear that Fried's writings on painting also engage drama theory, as they have their theoretical point of departure in the work of Denis Diderot, for whom painting and drama are intimately connected.[10]

Later, in the 1830s and 1840s, realism—particularly that of Courbet, Fried suggests—would develop another, different strategy to the same end. Courbet's paintings, Fried argues, seek to draw the spectator *into* the space of the painting, suggesting a continuity between the spectator and the represented scene.[11] As Fried reads it, the immersion of the spectator in the canvas—Courbet's realist strategy—has, like the absorptive strategy of the earlier period, the effect of denying the presence of the spectator before the canvas. By the middle of the nineteenth century, however, a mode of visual representation came into vogue in which the fourth wall becomes permeable or nonexistent. "Theatricality," in other words—the painting's acknowledgment of the spectatorial gaze—lost the stigma attached to it in the eighteenth century, and became an accepted, even desirable, strategy. With regard in particular to paintings of the 1860s, Fried argues that the "radicalization" of theatricality is expressed in the "facingness" of the picture surface, in the attempt to "make every portion of the picture surface face the beholder as never before."[12] Fried reads the stance of radical frontality or "facingness" in the context of flatness, reading the frozen pose as a modernist gesture. For these reasons, he sees Manet's work as initiating modernism in painting.[13] It should be added that facingness facilitates spectatorial awareness of the painting *as* painting.

We will return, then, to the painterly origins of the discussion of the direct look out of the frame in film, reading this look in pictorial as well as filmic terms, specifically in the relation of the spectator to film space. Calling into review a number of different moments in Hitchcock's films that feature the gaze out of the frame, I will suggest that these moments figure a hesitation between the self-conscious frontality of a typically modernist stance and the attempt to enter the space of the frame such as we find in Fried's expanded notion of realism.[14] Here realism implies the attempt to suggest the (figurative) collapse of the image with the real: in Hitchcock's interrogation of vision, the look out of the frame is only one part of the story. My thesis concerning the coexistence of this realist collapse with the modernist strategy of the direct look in Hitchcock's films accords with Deleuze's sense of Hitchcock's pivotal position—as both "pushing the movement-image to its limit" and inventing the mental image that "makes relation itself the object of an image." Further, it accords with his observation that Hitchcock "implicates the spectator in the film."[15] This account, then, is heavily weighted toward theories of spectatorship, drawing on notions of beholding in art theory in order to supplement the discussion of cinematic spectatorship. Considering the central importance of painting to Hitchcock's filmmaking, this approach seems long overdue.

Portrait, Window, Mirror

"Film is like a mirror," Christian Metz claims in a seminal text for psychoanalytic film theory in the 1970s, but "there is one thing and one thing only that is never reflected in it: the spectator's body. In a certain emplacement, the mirror suddenly becomes clear glass."[16] In Hitchcock's films, we repeatedly encounter moments when a mirror becomes a window and when a character's look into a mirror is not contained by its surface but instead becomes a direct look out of the frame. At such moments, character and spectator become mirror images and, although the spectator is not literally present in the film, she might be said to be reflected in it. At one and the same time, the spaces of character and spectator are suggested to be permeable to one another. More recently, Zizek has claimed that the spectator is "inscribed in the picture," and that it is precisely this inscription that is of significance: "this ontic 'umbilical cord' of the ontological horizon is what is unthinkable for the entire philosophical tradition."[17] And in fact, it is not primarily the psychoanalytic dimension of these arguments that concerns us here, but rather the ontological and representational issues surrounding them. As suggested earlier, the typical Hitchcock film takes pleasure in the manipulation of ontological registers.

As images, "window" and "mirror" suggest the two attitudes that painting takes with respect to the world, so it is of particular interest that in Hitchcock they often meet in the portrait. An early instance of Hitchcock's interest in frontality and its containment is to be found in *The Lodger* (1927). Rothman has called our attention to a telling shot in this film that includes both Ivor Novello's lodger and a female portrait.[18] Although this shot initially suggests that the portrait we see is located behind the lodger, when the lodger begins to move we realize that he is moving toward this portrait on a wall in front of him. As the lodger's image enters the space of the mirror behind him, it is confirmed that the portrait we see is merely a reflection in the mirror.[19] The lodger, then, is momentarily located in a charged space: he is positioned between two portraits, between the one that hangs in front of him (not visible to the spectator), and its visible image reflected in the mirror behind him. For the moment, the lodger is located within a specular space that is the mirror of art. It is figured as a contained, sealed-off space. The lodger's position occupies a complex relation to the film's spectator. On the one hand, this shot posits a fourth wall suggestive of Fried's absorptive mode, because it indicates by means of the reflection in the mirror that there is a literal wall between the spectator and the action. This fourth wall is the wall upon which the portrait actually hangs and, in the construction of this space, it is located between the film's spectator and the scene of the action. In one sense, this shot is figured as an "impossible" shot, because the position of the camera is coterminous with the wall: it depends upon the mirror reflection for its meaning. The film's next shot shows the lodger more closely examining the female portrait in front of him, although this is shown from the side. In the subsequent shot, however, the lodger is once more shot frontally as he walks toward the window located in the wall that separates the spectator from the scene of action. For a brief moment, the lodger looks through the window and straight out at the camera and the spectator.[20] Contained by the glass panes—the window in the wall through which the camera shoots him—the lodger is positioned in a space to which the spectator gains admission by virtue of the window's transparency. At this moment in the film, the lodger looks straight through the "looking glass" that also portraitizes him. The lodger engages the film's spectator in a specular relation, anticipating the moment in *Rear Window* in which, in Zizek's terms, the window contains the blot and returns the gaze.[21] In this early film, however, the continuity of the real with representation is already suggested: the fourth wall is opened up by means of the window, and the specular relation of lodger and spectator briefly replaces the portrait and its mirror reflection. Indeed, earlier in *The Lodger* a window literally functions as an eye or gaze when a shot of a police van from behind reveals two heads—resembling pupils—in each of its two rear windows.[22]

As mentioned earlier, the portrait of the jester in *Blackmail* (1929) is one of the first portraits that pointedly "looks out at us" in Hitchcock's films. The first of its diegetic beholders is Alice, the central character, and she looks at it once before and once after she stabs the artist who has attempted to rape her. Mocking and accusatory, the jester with his pointing finger seems the representative of a carnivalesque inversion of the law. But of *which* law? we may ask. At the very least this most theatrical of characters is an emblem of the aggressive theatricality—and hence modernity—of the portraitized figure. His gesture is a direct address of the spectator, and Alice mirrors it by pointing back at him. But it should be noted that the portrait of the jester has another beholder: shot from below, the portrait looks directly out of the frame and at the spectator of the film. Our first view of the portrait, a close-up of the jester's face, is followed by one of Hitchcock's surprising reverse tracking shots, a shot, as Zizek puts it, that typically "begins at the uncanny detail."[23] Here it begins in the eye of the jester, accentuating the power of his gaze directly at us, and rapidly tracks out to reveal the rest of the painting. Because of this radical stance of facingness and the surprising speed of the tracking shot, the camera's movement can be read both as the jester's approaching gaze *and* as the retreating movement of the spectator at its encroachment, suggesting fleetingly that the spectator has entered the cinematic frame. For a moment, jester and spectator are bound together in this double motion, with the "entry" of the spectator into the space of the film expressed by the camera's simulation of bodily movement. The realist strategy suggested by the ambiguity thus inscribed in the tracking shot complements the modernist stance of direct and aggressive looking. As its diegetic spectator, Alice herself manifests a realist attitude toward the painting of the jester: after her second viewing, she claws at the portrait with her fingers. In thus slashing the painting, Alice conflates the actual body of the artist with the body in his mocking portrait. But her gesture also responds to the mocking gaze itself: it is the counterpart of the jester's aggressive gaze. The scene of art in *Blackmail* links realist with modernist strategies several times over.

Although it is not represented in a portrait, the famous instance of the frontal gaze in *Strangers on a Train*, mentioned above, is clearly marked as the space of painting. It is Bruno, the protagonist's dark double, who sits staring directly into the camera while a tennis match is in progress. During this sequence, Bruno is seated facing Guy, the protagonist and his double. Both are spectators of the match that takes place within the containing space of their mirroring gazes. The axis formed by their looks is bisected by that of the ball's back-and-forth motion—a lateral motion that we do not see, but that is suggested aurally by the hollow and aggressive sound of the tennis ball as it is hit and returned.[24] Throughout this scene, its acoustical counterpart—the repeated "thunk" of the ball—accentuates the charged character of the exchanged—or mirrored—gaze. The space created by these two axes—that of the returned look and that of the returned ball—functions as an enclosed, theatrical space: it has four "sides." On one side Bruno sits immobile, in marked contrast to the other spectators, whose heads follow the ball back and forth in synchronized engrossment in the action. Against this sound and the mechanical motion of the other spectators, we are struck by the uncanniness of Bruno's immobility, the frozen figure's perverse lure. The figure's stillness within the rhythmic movement of the rest of the frame, together with his radical frontality, create the feel of a portrait here. In this sequence it is truly a picture that looks back at us: accentuated by the other heads turning in unison, Bruno's pronounced lack of movement reinforces his placement within a different kind of space, a painterly space such as we find in Manet's portraits. This is the image in which Zizek anchors his claim that the stain in Hitchcock's films "ultimately coincides with the threatening gaze of the other."[25] Here it is important to note again that the Lacanian gaze is not to be understood as coterminous with the look, that the gaze is on the side of the object, standing in for "the blind spot in the field of visible from which the picture itself photographs the spectator."[26] Bruno's motionless head—indeed his "motionless gaze," as Zizek puts it—creates the effect of "sticking out like a strange body and thus disturbing the image, introducing a threatening dimension."[27]

But the Lacanian gaze does not constitute the only vantage point for explicating this sequence in *Strangers on a Train*. Reading it in painterly terms seems to thicken our account of what is going on. The shot of Bruno features two polarities in a state of tension. On the one hand, the spectator experiences the flattening of the image: this is a moment when the two-dimensional properties of the image dominate its three-dimensional qualities, a moment when the ontological disjunction between viewed object and spectator is stressed. At one and the same time, however, we are conscious of the tennis ball hit and returned by the players on a lateral axis, perpendicular to the plane of representation that intensifies the looks exchanged from back to front by Bruno and Guy. It is yet another figure for the cross—or, rather, the "double" cross—upon which this film is structured. It is important to note, however, that it is not only the look out that seems to penetrate the fourth wall. When Bruno nearly strangles a party guest, for instance, Guy's fist, aimed at Bruno's chin, is seemingly thrust directly out of the screen and at the spectator, who here assumes Bruno's place. Later on in the film, Guy will play Reynolds in the decisive match that will decide not only the tennis championship, but also the possibility of preventing Bruno's double cross. During this sequence, on more than one occasion the ball is hit directly into the camera, "out of the frame," and at the spectator.[28] The modernist frontality of the figure in the first tennis sequence is visually echoed as the ball figuratively enters the space of the spectator in the second, promoting the illusion of movement into the space of the movie theater. But here it is the illusion of an actual penetration of the screen that is at issue. The tennis ball and the fist are not simply stand-ins for the gaze even though—like the gaze—they are aggressive. Hitchcock's play with illusion is reminiscent of similar moments in early cinema, notably in Edwin Porter's "Uncle Josh at the Moving Picture Show" (1902), where the naive spectator, Uncle Josh, fears that the image of a train on screen will enter his space.[29] As in the look out of the frame, the object of such shots is the figured merger of screen space with spectatorial space, of reality with representation. Here, however, the merger of two registers occurs at the level of the literal.

With the tennis ball in mind, the astonishing moment in *The Birds* (1963) when the seagulls famously enter the frame from the place of the spectator can now be read as more than a return of aggression in the form of the returned spectatorial gaze.[30] Of greater interest to our discussion here is that once again both movements—into and out of the frame—figure the collapse of representation with the real: the tennis ball's trajectory takes it "out of the film" and thus figures an assault on the spectator, whereas the birds enter the space of the film from the place of the fourth wall. Indeed, the emergence of the birds out of the space of the spectator—the real world—and into the space of the frame calls to mind a particularly interesting analogy concerning illusionism in visual representation, a story referred to by Lacan in his seminar on the gaze. It recalls Pliny's parable of realism, his famous tale of the contest between the artists Zeuxis and Parrhasios concerning who could create the most illusionistic painting. Zeuxis, as the story goes, painted a bunch of grapes so true to nature that it lured a flock of real birds out of the sky—birds that pecked away at the painted fruit.[31] But Pliny's tale ends as follows: Parrhasios wins the contest, having fooled Zeuxis with his trompe l'oeil curtain or canvas—on whose surface Zeuxis then asks him to produce a painting. Thus, having deceived even the artist's eye, Parrhasios' representation is the more successful, his illusion more complete. In calling attention to his medium by painting its support, one might anachronistically say that Parrhrasios performs a modernist gesture. And he does so, significantly, in a theater space, a space specifically designed to confound the perception of real and imagined.[32] *Spellbound*, as we recall, opens with a Dali sequence involving eyes painted on a curtain, ambiguously figuring the look out of theatrical space.

The "Reality Bleed" and the Spectator in the Film

Like many other Hitchcock films, *Rear Window* (1954), as John Belton points out, "plays with the differences between theatrical and cinematic film space."[33] Belton defines cinematic space as "a space that is 'other' for the spectator, who is necessarily segregated from it, physically prohibited from entry into it."[34] But we have been expanding Belton's claim that "only spectators *within* films may enter into it, as in *Sherlock, Jr* and *Purple Rose of Cairo*,"[35] to consider *figurations* of entry into films, for they have a great deal to say about spectatorial relations. Let us consider, for the moment, the degree to which *Rear Window* is governed by a deliberate frontality, by the facingness of Jeff with regard to the theater space before him. The spectator and the camera, of course, are placed on what Michel Chion calls "the fourth side"—or fourth wall—of a theatrical set,[36] that is, in the space of Jeff and his voyeuristic activities. At the end of *Rear Window*, as Chion puts it, Jeff the character who is also a spectator "[falls] into the picture," and locates himself within its space.[37] In my reading, on the other hand, I will stress the fact that Thorwald—the figure in Jeff's "picture"—will enter Jeff's space from the place of the film's spectator, the space of the fourth wall.

What is so threatening about Thorwald's entry into this space is that he invades the scene from the place of the spectator. In the theatrical economy of this film, Thorwald enters Jeff's apartment from a position outside the hypothetical fourth wall. Granted, several characters enter and leave the apartment through its door, understood to lead to the off-screen New York streets whose noises we hear. But it is not Bazin's idea of off-screen space to which I refer here, with its sense of continuous space only partly revealed by the cinematic frame. Instead, it is a sense of space that has its origins in theater, in the classical stage. Only Thorwald's entry that fundamentally disturbs the facingness of Jeff toward the courtyard: at the point of Thorwald's entry, Jeff "turns around," as it were,[38] to face a threat that comes from behind, from the space of the audience. Having entered the film from the place of its spectator, Thorwald in some sense becomes a representation of this spectator, now entering the space of the film. In the mirroring relation set up between Thorwald and Jeff at the moment when Thorwald's direct gaze is visible in the "picture window" across the courtyard or is represented by the glow of his cigarette in the dark, we are aligned with Jeff, whose penetrating look Thorwald returns. But now the look of the other comes from our place as Thorwald's radical frontality is replaced by his—or our—figured entry into the text. Here, at the film's most terrifying moment, the modernist gesture of facingness is followed directly by the (figured) realist entry into the picture plane. Thorwald's realist entry will be mirrored by Jeff as Thorwald pushes him out of the window and into the space of the spectacle he has been obsessively watching.

At this point, it will be useful to describe a mediatic trope of central importance to our concerns, a trope defined by William Egginton as "bleeding." By means of this trope, Egginton describes an "obsessive concern" of spectacle from the time that it was "organized in such a way as to presuppose an ontological distinction between the space of the viewer and the space of the character."[39] With his focus on the strategies that make representation appear realistic, Egginton distinguishes between a mode that insists on the "reality" of the medium, "presenting the medium (the film image) as if it were the object—reality itself,"[40] and one that suggests to the spectator that the object she or he sees stands in for another object. Whereas the first mode is predicated on the separation of spectatorial space from diegetic space, Egginton argues, in the second mode this separation is often undermined. The resulting collapse of spectator space and diegetic space in the first mode results in a "reality bleed," a term Egginton takes from Cronenberg's *eXistenZ* (1999), where it refers to the phenomenon in virtual reality games wherein the "real world" enters the world of the game—very much in the tradition of Courbet's realism as read by Fried. Egginton describes "bleeding" as a collapse of the distinctions between two levels of reality, usually a sudden collapse that catches the spectator off guard. The tension created by the direct look out of the frame—not specifically addressed by Egginton—is certainly one such moment in film. As an example of this collapse, Egginton mentions *Pleasantville* (1998), where the bleeding of one fictional world into another is produced "quite literally as a color bleed."[41]

The trope of "bleeding" is useful in describing the collapse of ontological registers in Hitchcock films, as well as in the merger of spectatorial reality with film that we have variously examined above. Its specific designation as a "color bleed" is actually useful as well, as a few of the sequences containing the movement out of the frame in Hitchcock's films are accompanied by flashes of red just barely motivated by the diegesis. This is color as flashes of light—conveniently the color of blood—rapidly emanating from the center of the frame as though spurting from a wound. Returning briefly to *Rear Window*, we recall that it is flashes of red that mark the scene in which Thorwald enters Jeff's space. In this scene the film image includes the afterimage experienced by Thorwald as Jeff resorts to a series of flashes to blind him, the suffusion of red suggesting the conjunction of body and image produced by the optical imprint a flash leaves upon the retina. The looks registered as Jeff's, with which Thorwald's alternate in shot-reverse-shot, are a series of blanched images. Not only has Thorwald entered the scene from the place of the spectator, but he and Jeff (doubles from the first) have merged within their embodied looks, at the level of physiological perception itself. In this alternation of point-of-view shots, the spectator sees more viscerally than usual through the eyes of Hitchcock's characters.

Another instance of "color bleeding" in Hitchcock's films deserves our particular attention with respect to facingness. It occurs in the sequence of the gun barrel in closeup that fires directly out of the frame in *Spellbound* (1945).[42] Here, too, the film penetrates spectatorial space as the gun goes off "in our faces." As the bullet is figuratively shot into the space of the theater, a single flash of red perforates the otherwise black-and-white images of the film, as though to suggest that the film frame was indeed bleeding into the space of the spectator, momentarily triggering the collapse of representation and reality into one another. Equated with Dr. Murchison as he points the gun simultaneously at himself, at the camera, and hence at the spectator, the spectator has figuratively become the suicides's (blinded) victim. Once again a flash of red marks the image of the gun at the moment of shooting, suggesting that it is Murchison's retinal image that we see.[43] This is a subjective shot, of course, seen through the eyes of a character at the point of death. But the sequence begins with an extreme close-up from behind of a hand holding a gun. As we see the gun from the point of view of a murderer, the scale and position of the hand suggest that it is an extension of our own bodies. When the gun is slowly turned around to face Murchison—and the spectator—it shoots us both in the eye. Here, too, the red-suffused shot that follows immediately upon its firing figures the physical merger of character with spectator at the level of perception. This, too, is a realist move in Fried's sense, resembling the corporeal realism that Fried locates in Courbet.[44] In this scene, too, we find an instance of self-conscious, modernist facingness—that of the gun—conjoined with the realist goal of embodiment.

But it is in *Psycho* that the picture confronts the spectator with the most uncanny power. The lure of a collapse of representation with the real is held out repeatedly in this film: "*Psycho*'s fiction," William Rothman has notably remarked, "is that its world is real."[45] One of the trailers released for *Psycho* sheds light on Hitchcock's project in this film, featuring Hitchcock as he gives a six-minute "house of horrors" tour of the Bates motel. When he suddenly pulls back the shower curtain to reveal a blonde screaming to the accompaniment of screeching violins, it is not only the theater curtain that is being pulled aside here, it is the fourth wall itself.[46] Hitchcock's direction for the shower scene is telling in this regard: Norman/Mother's knife should slash, he writes, "as if tearing at the very film, ripping the screen," opening up a space for us that resembles the eye-shaped peephole that Norman has carved into the wall.[47] As Zizek reads it, in *Psycho* we have finally reached—descended to—"the level of the real"[48] at the moment when Norman's psychosis compels him to take the mother's place. If, in its most extreme form, the "collapse of fiction with reality defines the psychotic universe,"[49] then this collapse can only be suggested here. In the moment of Norman's frontal gaze, his atrocious hybridity confronts us, perhaps even mirrors us, but his psychotic gaze is not penetrating: Norman's look is as unseeing as that of the blind. While the inquisitive camera tracks in to meet it, Norman's look remains turned in on itself, refusing to allow the continuity of character with spectator that occurs elsewhere in Hitchcock's films. Boundaries have been drawn. Whereas Norman himself figures the collapse of fiction with the real, Hitchcock stops just short of extending psychotic fusion to the spectator. Hitchcock's last filmic gesture—the final image of his final film, *Family Plot* (1976)—has some light to shed on that ultimate hesitation. In this dark comedy, Hitchcock definitively pulls back from the darker implications of his realist project. In *Family Plot* the direct look out of the frame is a wink, a signal by which the character Blanche lets us know that she is not, after all, a psychic. Blanche is not a medium, as she has pretended to be throughout the film: it has all been a performance, part of a scam. Tracking in on her look, does the camera signal that film is the genuine medium, the one that truly effects a continuity between living audience and ghostly image, or is this, too, performance and scam? In its undecidability, it is a genuine Hitchcock moment, a final wink at the audience in which all is seemingly relativized, rendered safely cinematic. But is it?

As we have seen, Hitchcock's films variously gesture towards the continuity of real and represented, extending to suggested representations of the spectator within the text—such as in the figure of Thorwald, for instance, as he enters the scene from the space of the spectator, and in the physicality inscribed in some point of view shots through camera movement and color. (In *Vertigo*, as I have already suggested, Hitchcock may go even further.) But the deliberate interpenetration of representation and the real—and the ultimate realist goal of embodiment—is most obvious, perhaps, in the Hitchcock cameo that occurs in nearly all of his films, the moment in which Hitchcock's body is present and recognizable in his texts. Although he never participates actively in the diegesis, Hitchcock is nevertheless in costume, hence comfortably within his fiction. The cameo both signals the incorporation of the "real"—it is the director, Hitchcock—and yet it is easily subsumed within representation as Hitchcock's body performs a simple, but appropriate, action within it. In its liminal position, the director's body as revealed in the cameo serves as a linchpin for Hitchcock's obsession with the juxtaposition of ontological registers. Hitchcock realizes Courbet's project of entering his text.

Oscillating Effects

In "Spatial Systems in *North by Northwest*," Fred Jameson's goal is to analyze Hitchcock's film "objectively," in terms of scenotopes organized as a spatial language. At a pivotal moment in his argument, Jameson suggests that "aggressive movement of the screen towards the audience" may have as its structural opposite the "plunging" of "cinema" into the space of the screen.[50] Indeed, a close look at *North by Northwest* reveals that the picture is "thrown out at us" by means of at least three aggressive gestures. The first of these is the oil truck that seems to come directly out of the screen to hit the spectator, now in the position of Roger Thornhill; the second takes place in the lodge, when the policeman's fist hits directly out at us as we again occupy his space; and the final example occurs in the form of Van Damm's fist as it aims for Leonard and hits the spectator, now in his place. But what of the opposite effect—that of the real plunging into the space of the screen? As an example of this opposite movement, Jameson specifically refers to the scene in which the Cary Grant character drives while intoxicated, and "the audience sits behind the wheel of the careening limousine as the screen itself veers giddyingly into space, taking the entire cinema with it out of control."[51] Perhaps with Cavell in mind, Jameson reads this sequence as an attack or "aggression of the camera upon the space within the screen" and postulates as its counterpart an "aggression" of the space toward the camera.[52] Somewhat tentatively, Jameson reads such spatial effects as residual traces of Hitchcock's experiments with 3 D movies in the early 1950s—and indeed, as Michael Kerbel points out, 3 D's two major claims were just these—that "1. it put you in picture . . . and 2. that it threw the picture out at *you*."[53] Interestingly, however, these technologically produced effects actually reproduce effects that Hitchcock had already attempted to create much earlier in his filmmaking career, as even the camerawork and the portrait in *Blackmail* make evident.

Jameson's concern is with the kinesthetic system of *North by Northwest*, but the scenotopes that he examines most closely are those imbued, as he puts it, "with the sense of the 'aesthetic' as such."[54] Mentioned specifically in this context are the scenes in the cornfield and in the pine woods. With its 3 D depth of field and the vertical lines of tree trunks that negate Bazinian depth, the scene in the pinewoods is one that, for Jameson, evokes "a distinctive Cézanne landscape."[55] And of course Cézanne's landscapes do in fact themselves set up an oscillation between a Cubist three-dimensionality and the flattening of space suggested by an emphasis on outline. The pinewoods scene in Hitchcock's film does likewise, as the vertical lines of the tree trunks at one and the same time create depth and ask us to read them simply as lines, their framing—they are cropped at the top—contributing to the overall sense of flatness. Dominating the middle of the frame, large trees create a split-screen effect that contributes to this impression. Like the famous cornfield sequence in the film, this painterly scene is about three-dimensional effects and their negation, about the collapse of scenographic space. The human bodies of the actors positioned within the pines, unnaturally far apart, seem trapped behind their trunks, much as Gerhard Richter's *Stag* (1963) is interrupted and fixed in place by similarly drawn trees. Their three-dimensional bodies, like those of the cars in this scene, are literally out of place, accentuating the artifice of the scene.

From the start, Saul Bass's title sequence signals the problematic of three-dimensionality and flatness in *North by Northwest* as the maplike grid upon which the titles are inscribed gradually dissolves into the three-dimensional image of Mies van der Rohe's Seagram Building. Repeatedly in this film, modernist spatial relations produce a striking, if momentary, flattening of the depth of field in the image. It is in these modernist painterly moments—when the planar qualities of the image assert themselves over its illusory qualities—that the spectator experiences a flattening of the frame, and the screen is reduced to the status of material support. We should note, however, that in this title sequence the writing on the grid is ironically replaced by the three-dimensional Mies van der Rohe building (I say ironically, because Mies is a modernist interested in pure space), which takes on shape and volume behind it. Then, however, the glass wall of the building becomes a reflecting surface—a screen—as it mirrors the pedestrians passing in front of it. But, in the end, in *North by Northwest* all moments of modernist flatness may be said to occur against the backdrop of the gigantic presidential heads carved into Mount Rushmore, bas-reliefs that function as their counterweight, as grand assertions of the potential for three-dimensionality in sculptural portraiture and in film. Fittingly, Cavell refers to these heads as a "crazy American literalization."[56]

Saul Bass's credit sequence for *Vertigo* also speaks to our topic. Here, too, we find a three-dimensional, filmic counterweight to modernist images. The sequence begins with the image of part of a woman's face, panning up from the mouth to zoom in on the right eye. As the camera focuses on the right eye in extreme close-up, the film frame becomes suffused with red, and the graphic spirals signalling vertigo begin to emerge from it. These spirals and whorling shapes all have a connection with the eye itself, for they tend to be organic shapes that, although abstract themselves, take the eye for its model. In their implied movement out of a kind of "deep space" and back into it again, these spirals mimic the perceptual shift that signals the collapse from the three-dimensional into the two-dimensional. And their movement visually echoes the famous dynamic that structures the vertigo shot. But this series of spirals ultimately returns to the filmic image of the eye in which it had originated. Although the whorls and spirals graphically announce the theme of vertigo as a traumatic disturbance displaced into the field of vision, it is likewise suggested by the eye in extreme closeup—it opens wide, it blinks and twitches—that vertigo has a physiological as well as a psychological dimension.

It is quite possible that Hitchcock's pivotal position in film history, as Deleuze terms it, accounts in some measure for this tendency in his films to accompany realist with modernist gestures. Interestingly, the same juxtaposition occurs in the films of Fritz Lang, with whom Hitchcock notably worked early in his career and from whom he learned a great deal about matters visual. We may, therefore, wish to read the presence of this dynamic in the films of both directors as a question of influence. Whether we choose to do so or not, however, we must keep in mind that not all filmmakers whose work spans the same period as Hitchcock's and Lang's are fascinated by these effects. We might well ask, then, in what other ways we can contextualize the coexistence of realist and modernist representational strategies in Hitchcock. It would not appear that the one is particularly privileged over the other in his films—they simply tend to occur in tandem, as though to cancel one another out or to hold one another in a state of suspension.

Here another art historical analogy may be productive in constructing a context for Hitchcock's strategies. Perhaps "representation anxiety," a term that Harry Berger has used in connection with Dutch art, may shed some light on the effects that we have been describing. In his work on Dutch painting of the seventeenth century, Berger reads a similar oscillation between "the force of mimetic illusion and its illusoriness" in Dutch painting as expressive of "representation anxiety," an anxiety involving both the artist's fetishistic desire to make the painting as "real" as possible *and* the fear that his work is *too* successfully illusionistic, too "real."[57] For Berger, this explains the tension between minute attention to detail in the rendering of reality and the self-conscious effects that disrupt illusion. With *Vertigo* in mind, one might easily characterize Hitchcock as a modern-day Pygmalion—one who exults in the fact that his creation is somehow "made real" yet, shuddering at the very thought, takes pains to undermine these effects.

The vacillation between the desire for a work's mimetic *success* and a fear of its uncanny mimetic *excess* finds another art historical frame of reference in the problematic surrounding trompe l'oeil. Trompe l'oeil, the extreme endpoint of the realist impulse, constitutes what Baudrillard has termed the "realist hallucination."[58] For Baudrillard, "reality" persists in trompe-l'oeil as the simulation of tactility, "as a vertigo of the sense of touch," produced by the manner in which the represented object pushes forward into the space occupied by its beholder.[59] Because trompe l'oeil pushes the world of the painting into the space of the real, it inverts the force that takes the eye into the vanishing point of Renaissance perspective, the perspectival system that determines film space. In Baudrillard's reading, the vertigo that trompe l'oeil generates is the result not of an excess of reality, but of a sudden failure of illusion that results in the deflation of the image. Realism in Fried's sense figures a movement into the canvas or frame, audaciously suggesting the continuity of representation with the real that is outside representation. In the direct look out of the frame, however, this continuity is expressed by way of a moment of modernist self-consciousness.

As in trompe l'oeil, the movement produced by the modernist direct look is out of the frame and into spectatorial space. If modernist moments in film call their constructedness to our attention, flattening the scenographic space that film inherits from the Renaissance, in moments such as the direct look out it is nevertheless the permeability of the screen that is at issue. For Baudrillard, trompe l'oeil extends far beyond painting and architecture to become more generally a "game with reality" indeed, "a metaphysical category—in the face of reality and against it."[60] Trompe l'oeil takes the game with representation and the real to its extreme endpoint. But, short of this, the game with reality has been being played in the arts, if not from of the time of Pliny, then at least from the sixteenth century on. If we prefer not to have recourse to psychoanalytic explanations for its occurrence, we might very well—with Egginton and Baudrillard—opt for a philosophical interpretation: realism becomes an issue as soon as reality becomes plural, as soon as ontological distinctions among realities can be made, as soon as we can distinguish between bodies and characters. The New York apartment setting of Hitchcock's *Rope* (1948), for instance, is full of paintings. A Milton Avery portrait of a girl—flat and modernist, her body broken up into various planes—is often picked up by the camera's eye. But the only painting that is mentioned by the characters is referred to as "a new young American primitive:" it is a trompe l'oeil still life of objects hanging on a wall, a painting in the manner of William Harnett. Late 1940s' chic may very well have dictated the apartment's hall wallpaper, complete with trompe l'oeil architectural elements: the trompe l'oeil balustrade in the neoclassical style is continuous with an actual shelf on which a sculpture is placed. Yet more may be at stake. In Hitchcock's work, the game with reality is played for mastery.

6

Kubrick and Kafka: The Corporeal Uncanny

Photographs and Stories

"The necessary condition for an image is sight," Gustav Janouch claims to have said to Kafka. Kafka supposedly smiled and replied: "We photograph things in order to drive them out of our minds. My stories are a way of shutting my eyes."[1] Photography as exorcism, performed "in order to drive things out of our minds." In a typical paradox, Kafka transforms the photograph from a monument to a thing or moment in the external world, a vehicle of remembrance, into a means of expelling a "thing"—a place, a person, a demon?—from the mind itself. Given material expression in the photograph, the image is separable, detachable—not only from its referent but, as Kafka is supposed to have put it—from the "mind." In Kafka's formulation as transmitted by Janouch, stories are "a way," a means of shutting the eyes, of not looking at what we do not wish to see. But this paradox ensures that the link between photograph and work of fiction remains ambiguous. On the one hand, stories are seen *in contradistinction* to photography—not as a means of exorcising demons, but rather as a means of shutting them out, of erecting a textual barrier between self and world. On the other hand, it is the *relatedness* of story to photograph that is intriguing, the sense in which writing, too, may be an exorcism. "Shutting the eyes," as an act entailed in writing, would render narrative an effort both to expel and shut out the images that photography fixes. In this reading, narrative is complicit with photography in its attempt to keep the "things" that haunt us at a distance. But is the "necessary condition for the image" really sight, as Janouch postulates? Surely it is also suggested that some images exist in the mind's eye alone.[2]

What then, might keeping one's *Eyes Wide Shut* imply? The title of Kubrick's last film almost certainly refers to this exchange between Kafka and Janouch, albeit indirectly.[3] Adopting Kafka's tendency to speak in paradoxes, Kubrick shrouds the relations between photograph and narrative in further ambiguity. Where to look for enlightenment? Quoting Kafka and Janouch in *Camera Lucida*, his meditation on photography, Roland Barthes muses that the best way to look at photographs may be to look away, to *close* one's eyes. "Absolute subjectivity," writes Barthes, "is achieved only in a state, an effort, of silence. Shutting your eyes is to make the image speak in silence," he continues, "to say nothing, to shut my eyes, to allow the detail to rise of its own accord into affective consciousness."[4] The detail to which Barthes refers is of a particular kind: it is what Barthes calls the *punctum*, an element that "shoots out of the [the scene] like an arrow and pierces me."[5] The marks or wounds created by the punctum generate affective responses: "a photograph's *punctum* is that accident which pricks me (but also bruises me, is poignant to me)"; it is that which "attracts and distresses."[6]

With reference to Barthes's reflections, then, keeping the "eyes wide shut" refers to the insight that comes from sustained meditation on the image that a photograph leaves in the mind's eye. It is when all else is excluded—what Barthes calls the "noise" that surrounds the image—that the significant detail, the wounding punctum, brings insight in the form of affective response. Barthes, then, takes Kafka's words literally, applying them to the photograph rather than to the story. "Shutting his eyes," Barthes *restores* the image of the exorcised "thing" to the mind. Reconnecting with the wounding "thing" and viewing it in the mind's eye once more, Barthes savors affects that Kafka prefers to keep at bay. Could it be that *Eyes Wide Shut*—a film whose title was chosen by Kubrick, remaining enigmatic to his screenwriter—contains a punctum, something that attracts and distresses Kubrick? Something once exorcised—only to be internalized and viewed with "eyes wide shut" after all? What is it that attracts and distresses; what is it that produces affects, both pleasurable and unpleasurable?

Kubrick's films reveal a fixation with the writers and artists of the Hapsburg monarchy; the "Blue Danube Waltz" and Strauss's "Also Sprach Zarathustra" only momentarily seem out of place in the aural texture of *2001*. In interviews, Kubrick invokes in particular the names of its Jewish writers and intellectuals—of Kafka, Stefan Zweig, Arthur Schnitzler, and Freud.[7] The Stefan Zweig story that took Kubrick's fancy was never made into a film, but the adaptation of Schnitzler's *Traumnovelle* intrigued Kubrick for decades before its realization.[8] Frederic Raphael, screenwriter for *Eyes Wide Shut*, was given books of paintings by Egon Schiele and Gustav Klimt and asked to study Freud.[9] Years before, collaborating on the screenplay for *The Shining*,[10] Kubrick and Diane Johnson read Freud's essay on *The Uncanny* together, and Kafka was also on Kubrick's mind.[11] How intriguing, then, that in an essay written years before the release of *Eyes Wide Shut*, Michel Ciment suggests that Kubrick's "unfulfilled ambition" of filming the Schnitzler text may have "found an outlet" in *The Shining*.[12] As I will claim, the points of connection between *The Shining* and *Eyes Wide Shut* are mediated by the presence of Kafka.

In Kafka's writing, at once so allegorical and yet, as Kubrick put it, "simple and straightforward, almost journalistic" in style, Kubrick thought he had found the "perfect guide" for a "realistic approach."[13] Critics who have sought the "missing auteur" in Kubrick's work might look to the extreme anonymity of Kafka's narrative technique—to what Kubrick refers to as Kafka's "journalistic" style—as a model for what is read as the filmmaker's authorial "absence."[14] If Kubrick is said to have "eviscerated the affective surfaces" of more than one novel,[15] it is equally claimed of Kafka that he "affectively neutralizes" what his stories are at pains to represent.[16] But oddly, perhaps, it is two minor scenes in *Eyes Wide Shut* that most obviously cue Kafkaesque concerns in Kubrick. Of course Schnitzler's *Traumnovelle* contains the scenes to which I am referring—the scenes in the costume shop—but readers of Kafka will agree that these scenes might well have come straight out of *The Trial*. In both their fictional and filmic versions, they play themselves out against the background of sexual antics performed by a young girl with two men in wigs—antics that take place behind and under furniture and have both the offhand and yet grotesque effect of similar couplings in Kafka's fiction. For Kubrick, I will suggest, the Kafkaesque overtones of these scenes in Schnitzler's novella contitute what Barthes's punctum is to the photograph: that which "pricks me, bruises me, is poignant to me." We will return to this topic later.

Material Images

A meditation on the nature of the still image lingers even in the midst of Kubrick's most kinetic films,[17] not surprising in a filmmaker who began his career as a photographer. Kubrick's concentration on the still image is the natural counterpart to his fascination with cinematic movement; we find it in the thousands of preproduction photographs in which most of Kubrick's films have their visual origins, of course, and we find it variously expressed in the films themselves. *Barry Lyndon*, the most painterly of Kubrick's films, repeatedly features the static image, usually in the rendering of painting: it is present in the compositions from Gainsborough and Hogarth, and in the homage to Reynolds that occurs in the static shots especially of the Lyndon residence, picturesque shots of the real Castle Howard. We find it in the careful composition of each frame, in the manner in which movement itself becomes an "actor" in some frames, often beginning in the middle of an otherwise still frame, and then gradually subsuming the frame from within, in the manner of F. W. Murnau. An interest in the still image as the basis and foil for cinematic motion is evident in *2001*, as well. Although the film is indeed "a formal statement on the nature of movement" as Annette Michelson has pointed out, the orchestrated, abstract nature of this movement admits its reliance on the still image—hence our sense, as Michelson puts it, that we are viewing another *Ballet Mécanique*.[18] We find the still image likewise in the transparencies used for the "Dawn of Man" prologue in *2001*: they are "picture postcards" that provide sublime backdrops for these scenes, of course, but they also endow each of them with something of the photograph's atemporality, its "moment of time" feel in a series of incomprehensibly distant moments of the past.

In *The Shining* (1980), the static image as photograph is basic to the evocation of the uncanny and the supernatural. Perhaps Kubrick himself had the intuition expressed by Kracauer that the photographic rendering of human bodies produces portraits of ghosts and ghostly images.[19] Or perhaps it was Barthes's assertion in *Camera Lucida* (also 1980) that the *eidos* of the photograph is death that suggested the particular possibilities of still photography for rendering the supernatural to Kubrick.[20] Certainly Freud's work on *The Uncanny* would have triggered an interest in the effects that mechanically rendered motion can have on the spectator, reminding Kubrick of early film's preoccupation with its capacity to set images of the human body in motion, to efface the divisions between life and death.[21] Or it may in fact have been Kafka's suggestion to Janouch, mediated by Barthes, that photography is a kind of exorcism. Whatever the source, *The Shining* is haunted by photography: photography itself resurfaces as an aspect of the film's imaginary, as a return of the repressed—or, as Barthes puts it, a "return of the dead."[22]

Most intriguing, perhaps, is the almost maniacal, willed insistence on photographic indexicality that persists in film's relation to photography in

Kubrick: it is here that the body enters film. Photographs in *The Shining* become "material." Jack's "visions" or mental projections—his experiences with the dead—take their subjects both from newspaper photos and from the myriad black-and-white photographs that adorn the walls of the Overlook Hotel. These images take on lush colors as Jack brings their dead imaginatively to life, as he "realizes" the photographs and enters their spaces, interacting with the ghosts who populate them.[23] Jack has a "visionary" power that resides in the capacity to animate photographs from the past, to animate them narratively in the manner of cinema. But of greatest importance to this reading is the film's insistence on the (figured) materiality of these images, on the manner in which they evoke the body. In one of his "visions," Jack "recognizes" the former caretaker from his photograph in the newspaper and, as Fred Jameson puts it, "the film public palpably gasps when the conventions of the ghost story are violated, when the hero physically intersects with his fantasmagoric surrounding and he collides with the *material body of a waiter* whose drink he spills" (italics mine).[24] Another case in point is the allusion to *Faust I* as Jack sits down at the ballroom bar: "I'd give my goddamned soul for a glass of beer," he announces. A moment later, his own reflection in the mirror is replaced by the image of the bartender, a devil clothed in red. Just as Goethe's Mephisto plays to the students' bodily desires by conjuring up an image of wine real enough to guzzle down,[25] the bartender produces a drink for the "parched" Jack in an atmosphere that similarly insists upon the materiality of illusion. Drinks are spilled and consumed, music listened and danced to, lust is aroused, disgust produced. The horror film, as Linda Williams has famously said, is one of the "body genres."[26] The ghost materializes and is revealed to have a body; Kubrick's uncanny is decidedly corporeal.

Using language that suggests the indexical relation of the photograph to the real, Mr. Halloran tells Jack's son Danny that the violent events perpetrated in the hotel have left "their trace." The photographic nature of certain images will be evoked visually several times later on in the film, each time juxtaposing the photograph's "flat Death" with an uncanny materiality.[27] One notable incidence occurs in the "Thursday" sequence, when the film camera moves in on Jack's crazed face with its motionless grimace—an image that is a freeze-frame—until Jack arches his eyebrows diabolically. This moment of controlled movement exemplifies the possibilities both of arresting action and of killing off the moving, hence seemingly three-dimensional, image into the photograph—and of bringing it to life by the introduction of movement once again. Macabre in the extreme, the "frozen" moment and arrested action of the photograph are suggested quite literally in the ice sculpture that Jack's body—very much a material image—will become. How fitting, then, that the film camera, moving ever closer, will discover Jack at the center of the group photo of Overlook guests at a 1921 ball. Now himself a ghost, Jack has been exorcised into the space of photography.

Like father, like son. Danny's visions also have a photographic dimension: the first one features the oceanic, silent eruption of blood out of the elevator, with the two Grady girls not yet part of the scene. Instead, the image of the elevator is cut with a very briefly held still of the two murdered girls: their frontality and the directness with which they look out of the frame suggest a family snapshot, while their near-doubling—they are not twins—nevertheless alludes to a photograph by Diane Arbus, "Identical Twins, Roselle, N.J. 1967." Later, Danny will turn around to see the Grady girls behind him as he is playing darts. Although they have now "materialized"—become more filmic and entered the space of the narrative—they continue to assume a frontal pose. Even as they turn around they hold hands and maintain their "frontal" configuration: they are silent images only partially released from a photograph. In the "Tuesday" sequence, the Grady sisters will appear to Danny again as figures in a photograph, but in the "Thursday" sequence he will come upon them at the end of a corridor, and this time they will speak to him—in tandem and in the formulaic language of fairy tales. Terrified by these images, Danny recalls what Mr. Halloran had told him—that the images he sees are "just like pictures in a book."

A number of Annette Michelson's assertions concerning *2001*—that it dissolves the opposition between body and mind, that "things seen" are supplemented by "things felt," and the camera has a great deal to do with both[28]—hold true for *The Shining* as well. The film camera is a "presence" in *The Shining* from its first frames, of course, when its eccentric trajectory seems to stalk, then lose interest in, the family in the VW below. Swooping over a cliff rather than keeping its prey in focus, the camera emerges as a character rather than as an embodiment of authorial presence—unlike the camera in a Hitchcock film, for instance, it is less voyeuristic than predatory. The familiar Dies Irae melody with which the film begins conjures up Dreyer's *Day of Wrath*, reinforcing a connection with the earlier film in its use of a mobile camera.[29] Here, as in *Day of Wrath*, the camera seems to have the "evil eye" as well as the witch's power of invocation, the power to call up "the Quick and the Dead." Its sinister playfulness is continued in many interior shots of the hotel, where, rather than keeping the Torrances in frame, the camera often disappears behind pillars, only to bring them into focus once more as it wends its sinuous way along confining corridors.

The point here is simply that the film camera does not play to the eye alone. During long takes the steadicam tends to track rapidly backwards, retreating in front of the characters who are moving toward us, thus doubling the effect of speed and motion, and producing spectator vertigo. Although the camera is rarely aligned with Jack,[30] and prefers to shoot characters frontally, it is often located behind Danny—sometimes seeming to share his point of view, sometimes in pursuit—most notably during the dizzying sequences when he is on his tricycle. In *The Shining*, the affective response missing from the film's unlocalizable narrative "voice" is displaced into the spectator, in whom camera movement and imagery produce sensations of vertigo and nausea.[31] Kubrick ensures that his spectator is embodied.

At times the film camera crosses to "the other side." Moving "through the looking glass," it may playfully juxtapose the uncanny mirror image with the (diegetic) real,[32] as when in the crucial sequence titled "A Month Later," Wendy brings Jack breakfast in bed. In our first view of Jack, the camera pulls back from a frontal shot, only gradually revealing to us that what we see is his reflection in the mirror. Next the "real" Wendy enters the frame, and then the camera moves back into the space of the mirror. There follows a shot of Wendy from the point of view of Jack that emerges from an "impossible" place—out of the mirror itself, a Dreyer moment, recalling the impossible point of view of the corpse in *Vampyr*. The mirror will likewise be the site of the uncanny when Jack enters Room 237. A shot of Jack shows him in happy anticipation as a young and beautiful woman approaches him. But as he embraces her, he glances into the mirror in which their bodies are reflected. As the woman's body visibly ages, disintegrates, and decays in the mirror, telescoping time, we hear the cackle of a witch. Once again illusion asserts its connection to corporeality, a corporeality that corrupts the image from within. The witch as temptress and hag recalls *Day of Wrath*, to be sure. But the image in the mirror—a trope of the supernatural—more importantly points to the abject maternal body, alive and dead, equally the object of desire and of horror.

"Canniness" or the Vital Domain

Citing Freud as his source, Winfried Menninghaus reminds us that fairy tales can represent uncanny situations and occurrences without bringing them fully into affective consciousness. Just so, Kafka's stories have the ability, as Menninghaus puts it, "to render virtually invisible and affectively neutral what his fictions are continuously at pains to represent: disgusting bodies, gestures, and actions."[33] Eating and sex, two canonical acts of the grotesque, are closely associated in Kafka, and carnality—both in its sexual and gustatory forms, approaching even cannibalism—evokes strong affective responses in the male characters who populate his texts. Similarly—Deleuze's insistence on Kubrick's cinema as a "cinema of the brain" notwithstanding[34]—critical response to *The Shining* has noted its corporeal concerns, variously connecting the Overlook Hotel with the womb,[35] its labyrinth with the intestines,[36] and pointing out that its dominant color is blood red.[37] As in Kafka's texts, disgust and nausea are often linked in the genre of the horror film to a complex relation to the female body.[38] But even beyond this clichéd common concern, the nature of Kubrick's obsession with the female body points to an unexpected dimension of Kafka's significance for his work.

In *Camera Lucida*, Barthes recalls to mind Freud's observation that the maternal body is the one place of which we can all say with certainty that we have been, suggesting that the landscape of desire is *heimlich*.[39] "It's all very homey," says Jack Torrance on first surveying the cavernous spaces of the Overlook Hotel; "homey" in the sense of comfortable, gemütlich, is precisely what the Overlook is not. A month later, when Jack claims to have fallen in love with the hotel right away, to have felt as though he "had been there before . . . as though he knew what was going to be behind every corner," we know what his remarks are intended to suggest. "Homey" is *heimlich*, canny, and as Ciment too reminds us, a sense of déjà vu suggests that the familiar place has been connected with the maternal body.[40] Further, in *his* visions, Jack's son Danny repeatedly sees "torrents" (Torrance?) of blood pouring out of an elevator. Blood is first seen seeping out from behind the doors, then gushing forth (the cinematic allusion here is to *Metropolis*), and the narrative overtly connects this blood with a paternal violence against children that transgresses our most rigid taboos. But visually, this scene accomplishes something else: by suggesting that the corridors of the hotel are corporeal passageways—arteries for the transport of blood—it turns the hotel itself into a body. What is more "homey"—*heimlich*, canny—than the body of the mother? And yet this scene is violent: the gushing of blood surrounds the deaths of children, as though to suggest a perverse inversion of the nourishing placenta.

Indeed, as in Kafka, perversion and disgust infiltrate the domain of nourishment and eating from this film's beginning when a conversation about the snowbound Donner party cues the theme of cannibalism. Foreshadowing the desperate circumstances of the snowbound Torrances, this theme persists during the tour of the meat freezer, and we feel relief that Danny, when asked which meat is his favorite, replies "French fries and ketchup." The suggestion of cannibalism infects the act of eating so profoundly that it comes into play even as the sympathetic African American chef, Mr. Halloran, serves Danny chocolate ice cream, and we might add that his father Jack's preferred drink is Jack Daniels. Cannibalism resides in the domain of Kristeva's abject, a prime example of the "crossing over of the categories of Pure and Impure,"[41] a perversion of the infantile desire for incorporation.

If Danny experiences nausea as well as terror at the images of his bloody visions, his reactions only serve to make the connections between the digestive and the uterine domains more fluid. And then there is Tony, Danny's imaginary friend and double, the "author" of his visions, who lives, as Danny puts it, in his "mouth" and in his "stomach." In keeping with Otto Rank's insights concerning the double, Danny gives birth to Tony in order to ward off death, in turn keeping Tony "safe" in his "stomach," as he puts it, his metaphorical womb. From the child's point of view, Tony—both a voice who speaks through Danny, and the "source" of Danny's ghastly visions—inhabits his body rather than his mind. Thus, Danny's visionary power—"shining"—is by its very location identified with the "desirable and terrifying, nourishing and murderous, fascinating and abject inside of the maternal body."[42] Danny's visions both figure and produce substances—blood and vomit—that Kristeva relegates to the domain of the mother, the domain of the body. From what source, we may well ask, does the heartbeat that makes its way into so many of Kubrick's soundtracks emanate? And why does the color red tend to dominate the visual field?

The maternal body itself is abject, and we must break with it through the power of language.[43] Small wonder, then, that Jack Torrance, would-be writer, imprisoned within the maternal body that is the Overlook Hotel, has a disturbed relation to the symbolic. Jack comes to the hotel armed with an album into which he has carefully pasted newspaper clippings—both photographs and stories—intending to use these as a basis for his novel. But Jack cannot write, he can only type, his typewriter has become a mechanical writing machine. In the manner of concrete poetry, Jack uses language as though it were a nonsignifying material, creating a series of typographical variations on a single sentence—a sentence not even of his own devising. Page after page piles up, producing a modernist text that is a material object, a sculpture—a text whose relation to temporality is distorted in favor of the image.

"Shutting the Eyes"/"Eyes Wide Shut"

In Schnitzler's *Taumnovelle*, the two men engaged in sex with the young daughter of a costume-shop owner first appear as judges of the Vehmic court, dressed in the red hats (*Talare*) and pleated robes of this office.[44] The judges are seated at a table from under which the young girl slithers to escape her approaching father. In this first scene at the costume shop, the father admonishes the girl and chastises the judges who, as they leave the shop in evening clothes, are revealed to have been in costume—not judges at all. The next day, when the hero of Schnitzler's story returns to find one of them leaving the young girl's room, the father will reveal himself to have been in complicity with their behavior: it had never been his intention to have recourse to the law at all. Indeed, the father is his daughter's pimp. Schnitzler's scene is a scene out of Kafka.

Kubrick's film both masks and intensifies this connection. The daughter's lovers do not even pose as judges: Kubrick's modern-day New York version of this scene transforms the costumed "judges" into Japanese tourists in wigs; one of them is wearing red bikini briefs, and the other emerges naked from behind the sofa where he has presumably been having sex with the young girl. In Kubrick's film, the costume-shop owner is a man named Milich who speaks in a heavy accent that permeates the scene with a Middle-European atmosphere. The bathrobe that Milich wears is worn by Schnitzler's shop owner as well, a sign of the not-quite-respectable nearness of the body that evokes memories of many Kafka texts. Further, the film introduces a Kafkaesque "gatekeeper" aspect into the initial encounter between Bill Harford, the protagonist, and Milich: Harford bargains with Milich for access to his shop at an actual wrought-iron gate, while Milich—jangling his keys—claims "one can't be too careful." Milich, we might add, is played by Rade Scherbedgia, an actor who resembles Kubrick himself, suggesting that a personal concern may inform the costume-shop sequences.

In his memoir of the collaboration with Kubrick, Frederic Raphael repeatedly recurs to the topic of "how thoroughly Schnitzler's story is impregnated with Jewishness."[45] Although the topic of Jewishness came up between Kubrick and Raphael time and again, Raphael complains with more than some regret, that Kubrick "forbade any reference to Jews"[46] and that Jews are not featured in any of Kubrick's films.[47] But Jewish culture must at least have had a part to play in the affinity Kubrick apparently felt both with Schnitzler and with Kafka.[48] It is present in Kubrick's intensification of the Kafkaesque scene embedded in the Schnitzler text,[49] and perhaps in his decision to delete what may have been most meaningful to him (just as Barthes omitted his mother's photograph from *Camera Lucida*) but nevertheless to retain a reference to Kafka by other, more easily recognizable, means.

Let us return now to Schnitzler's young men dressed as Vehmic court judges. Their relations with a young girl are shocking in the Schnitzler story at least in part because of the nature of the office that they appear to hold: they appear to be the contaminated representatives of a law that is itself rendered contaminated by their acts. Nevertheless, the law is not cleansed of this contamination when the men are revealed as impostors: on the one hand, their fantasies suffice to contaminate the law and—equally important—paternal law itself is "infected" when the father's complicity becomes apparent.

Citing Reiner Stach's work on Kafka, Slavoj Zizek reminds us that the "trespassing of the frontier that separates the vital domain from the judicial domain" is a characteristic of Kafka's universe.[50] In *The Trial*, for example, the court is located within the "vital promiscuity" of the workers' lodgings; it is a sexually enticing washerwoman who allows K. entry into the interrogation chamber and, as K. stands before the tribunal, he dimly sees a man and woman locked in an embrace.[51] Zizek puts it thus: "Smeared by an obscene vitality, the law itself—traditionally a pure, neutral universality—assumes the features of a heterogeneous, inconsistent *bricolage* penetrated with enjoyment."[52] Zizek reads Kafka's reaction to the separation of these domains as a sign of his embeddedness in Jewish culture: the Jewish religion, claims Zizek, "marks the moment of the most radical separation of these domains. In all previous religions, we encounter a place, a domain of sacred enjoyment (*in the form of ritual orgies, for example*), whereas in Judaism the sacred domain is evacuated of all traces of vitality and the living substance is subordinated to the dead letter of the Father's law" (emphasis mine).[53] Reacting against this separation, writes Zizek, "Kafka trespasses the divisions of his inherited religion, flooding the judicial domain, once again, with enjoyment."[54]

It is as though *Eyes Wide Shut* had been made with this quotation from Zizek in mind. Certainly Kubrick's film celebrates the impure in a ritual of defilement.[55] The formal aspects of the ritual—the geometric arrangement of bodies in patterns; the sculptural masks that obscure the human face; the slow, precise motions that govern these bodies—all contribute to an absorption of the body by art. Arrested erotic poses break into motion as tableaux dissolve into ritual actions. Tellingly, the elaboration of the ritual orgy in *Eyes Wide Shut* culminates in the moment when its participants take on the role of judges as Bill Harford stands before them in the crimson circle, unmasked and brought to judgment. Surely this is a masochistic scenario par excellence. In Schnitzler's story, the mock "judges" who participate in the orgy with the shop owner's daughter anticipate this moment, of course.[56] Although Kubrick has disguised Schnitzler's mock judges as businessmen, *Eyes Wide Shut* features the permeability of the judicial and the vital domains that both Schnitzler and Kubrick read in Kafka, transposing it to the scene of a ritual orgy enacted by powerful men participating in a quasireligious rite.

It remains to suggest in what sense Kafka's merging of these domains might constitute a punctum for Kubrick. What, for Kubrick, might the implication of "flooding the judicial domain with enjoyment" be? If, as Zizek contends, in Judaism "the living substance is subordinated to the dead letter of the Father's law," then Kafka presents the reader with the counterexample of a textuality that is anything but dead—yet whose sensuality is masked by the glossy surface of a distanced, opaque, *modernist* style. It is a style of "proverbial purity," whose effect on the reader, as Zizek sees it, may be otherwise: "It is as if," Zizek writes, "Kafka's text were a coagulated, stigmatized, signifying chain repelling signification with an excess of sticky enjoyment."[57] The "stickiness" of this text is that of unmentionable bodily substances— of the body of the sexual woman, of Kristeva's abject mother, and of the Bakhtinian grotesque who ingests, excretes, and fornicates.

In any art form, Annette Michelson has suggested with reference to Kubrick's *2001*, the perception of "lived reality" is not easily compatible with the "movement towards abstraction which animates the style and esthetics of modernism"[58] As we have noted, Jack Torrance's typewriter is a machine that can only produce mechanical writing on stacks of paper, while in his *Penal Colony*, Kafka notoriously offers his reader a writing machine that inscribes human flesh. Kafka's bleeding script points to modernism's Other, its counterpart and complement. It is the vital domain itself—the stuff of representation become its surface—reversing the relation between the photograph and its inscription by the body as trace. What Kubrick sees in Kafka's stories is a relation between style and content that is antithetical in the extreme. If, as Kafka puts it, his stories are a way of "shutting his eyes," Kafka may also be referring to the manner in which his "pure" style acts as a kind of sealant, covering over—even entrapping—his subject under a veneer that represses it, contains it, and gives it an auratic glow. To have one's eyes "wide shut," then, is, like Kubrick, to be aware of Kafka's project—and to imitate it.

7

The Castrato's Voices:
Fassbinder's *In a Year of Thirteen Moons*

Resembling Roland Barthes's description in *S/Z* of the realist text as a "weaving of voices," an "obliterated network . . . a vast 'dissolve,' which permits both overlapping and loss of messages,"[1] Fassbinder's film presents its spectator—and auditor—with a multilayered and sometimes opaque textuality. Barthes's "voices" or codes, as we recall, structure the multivalent text, creating a "stereographic" space of writing that refers to a chain of prior textualities: in this system, "reality is what has been written" and its origin is lost in the chain of signification.[2] Famously based on Balzac's *Sarrasine*, Barthes's analysis focuses on the realist text's discontinuous meanings—its pluralities—smoothed over by the "natural movement" of its sentences.[3] In the case of *Sarrasine*, this "natural" style notably covers over a "shocking" rupture in the chain of signification, as the body that anchors its symbolic field is that of the singer Zambinella, a castrato, and, as Barthes would have it, "castration jams all metonymy."[4] In contrast, Fassbinder's postmodern film—the story of a transsexual in whose significatory chain *S/Z* itself is surely a link—lacks Balzac's "natural" or *naturalizing* style: it lacks a "skin" to contain its heterogeneous parts. Its textual body is flayed and open to the view.

Indeed, *In a Year of Thirteen Moons* (1978) has left one of Fassbinder's most astute critics, Tim Corrigan, suggesting that it is illegible, "a movie . . . about textualities that lose their ability to naturalize and balance the materials of signification with a sense of meaning," leaving us with a "dense overabundance of materialized markers."[5] Against the backdrop of Corrigan's comments, this chapter reads the film's "voices" or codes through several specific instances of the human voice and delineates the material and symbolic aspects of exchange in *Thirteen Moons* through the multiple relations of sound and image, word and flesh, self and other that it establishes. The film's strategy, it is argued here, is to collapse the binary oppositions that structure these relations, transforming the "either/or" of binarism into a "both/and" of mutuality or simultaneity. As word and flesh, self and other are collapsed, the film embraces the condition Kristeva calls abjection.[6] But the question of whether Fassbinder's text is "realist," allegorical, or "oscillating between different referentialities,"[7] I will argue, remains suspended as the eroding distinction between self and other takes on the ideological task of imaging German-Jewish relations. What light, this chapter will also ask, can *Thirteen Moons* shed on the controversy over Fassbinder's alleged anti-Semitism?

Textualities, the Voice, and the Real

Let us begin at the film's beginning, with the (failed) sexual encounter between Elvire and the male prostitute, a scene whose indistinct, even veiled, images are accompanied by a nondiegetic five-minute excerpt from the Adaghietto of Mahler's Fifth Symphony, an obvious homage to Visconti's *Death In Venice*. Here is a link, to use Barthes's term, in the code of Art. Art, the (gay male) body, and death are simultaneously evoked, of course, in the multiple references that the music generates: Visconti's film leads us directly to Mann's novella, leads through the novella's dichotomies of Apollonian (sculpture) and Dionysian (dance) to Nietzsche's *Birth of Tragedy* and back to Winckelmann. Nondiegetic music—incorporeal, unlinked to the ambient sound of the scene—conjures up a clichéd chain of textualities (for the German spectator, at least), signifiers of a German tradition of high-cultural sublimation, in which the erotic, disease, and death are re-covered in the realm of the aesthetic. Exploiting the affective impact of its poignant strains, the film uses Mahler's music as one strand of the aural texture of this scene, while diegetic sound—angry words in Czech, the dull thud of blows—serves as its counterpoint. Here the human voice in "acoustic close-up" features "the breath, the gutturals, the fleshiness of the lips" in a way that introduces the material body into speech.[8] Simultaneously, the image track reveals and yet does not reveal the missing body part upon which signification and symbolization depend. Violence to the body puts an end to the haunting strains of Mahler; the scene terminates in a chilling moment of desublimation, a material blow to the aesthetic.

On to the next scene: Elvire, rather badly beaten up, enters the apartment, whereupon she speaks a series of quotations—or perhaps we should say that Fassbinder's speaking subject "is spoken" by German culture. Again the quotations are clichéd: one of Marlene Dietrich's theme songs from *The Blue Angel* ("Von Kopf bis Fuss") is followed first by a passage from *Rumpelstiltskin*, then by an expansionist military folksong that links the Fatherland with the banks of the Volga, and then concludes in the famous opening lines of a Schiller poem ("The Ring of Polykrates") familiar to German schoolchildren. Sentimental, ominous, and even mock heroic, these quotations—torn from their context—seem to serve Elvire as assurances of a culturally generated subjectivity. Punctuated with sobs and cries of pain, the performance of these quotations is also marked by the "grain" of Elvire's voice, by "the materiality of the body speaking its mother tongue."[9] When the next sound, the flushing of a toilet, announces the physicality of another body, the aural suggestion is made that the detritus of German culture, too, has been evacuated. This postmodern gesture, an emptying out of significance, gives priority to the material body while retaining the possibility of an allegorical function for sound. The oppositional relation, then, of nondiegetic music (the "chain of Art") to closely miked (if not indexical) dialogue and sounds of pain in the opening scene,[10] is repeated in another key: a series of quotations (the "chain of Art") is undermined by the grain of the voice and ambient sound. Although the drives and affects, indeed the body itself, create ruptures in the symbolic order, these very ruptures (the flushing of the toilet) may be recuperated for signification.

But it is in our third example, the abbatoir scene, that the layering of sound and image and the juxtaposition of the symbolic and the material take their most shocking form. Here a long, characteristic tracking shot reveals a row of slaughtered and dismembered animals: this steaming, bloody meat is the real itself. The violence of this sequence is not performed—it is recorded. And yet it, too, is multiply under the sign of Art, for the carcasses are on display, at least to the moving camera and for the spectator. Suspended from hooks, they constitute a (literal) still-life, a "cinematic *nature morte*"[11] of opened and flayed beasts, announcing a subject in painting of which Rembrandt's versions of the "Slaughtered Ox" (1643; 1655) constitute only the best-known examples.

Fassbinder's film eerily silences the cattle's cries of pain, the sound of blows or gushing blood. Instead, the soundtrack substitutes a voice-over, taken from Elvire's taped interview with a journalist, which relates the story of her relationship with her erstwhile actor lover, Christoph. But it is not the occasionally glimpsed image of Elvire in this scene that supports her voice, nor is the voice strictly acousmatic.[12] Rather, as Kaja Silverman has argued, "the corporeality which supports that voice is provided by the waiting and dying animals."[13] In this scene, too, the voice registers pain, rising to a hysterical pitch as she reaches the high point of her story, a recitation of Tasso's famous speech in Goethe's play, *Torquato Tasso*. But the voice speaks words at several removes, as Elvire performs Christoph rehearsing his lines as Tasso. And since Tasso's speech in this play is said to have held autobiographical significance for Goethe, this chain leads to Goethe as poet and, by extension, to Fassbinder himself, very much the auteur of this film.[14] In her excerpt from Tasso's speech, Elvire's voice-over describes the poet through the metaphor of the sacrificial beast: the artist is a beast to be sacrificed on a (political) altar. What is consigned to the realm of metaphor by Goethe is played out in the real by Fassbinder.

Along with sacrifice, aesthetic sublimation is again a theme ("And when man is silenced in his agony/A god enabled me to speak my pain"; "Und wenn der Mensch in seiner Qual verstummt,/Gab mir ein Gott zu sagen was ich leide"). Invaded from within by the "code of Art," Elvire's narrative is the story of a culturally constituted subjectivity. But once again language itself is infiltrated by the real (of hysterical anguish) through the medium of the voice. Nondiegetic strains of a Handel organ concerto accompany Elvire's recitation, creating a liturgical "aural bath" that effects by means of contrast a connection between the bleeding carcasses and Elvire's harrowed voice.

There is a further, more ominous, link in this chain, one that again undermines signification with an evocation of the real: the slaughterhouse scene in Fassbinder's film recalls another—infamous—abbatoir sequence in cinema, a scene from the most vile anti-Semitic film in the Nazi arsenal, Fritz Hippler's *The Eternal Jew* (1941).[15] In the corresponding scene of this Nazi film, a male voice-over speaks horrifying anti-Semitic commentary over documentary images of kosher butchering complete with sounds of pain emitted by the dying animals. In *The Eternal Jew*, the agonizing images and sounds of this sequence are preceded by a warning to "sensitive viewers" to avert their eyes, and they are followed by Hitler's speech to the Reichstag (January 30, 1939) in which he foretells the annihilation of the Jews. Thus Hippler's film obliquely establishes a connection between kosher butchering practices performed by Jews in accordance with dietrary law and the slaughter of the Jews in the Holocaust, outrageously suggesting that the (kosher) butchers must themselves be butchered. By stretching cinema's affective possibilities to their outermost limits, *The Eternal Jew* attempts to transport its spectators out of the realm of reason into that of bodily response and emotion. The disgust and nausea experienced by its spectators are—paradoxically—intended to move them to acquiesce in a far greater violence.

What, we must ask, is the significance of Fassbinder's allusion to this propaganda film? The controversy over anti-Semitism in Fassbinder's *Garbage, the City, and Death*,[16] a play with which *Thirteeen Moons* has been compared,[17] must give us pause. But as the sensibility of Fassbinder's film clearly emerges on the side of both the suffering Elvire and of the slaughtered beasts, can we perhaps assume that this allusion carries philo-Semitic ideological weight? Fassbinder's film yokes German idealist culture—the extended quotation from Goethe's *Tasso*—to the most vile anti-Semitic propaganda, in both instances by means of a voice-over spoken to accompany images of the suffering animal body. The slaughterhouse sequence of *Thirteen Moons* thus suggests a cultural continuity between idealism and Nazism that it then radically critiques by stylistic means—by bridging the gap between word and flesh through the medium of the hysterical voice. We will return to the ideological implications of this strategy later.

The Maternal Voice: Word into Flesh

Unlike Balzac's fictional castrato, a singer on the eighteenth-century Italian stage, Fassbinder's transsexual does not sing. As in *Sarrasine*, however, in *Thirteen Moons* the voice also notably has a (suppressed) erotic dimension, suggesting yet another link in the chain of art. As Alice Kuzniar and others have noticed, during the crucial scene in which Elvire visits Anton Saitz, the man for whose sake she has become a transsexual, she is wearing the black dress and hat with veil famously worn by Zarah Leander in Detlev Sierck's (later Douglas Sirk) *La Habañera* (1937), and she speaks with Leander's deep, soft voice.[18] Once again the links are multiple, connecting Elvire to Zarah, film star and singer in the Germany of the 1930s and 1940s. Although herself female, Leander continued after the war to function as a source of identification for gays and transsexuals—primarily through the medium of her baritone voice.[19] As Leander aged, she deliberately performed the ambiguity that her voice seems to have conjured up from the start, playing to her transgendered image among these audiences. Kuzniar's analysis reads Zarah Leander as a "ghost" that haunts several Fassbinder characters in the late 1970s and early 1980s, the period when Fassbinder was intrigued with melodrama in the style of Sirk.[20] Interestingly, however, writings and interviews by Fassbinder omit all mention of Sirk's former identity as Detlef Sierck, who directed Leander in films of the 1930s before fleeing Germany with his Jewish wife in 1937.

Throughout Sierck/Sirk's career, music had a major role to play in the staging of melodramatic emotion,[21] and Fassbinder's acknowledged indebtedness to Sirk provides us with yet another layer of aural reference in *Thirteen Moons*, which the "ghostly" presence of Leander eroticizes. It is by way of reference to Leander that Fassbinder's castrato sings, after all. Finally, Sirk's suppressed past as Sierck reintroduces the ambiguity of political affiliation into the ambiguity of identity more generally in the discourse of this film.

In some sense also standing in for the castrato's voice, the prepubescent voices of the Vienna Boys Choir are the voices most obviously connected with desire for Elvire, because they create the acoustic space of her masochistic masturbatory fantasy. Yet the voices of these young boys do not have the simple function of evoking homoerotic desire in Elvire (which, after the sex-change operation would no longer be homoerotic, in any case) but seem, rather, to transport Elvire back into an eroticized childhood space and time. It is "Lo How a Rose E'er Blooming," from the Choir's Christmas album, to which Elvire repeatedly listens. With its message of the Virgin birth, this hymn's evocatory power is both erotic and masochistic: evoking an idealized childhood, the boys' voices double Erwin/Elvire's own childhood voice while conjuring up the fantasy of the maternal voice as a lost object of desire.[22]

Although the affects that this hymn evokes in Elvire may not be surprising in one who spent years in a Catholic convent orphanage where questions of origin might reasonably find a religious articulation, there is more at stake here. As if to signal another intertextual moment, Fassbinder makes use of the iconography of the *hortus inclusus*, the enclosed garden in which the Virgin is so often represented in visual art, for the setting in which we first discover Sister Gudrun. It is Sister Gudrun, of course, who will narrate the story of his/her childhood to Elvire who, having repressed its painful memories, can even now not come "to terms" with its events. Sister Gudrun's narration—one of Fassbinder's relentless embedded narratives, not imaged by the camera—is paralleled by the camera's enunciatory tracking movements that keep the speaking Gudrun in frame. But Elvire escapes the double syntax of Gudrun's narrative and the tracking camera by moving out of frame, evading the camera as she escapes the wounding knowledge imparted by language. In what seems an almost parodically Kleistian moment, Elvire—like Kleist's *Marquise of O.*, who likewise finds herself in settings and scenarios that recall the Virgin birth—falls unconscious during Sister Gudrun's narration. The body asserts itself to protect the suffering mind; the flesh triumphs over the word.

The setting of the enclosed garden notwithstanding, the fantasized mother is precisely what Gudrun is *not* during this scene, the irony being that her character is played by Fassbinder's actual mother. Gudrun's demystifying narrative, her linguistic cruelty, aligns her with the enunciatory function of the father over and against the "sonorous envelope" created by the maternal voice.[23] Instead, it is the prostitute Zora's voice that most closely resembles the maternal "sonorous envelope" while it tells a fairy tale. The setting of Zora's tale—the dimly lit bedroom in which Elvire lies in a state of drugged semiconsciousness, half asleep—contributes to the atmosphere of enclosure produced by Zora's soothing, uninflected tone. And the genre of her narrative—the fairy tale, the maternal narrative par excellence—underscores these connections. Its content—the story of a brother and sister who have been transformed into a snail and a mushroom, causing one to eat of the other in a moment of hunger—has all of the horrifying literalness of the fairy tale. A story of incorporation, it recalls the oral phase of infancy, in which the infant does not distinguish between its own body and that of the mother. Thus, a maternal voice serves as a vehicle for a regression to a prelinguistic state of plenitude during which the relation to the mother is structured by ingestion/incorporation.

One more permutation of the maternal voice needs mentioning here: these are the disembodied, ethereal human voices that we hear in moments when, according to one critic,[24] the trauma of castration is evoked by the soundtrack. Composed for the film by Peer Raben, the music is atonal; these voices do not sing words, only tones distorted to heighten their emotional impact. Yet their sounds evoke celestial voices, voices akin to the maternal voice that bathes the child in a "celestial melody"—as Silverman puts it, rephrasing Guy Rosolato—"whose closest terrestrial equivalent is opera."[25] Like Zora's, these voices too call up a nonlinguistic state. Whether evocative of a prelinguistic plenitude, or of a radical divestiture that symbolically excludes the subject from the symbolic (castration; abjection)—in either case an unrepresentable condition—these tones are appropriately nonverbal. Here, then, we find another turning away from the realm of language toward the radical materialism of abjection. As a means of return to the body of the mother, abjection is aligned with the flesh and its dissolution, with viscosity and bodily fluids—and with death.[26] Further, as Kristeva points out, in abjection the corpse escapes the symbolic order, as it has been rendered an object, a thing.[27] The transsexual, likewise outside the symbolic order, is read similarly: for Christoph, his lover, Elvire, is a " 'thing' that has no 'soul,' with brains that are 'nothing but jelly.' "

Tableau: Elvire's Passion

As Bataille points out, the origin of the slaughterhouse is the temple, a location in which the preparation of meat both for food and for sacrifice goes forward: "The slaughterhouse emerges from religion insofar as the temples of times past . . . had a dual purpose, being used both for supplication and for slaughter."[28] Having worked as a butcher earlier in life, Elvire is not distressed by the carnage she sees in the slaughterhouse. Reading the slaughter of the beasts as part of "life itself," she attempts to recuperate these bloody deaths as "giving meaning to" their lives. For her, the animals have a part to play in the cycle of life and death more generally. Attempting to transform the real into the spiritual, she asserts that the beasts' "screams of pain" are actually "screams for salvation." Although Fassbinder's film as a whole will not permit salvation, we should note that Elvire identifies both as butcher and as beast and that the return to the scene of the slaughterhouse is a stage in a Passion that has Christological overtones and will culminate in her death.

Let us linger for a moment with the theme of food and ingestion, a theme that occurs in several guises in the textual fabric of Fassbinder's film. It is evident in the offering of food—bread, wine, and cheese—that Elvire brings to Anton Saitz, the man for whose sake she became a transsexual. It is present in the iconography of the Last Supper that composes the garden scene in which Elvire finds her daughter and wife consuming a meal that also includes bread and wine. Food and ingestion are featured as well in Zora's fairy tale about the sister, a snail, who eats of her brother, a mushroom. And not only the abbatoir scene effects a connection between the slaughtered beasts and Elvire: during their argument, Christoph, her lover, calls her a "horrible, ugly piece of meat." If, for a moment, we read Christoph's angry words that she is a "piece of meat" with the images of the butchered animals in the slaughterhouse, then these words contain the suggestion of cannibalism.

This is not a literal cannibalism, to be sure. But the topos is also present, in barely disguised form, in Zora's fairy tale of the lost children mentioned above, in which the sister/snail takes a bite of her brother/mushroom. As a wild mushroom, the mushroom is doubly dangerous to eat, both because it may be poisonous—and because it is the body of the brother. But the greatest danger lies in the boundary crossing this act signifies: the sister's act of consumption is wholly marked by the abject, for it collapses the boundary between self and other, inside and outside.[29] In cannibalism, the symbolic is transgressively relinquished in favor of abjection.

In the Christian sacrament—especially in the literalist position of early Christianity—bread and wine are thought actually to *be* the body of Christ through the doctrine of transubstantiation. Just as, for the Christian, God's word becomes flesh in the body of Christ, so the sacramental bread and wine become the flesh and blood of Christ. For the believer, their metaphorical character is temporarily overcome—only, of course, to be raised to a higher level of metaphoricity thereafter. In the case of Elvire, however, the conversion of word into flesh goes no further, and once again incorporation is revealed to be the operative dynamic in Fassbinder's film. The masochistic "ecstasy" of excorporation—a "taking outside of" the self in the heteropathic identification stressed by Silverman[30] might make "salvation" of a sort possible. But the entrapment within the body suggested by the repeated metaphors of ingestion and incorporation—by multiple figurations of the return to the maternal body—imply that for Fassbinder the body, the real, is not convertible into the symbolic. Bataille's temple, once a space of sacred as well as profane slaughter, is now merely a slaughterhouse.

Mute Body/Flayed Text

Without the attendant redemption, Christ's Passion and Crucifixion play a prominent role in the fantasmatic that structures a number of Fassbinder's films, generating masochistic erotic situations and tableaux in *Berlin: Alexanderplatz*, *Despair*, and *Querelle* as well as in *Thirteen Moons*. Indeed, the fantasmatic of these films is structured on the Passion of Christ as Slavoj Zizek reads it, as the "fantasy-scenario which condenses all the libidinal economy of the Christian religion."[31] And the role played by abjection in *Thirteen Moons* accords with Zizek's contention that Christianity embraces abjection in the figure of the saint. If the saint "occupies the place . . . of pure object, of someone undergoing radical subjective destitution,"[32] then the resemblance of the saint's position to that of Elvire is obvious. Moreover, the analogy drawn between the tableaux of (real) flayed beasts and Elvire's masochistic psychosexual position gains in significance. But these identifications structure a purely personal fantasmatic. If the fantasmatic has a sociocultural dimension, absorbing "social and political alignments,"[33] how does this play itself out?

Thomas Elsaesser has alerted us to the manner in which the theme of personal guilt for the death of Fassbinder's lover Armin Meier is radically expanded in *Thirteen Moons* to encompass German guilt and responsibility for the Holocaust. As Elsaesser suggests, Fassbinder's film allegorizes German-Jewish relations after Auschwitz, and does so as "a matter of love."[34] The fantasmatic of Fassbinder's film, as we have seen, is governed by materialism, by abjection or, in Kristeva's parlance, the realm of the mother. It is here that "subject and object push each other away, confront each other, collapse and start again—inseparable, contaminated, condemned, at the boundary of what is assimilable, thinkable: abject."[35] In this condition, self and other collapse; Elvire/Armin and Saitz/Fassbinder—lover and beloved—are also Elvire/Fassbinder and Saitz/Armin.[36] Elvire is both butcher and beast; within the logic of abjection, the two are inseparable, indistinguishable in mutual contamination. Through the topos of the Passion, Elvire is both Christian and Jew, just as she is both a German and the victim of her own Germanness.[37] But how can an ethics or a politics emerge from the negation of distinctions? Amid the collapse of dichotomies that governs this scenario, the political would seem to be subsumed within the structure of the drives, which are insusceptible to ethics.

At this point we must look again at the presence of Hippler's *The Eternal Jew* within the chain of textualities that relates to *Thirteen Moons*. And again it is "sacrifice" that is the operative term. As Zizek sees it, it is the idea of sacrifice that most radically distinguishes Christianity from Jewish structures of belief. Although kosher butchering is not a religious practice, but simply mandated by dietary law, the insidious propaganda of *The Eternal Jew* suggests that kosher butchering does not adequately sever the slaughter of animals for food from their slaughter for sacrificial purposes. Indeed, the images of lambs we see cavorting in the meadows carry another—albeit subliminal—message beyond that of impending cruelty to animals, calling to the minds of Christian spectators the crucifixion of the "Lamb of God." Not only does Hippler's film heighten spectatorial affect by acts of violence and cries of pain, then, it also intensifies affect by attaching it to the domain of the sacred and to ideology.

We have already seen the manner in which Fassbinder's radical materialism makes use of the imagery of the Passion only in order to disconnect death from sacrifice as well as from salvation. The "perverse, Wagnerian scenario," as Eric Santner puts, sees the "final solution" to "the Jewish question" in the resolution of tensions by a Christ-like redeemer.[38] In *The Eternal Jew*, this role is obviously assumed by Hitler in his speech before the Reichstag, a speech that culminates in the fateful words "annihilation of the Jewish race in Europe." Hippler's film ends with words of exhortation delivered by its anonymous male narrator in voice-over, urging the German people to "keep the race pure" and to unify. Harnessing its constituent textualities, Fascist film covers them over in a paternal voice that interprets the image, speaking on behalf of purity and organic wholeness.

Fassbinder's text, on the other hand, refuses to its very end to harness image and voice, choosing instead to lay its textualities bare. During the final minutes of *Thirteen Moons*, the multiple layers of its sound track are at their most prominent, and music never has the function of linking voice to body.[39] The sound of traffic and other noises, a pop song, the strains of the Vienna Boys Choir, the disembodied "celestial" voices, and various diegetic conversations are accompanied by Elvire's emotionally charged taped interview, a monologue that, running in real time, lends the final minutes of Fassbinder's film a nearly unendurable sense of anguish. As the taped voice of Elvire contemplates suicide, that voice's severance from its source in the body becomes hopelessly final as we come to realize that she is already dead. While the recorded voice, separable from the body, continues it search for significance, the body itself has become a corpse beyond significance, wholly consigned to abjection. When, at the end of the film, the Vienna Boys Choir's Christmas record skips, they sing the words "quietly falling" ("leise rieselt") over and over again. Neither the skipping record that "voices" the jamming of all textualities nor the taped interview is anchored in a body. Instead, the body is rendered mute and the voice—its residue—sings on, embalmed in the mechanisms of technology.[40]

Deliberately tearing the skin that would make the textual body whole—and, therefore, consonant with the aesthetic ideology perverted by Nazism—Fassbinder presents the spectator with a masochistic, "flayed" text, a filmic body that bears the marks of (self) flagellation. Thus, Fassbinder's film accomplishes at the level of style what it cannot do at the level of its structuring fantasy: it severs itself from the contaminated aesthetic of fascism. If the spectator is taken aback by the film's abrupt termination in a few unexposed black frames, it is because this end to all signification leaves us with mere material, with film stock. It is as if the film itself had died—or been tortured to death.

PART III ART AND EMBODIED SPECTATORSHIP

8

Violence and Affect: Haneke's Modernist Melodramas

Part One: Bourgeois Tableaux

The dissolution of the family is one of Michael Haneke's favored subjects, our postmodern condition in late capitalism its context. Haneke's subject is especially prominent in the group of films he subsumes under the title *Civil War (Bürgerkrieg)*—or, more literally, *Bourgeois War*—a title that cues their generic context as the tradition of eighteenth-century bourgeois drama. Joined together in the sibling relationship of the trilogy, *The Seventh Continent* (1989), *Benny's Video* (1992), and *71 Fragments of a Chronology of Chance* (1994) are films in which the fragmentation of the family as an organic unit plays itself out in astonishing acts of violence to the body, as if to amend Diderot's dictum that excludes the dramatic turn of events—the coup de théâtre—from the domain of bourgeois drama. Although the space of the patriarchal nuclear family occupied by Diderot's melodrama is the space of early capitalism as defined by Habermas, the conditions that shape it from without are not at the center of Diderot's concern. Instead, Diderot's interest is determined by the sentimental realism of Samuel Richardson, whose novels come in for praise because they do not "cover the walls with blood," and hence evoke in their readers feelings with which they are at home.[1] The "dramatic turn of events" is a theatrical, if not an untrue, representation of bourgeois life, claims Diderot, and the realism that Diderot reads in Richardson is so designated because its privileged space excludes such excess. Instead, this form of realism plays upon spectatorial affect to another—ethical—end, so that the reader will "experience a revulsion"[2] not at bloodied walls, but at injustice per se. In an island utopia described by one of Diderot's fictional characters, people go to the theater to see plays that teach them to fear the more violent expressions of the passions. This is familiar ground, defined by the bourgeois ethos and the affective aesthetics of the eighteenth century's Age of Sensibility. In the German dramatic tradition most familiar to Haneke, it is Lessing, translator of Diderot, who promotes the bourgeois drama with its aesthetics of affect.

Instead of dramatic action, Diderot's aesthetics mandate the *tableau*—a static scene resembling a painting—for the expression of emotion in bourgeois melodrama. Held at a moment of emotional intensity, the content of the tableau *is* that emotion,[3] Peter Szondi points out in a famous essay. Emotion expressed in the tableau speaks emblematically to the audience, whose response is empathy. As the operative strategy of these plays, of course, empathy does not elicit the violence of civil war or revolution. "As long as the bourgeosie does not revolt against absolutism, and make a bid for power, it will live solely for its emotions," Szondi argues, "bewailing in the theater its own misery."[4] In the context of Szondi's critique, Haneke's *Civil War* trilogy stands revealed as a darkly ironic title. The acts of violence that punctuate his trilogy are the expression of sociopolitical circumstances, it is true, but they, too, are not political acts. In keeping with the violence of bourgeois melodrama, the violence of Haneke's films arises out of social paralysis and takes the irrational, even self-directed forms characteristic of the former genre.[5] The bourgeois drama's aesthetics of affect lingers in more contemporary domestic melodrama, and it will be seen that Haneke's description of *The Piano Teacher* (2000) as a "parody of a melodrama"[6] is suggestive for his earlier films as well.

In *The Seventh Continent*, the first film in Haneke's trilogy, the nuclear family never arrives at its island utopia—Australia—a utopia that was in any case ironic. Instead, the consumer culture of late capitalism, the film suggests, causes them to commit a bizarre coup de théâtre, a ritualized family suicide which begins with the systematic destruction of their earthly possessions, includes the sustained flushing of banknotes down the toilet, and culminates in the death of all three family members, including the little girl. Surely the film's point is the senseless masochism of this suicide, a melodramatic act that stands in place of political action. *Benny's Video* features shocking violence, as well, complete with the bloodied walls that so offended Diderot and ending in the destruction of the family as Benny turns himself and his parents over to the police for a murder in which the parents are accessories after the fact. The killing spree that takes four lives in *71 Fragments* is arbitrary, yet nevertheless emotionally prepared for as each chance victim is shown within a set of difficult family relations as well as in a social order defined in familial terms, a reduction typical of melodrama.[7] We the spectators of these films are moved, our "passions" quite deliberately called into play though held in check, disciplined even as they are aroused by the manner in which image and narrative are subjected to various forms of askesis. At the level of style, too, acts of violence are performed. As one Austrian critic has written concerning *71 Fragments*, "its 'anorexic' images seem to have been carved with the surgeon's scalpel from the 'fatty images' of a voyeuristic cinema."[8]

The content of bourgeois melodrama is distanced, then—parodied—by a visual style in the tradition of modernism, one that deliberately emulates the cool detachment of Bresson, whom Haneke cites repeatedly in connection with his own films. Haneke's emphatic affirmation of modernism's refusal of psychology intersects parodically with the bourgeois family as their defining subject matter. As I will argue, it is the bourgeois drama's—melodrama's—self-containment within the personal that is the object of critique and is opened up by modernist techniques. This is an interesting choice, especially when we consider how rarely drama is mentioned in the modernist canon. As I will further argue, Haneke's other topic—the mediatization of the public sphere that characterizes the postmodern period—is likewise countered by formal means. In Haneke's films, sound assaults the sensorium and promotes perceptual and emotional realism in the spectator and thus wages war against the inauthenticity of postmodernity. In these films, modernist technique remains the source of filmic vitality, revising and making new the bourgeois realism of an earlier era and charging postmodern simulation with the energy of the real.

Cold Image; Hot Affect

Haneke's writings and interviews place a great deal of emphasis on the reception of his films. With regard to visual style, he repeatedly suggests that his radically pared-down images function as provocative substitutes for the consumer images produced by Hollywood. It is the formal rigor of modernist sources and strategies that Haneke invokes, Joyce, Straub and Huillet, and Alban Berg all come in for praise, and Austrian modernists come to mind as well, chief among them Kafka. By way of Adorno, Schönberg's formal rigor comes into play as well: Haneke notes that his screenplays are structured according to musical principles.[9] In Adolf Loos, who isn't mentioned,

Haneke may well have found the convergence of visual restraint with political beliefs that he himself espouses. Loos's insistence on rationality in architecture, on an architecture without ornament, also arises in opposition to commodity fetishism.

It is the "Jansenism of the image"—to cite Bazin's famous formulation for Bresson's visual style—that Haneke hopes will generate an interactive relation with a spectator whose imagination will complete it, or—better yet—flesh it out.[10] Although lip service is paid to self-reflexivity as a means of spectatorial "emancipation"[11]—that is, to the cognitive aspect of spectatorial response—what matters at least equally is that the spectator's "fears, desires, and fantasies" be mobilized.[12] As Haneke sees it, "the author of the film puts markers and signposts into place; the spectators' potential for fantasy and emotion then unfolds between these markers."[13] Although detachment and control characterize the attitude of these films toward their material, this is not the attitude that Haneke hopes to generate in the spectator.[14] Indeed, these films elicit a spectator who is provoked, feels irritated, on the defensive, and in a situation of conflict,[15] thus moving considerably beyond Brecht's intellectual provocation into the realm of programmed emotion. It is in this affective and corporeal sense that Haneke's films are "interactive," but given the manner in which their spectator is manipulated, Haneke's claim to an interactive model at the cognitive level may seem naive at best.[16]

Haneke's famously ascetic cinema refuses the choreography of violence, the special effects and other aestheticizing means that render extreme violence cinematically pleasurable, techniques that call to mind films by Peckinpah, Kubrick, and Quentin Tarantino. But if the spectator is generally spared graphic images of violence to the body—if not always its horrifying results—the film's sound track is at pains to evoke affect in their place. As Haneke writes in his notes to *71 Fragments*, "the ear is fundamentally more sensitive than the eye . . . the ear provides a more direct path to the imagination and to the heart of human beings," whereas the "reception of images seems . . . more filtered by the intellect."[17] Sounds of traffic and of machinery, cries of pain, screams, and diegetic music variously act upon the corporealized spectator whom Haneke's films call into play. Sound in Haneke's films deliberately assaults the senses as well as the sensibilities. As in the films of Bresson, sounds are intensified and remain distinct, frequently occur in voice-over or issue from off-screen, and Haneke's sound track refuses the homogenizing effects of extradeigetic music. Like Bresson's, Haneke's spectator is caught between a visual askesis and an affective soundtrack, one that intentionally acts upon what the director takes to be the more sensitive sense organ, the ear.[18]

"Aesthetics," Terry Eagleton has famously claimed, "is born as a discourse of the body."[19] Although this chapter acknowledges the body of the text, its shape and materialities, and the bodies of the fictional characters whose stories are being told, it focuses primarily on the body of the corporealized spectator whose senses the text calls into play.[20] Another aspect of eighteenth-century writing is of interest here: the non-Kantian aesthetic discourse of this period is concerned with the appropriateness of response to sensory stimuli—some responses are decorous, others are not—promoting an aesthetic ideology that is reflected at the formal level, in style. (It is for this reason, for example, that the tableau scene in bourgeois drama insists upon the fiction of the theatrical fourth wall, the figurative curtain that maintains the "privacy" of the theatrical characters whose emotions are on display to their audience.) Stressing problems of corporeality in relation to those of style, then, this chapter examines the position of the spectator evoked by films in which scenes of violence are distanced by means of a rigorous modernism, yet nevertheless engage affect.

Fred Jameson joins others in claiming that because movies are a physical experience, the memories that they produce are of the body.[21] The experience of film, in other words, is affective. From the standpoint of eighteenth-century affective aesthetics, affect is the joint product of the sensorium and the affective imagination, and for the eighteenth-century affective imagination, whose site of interest is the passions, the senses provide the stimuli that associationism interprets for the subject. In exploring spectatorial affect, then, I take up the current interest in the perceptual as well as cognitive aspects of film spectatorship, especially in the work of Torben Grodal[22] and Greg M. Smith. Smith's model of the emotions is of particular interest for my concerns because, like Addison's, it is associative. For Smith, emotions evoke thoughts and memories, as well as physiological reactions, combining cognition, involuntary reactions, "action tendencies," and even facial expressions.[23] Equally important, Smith frees emotion generated by film from a necessary connection with human actors, recognizing the part played by formal considerations such as choice of music and mise-en-scène.

Another context for this chapter is Vivian Sobchack's semiotic phenomenology, in which the spectator perceives "the visible, audible, kinetic aspects of sensory experience to make sense visibly, audibly, haptically."[24] This is the insight, for example, that decades ago informed Hitchcock's remark to the screenwriter Ernest Lehman that "we're not making a movie, we're constructing an organ, the kind of organ that you see in the theater . . . we press this chord and now the audience laughs, and we press that chord and they gasp, and we press these notes and they chuckle. Someday," says Hitchcock, "we won't have to make a movie, we'll just attach them to electrodes and play various emotions for them to experience."[25] When asked by Peter Bogdanovich what the term *pure cinema* might mean to him, Hitchcock referred to a short sequence in *The Birds* in which the mother catches a horrifying glimpse of her dead neighbor's gouged-out eyes. Instead of using the conventional tracking shot to simulate her approaching gaze, Hitchcock resorts to three quick and increasingly closer cuts, explaining his choice thus: "The staccato cuts are about catching the breath. Gasp. Gasp. Yes."[26] In referring to horror, melodrama, and pornography as the cinematic "body genres," Linda Williams reminds us that such films not only elicit certain affects from their spectator, but may evoke sounds and stimulate bodily fluids, as well.[27] Cinema produces affects accompanied by involuntary responses, by gasps or cries of horror, tears, sweat, vomit, and the like.

Effects of the Real

Distinguished by *Cahiers du Cinéma* critics as one of the thirteen most noteworthy films of 1993, yet nearly subjected to censorship in Switzerland, *Benny's Video* opens with the videotaped slaughter of a pig, a sequence notable for the relentlessness with which the video camera pursues its object. Rendering these images nearly unendurable are the pig's squeals of pain, sounds that provoke a moral response inseparable from the affective one the spectator experiences: the spectator's auditory suffering is relieved when the scene of the animal's suffering comes to an end. Even after its conclusion, our senses remain negatively involved with the film: the end of the video sequence is signaled by "snow" that baffles our sense of sight and grates upon the ear. A palpable sign of the termination—the death—of the image chain, the video snow underscores the death of the pig. In *The Seventh Continent*, snow on the TV screen has an even more horrifying message to convey, for it is "watched" by spectators who are dead. Signaling the materiality of the video image and of the screen itself, the absent images for which the snow stands are reflected in these spectators' unseeing eyes, while the noise that substitutes for sound falls on deaf ears. Haneke's interest in spectator affect is mirrored in the modernist strategy of privileging the materialities of the medium, another feature that Haneke's films share in common with Bresson's.

Benny's Video, the film, revolves around a postmodern consciousness for which representation and reality are nearly indistinguishable, in which "experiential time" is constantly recorded.[28] Benny's video footage documenting the pig's slaughter is coded as amateurish documentary: it is unedited, steadily marked by hand held effects, ends abruptly, and hence marked as "real."[29] More importantly, as in other films featuring slaughterhouse violence (Fassbinder's *In a Year of Thirteen Moons* is discussed in the previous chapter), it records a real death, not one enacted for the camera, and its impact on Benny and on the spectator derives from this knowledge. If the definitive scene of graphic realism is, as Michael Fried has said of painting, one that the viewer can't bear to look at—or listen to—then this is realism par excellence.[30] But this footage is not simply marked as real, but is variously manipulated—subjected to slow motion, rewound, briefly frozen. This is a sequence in the process of being viewed, not only by the spectator of the film, but by a diegetic spectator, as well. It is being scrutinized by the fourteen-year-old Benny, who is using video technology to examine the process of dying. Soon he will shoot a young girl with the same weapon that was used to slaughter the pig, the event will be recorded by the video camera that seems always to be running in his room, and he will subject this footage to similar scrutiny.[31] Benny will perform all of these actions seemingly without any response, affective or moral.

Obvious allusions are made here to Baudrillard's insights concerning a postmodern subject who cannot "produce himself as a mirror," only as screen,[32] but, additionally, Haneke's film provides us with a wealth of sociological detail designed to suggest why this adolescent's life might be devoid of feeling, and how, for him, perception comes to be mediated by the technology with which he is surrounded. The teenager finds replacements for his absent parents, Haneke suggests, in the eyes of the video camera and in the movement of video images. For Benny, videotaping is an act of perception, with images on a monitor substituting even for the obscured view of the outside world through his bedroom window. Benny seems incapable of relating to anyone—even, one scene suggests tellingly, to himself—except through its mediation, while the sounds of TV and Rock form an aural space that envelops him. Because Haneke refuses psychological realism, Benny, like many other Haneke characters, projects an opacity that renders individual motivation inaccessible.[33] Yet social commentary lies within Haneke's purview and, when the film points an accusing finger at Benny's parents, one wonders to what extent psychology has been invalidated, after all.

The media also come in for a share of the blame. Television reportage, Haneke's films suggest, has anesthetized our capacity to respond to scenes of suffering. Benny spends his time watching the aestheticized violence of action movies and the restrained, "normalizing" television reporting of scenes of death in Bosnia. Providing violence in another register—but real violence as well—these news programs present images of carnage accompanied by voices of commentators carefully trained to exclude all emotion, thus rendering a sanitized version of the real precisely where the spectator has come to feel that she has access to immediacy. If the realism of film is conceptualized in spatial terms, Mary Ann Doane has argued, the realism of television lies in its relation to temporality, to its sense of "liveness."[34] The third film in this trilogy, *71 Fragments*, will undermine precisely that when we see the same news broadcast more than once, suggesting our entrapment in a loop that only the end of the film cuts through. Television coverage works hard to keep the shock of catastrophe at bay, and in *Benny's Video*, Benny's vacant expression reflects the TV commentator's calm detachment.

For Benny there is no difference between a death marked by "ketchup and plastic," as he says of death in the movies, and one that produces real blood. But he knows the difference between his video and feature films. Benny returns compulsively and with evident fascination to the documentary images, holding the images of the pig's death agony in freeze frame. Necrophilic fascination may be one explanation for his behavior, but another aim is the control of narrative flow and time: Benny manipulates this footage in order half-seriously to interfere with the inevitability of its narrative and to reverse "reality." (Haneke's *Funny Games* will briefly succeed in doing just that, only to suspend all plausibility by "rewinding" the action.) Benny's scrutiny of these scenes seems scientific and epistemological, an attempt by technological means to discover the secret of life and death. Later, he will repeatedly view the images of the murder he commits. But the video camera is stationary in the murder scene, only accidentally trained upon its players who move in and out of the frame. Emulating the restraint of Bresson's images, Haneke's images deny their spectator the spectacle of violence that they critique in other media. For the spectator, as for Benny, his act is elusive, incomprehensible.

Haneke's bitter indictment of the upper-middle class Austrian family continues as the businessman father and art dealer mother attempt to cover up Benny's act of murder as much for the sake of their careers as to protect their son. Yet when Benny attempts a "flight into Egypt" with his mother—while his father remains behind to dispose of the corpse—their trip, despite its macabre motivation, takes on some of the qualities of a utopian space and time.[35] As is evident from videotaped images of Benny shooting video, his mother herself films with a second camera. Although the relation of mother and child is mediated by the video camera—indeed, their meeting ground is the collaborative work of the videotape itself—the very fact of their relation seems to confer a redemptive effect on this medium. Later, while channel-surfing in the hotel room, Benny stops at a broadcast of a Bach concert featuring "Liebster Jesu, wir sind hier." This diegetic music continues as he moves to the window and, in one of the rare point-of-view shots in this film, with Benny we see the image of the nighttime harbor while the organ continues to play. Superimposed upon the organ music, with the image of the harbor still in view, we hear the voice of Benny's mother as she enters the room: "Greetings from Papa." As Benny answers "How is he?," their conversation becomes the fragile rendering of a family reconstituted. Even though their "reunion" takes place within a formulaic exchange and in voice-over, it is solemnized within the auratic aural space of the Bach prelude, of religious high art.[36] Although the warm colors of Egypt suggest that even these gestures can only take place in "warm" Third World locales, not in the cold urban spaces of Vienna, this space nevertheless remains the private space of familial love, sanctified by religious feeling—the "flight into Egypt"—as well as by high culture. Haneke gestures toward a redemptive space but, unlike Bresson, he can go no further.

As the title of Haneke's film suggests, the boundary between the film and Benny's video is repeatedly revealed to be permeable, as though to suggest that visual restraint cannot spare even Haneke's images the charge of being tainted. At various moments, the spectator is only retrospectively aware that the sequence we're watching belongs to Benny's ongoing video rather than to the film's diegesis. Blurring the boundaries among a variety of images once again points to their different, though temporarily indistinguishable materialities, while space and time are blurred in a gesture that includes both postmodern and modern velleities. One of the most effective confusions of this kind occurs at the end of the film when we see a scene shot from within Benny's dark room, looking through the partly open door into a more brightly lit space—one of Haneke's signature shots. Here, too, the materiality of the cinematic medium is at issue, for the light that permits the image enters the "dark chamber" from which it is shot through a partly opened door, which suggests the work of the shutter that admits light into the camera itself. In this scene, we recognize both image and sound track, for we have seen and heard them separately before. It is Haneke's strategy initially to obscure the context of the image—does it belong to the film or to the videotape?—and consequently to allow sound to fix its meaning.

Toward the end of the film, the spectator hears once more the desperately calm conversation in which Benny's parents discuss how best to dispose of the body of the young girl Benny has killed. A few seconds later, with an even greater sense of shock, we realize that Benny's video is once again being viewed, this time with a voice-over conversation between Benny and the policemen with whom he is viewing it. The parents' conversation will serve to indict them as accessories after the fact for the murder that their son has committed. As Benny turns himself in, the videotape becomes not only a document of violence, but its instrument as well. In keeping with the film's trenchant critique of contemporary mores, it remains unclear whether Benny's act is a moral act—a Bressonian assumption of guilt, with religious overtones—or merely an act of violence against his parents, the flipside of the utopian space suggested in Egypt.

The final frames of *Benny's Video* represent the scene in the police station as multiple images on the monitors of a surveillance system. Doubly mediated by technology, these cold, impersonal images are on view for the benefit of an anonymous spectator representing the Law, and for us. The film's final images—images shot from above, the "God shot"—are filmic images that frame and control the video images that they contain. Haneke's film opens with Benny's video images presented directly to the spectatorial view, whereas in its middle section the nature of its images—film or video?—is often initially ambiguous. Finally, when Haneke's film definitively subsumes Benny's video and the images produced by the surveillance cameras, the cold formalism of Haneke's cinema contains and masters video. If Haneke's camera encompasses and transcends even the eye of the Law, whose eye does it represent? If these images are meant to gesture toward a higher authority, its identity remains enigmatic.

In the third film of Haneke's trilogy, the closure and control that characterize *Benny's Video* are once more the objects of his formal attention. In *71 Fragments of a Chronology of Chance* even more obviously than in *The Seventh Continent*, narrative is disrupted and distorted by an emphasis on duration, by abrupt cuts, and by black footage of varying lengths. The series of cuts to black disrupts the continuity of the viewing experience and spectatorial investment in narrative flow, accentuating the similarly varying lengths of its narrative fragments. These fragments of a puzzle that the spectator struggles to piece together are antidramatic, again in imitation of Bresson, but arranged in linear fashion. Although attenuated stories gradually emerge out of these fragments and merge in the act of violence in which the film culminates, Haneke's film frustrates our desire to read it as a unified whole.[37] One recurrent image in the film—the emblem of puzzle pieces with which two students create various shapes—is held out tantalizingly to the would-be interpreter. The image of the cross that these pieces are repeatedly made to form may or may not be an interpretive red herring.[38] The puzzle, which creates form out of fragments, produces commercialized images, images over which money changes hands as the students place wagers. But these students also play pickup sticks, a game whose goal is the destruction—or deconstruction—of random arrangements. Are these games figures for the film itself? If so, which one—the deliberately constructed arrangement, or the random assemblage so deliberately dismantled? Modernism's tension between the fragment and the whole shapes this question. It is simultaneously answered and rendered moot as the students devise a computer game equivalent for the puzzle, suggesting its transposition into the virtual reality of the postmodern. To the question of which activity—the construction of forms or their dismantling—is a model for spectatorial activity, *71 Fragments* provides no answer. If game playing per se stands in for the cognitive dimension of spectatorship, however, then it is clearly an insufficient model for the spectatorship solicited by Haneke. In the affective model of spectatorship, cognition is supplemented by bodily responses and emotions.[39] In lieu of the spiritual whole that replaces fragmentation in Bresson, Haneke offers us affect.

As if to confirm this insight, *71 Fragments* assaults the senses with an even greater force than *Benny's Video*, almost as if to fragment the spectator's body in the process. Haneke's tactile assault is most obviously in evidence in the much-cited table tennis episode of *71 Fragments*, a scene in which Ping-Pong balls mechanically emitted from a practicing device are repeatedly smashed by the player out of deep space and toward the screen and the spectator. Typically for Haneke films, the sound track—a loud and repeated "thunk" that dominates this scene—is in itself aggressive. Intensified by its duration—a full three minutes—this sequence creates a painful sense of real time that promotes our self-awareness as corporeal, perceiving presences. The Ping Pong balls repeatedly smashing toward us play to our fear that the image is real and will emerge to occupy our space. Repetition and duration combine in this sequence to reinforce the spectator's physical presence before the screen:[40] Haneke admits that his strategy is to prolong such moments for the spectator "until it hurts."[41] Interestingly, the lower right-hand corner of the frame makes visible a portion of the machine that is the practice device, the machine that emits the Ping-Pong balls mechanically and in quick succession. The reference here, quite pointedly, is to the film projector itself, a machine that similarly projects its images. In this modernist moment, the film sets up a mirror relation between character as both player and spectator (who receives images/Ping-Pong balls), and the spectator of the film.[42] Hence, the point at which the film's spectators are most aware of themselves as corporeal is also its most self-reflexive moment, a moment when the film points to its apparatus. In this sequence, image and sound collude in their attack on the spectator as well as in self-critique.

Thematically and ideologically, of course, it's clear that the Ping-Pong ball sequence is concerned with the mechanization that this practice machine imposes on the body, not just on the filmic body per se, but on the body of the increasingly alienated student who will later run amok.[43] Herein it recalls the car wash sequences of *The Seventh Continent*, which occur once in each of this film's three parts, each time more loudly and threateningly. Much of the scene that opens this earlier film is shot from the back seat of the car, where the spectator is figuratively placed until the credits are superimposed over the image. Here and in the two other car wash sequences, the bodies in the car—as well as that of the spectator—are subjected to a working over by this mechanized process, their bodies battered by sights and sounds. The assault of the senses wears down resistance, generating emotion as well: in the second of these sequences, the water that washes over the car and windshield also releases the mother's tears. As in the videotaping by mother and son in *Benny's Video*, even interiority—figured literally by the enclosed space of the car, as well as by her tears—is a product of technology. In the film's spectator, a different kind of affect is generated by the loud and threatening sounds of the car wash machinery, whose impact produces intense discomfort.

Returning now to *71 Fragments*, we note that Haneke's subject matter is once again the bourgeois family in crisis, a crisis that only indirectly promotes the act of violence in which the film culminates. It is suggested that the rampage in which the student randomly murders three people in a bank and then turns the gun against himself is attributable to the pressures of his personal life as well as to those that the social world imposes upon him. Within the ideological framework of Haneke's film, it is no accident that his outburst is preceded by the thwarted effort to withdraw money from an automatic teller machine, or that it takes place in the locale par excellence of capitalism, a bank. Scenes of violence in Serbia, Haiti, and Ireland, purveyed by the television newscasts that periodically punctuate the action, contribute to an atmosphere of generalized violence in which private, melodramatic excess is more easily vented. But the scenes of violence outside Austria are *politically* motivated, the expression of class conflict or ideological strife, whereas the Austrian story that Haneke's film tells remains framed by the narrative of nation as family. The rift between a tired couple with a baby, the antagonistic relationship of the elderly father and his adult daughter, and the student who hides his growing despair from his mother over the phone are the narrative fragments of which the film is comprised. In the context of these divided families, perhaps, the couple that wishes to adopt a child as though in an effort to make the relationship whole may seem misguided, but in some ways this couple is the ideological center of Haneke's project. Adoption makes a whole of heterogeneous parts, particularly in this instance: it is difficult not to read the couple's sponsorship of a Rumanian orphan as a political statement about the integration of immigrants into Austrian society. Indeed, the boy first comes to their attention by means of a human interest story on television, fleetingly suggesting another redemptive function for the media. But the Rumanian boy's adoption precludes that of the little Austrian girl whom the couple had earlier courted and promised a home. The film excludes the scenes of her suffering, although it surely implies that such integration comes at the expense of native Austrians. The wholeness of the bourgeois family as a guarantee for the wholeness of society is a familiar theme from the bourgeois dramas of Diderot and Lessing. The latent conservatism that emerges from the relationship of mother and child in *Benny's Video*—where it is certainly implied that, had his mother spent more time with him, Benny might have been saved—now finds its counterpart in *71 Fragments*. But if adoption is the functional metaphor of Haneke's film as it is of Lessing's famous bourgeois drama, *Nathan the Wise*, the family that is created suggests legislated in place of biological wholeness, and thus makes room for a modest political reading, after all.

But where does this leave Haneke's spectator? In their affective impact on the spectator, film experiences are real experiences, perceptual theory argues. For the spectator, the bombardment with sound and images, the effect of abrupt cuts that terminate narrative fragments, and the obliteration of the image by black provokes physiological responses identical to those provoked by similar stimuli in the real world. This is the stuff of an emotional realism[44]—a realism, however, that is painful. From Haneke's point of view, assaults on spectatorial perception hold out redemptive possibilities; in contradistinction to Brecht, Haneke believes that affect stimulates thought. Art as an act of violence originates in the aesthetics of Dadaism, futurism, and surrealism, where it launches a deliberate assault on the spectator because, as Susan Sontag puts it, "the relation of art to an audience understood to be passive, inert, surfeited, can only be assault. Art becomes identical with aggression."[45] In *Funny Games*, Haneke's next film, the intense emotional battering and physical violence its characters suffer have their counterpart in formal strategies that intensify this attitude of assault.

Part Two: Assaulting the Spectator and Other Games

On the surface, *Funny Games* (1997) appears to exemplify Stephen Prince's idea of responsible filmmaking, according to which "a critique of violence may be best pursued in its absence, that is, by not showing—at least not in graphic detail—the very phenomenon that a film would address."[46] By way of its visual discretion, the style of this film seeks to interrupt the chain of imitative behaviors that it sees between media violence and the sociopathic behavior of contemporary Austrian youths who cannot distinguish, as the film claims, between fiction and reality. But *Funny Games* manages not only to elicit an intense somatovisceral response from its spectators, I will argue—a response that actually sets up an equivalence between the spectator and the film's diegetic victims—but, by means of modernist strategies such as the direct look out of the frame, it establishes a complicity between the film's spectators and the murderers depicted in its narrative. It takes, therefore, an aggressive—not to say sadistic—posture toward its audience.

In Haneke's films, the corporeality of the spectator—her tactile proximity—tends to be counteracted by the formal structure of games, both diegetic and cinematic, which we have connected to the cognitive dimension of the film. Distance, of course—the sense of detachment that results from modernism's formal constraints—may in itself be cruel.[47] Allegations of cruelty have been notoriously leveled against Bresson and Hitchcock, of course.[48] But perhaps we believe with Freud that artistic activity is a product of the same imagination that is operative in children's games: in these games, too, cruelty may be in evidence, violence enacted, and structure have the power to entrap. An assault on the senses, formal detachment, and the coersive structure of games: in *Funny Games*, Haneke plays these connections out.

Funny Games opens with an aerial long shot that tracks a car as it moves along a country road by a lake, signalling the genre films with which it seeks both to ally itself and to break. Clearly an allusion to Kubrick's *The Shining*— but with a difference: the camera is never eerily out of control, and there are no strains of "Dies Irae" to conjure up the supernatural. Nevertheless, moving into the country from the city, the people who inhabit this car will soon experience the extreme violence visited upon countless characters in American horror movies who do likewise. In the meantime, however, Georg and Anna are engaged in a game that characterizes them as the members of the Austrian educated bourgeoisie—the *Bildungsbürgertum*—that they are: placing DVDs into the player of their Range Rover, Anna invites Georg to identify the composer, the piece, and its performer. This display of cultural capital in a car that flaunts their consumerism seems alone to condemn these characters to a period of extended torture and to death since, as the film will make abundantly clear, they are in other ways unobjectionable—even "nice." While Georg deliberates whether the aria that they—and we the spectators—are hearing is by Tebaldi, the diegetic music is drowned out for the spectator alone by the angry, convulsive music of John Zorn. These abrasive sounds accompany a title sequence whose red letters superimposed upon the image already foreshadow blood on a screen. Perhaps it is high, or higher, culture—Adorno's "On the Fetish-Character in Music and the Regression of Listening"—that seals their fate, for surely this is regressive listening, listening arrested at the infantile stage.[49] For Adorno, their listening habits alone—fetishizing the leitmotif rather than listening for the structural unity of the whole—would characterize Anna and Georg as commodity fetishists.

If the late adolescent murderers-to-be base their acts of torture on children's games—"hot and cold," "cat in the sack," a version of "eenie-meeenie-minie-mo"—they do so only after the trope of violence as play has been cued by Anna, who resorts to a commonplace to excuse her dog's wild barking at their approach: "he just wants to play." "Funny game," says one adolescent in response. Other instances of linguistic manipulation—calling a knife a toy, for instance—and the repeated, though relatively unobtrusive use of cliché, suggest a critique of language reminiscent of Haneke's fellow countryman, the writer Peter Handke.[50] Games address the cognitive level of perception even when they structure violence: the acts of torture perpetrated by Peter and Paul adapt a variety of plots and structures: clowning or mime (the egg game), betting ("we bet that none of you will be alive at nine o'clock tomorrow morning, and you bet that you will"), and pulp fiction (Anna is to play the "loving wife" as she watches her husband's brutal murder). But they have another dimension as well. In this film, games, performance, and plot are acts of torture from which the spectator is not excluded. Mocking a variety of sociopsychological explanations for their behavior—poverty, drug addiction, abuse of all sorts—that are clichés in their own right, Peter and Paul construct scenarios of inexplicable violence, scenarios that they observe with detached—and, indeed, aesthetic—pleasure. "Here are the Rules of the Game," they tell their victims in a barely veiled allusion to Jean Renoir.[51]

The director has a game to play, as well, and it is cat-and-mouse.[52] "Form and content must be absolutely identical," pronounces Haneke. Recalling references to self-reflexivity in Haneke's interviews, to the mobilization of the cognitive aspect of spectatorial response, we may wonder whether it is in this light that we are to read the modernist efforts at distanciation in *Funny Games*. Media consciousness permeates this film, of course. We find it in the aliases adopted by the murderers—Tom and Jerry, Beavis and Butthead—and we find it distressingly present in the film's Tom Twyker moment (keeping in mind that *Run, Lola, Run* is obviously the later film), the moment at which it seems that one of Haneke's characters at least, Anna, is able to break through the "no exit" structure of the deadly games to which she has fallen prey. Seizing the rifle, Anna shoots and hits Peter, presumably killing him. But if the spectator feels relief at her action, it is momentary only, for Paul simply picks up the remote and rewinds the action, which then follows its deadly and predictable course. Games of violence, Haneke would have us know, can be played by the director, too. Manipulating the narrative as if the film were a video and he its spectator, Haneke makes it abundantly clear both that he is in control and that media violence is one object of his critique.

Of the slightly tired self-reflexive strategies to which the films resorts, it is perhaps the look out of the camera—the look that famously flouts film's dictum against breaking through the fourth wall—that strikes the spectator with greatest intensity. (The fourth wall functions as the figurative "curtain" that protects the privacy of the characters in bourgeois drama.) At a number of moments in the film, Paul winks conspiratorially out of the frame and addresses the spectator directly. Given the exigencies of Paul's behavior and the tortured sounds of pain with which the sound track repeatedly inundates the spectator, this suggestion of conversational intimacy—if not complicity—between murderer and spectator is repulsive in the extreme. Here our affective responses are engaged within the context of belief—a cognitive approach to affect. But our moral repugnance at the structural trap created by this direct address provokes—at the very least—anger at our enforced complicity. In some spectators with whom I have viewed the film, in fact, these moments produced the desire to react violently themselves, a response that paradoxically actualizes their connection with the characters.[53] Perhaps this is the effect that Haneke has in mind, for his film also ends on the direct look out at the camera, held in freeze-frame, while the blood-red letters of the credits are inscribed upon it. When, as in the title scene, Zorn's loud and disturbing music blares out in intensified auditory assault, it joins this disturbing frontal stare.

In and of themselves, the moments that harness the direct look out are disturbing and coercive, if somewhat heavy-handed. In this film, modernist reflexivity appears in the guise of black humor, the interest in the materiality of film diminishes, the image is perceptibly less acetic, the narrative more conventionally shaped, and filmic intertextuality more prominent. (It may be for these reasons that *Funny Games* is the first Haneke film to have been nominated for a prize at Cannes.) Keeping in mind the allusion to *The Shining* in the opening frames of the film, the spectator may recognize another reference to Kubrick in these moments of direct address: they recall the famous publicity still for *A Clockwork Orange* (1971)—its opening shot—the close-up in which the droog, Alex, looks out from the frame and directly at the spectator. By this means the film seems to suggest that in some sense Kubrick's opening shot and its own final shot are bookends, implying that the films are somehow coextensive. And, indeed, *Funny Games* recalls *A Clockwork Orange* in a number of ways that have a bearing on our reading of Haneke's film. They share in common the attitude of game playing and theater imposed upon acts of violence, of course, regardless of whether the white makeup of Kubrick's droogs, their white mime's garb and clown masks, have been reduced to tennis whites and surgical gloves in Haneke's film—and they recall as well the merry pranksters of Antonioni's *Blow-Up* (1966), another text in the modernist canon to which we will recur later. Like Peter and Paul, the members of Alex's youthful gang are without remorse and without motivation: like Haneke's film, Kubrick's ultimately invalidates sociopsychological explanations. It should be added that *A Clockwork Orange* is arguably as well known for the uproar that it created among critics and censors—its *X* rating in the United States, its censorship in Britain—as it is for the new and shocking quality of its violent images or provocative narrative.[54] Its reception exemplifies a condemnatory attitude toward violent material in film that Haneke himself professes to share.

Interestingly, the famous "Ludovico Treatment" in *A Clockwork Orange* gives expression to the problem of association in aesthetic response as well as in behavioral conditioning more generally. Most significant for Haneke may be the role of music in that conditioning: the meeting of high and low culture—Tebaldi and Zorn; Beethoven and the Hollywood musical—is no doubt only one aspect of this interest. Alex's favorite composer is the "lovely Ludwig van," of course, and the sadistic behaviorists who promote the Ludovico Treatment use its affective power over Alex as a cue to arrest negative behaviors before they fully begin, thus depriving Alex of his enjoyment of Beethoven's Ninth.[55] When the liberal writer who suffers at the hands of Alex and his droogs later identifies him from the song he sang while raping and killing the writer's wife, even this liberal is moved by the power of music to take revenge. Appropriately, perhaps, the association of music with visceral response became a topic of debate in the reception of Kubrick's film as well when one critic complained that Gene Kelly's "Singing' in the Rain" had been forever spoiled for her by the acts of violence that Alex committed while singing this tune. She would never be able to hear it again, she wrote, "without a vague feeling of nausea."[56]

Another point of convergence between Kubrick's and Haneke's films requires mentioning here. Significantly and predictably, the violent images with which the Ludovico Treatment connects the Ninth Symphony are images taken from films. As Alex puts it, "its funny how the colors of the real world only seem real when you viddy them on a screen." From here Peter and Paul's final dialogue in *Funny Games* is not far to seek. After having disposed of Anna by tossing her into the lake, Haneke's dynamic duo holds a conversation about reality and fiction during which they conclude that "fiction *is* reality." As a comment on the inability of Haneke's characters to tell the two apart—this is a topic familiar from other Haneke films, not to mention from Baudrillard—this conclusion is not profound. But their conversation is actually more nuanced and suggestive than these remarks would indicate, and it differs from Alex's paradoxically more postmodern reaction. Their conversation begins with a science fiction film whose plot Peter is relating to Paul, a film in which the hero finds himself in a universe that is real. Paul interjects that fiction *is* reality, explaining that, since one actually sees this universe—if only in a film—it is just as real as the reality that you see in the same way. Paul, then, is speaking—and I say this in jest—as a proponent of Bordwellian constructivist cognitive theory, which holds that spectators use the same set of assumptions for understanding film as they use for understanding reality. Or, to put it another way, fiction and the real meet in the affective response of the spectator who is moved, programmed—even coerced—into responding somatically. It is in the spectatorial body that the film becomes "real." Significantly, the film that Haneke's characters discuss is a science fiction film, a genre known for the intensity with which its special effects act upon the body.

If the affective aesthetics of the bourgeois melodrama are in evidence in *Funny Games*, we might well ask whether the film contains other traces of this genre. Might this film, too—like *The Piano Teacher*—be called a "parody of a melodrama"? The fact that the nuclear family is cohesive in this film, that the bond between parents and child and with one another seems strong and loving, and that it is only the murderers who seem actually to suffer the negative effects of mediativization, should not sidetrack us. The ideological project that characterizes Haneke's bourgeois trilogy is still in place in this later film and, as mentioned above, it remains critical of the *haute bourgeois* consumer society in which its narrative devolves. Its initially negative emphasis on a commodity culture notwithstanding, this film takes place in a country house from which the austere modernism of Benny's apartment, for example, is conspicuously absent. Its furnishings are augmented by peasant appurtenances, and its warm palette has more in common with the Egyptian sequence in *Benny's Video* than it does with the bluish tints of urban spaces. This is a modern rendering of the eighteenth-century domestic idyll, complete with a country kitchen in which actual cooking takes place. But these nostalgic images are finally ironized: the property is enclosed by a high electronic gate that entraps its owners rather than protects them.

The irrational outbursts of violence during which Peter and Paul kill the family at its country retreat—they have already killed one set of neighbors and are poised to kill another as the film ends—are tellingly not the products of class conflict. Peter and Paul's manner of speaking and their familiarity with its codes of behavior leave no doubt as to the social class in which they were raised. Indeed, it is their very knowledge of the decorum that prevails among its members that allows them to acquire a foothold in the houses in which they wreak mayhem. No gate keeps them out because these gates are not intended for the likes of them. It is not class ressentiment that motivates their rampages—and here is a major point of divergence from *A Clockwork Orange*. Rather, these outbreaks of violence are once again situated within a familial—and melodramatic—context. When the family remembers that their neighbor has a nephew of roughly the age of Peter and Paul, the young men's appearance on the scene is naturalized for them. By this means, the spectator is given to understand that the acts of violence take place within a quasidomestic framework, after all—which is to say, once again, that these are not the coups de théâtre of political uprisings. Significantly, these acts have a theatrical aspect resembling the tennis games of Antonioni's *Blowup*, where the tennis players participate in a theater of illusion—merely a "happening"—while political assassination is committed by other actors (by Vanessa Redgrave, in fact). Insofar as the victims themselves come in for blame—especially Georg—it is for upholding the bourgeois decorum that leaves them passive in the face of danger. The film suggests that their victimhood is attributable to their "niceness."

Let's recall Hitchcock's self-description of the director as an organist, playing affective chords upon the body of the filmic spectator. Hitchcock's metaphor of the cinema as a behavioral programming device is a version of the Ludovico Treatment, although clearly not administered by the State or as far-reaching or long-lasting in its effects. But it's been repeatedly suggested that Hitchcock's films—his "anguish-producing machines," as André Bazin has called them—take pleasure in making their spectator suffer.[57] "Hitchcock," writes Bazin in *The Cinema of Cruelty*, "sometimes makes you hear, over the victim's terrified screams, the true cry of joy that does not deceive you—his own."[58] Given Haneke's renunciation of psychology, it may seem inappropriate to suggest that his cold formalism arises from the distance of the sadist, for whom intimacy can only be established through the pain of the other—that of his spectator. But, metaphorically at least, the termination of Haneke's training as a concert pianist, while sparing him the sadomasochistic tortures of an Erika Kohut (*The Piano Teacher*), only left him more fully in the position of Hitchcock, playing his torturing chords upon the mind—and body—of his spectator. Expressing their excess intermittently in acts of diegetic violence, these visually austere films provoke intense reactions in their spectators. Coldness and violence coexist in Haneke's films, films of which it has been claimed that they "prick the wounds of cinema, and renew themselves."[59] Renewal may very well lie in restoring an affective charge to film. If so, however, it comes at a price.

Looking and Pain

Is it truly possible to represent variations on sadomasochistic behavior in film in a manner that makes the participants in this scenario insusceptible to being psychologized? In *The Piano Teacher* (2001), which received the Grand Prix at Cannes, Haneke very loosely adapts Elfriede Jelinek's novel of the same title (1983), omitting its feminist thrust and, notably, its critique of high culture.[60] But the film remains the story of a sadomasochistic relationship or two, presenting in its diegesis the power structures that *Funny Games* cloaks in another narrative. What did Haneke mean when he called *The Piano Teacher* a parody of melodrama? Masochism is not foreign to melodrama, of course, whose generic characteristics include its masochistic cast: it is the victim who constitutes the emotional center of its story.[61] When we recall that melodrama's etymology is melos-drama or music drama, we realize that choosing this genre for a narrative about music performance involves a literalization of the figurative. For Haneke, the parodic dimension of this film lies in its refusal to explain, but also in its attempt to present "the unreal as real."[62] His remark is tongue-in-cheek—parodic—and, were it not for the modernist high seriousness of this film, one might be tempted, with Jameson, to read postmodern reification in Haneke's claim.[63] Indeed, Peter Brooks's reading of melodrama as a *failure* of literalness, a failure of the codes of realism, seems more to the point.[64] For Brooks, melodrama of necessity spills over into the metalanguage of metaphor. Similarly, for Geoffrey Nowell-Smith, the melodramatic text "somaticises its own unaccommodated excess"—the "hysterical moment" of the text being the moment at which realism's mode of representation breaks down.[65]

But excess does not spill over into the mise-en-scène of Haneke's film. Instead, extreme rigor and aesthetic control dominate *The Piano Teacher* at the formal level. Although the narrative portrays a series of perverse acts, their perversity is not expressed in the tone of the film, which is without affect, completely deadpan. Although the modernist strategies to which Haneke resorts in this film are more naturalized here than in his bourgeois trilogy, *The Piano Teacher* repeatedly draws on them to achieve its ends. Once again an emphasis on duration retards the momentum of narrative and intensifies spectatorial affect, as for instance in the bathtub scene in which Erika Kohut, the protagonist, slices away at her private parts with a razor blade. The painful protraction of this scene is just that—painful—although the sensationalism of the action is played down as much as it is possible to do so. We don't see the actual wounding and hear only muted sounds of pleasure/pain that are almost insusceptible to categorization. Blood is visible in the tub only in the course of being washed away: for the spectator, shock lies as much in the unemotional presentation of the action as in the action itself. The austere visual compositions of Haneke's earlier films—the Bressonian shots of feet walking across the floor, for instance—are markedly in evidence here. One sequence features a nearly abstract juxtaposition of shapes in black and white with a grand piano in the foreground, Erika with her back to the spectator, and a portrait of Schubert on the wall. Here the human figure functions as just another object—recalling Bresson's admiration of this technique in the paintings of Cézanne—and our only access to the human is subsumed within the thing.[66] In *The Seventh Continent*, the Haneke film in which Bresson is most in evidence, it is only letters that tell us the film's plot. The distancing effect of letters read in voice-over is displaced in *The Piano Teacher* into the shocking letter that spells out the masochistic contract. And although this film seems less interested in the visual materialities of film than in the earlier films, it becomes clear that classical music—both as a form of expression and by virtue of its structure—stands in for film per se. As we recall, Haneke confesses to basing his films on musical structures.

But music is not the only stand-in for the moving image, for its low-cultural equivalent is present as well. As in the earlier films, in *The Piano Teacher* the drone of the television announcer is constantly in the background, and once we hear the sound track of a domestic drama. For brief moments, Erika—and the spectator—voyeuristically watch footage from a pornographic film. We are reminded, in other words, of the degradation and commercialization of the moving image, and are no doubt meant to read the act of fellatio so graphically displayed to our view in contradistinction to what is in fact *not* shown in the public restroom where it is briefly performed by Erika. (In the restroom scene, framing keeps the erect penis out of view.) Thematizing the issue of voyeurism even more directly than the scene in the video shop is a sequence set in a drive-in movie theater. Indeed, the visual relationships here deserve a closer look. The couple having sex in the back seat of the car is, of course, not looking through the windshield at the movie screen, although the point may be that they have been moved to have sex by images they have seen.[67] Watching the couple through the window, Erika looks through glass, if not through a lens, at a framed hence visually composed scene—not at movie images of sex, but at the "real thing," rendered an image for Erika by virtue of the window's glass and frame. The "real" bodies in the car serve as a graphic reminder of pornography's resistance to representation, of its status as a "fantasy of the real at the verge of symbolization."[68]

Having witnessed the effects of this experience on Erika—she responds physically to the sight of the lovers by urinating—how can we avoid the conclusion that her sexual development has been arrested at the infantile stage? It is unlikely that scenes such as this one can be read without bringing a knowledge of developmental behavior, if not psychoanalysis, to bear. *The*

Piano Teacher actively solicits explanations precisely because, as Haneke has claimed, the film itself does not explain the perverse scenarios that it displays to the view.[69] What would it mean to take at face value the shockingly melodramatic scene in which Erika, who shares a bed with her mother, attacks her mother sexually in the darkened room, sobbing spasmodically all the while?[70] If Erika's engagement in other forms of sexuality—voluntary as well as forced—is only partially displayed to the spectator's view, we are nonetheless confronted with the urine, sperm, vomit, and bloody noses—the secretions of the body that accompany it. Whether these scenes constitute pornography—Haneke denies it, Jelinek asserts it[71]—must be left to the discretion of the spectator. Regardless of whether the spectator is aroused or disgusted by these scenes, Haneke's "parody of melodrama" remains very much a body genre. In any case, the spectator is punished by the psychic and physiological pain that surrounds the presentation of sexuality in this film. The spectator is structurally placed in the masochistic position.

We would be morally defective, Susan Sontag tells us, if, in watching the pain of others, we did not ourselves suffer.[72] Emotional suffering is what is at issue for Sontag, of course, not literal pain. But what we might call affective pain—pain both emotional and physical, combining aspects of the two—is produced in the spectator of *The Piano Teacher* by virtue of the collaboration between the narrative events, music, and formal control in evidence here. The irruptions of the Lacanian real orchestrated at the level of the film's narrative are not allowed expression in the mise-en-scène, not displaced into it as is usual in melodrama. In Haneke's films, rather, spectator affect is aroused by narrative events, then constrained, controlled, one could almost say *rejected*, by what critics repeatedly refer to as the coldness of their images. "The quality of coldness is imperative to masochistic control of desire through suspended passion," Gaylyn Studlar writes in the most comprehensive account of the masochistic aesthetic in film,[73] using language that might well describe the relation of text to spectator in Haneke's films. Even more pertinently, Deleuze tells us that masochism speaks directly through formal control: characterized by its coldness, it is masochistic fantasy that plays itself out in formal patterns, in "a particular kind of formalism."[74] This quality of formal distance or coldness is intensified in *The Piano Teacher*, where it in some sense replaces Jelinek's critique of high culture. Indeed, Jelinek herself calls Haneke "one of the coldest auteurs who ever existed."[75] "Do you have no ear for what coldness is?" Erika Kohut, Sacher-Masoch's "Venus of ice," demands scathingly of her student Fräulein Schober as she plays a song from Schubert's *Winterreise*.

It is by formal means that the atmosphere of coldness is most profoundly sustained in this film. In particular, it is Isabelle Huppert's modernist acting style that enables distance, invoking Bresson's preference for nonexpressive acting in film,[76] and for what Bazin refers to as the "sheer epidermis" of the human face in Bresson's films.[77] For the most part, Huppert plays Erika with the impassive expression of a mask, with a minimalism that is as different from melodrama's expressiveness as possible. Bresson's emphasis on the skin is a reminder of the flesh and blood that lies behind it—and hence of our common humanity. Haneke, on the other hand, stresses the sculptural quality of Huppert's face as though to conjure up the "woman of stone" who is the ideal of his fellow Austrian, Sacher-Masoch.[78] Only once, notes Haneke, did he insist that Huppert's face display expressivity: against her will Huppert grimaces during the final scene of the film as she inserts the blade of her kitchen knife into her breast. In this moment theatricality is foregrounded.[79] It is no accident that it takes place against the backdrop of Vienna's concert hall, calling to mind the tradition of melodramatic suffering of abandoned lovers in theater and opera. Although it is in marked contrast to the lack of emotion on Huppert's face during most of the film, in a sense her grimace simply replaces her mask of impassivity with the tragic mask of the Greeks. Thus, her grimace allows Erika to remain a "woman of stone" after all, even as the theatricality of masochism finds expression and melodrama assumes the aspect of tragedy.

The Masochistic Tableau

Arrested actions and sculptural display are central to the sexual perversion that is masochism. Erika Kohut's abrupt termination of the sex act she performs leaves her lover's penis painfully erect, and she demands of him that it remain that way. The deferral of desire characteristic of masochism originates in the masochist's disavowal of pleasure through suspended action. As Deleuze points out, it is the moments of suspense in Sacher-Masoch's novels that are privileged, in part because the woman of stone—the torturer—assumes postures reminiscent of statues, paintings, and photographs."[80] Such moments are tableaux and, like the tableaux of the bourgeois drama, they, too, have the function of arresting narrative and intensifying emotion. These are sculptural moments, moments when postures are held and gestures take on a heightened significance. Iconicity, Studlar suggests, constitutes a central aspect of the masochistic aesthetic's reliance on art as an ideal. Within the framework of this aesthetic, paintings, statues, and the held pose "exemplify the iconic suspension of spatial and temporal laws, the delay of gratification, and masochistic contemplation in the art model."[81] Whereas Huppert's acting has a sculptural quality, Haneke's mise-en-scènes are generally speaking not iconic. Schubert's portrait on the wall of the piano room is a notable exception, serving to anchor the "art model" of *The Piano Teacher* in music. As we shall see later on, however, in this film music itself takes on the function of the icon.

As in the case of bourgeois tragedy, the tableaux of Sacher-Masoch's novel rehearse a family drama. But it is a perverse drama that is enacted time and again in masochism, one in which qua Deleuze, the death-bringing oral mother, holds sway. Nevertheless, the intensified emotion and affect they hold in common links the moments of stasis in masochistic scenarios to similar moments in bourgeois dramas. We might say that in *The Piano Teacher* a rather different relation to bourgeois melodrama plays itself out, one entirely in keeping with Haneke's notion of parody. The strategy of the *Civil War* (*Bürgerkrieg*) trilogy was in some sense to displace the emotional but statically rendered visual tableaux of bourgeois drama into a distancing formalism, on the one hand, and into diegetic acts of violence, on the other. In *The Piano Teacher*, the implied tableau of the erect male organ would express the heightened affect of the tableau physically—literalizing it, turning it pornographic—were it not merely discussed, mediated by language rather than available as image.

Released during the same year as *The Piano Teacher*, Haneke's made-for-television adaptation of Kafka's *The Castle* is continuous with the sadomasochistic world of *Funny Games* and *The Piano Teacher*. Because Kafka's novel fragment itself has a masochistic register, Haneke's television adaptation need not justify its particular interest in sadomasochism and thus effectively closes itself off to psychologizing [82] In this version of *The Castle*, Haneke makes brilliant use of the disadvantages of the televisual medium—its flatness or lack of deep space and its reliance on the medium shot and medium close-up. Televisual style is exaggerated and used to greatest effect in a series of snow-filled outdoor scenes in which K. in medium shot repeatedly walks back and forth across a row of doors and windows, from left to right and vice versa. These snowy scenes perfectly exemplify the icy scenes of Sacher-Masoch's *Venus in Furs*. Moreover, by throwing continuity to the winds, these sequences disorient the spectator in the same way that K. is disoriented, distorting time as well as space by virtue of their repetition, and ultimately rendering time as a spatial pattern. Because we never completely see the building to which the doors and windows belong, the flatness of their surfaces is accentuated, producing the effect of stage sets—of painted representations that call both Studlar's "art model" and the theatricality of masochism to mind. Indoor scenes are likewise spatially ambiguous: the rooms in which the action takes place have no discernible contours and, in adherence to Kafka's text, the relationship of spaces to one another remains unclear. In Haneke's film, the beams and other wooden structures within interior spaces function ornamentally and fetishistically, recalling the plasticity of von Sternberg's interiors. In contrast to the icy cold of the outdoors, human bodies produce a stifling heat indoors. In these tactile, uterine, and abject spaces, unfettered sexuality reigns. In accordance with Kafka's text, sexuality displays the elements of masochistic fantasy, complete with Frieda wielding a whip and a barmaid whose ample breasts and the beer she serves are continuous with the oral-stage fantasies of masochism.[83]

If its televisual style seems to single *The Castle* out from other Haneke films, it should be pointed out that it also has formal strategies in common with them. The cuts to black with which we are familiar from *The Seventh Continent* and *71 Fragments* also puncture *The Castle*, whose voice-over of Kafka's text is cut abruptly, in midsentence, at just the point where its written model breaks off. In keeping with the aesthetics of masochism, as well, Kafka's text is fetishized, fragmented, and permanently suspended in the incomplete sentence. Returning to Haneke's earlier films after *The Castle*, we might now retrospectively read what we have called their modernist style somewhat differently. The close-ups of body parts—feet getting into slippers, hands preparing tea—that recur so frequently in *The Seventh Continent* might now be read not only with reference to Bresson, but also in relation to fetishism. In this context, the narrative fragments of *71 Fragments* with their cuts to black take on the aspect of cutouts against a black field, fetishes that undermine narrative development by their stress on spatiality. The control that Benny exercises over his video would now appear to function as the disavowal of narrative progression characteristic of masochism. At the thematic level, the "last supper" eaten by the family of *The Seventh Continent* suggests the connection of masochism with martyrdom, while Benny's "flight into Egypt" seems an elaboration of the Marian fantasy.[84] From this point of view, the cross repeatedly pieced together by the students in *71 Fragments* is not just an allusion to the final image of Bresson's *Diary of a Country Priest*, but may have christological—and perhaps masochistic—significance, after all.[85]

At the level of plot, K's voyeuristic assistants in *The Castle* surface as Peter and Paul in *Funny Games*; Frank Gierig, the actor who appears in both films, physically underscores their connection. Peter and Paul exist within a sadomasochistic dynamic that makes them act with a mutual aim; it is claimed that K's assistants are nearly identical. Interestingly, it's been suggested of Jelinek's novel that its ending is a grotesque parody of Kafka's *The Trial*.[86] When Joseph K. is stabbed, he prepares to die like a dog, but Erika in Haneke's *Piano Teacher* is not likely to die at all: the knife does not enter her heart, but merely pierces her shoulder. Yet the final images of Hanke's film reveal Erika walking from left to right in medium long shot in a composition that recalls the outdoor shots involving K. walking back and forth in Haneke's version of *The Castle*. In *The Piano Teacher*, the stage sets that conjure up the icy "art world" of the masochistic text have been replaced by "documentary" images of the Viennese concert hall itself. In representing an overtly perverse relationship, therefore, *The Piano Teacher* also illuminates the pathology that lies just beneath the surface of Kafka's texts, those canonical texts of Austrian high modernism. But whether the sadomasochistic register of Haneke's films is most crucially a matter of adaptation, intertextuality, or disposition itself remains permanently suspended.

Sentiment, Music, and the Real

Let me begin by summarizing briefly the argument developed in the first part of this chapter. It starts with the assertion that a number of Haneke's earlier films are composed against the generic backdrop of the bourgeois melodrama and that the acts of violence that punctuate these films are in defiance of eighteenth-century conventions that bar dramatic events (coups de théâtres) and acts of violence from bourgeois drama. Violence is reserved for tragedy, in which political events have a place and that is not located in the domestic space of the middle class. Bourgeois melodrama of the eighteenth century, the argument goes, confines itself to the private domain of the family and expresses it moments of dramatic climax not in dramatic action, but rather in the static pictorial arrangements of the tableau, arrangements that typically occur at moments of significance to family life, such as death-bed scenes or scenes of reconciliation. Dramas such as these, Peter Szondi argues, have traditionally diverted the middle class from political action by channeling emotion that might lead to political action into feelings of sympathy or empathy.

Although Haneke's films seem deliberately to introduce acts of physical violence to the bourgeois melodrama and to displace its static arrangements into a modernist formalism, this violence does not open up the space of melodrama to the political. Acts of violence in Haneke's films are often directed against the self or otherwise remain in some sense familial. Insofar as a political agenda is expressed in Haneke's films, it may very well lie in demonstrating the inefficacy of such acts. The stasis of the tableau as it offers itself up to contemplation, its distancing effect, and its control of narrative progression: these characteristics of the tableau in bourgeois melodrama find expression in the modernist style that produces Haneke's "cold images." Like the fourth wall of eighteenth-century melodrama, their coldness in some sense protects the privacy of those whose suffering is on display. This insight accords with Haneke's critique of the media as depriving the victims they expose of all dignity and self-respect.[87]

Interestingly, a recent essay by Ed Tan and Nico Frijda takes up the question of spectator response to the suffering portrayed in sentimental literature, specifically to the bourgeois drama and novel of the eighteenth century. In their essay, Tan and Frijda confirm from the perspective of perceptual psychology that the spectatorial position involved in watching such plays—or films modeled upon them—evokes what they call "witness emotions," empathic or sympathetic emotions, feelings of compassion that render the spectator passive and usually move her to tears.[88] Tan and Frijda claim from their behaviorist perspective precisely what Szondi suggested years ago in his essay on the social psychology of bourgeois drama: that sentimental feelings such as sympathy are associated with helplessness, submissiveness, with "a sense of being discharged of any obligation to act."[89] Basing their conclusions on the affective—both emotional and physiological—responses to sentimental scenes, Tan and Frijda ascribe to sentimental feelings the tendency to suspend "control mechanisms" and to produce the feeling of "yielding" in those who experience them.[90] It is by means of the extreme physical violence that bourgeois drama ordinarily excludes from within its parameters then, I am arguing, that Haneke's films wrest their spectators from passivity by preventing the tears that the melodrama seeks to solicit. Although these scenes of extreme violence provoke fear or disgust, Haneke's films do not give their spectators an outlet for the affective tension they create.

As Torben Grodal points out, art films may deliberately block the progression of narrative, or what he calls its "downstream" flow.[91] Often in such films, the flow of music—its temporal unfolding—stands in for the missing narrative development, promoting the unfolding of emotions that the narrative temporarily blocks. In narrative cinema, music often has the function of creating sound bridges over scenes of disparate narrative content. In *The Piano Teacher*, for instance, Haneke uses sound both to create affective continuity and to produce shock at the yoking together of the narrative spaces so linked. The most notable instance of this occurs when the sounds of Schubert's Trio in B Flat, which Erika has been performing at the piano, continue as nondiegetic music into the next scene—the scene in which she watches a pornographic movie in a video store. The nature of the continuity here produced is initially perceived as disjunctive, as it joins classical music—identified with the world of the "spirit," purified of sexuality—with the barely representable real of pornography.

But it is precisely the point of *The Piano Teacher* to remind its spectator that music always involves the body—that, actually, it involves several bodies: the body of the composer, the body of the performer, and the body of the listener. The coldness of Schubert's music, asserts Erika in her role as piano teacher, must be understood by the pianist who performs it. Its precise structure must be transposed into the precise movements of fingers and phrasing expressed through the body language of back and arms. Thus the performance of Schubert must involve a continual holding back, a suspension of passion that has a special resonance for Erika as masochist. Interestingly, when Erika begins to respond sexually to the advances of the student, the performance of classical music disappears entirely from the film. Passion and its withholding are displaced into performances of other kinds. *The Piano Teacher* is about the control of passion in art, and it exemplifies its subject by way of its formal procedures.[92]

Where in this film, then, is the iconicity associated with the masochistic aesthetic? In answer to this question, let me suggest that it is musical structure that functions iconically in Haneke's film. The structure of Schubert's music is crystalline—not vegetal—Adorno claims in 1928, in his first essay on a musical topic.[93] Schubert's music is not organic, writes Adorno, nor is music the poetic representation of psychological content in Schubert. Rather, there is a connection between what music intends at the symbolic level and its "material concretion," its form—and form, Adorno claims, has a relation to the world. As Adorno describes it, Schubert's music is produced through the dialectic that is almost vampiristic: it is a subjective "sucking-in" (*saugen*) of images from the objective world that sometimes in their musical expression—and here Adorno resorts to a photographic metaphor to make his point—fortuitously yield "das getroffene Abbild . . . wie eine Photographie." That is to say, Adorno claims that Schubert's music can produce telling (musical) images that are expressions of the real world, expressions so real that they seem to be literal impressions (Abbild) of the referent, such as occur in the photograph.[94] Adorno's description suggests that musical passages or ideas can retain an imprint of the real—can be indexical, in the way that photographs and film images are.

In and of itself, the metaphor of the photograph is of interest, but even more to the point is Adorno's formulation concerning the emotional effect of Schubert's music on his listener. On hearing Schubert's music, writes Adorno, tears pour out of the eyes without ever having moved the soul, "so literally and real does his music enter us."[95] Although I cannot possibly contend that Haneke, who cites Adorno frequently, nevertheless has any knowledge of this particular early essay, its reading of Schubert is congenial to Haneke's thinking. It is because Adorno reads Schubert's music as having a literal relation to the real that he is prompted to suggest that the reaction it triggers in the listener is purely physiological. The listener's reaction exists only as tears, not as the product of emotion, never moving the "soul," never becoming mere sentiment. Ideologically, it is important to Adorno that the imprint the real world leaves in music triggers a material response rather than a sentimental condition: the tears of bourgeois drama are not the tears that Adorno is describing. Adorno's tears are the products of affect deprived of association, the direct assault of art on the bodies of its audience. This is the assault on the audience by the real, the puncturing of the wound that—for Haneke, at least—is capable of renewing film.

9

Images of Horror:
Taste, Cannibalism, and Visual Display

Touch, Taste, and Vision

This chapter takes up the concerns of several earlier chapters in positing a relation of reciprocity between spectator and image, a relation that constitutes one aspect of the interface between representation and the real. With Merleau-Ponty, I have argued that we must "make the contact between observer and observed enter into the definition of the 'real.'"[1] Following Vivian Sobchack's semiotic phenomenology and the contemporary interest in the physiological, perceptual, as well as the cognitive aspects of film spectatorship, this chapter supports and expands upon the contention that the perceiving mind that makes film experience possible is an embodied mind.[2] It is by means of the spectator's somatic responsiveness, I have argued, that the material aspects of embodied spectatorship carry over to or are projected upon the image most fully, lending the image itself the semblance of materiality. And it is materiality that is problematically at issue in cannibalism, its limit case. Examining figurations of cannibalism, we take up a shocking and different collapse of boundaries and explore its function in the horror film. Pursuing the concern with material images, we investigate the perverse "works of art" cathected upon and produced by some notable cannibals of horror film, reading in their activities the psychotic extreme endpoint in the pursuit of "realism." Needless to say, the question of taste in both its figurative and literal sense will also be the object of our scrutiny. The imbrication of the senses that the horror film in particular promotes and encourages a spectrum of spectatorial responses to the image, including tactile and gustatory experiences, with the result that disgust is one of the central affects that horror films produce.

But while the horror film in particular relies on synesthesia for its effects, the interrelation of the senses in aesthetic response has its antecedents in the pre-Kantian seventeenth and eighteenth centuries, in Locke and the English empiricists, and is famously contained in Baumgarten's formulation that aesthetics is the science of sense perception (*Aesthetica*, 1750). Although vision has a central role to play, touch is likewise featured in the aesthetic arena as, for instance, in Denis Diderot's "Letter on the Blind" (1749), which gives touch an importance equal to that of vision. Touch helps to shape the categories of Edmund Burke's *Philosophical Inquiry into the Origin of Our Ideas of the Sublime and the Beautiful* (1757), and is stressed by Johann Gottfried Herder, whose essay on sculpture (1778) displays a preference for the haptic over the optical.[3] Toward the end of the eighteenth century, tactility is featured as one of the qualities of visual experience by theorists of the picturesque, to whom we recur below. Although Jonathan Crary bases the argument of *Techniques of the Observer* on the notion that vision becomes lodged in the physiology of the body only during the course of the nineteenth century—in the art of the Impressionists, for example—it is actually very much present in the multisensory acts of perception featured in the non-Kantian eighteenth.[4]

In the twentieth century, related ideas find their expression in diverse theoretical contexts. The tactility of the image is notably stressed in Walter Benjamin's canonical essay, "The Work of Art in the Age of Its Technological Reproducibility" (1936). Benjamin's materialism ensures that the optical regime will not lose its grounding in the body: the cinematic spectator responds viscerally to the image, much in the way that spectators of Dada performances had. It is its quality of violent assault, Benjamin points out, that makes the art of the Dadaists tactile, and the Dadaists themselves, committed to the plasticity of the word, concurred. The spectator of Dada art is hit by sensory impressions that resemble "missiles," producing in the spectator "a demand for film, the distracting element of which is also tactile."[5] During this period, French writing on vision and the other senses was stimulated by Henri Bergson's *Matter and Memory* (1896), whose position on the body's centrality to perception was elaborated by Merleau-Ponty's phenomenological approach, emphasizing the merger of spectator and world in a dialectic of perception and expression. If the supplemental function of touch and taste in the eye's attempt to apprehend the material world is featured in a key moment of insight in Sartre's *Nausea* (1938), this is an echo, perhaps, of Sartre's interest in the work of his friend Merleau-Ponty. As Martin Jay reminds us, for Sartre vision remains essentially negative: not surprisingly, Sartre's sense of the relentless hostility of the gaze, essentially sadomasochistic, informs Lacan's thinking concerning the aggressivity of vision and of the gaze imagined as emanating from the place of the other.[6] Tactility disappears from the disembodied gaze of Lacan's specular regime, its simulation in trompe l'oeil both a lure for the eye and a snare for the spectator.[7]

And what of the mouth in connection to the eye? Pre-Kantian eighteenth-century spectators are embodied spectators—witness Lessing's beholder in *Laocoön* (1766), who looks upon the ugly and experiences nausea, or Burke's comment concerning sweetness as "the beautiful of taste."[8] The intermingling of taste and sight occurs frequently in metaphors of looking in the eighteenth century, but especially, of course, in relation to figurative taste.[9] On a metaphorical plane, the pairing of literal taste with sight extends into the nineteenth century in which, for example, as Jacques Aumont notes, the theme of "occular digestion" describes the tendency of the eye to "swallow up" the landscapes that pass before it during train travel.[10] From yet another perspective and later, psychoanalytic readings of the oral stage find their way into analyses of the visual in which the drives are acknowledged. Formulations such as Lacan's "appetite of the eye" stress the relation of vision to desire,[11] a topic embraced by French film theory of the 1970s and applied, for instance, to the work of Hitchcock. In its reading of cinematic spectatorship as an oral-stage fixation, Jean-Louis Baudry's influential essay "The Apparatus: Metapsychological Approaches to the Impression of Reality in Film" (1975) draws parallels between the spectatorial fixation on the image and the infant's desire for the mother's breast. For Baudry, Bertram Lewin's elaboration of the dream screen as developed in "Sleep, Mouth and the Dream Screen" (1946) suggests an analogy to the cinematic screen.[12] Psychoanalytic film theory thus links the infant's desire for fusion—the desire to remain within the preoedipal, prelinguistic oral phase—with what it takes to be a similar regressive state in the cinematic spectator. The experience of film, it is argued, promotes a collapse of the boundaries between subject and object. For Baudry and others, the pleasures of film are viewed as regressive, passive, and as facilitating an "archaic mode of identification."[13] In this psychoanalytic reading of spectatorial experience, the visual orifice substitutes for the buccal orifice. Nevertheless, Baudry concedes that various acts of perception take place in the viewing of cinema, despite the fact that what is perceived is not reality itself, but rather the impression of reality generated by the cinema effect.[14] Concurrently with Baudry, Christian Metz distinguishes between two forms of the gaze: the projective gaze, in which vision resembles a "sweeping searchlight" analogous to the projector, and the introjective gaze, in which the eye resembles both screen and sensitive film strip.[15] Although Metz would never wish to make this claim, his formulation suggests that the gaze in its introjective form—as the taking in of images—is a form of physical incorporation that resembles ingestion.[16] We will return to this insight later.

Interestingly, it is in the field of a psychoanalytically inflected art history that we find a theory of art that has the imbrication of the senses at its base. In "Psycho-Analysis and the History of Art" (the Ernest Jones Lecture read before the British Psycho-Analytical Society in November of 1953), E. H. Gombrich argues for the "importance of oral gratification as a genetic model for aesthetic pleasure."[17] Gombrich asserts that the notion of "taste" in its figurative sense has too much of the Platonic emphasis on the spiritual, that social disapproval suppresses the fact of literal eating and drinking. Taking the French as the predictable example for cuisine raised to an art form, Gombrich reminds the reader that the French language refers to an artist's manipulation of his paint as his "cuisine" and to some paintings as "a feast for the eye."[18] But the connection of eating and looking does not remain at the level of metaphor alone. Although Gombrich is aware that painting has a multiplicity of dimensions and meanings, he nevertheless speculates that it may be through judicious eating that we learn about visual proportion. Taking spectatorial responses—including his own—to Bouguereau's nineteenth-century painting of Venus rising from the sea as his example, Gombrich notes that the sophisticated beholder experiences such paintings as "syrupy, saccharined, cloying." Further, this yoking of sight and taste does not remain at the level of figurative language: by way of such synesthetic metaphors, Gombrich claims to describe "our reaction to a surfeit of oral gratification."[19] While looking at paintings, he suggests, we transfer what we have learned in the arena of literal taste to taste in the visual arts:

> For it is here that we learn first that too much of a good thing is repellent. Too much fat, too much sweetness, too much softness—all the qualities, that is, that have an immediate biological appeal—also produce these counter-reactions which originally serve as a warning signal to the human animal not to over-indulge. Perhaps it could be shown that this warning signal shifts from a biological to a psychological plane.... We find repellent what offers too obvious, too childish, gratification. It invites regression and we do not feel secure enough to yield.[20]

Gombrich's speculative thinking suggests that taste may be transferred from the body to the mind—or, more accurately, perhaps, to the sensibility. Thus, Gombrich reconnects physiological response to aesthetic experience in what may very well be an anti-Kantian gesture.

Earlier than Baudry and Metz in the area of film theory, then, Gombrich concedes that there may be a correlation between what he calls aesthetic activity and regressive pleasure, contending that an appropriate balance between the two must be maintained. For the true connoisseur, Gombrich suggests, Bougeureau's work is too easy to read, hence more complex forms of gratification are required to satisfy the person of sophisticated taste. (Edith Wharton was well aware of the question of taste raised by Bougeureau's work when she chose one of his paintings to adorn the wall of the nouveau riche Julius Beaufort in *The Age of Innocence*; see Chapter 1). In making his argument, Gombrich cites Edward Glovers' "Significance of the Mouth in Psycho-Analysis," in which Glover builds upon the Freudian distinction between active and passive aims as constituting the difference between the "biter" and the "sucker."[21] Glover's distinctions, Gombrich suggests, can be profitably correlated with his own views linking softness with passivity and the "hard and crunchy" with activity. The biter, claims Gombrich, finds his gratification in post-Bougeureau art—in the aggressive primitivism of a Cézanne or a Picasso—with Impressionism the point at which the two forms of satisfaction overlap. At the end of his lecture, Gombrich acknowledges that he has deliberately oversimplified his account of changes in artistic style as "redistributions in the balance of gratification," and that the "real work of art clearly achieves more than the satisfaction of a few analysable cravings."[22] Nevertheless, Gombrich imaginatively suggests that there may be a broader sense in which taste—in its material permutation—may be at the center of aesthetic experience. Radical—and limited—as this may be, it returns to the idea that the origin of aesthetic experience is the body. In accounting for the history of artistic style by shifts in an attitude toward texture, Gombrich, like Walter Benjamin, may have been influenced by Alois Riegl.

We recall that in reading film as a tactile medium, Benjamin similarly blurs the boundary between the cinematic image and the world of the real spectatorial body, effecting this connection via the spectating body's somatic responsiveness. The reciprocity between the image and the real may be most apparent in genres such as the horror film, a genre that derives its very name from the affect it seeks to elicit.[23] It is horror's obvious intention to produce extreme effects in its spectator and, as we can see from the reception history of films such as Tobe Hooper's *The Texas Chainsaw Massacre* (1974),[24] spectators over the decades have dutifully complied. The contemporary American horror film launched in 1960 by *Psycho* openly declares its intention to enhance and broaden visual experience by means of the other senses, by an emphasis especially on touch and taste. In this project, it recalls late eighteenth-century thinking about the aesthetic category called the picturesque, whose proponents saw their task as making visually palatable, for example, distasteful images of the flesh. This was to be achieved, they argued, by expanding vision to include the other senses and by shaping spectatorial response to sense perception. In a passage in Uvedale Price's fictional *Dialogue*, for example, a side of beef in a butcher shop is praised for the "mellow tints" that allow its spectator to associate it with paintings by Rembrandt, perhaps with his renderings of the *Slaughtered Ox*.[25] Price and his fellow theorists of the picturesque strove to enhance visual pleasure by educating spectators to see the things of the world as they would see a painting. Predictably, the outcry against Price's aestheticization of the carcass is the standard one from opponents to realism in representation, who naturally complain that paintings such as Rembrandt's do not aestheticize enough. Entering this long-standing debate more recently, Mieke Bal may be aware of how thoroughly she speaks to the underlying project of the picturesque to incorporate the other senses into visual perception. In any case, Bal has claimed of precisely these paintings by Rembrandt that it is the "roughness" of the layered paint—and, one imagines, the evocation of tactility that this roughness produces, the perception of the paint itself as flesh—that elicits in their spectator the sensation of its "putrifying smell."[26] This is the same project in which the horror film participates when it reveals the opened human body time and again. Supplementing the activity of the eye with that of touch, taste, and sometimes even smell, the horror film engages its spectator in a multisensory, yet nevertheless aesthetic experience that promotes a certain kind of illusion. Horror, like the picturesque, overlaps with realism in its expanded sense, with a realism anchored in the response of a spectatorial body whose sensations and affects promote the effect that the image is real.

It may be useful to illustrate this claim with a self-conscious moment from a horror film that has become a cult classic, an example from the *Day of the Dead* (1985) by George Romero. The last film in a trilogy that spans three decades (from the 1960s to the 1980s), it is even more violently visceral than its predecessors. As in the case of the two earlier films, Hitchcock is not far to seek: *Day of the Dead* opens with a scene that conjures up *Psycho*'s conclusion with Norman Bates/Mother as the object of the investigative eye of the camera as it moves in on Norman's eyes in close-up. Romero's film begins with a variation on this scene from *Psycho*, a scene that it significantly recasts:

when the androgynous character with whom Romero's film begins reaches out to touch the eye that confronts her, arms and hands break through and out of the wall—through the screen, as it were—as if to grasp her in turn. This is a central trope of horror. Here sight elicits, is rendered and literally replaced by touch, as if to suggest that in a film whose affective center lies in the eating of human flesh, taste, touch, and the other "lower" senses must affectively and effectively triumph over the human eye. If in this sequence Hitchcock's gaze—the camera's gaze—has been rendered both material and tactile, this is a preoccupation not foreign to the master himself, even if it does remain at the level of suggestion in his films. In the horror film—indeed, in all of the body genres—aesthetic questions return with a vengeance to their origins in the discourse of the body, and sensory evidence always exceeds the apparatus that produces it. Only the horror film's exaggerated self-reflexiveness can protect its spectators from the full force of a reality effect anchored in the body.

I should add that this chapter in no way purports to be a systematic study of cannibal horror.[27] Instead, it aims to uncover some of the aesthetic issues that cannibalism in horror raises. Pursuing the pervasive but metaphorical evocation of cannibalism in Hitchcock, it looks both at the corpse as art and at the trope of "eating the body" in their connection to the undermining of metaphor that we call literalism. The second part of this chapter examines literal cannibalism by looking first at Hooper's *Texas Chainsaw Massacre*, both I (1974) and II (1986), in which cannibalism is a family affair and orality has its origins in Mum. Not surprisingly, Hitchcock's films are those most frequently alluded to by practitioners of horror: homage to Hitchcock is virtually de rigueur. Deeply indebted to Hitchcock, Hooper's films suggest disturbing parallels between sight and taste. These analogies are intensified and complicated by the proclivities of the literal cannibals who populate the final group of films under discussion, three films based on the Thomas Harris novels: Jonathan Demme's *Silence of the Lambs* (1991), Ridley Scott's *Hannibal* (2001), and Brett Ratner's *Red Dragon* (2003). In all of these examples of cannibalistic horror, the visual arts have a central and problematic role to play.

Hitchcock's Hunger:
Metaphorical Cannibals and Material Images

"It's called 'Hunger,' " says the sculptress in Hitchcock's *Rear Window* (1954) of her modernist yet curiously primitive piece. Featuring a cavernous hole in the middle of a torsolike rectangle of stone, her sculpture—reminiscent of a Henry Moore—has only the suggestion of a head. Here appetite is material, ungoverned by the mind. Largely unmentioned in the critical discourse on *Rear Window*, this sculpture as material image forms a counterweight to the song whose composition concludes with the end of Hitchcock's film. If it has become a commonplace to say that the fashioning of this song, "Lisa," underscores the process by which Lisa Fremont, the Grace Kelly character, has been rendered image—idealized, symbolized—for James Stewart's Jeff, it must be pointed out that in this film of desiring women, the sculpture with the gaping hole at its center participates in another project. Suggesting vacuities that cannot be filled, it gives shape to the appetites that "Mrs. Bates" in *Psycho* (1960) warns Marion not to sate "with my food and my son." At once abstract and primitive, the sculpture conveys a totemic quality, playing perhaps to the suggestions of cannibalism that occur at the intersection of dialogue with image in this film, as when, for instance, Stella's fascinated musings about cutting up women's bodies occur just as Jeff is cutting up his breakfast. *Rear Window* is far from being alone among Hitchcock's films in making such connections, of course. In the imagination of Daisy, the involuntary murderess of *Blackmail* (1929), the image of a knife conjoins a corpse with a loaf of bread. While eating a chicken leg, Jack Favell in *Rebecca* (1940) punningly comments on "fowl play" and suggests that he well knows what to do with old bones: "bury them." In keeping with its plot, *Lifeboat* (1944) is open about its suggestions of cannibalism. When, in *North by Northwest* (1949) Roger Thornhill is complimented by Eve on his "taste in women," his witty riposte is "I like *your* flavor." No matter the extent to which it is sublimated, in Hitchcock's films desire is expressed as a hunger for the body both as sexual object and as foodstuff.

The metaphorical deployment of cannibalism is pervasive in Hitchcock, and the linkages that it creates recall to mind Gombrich's contention that metaphors—especially synesthetic metaphors—should perhaps also be read as "indicators of linkages not yet broken," rather than as promoting the transfer of established meanings.[28] Cannibalism as a topic in Hitchcock is not entirely new: Tania Modleski has pointed to suggestions of cannibalism in *Frenzy* (1972), reading the film as an expression of extreme ambivalence toward women that originates in fear of the "devouring, voracious mother."[29] As argued by Modeski, woman in this film is variously connected with pollution, she is both edible commodity and inedible corpse and functions as the site of a male sexual inadequacy shared by murderer and detective alike. In fact, similar connections are made throughout Hitchcock's oeuvre, suggesting that this obsession may have something to say about representation in his films. What is indicated by the way Hitchcock figures these themes by collapsing the distinction between literal and figurative language, by means of a linguistic collapse that is underscored by the image? In *Frenzy*, the murders committed by Bob Rusk (a greengrocer still dominated by his Mum, for whom he was asked to peel grapes as a child) are framed by the eating of apples, an activity that suggests the consumption of the woman as it literalizes the metaphor—*the eating of the apple*—that we associate with man's Fall. Inspector Oxford's charming yet sadistic wife, enrolled in a gourmet cooking course, serves up body parts in elegant sauces and a *soupe de poisson* that might have been concocted by *MacBeth*'s witches, in which sea creatures seem still to be swimming about. Her husband, a steak-and-potatoes man, the film implies, is being "poissoned"; his wife's cooking is too "raw," the foodstuffs too incompletely transformed. While serving her concoctions, Mrs. Oxford enjoins her husband to find the murderer "before his appetite is whetted again," while she bites off pieces of a crunchy bread stick that has been verbally linked to the finger of a female corpse. In response, the inspector offhandedly remarks that "religion and sexual mania are closely linked," pointing, within the context of their meal, to a perverted form of communion. As Oxford's remark indicates, in *Frenzy* the spiritual collapses into the material realm of the flesh. The cannibalistic feast prepared by Mrs. Oxford—she herself partakes only of the breadstick—has no sacramental dimension. Although Hitchcock's Catholic upbringing no doubt creates a backdrop for these concerns, it does not fully explain the repeated references to eating the body.[30] Small wonder that Hitchcock chose no well-known actor for *Frenzy*—no body has the star's allure—for *Frenzy* is uncharacteristically direct and brutal, verging on the obscene. Bodies in *Frenzy* are reduced simply to material: when the sex murderer finishes off the apple that his victim had been eating, the allusion to Adam and Eve is negated and the human body equated with fruit. When, in *Psycho*, Norman Bates points out that Marion "eats like a bird," he stutters as he adds that this phrase contains "a falsity." Struggling to find the word "fallacy" (phallus-y?) in the presence of Marion, Norman exhibits an uneasy command of language. In his office, Norman and Marion are surrounded by the stuffed birds that literalize the slang expression of "stuffing birds," its sexual connotation rendered murderous. Chewing compulsively on candy corn throughout the film—and thereby linking his own body with that of the woman's or "bird's"—it is suggested that Norman is trapped in the oral stage, reluctant to sever the prelinguistic bond with the mother. With Lévi-Strauss, Julia Kristeva and others read dietary prohibitions as dependent upon prohibitions of incest: "Food is the oral object (the abject)," writes Kristeva, "that sets up archaic relationships between the human being and the other, its mother, who wields a power that is as vital as it is fierce."[31] In *Psycho*, Norman exhibits a desire for fusion with Mother in its psychotic form, containing within himself both Norman and Mother—in what Raymond Bellour refers to as the "incorporation of a metaphor-become-reality"[32]—until the final scene in which Mother triumphs over her son. Much has been written on this topic, and I will not repeat it here.[33] Suffice it to say that Norman's medium is the body—his hobby is stuffing things, such as the birds with whom his victim Marion is linked. This macabre "artist's" efforts at taxidermy include the body of his mother, in yet another appalling literalization. When "Mummy" becomes "mummy," Norman's psychotic production—the mummy as corpse and sculpture—*is* the thing it represents. But while the final abode of the actual mummy is the fruit cellar, Mother's voice and will reside within Norman's body. When, in the ultimate merger in which Norman is wholly subsumed by Mother—cannibalized by her, as Robin Wood puts it[34]—her voice speaks Norman's concern not to be thought "fruity," the (literalized) metaphor which motivated her placement in the fruit cellar is laid bare.

Suggesting a collapse of corpse and sculpture similar to that in *Psycho*, Roger Thornhill remarks to Van Damm, the villain in *North by Northwest*: "I didn't know you were an art collector. I thought you just collected corpses." From Norman's horrifying literalization to the tongue-in-cheek witticisms of Thornhill, there is also a broad spectrum of reference in Hitchcock's films that conflate the corpse with art, and I have suggested some of these in Chapters 4 and 5. Wit—and we might add, humor—in Hitchcock's work, provides the inner life, as George Toles puts it, "with a means of guarding itself absolutely in the very act of unveiling."[35] To illustrate Toles's seeming oxymoron, we might look to one of Hitchcock's dark comedies, *The Trouble With Harry* (1955), a more benign predecessor of *Frenzy* that simultaneously unveils, covers over, and connects the corpse with art and food. The signifying chain that links them is both on the surface and circuitous: connected by the theme of preservation, fruit, the female body, the male corpse, and visual representation are here conjoined. The artist Sam Marlowe's paintings—among them semi-abstract still lifes and landscapes, as well as a Modigliani-like female portrait—are for sale alongside jugs of cider at a farm stand. Sam barters his paintings for groceries, thus reinforcing the connection between works of art and fruit. Another term enters this relation: here, too, women are repeatedly connected

Images of Horror: Taste, Cannabalism, and Visual Display 169

with fruit as nourishment and temptation, offering men lemonade, blueberry muffins, and elderberry wine. Once again the allusion is to Eve's offer of the apple, of course, but the connection runs deeper: when the captain refers to Miss Gravely as "preserves that have to be opened some day," preserved fruit and the female corpse (grave-ly) are equated. Like Miss Gravely, the autumnal landscape is overripe—it is as though the blood of Harry's corpse had somehow stained the leaves of the sugar maples crimson.[36] While sketching in the woods, Sam comes across the body and makes a pastel of it, commemorating the (dead) face in a portrait. And when Mrs. Rogers suggests ironically that her husband's corpse should be "stuffed and put in a glass case," his body is once again rendered an objet d'art. There are many displacements here, of course: the corpse is not that of a mother, but that of a father by law. But the film takes care to point out that another father, Mr. Gravely, has been killed by a harvester, "harvested," that is, by a mechanical Grim Reaper that treats him as a food crop. As Lesley Brill points out, Harry's body, too, is repeatedly "planted and harvested."[37] Harry is connected, then, with Mother Nature's seasonal cycle. He is further feminized by being a man whose wife, in the parlance of the film, "didn't let him in."

In *The Trouble with Harry*, the corpse seems indeed to be Zizek's Hitchcockian blot, the "remainder of the real," the detail that "does not fit," that "sticks out" from the idyllic surface scene and denatures it, rendering it uncanny.[38] As Zizek notes elsewhere, the cool detachment—if not to say disregard—with which the characters treat Harry's corpse in their midst reveals the neutralization of this traumatic experience.[39] In Zizek's reading, the characters ignore the corpse because they cannot come to terms with the real—Harry's body must be recovered within the realm of the symbolic before its death can be acknowledged. And his body's representation in art has a similar effect when Harry's corpse is first casually sketched by Sam, who records it as part of the natural scene that he has chosen to depict. Later, Harry's "death's head" will be portraitized, covered over by representation, just as the corpse must finally be acknowledged in the rituals of a conventional burial. Consequently, during a verbal parody of psychoanalytically tinged art criticism performed for the deputy, Sam verbally transforms the portrait—now potentially evidence of a murder—into that of a sleeper rather than a dead man.

In simultaneously retouching the portrait and performing a verbal sleight of hand in which obfuscation masks exposure, the artist disposes of the corpse by symbolizing it, covering it over with words and embellishing it with lines. But for the film's spectators, Harry's corpse already exists in the symbolic—and not only because we see it in the images of a film. The many shots of his foreshortened body, complete with feet "sticking out" (to use Zizek's term) that is, with the feet in close-up rather than the head—are far from suggesting the "artless bluntness" attributed to them by Brill.[40] They are "artful" indeed, doubly situated within the symbolic: this is the famous angle from which Mantegna painted his dead Christ. But there is another twist in our reading, another irony that needs mentioning here: historically, Mantegna's rendering is considered transgressive because it represents Christ too realistically, as a corpse, not as a divine body soon to rise from the dead. There is also no hint of resurrection here. In *The Trouble With Harry,* Harry's unburied and artful corpse, feet "sticking out" like those of Mantegna's Christ, his corpse as blot, as a remainder of the real—is the final image of the film. In this image, the real of the corpse and artful allusion humorously co-exist.

One body must be laid to rest, another must be brought to life. As the Captain puts it, Miss Gravely is a well-preserved woman as well as a jar of preserves to be tasted, but Miss "Gravely" is also in some sense dead. A Galatea in a minor key, she is revivified or "renovated," as Marlowe puts it, brought to life by the artist as Pygmalion. This artist cuts her hair and does her makeup: like the mortician's, his art is performed directly upon her body. When later she enters the Captain's house, Miss Gravely will encounter another Galatea there: a large figurehead from the captain's ship, a "fine figure of a woman" with prominent breasts and a red dress. The Pygmalion-Galatea relation of *Vertigo* (1958), although comical and in a minor key, is fleshed out in this sequence: since the "painted" Miss Gravely is raised from the dead, she is the statue (figurehead) come to life. Like the statue, she is also sexualized. A benign version of the painted or scarlet woman, Miss Gravely literally wears her metaphorical red dress; presumably the preserves the Captain has in mind are cherry—or strawberry. This marterialist film consigns the woman to the world of objects; once again she is multiply figured as food, corpse, and sculpture.

When Marlowe decides finally to barter his paintings (now headed for the Modern Museum), he will receive in exchange two boxes of strawberries each month for Mrs. Rogers. For himself—to be shared with her—he requests a double bed. By rejecting money—a symbolic means of exchange—and continuing to act within the economic system of barter, Marlowe maintains the careful system of equivalences that Hitchcock has set up in this film, a system in which paintings are perceived as objects just as jars of preserves or human bodies are—both living and dead. Remaining within this

Images of Horror: Taste, Cannabalism, and Visual Display 171

materialist system of equivalences, Marlowe as artist may very well create modernist images, but his paintings are nevertheless realist in a thoroughgoing way. Although his art is not the psychotic art of a Norman, clearly, who preserves the body in another—and more horrifying—manner, Marlowe paints upon women's bodies as willingly as he represents the world around him on canvas. For Marlowe as materialist artist the thing and its representation appear to be of equal value, and this frame of mind is shared by nearly all of the characters who inhabit this New England village. It is only the outsiders—such as the "millionaire" and the art critic he brings along with him—who operate within a more symbolic system. Finally, I would argue, it is by virtue of their relentless materialism that the characters who populate Hitchcock's comedy appear not to feel anything when they all literally stumble upon Harry's corpse. Although it may be that—in Zizek's words—their attitude reflects a "neutralization of an underlying traumatic complex,"[41] there is actually nothing in this comedy to suggest trauma at all. What in fact seems apparent is that most of the characters in *The Trouble with Harry* act within a system in which—for a while, at any rate—a corpse and a rock shockingly share the same significance in the landscape. In an inversion typical of Hitchcock, the doctor of the village, a devoted reader of poetry, is the exception. For him, figurative language offers a respite from the materialism to which his profession consigns him.

We will conclude with a reading of *Rope* (1948), where metaphorical cannibalism is once again present and where the final substitution is only seemingly in favor of representation, of the figurative rather than literal. For Brandon, one of the murderers, the crime he commits is "a work of art, a masterpiece," his techniques enacted directly upon the flesh. In fact, Brandon's remark alludes to one of Hitchcock's favorite essays, Thomas de Quincey's "Murder as One of the Fine Arts," whose title Hitchcock quotes in his address to the Film Society of Lincoln Center in 1974, adding that "the best way to do it is with scissors."[42] Hitchcock's punning is understood to encompass both a literal meaning and a reference to cutting, or film editing practices. In *Rope*, cutting—the technique by which Hitchcock famously produces suspense—is kept to a minimum. There are cuts in *Rope*, but those that occur are necessitated by the technology of 1948 and half of these are masked, nearly invisible, thus enhancing the sense of real time conveyed by this film.[43] Indeed, technique in *Rope* seems in more than one respect to be in the service of a seemingly gratuitous realism. In his interview with Hitchcock concerning *Rope*, Truffaut refers to what he calls the "painstaking quest for realism" in its mise-en-scène.⁴⁴ Although *Rope* is theatrical—very much a chamber play—Hitchcock claims to have created its New York City setting by using a "magical . . . cyclorama with an exact miniature reproduction of 35 miles of New York skyline lighted by 8,000 incandescent bulbs and 200 neon signs."⁴⁵ More than one critic has wondered how on earth this could have been effected. The quest for an excessive, seemingly pointless realism is frequently a topic apropos of the set of *Rear Window* as well, for which Hitchcock made the claim that twelve of the apartments represented here—many of which the camera never penetrates—were nevertheless completely furnished.⁴⁶ Supplementing "the art of murder" as an art of technique, then, is the suggestion of a belief in the "magic" of mimetic accuracy, as though this attention to detail in and of itself—despite its unavailability to the eye—could magically impart something of the real to the body of the film.

In *Rope*, Hitchcock's Catholic upbringing is again in evidence, taking the form of a rebellion against convention, an undermining of the Eucharist's symbolic value. *Rope*'s narrative concerns a dinner party that covertly celebrates a murder. At the film's beginning, David Kentley is strangled with a rope by his two friends, Brandon and Philip, who place his body into a trunk from which they serve dinner to the dead man's father—a book collector—as well as to his aunt, his fiancée, and his former teacher Rupert. Ostensibly, the group has been invited so that Mr. Kentley may examine some rare books acquired by the two murderers. Here, clearly, is a sacrificial meal, albeit a deeply grotesque one, served upon the casket of a dead man, now become an altar of sorts with the addition of candelabra, lace cloth, and beautiful vessels. Inside the trunk is the corpse—the real—while on its surface we find the prepared dishes that substitute for it. Brandon and David are serving chicken, concerning which an anecdote is told that connects chicken both to the human body and to sexual practices. As in *Frenzy*, in this earlier film, too, Christianity, sexuality, and killing are linked, this time by means of a story told about Philip's "strangling the chicken" to the sound of Sunday church bells. Various forms of transgression—including cannibalism—are implied when, during the telling of this tale, one dinner guest—Mrs. Atwater, David's aunt—gives up the effort to guide her fork to her mouth. Once again figurative language—"strangling the chicken"—a slang term for male masturbation, is literalized in the anecdote (which doesn't acknowledge the slang expression—the idea is that Philip has actually strangled a chicken), as well as in the dish being consumed by the party guests. Placed over the hidden human body, the platter of chicken is visually, metonymically, connected to the corpse, which is then consumed as chicken.

Both word and image suggest a sexual—thus also material—relationship among Brandon, Philip, and the dead David.[47]

If the formal trappings of the dinner—the candelabra and lace cloth—turn trunk into altar, the consumption of chicken hardly promotes transubstantiation even if, once the dinner is cleared from the trunk, it is replaced by rare books—even if the body is covered by the word. These books are grotesquely tied together with the piece of rope that has strangled the rare book collector's son: the instrument of death links written text with corpse. Although they contain the word, the books also replace the chicken that has already stood in for the corpse, suggesting not that the flesh has become word, but rather, I suggest, that a literal language takes the place of the body. A book collector (Mr. Kentley) and a teacher turned publisher (Rupert Caddell, the James Stewart character) are the two "fathers" of this film, and both are connected with language and textuality. In the perverse version of communion orchestrated by Brandon, the body of the son is transformed into words when the rare books substituted for his body are given to his father. But this is far from being a symbolic transformation. The film's title almost certainly refers to "the 'rope' connecting 'words' and 'acts,'" as Zizek suggests, to the "cutting of the rope through which we achieve symbolic distance to reality"—a process which does not fully take place in this film.[48] Critics have repeatedly pointed out that the murder was committed precisely because Brandon, Rupert's former student, has taken his Nietzschean teachings concerning the right to kill *literally* or—to recur to Zizek's formulation—that for Brandon the symbolic "rope" connecting words and acts has not been severed. Here body, chicken, and language remain deeply connected. But the fact that the written word finally replaces the corpse does not mean that *Rope* embraces metaphor and the spirit: it merely means that language itself has been rendered literal or material—has produced a corpse, is one with it, and therefore is like the corpse in being material. Perhaps it is for *this* reason—because a literal language ultimately substitutes for the body—that the film's spectator is never allowed a glimpse of the trunk's contents when it is finally opened. It is the metonymic rope established by the film that links the body and the word, demystifying metaphor as symbolic. It will have become apparent that Peter Greenaway's *The Cook, The Thief, His Wife and Her Lover* (1990) is the direct offspring of *Rope*.[49]

The precarious relation between the word and its referent is marked more than once in this film, as when, on a more comic note, Mrs. Atwater tries repeatedly to remember the titles of films that she has recently seen: "He was thrilling in that new thing of Bergman's . . . what was it called now? The something of the something. No, no, that was the other one. This was just plain something." Surely the title that Mrs. Atwater can't summon to mind is Hitchcock's own *Notorious* (1946), and while her vague signifiers and missing words can't conjure up the title of Hitchcock's film for its characters, they do succeed in evoking it for its spectators. Mrs. Atwater's empty "somethings" don't only bring *Notorious* to mind. and Hitchcock himself is conjured up by words that do—but in some sense don't—miss their mark.[50] A recurrent image of writing in this film also gestures toward a complex relation between the word and its referent: although it has often been suggested that the blinking neon sign outside the window of Brandon's apartment reads "storage," the flashing "s" and the other letters we glimpse through the window never come together in a word. Even if the flashing letters were to come together to form "storage," the word would point ironically to the body at the center of the film. And while mystery resides in the broken letters, their periodic, rhythmic flashing marks duration, the real time in which this film takes place. Film is indeed writing in light, Hitchcock suggests here, but once again it is the "literal," visceral effect that seems to interest him more: the periodic pulsing of the letters works directly on the body of the spectator to produce a perceptual "realism" that assaults the sensorium. Once again, then, the material body serves to destabilize language.

What impulse underlies the various instances of what we have been calling a realist—or materialist—tendency in Hitchcock's films? We considered this issue from another perspective in Chapter 4, Part Two, where the figured permeability between real world and screen images is read against the backdrop of Michael Fried's writings on art. In taking a materialist position in *The Trouble with Harry*, however, Hitchcock experiments with a different point of departure, one that equates people with things, one in which the affects that normally attach to persons are suppressed or wholly missing. In *Rope*, as we have seen, literalism and lack of affect have deadly consequences. And what of the other extreme instances of what we are calling materialism, those that in *Frenzy* or *Psycho* take a horrifying, psychotic form? In accounting for them, a macabre anecdote involving Tippi Hedren leads us in another direction. According to Donald Spoto, the story goes as follows: While Hedren was rehearsing for her role in *The Birds*, Hitchcock had a life mask made of her face "and for a long time jealously guarded her delicate features, captured forever in perfect repose."[51] The actress thought nothing of it at the time, Spoto suggests, but it became clear what one purpose of the life mask

Images of Horror: Taste, Cannabalism, and Visual Display 175

had been when Hitchcock presented Hedren's young daughter, Melanie, with a pine box shaped like a casket. When Melanie opened this box—at the dinner table, the anecdote goes—she found a doll lying in it that was an exact replica of her mother in her role in *The Birds*, with Hedren's features modeled as precisely as on the life mask itself.

In presenting Melanie with an effigy of her mother's film image, doll, and corpse, Hitchcock does not appear to have had a consciously sinister motive. One can imagine the reaction of the little girl, however, at seeing this replica of her mother. In some sense, however, in making this presentation Hitchcock seems to have been identifying with the child, who could exercise a control over the replica not permitted by the living person. And how like the "representation compulsion," the mimetic drive of Goethe's collector mentioned in the Introduction to this book—how very like the collector whose urge is to surround himself with precise representations of the real. After commissioning realist paintings of objects, then portraits of his family surrounded by these objects, this collector commissions trompe l'oeil paintings and finally hyperrealist sculptures, ever pushing at the boundary that divides life from art. In pursuing his obsession, the collector's perverse goal is an ever-greater degree of realism, approaching life itself. It is Pygmalion's goal—and so often Hitchcock's. Here, however, something slightly different may be at issue. At one level, the Hedren doll is the product of an obsessive mimetic impulse: in modeling Hedren's features on a life mask, Hitchcock goes as far as possible in the direction of perfect mimesis, collapsing as far as it is possible to collapse the distance between sign and thing. As a contact image, the life mask closely approaches the status of *acheiropoetoi*, images not made by human hands. The contact image par excellence is the Veil of Veronica, on which Christ's features are said to have been perfectly recorded when he used it to wipe his face. Traditionally, then, the Veil of Veronica is the true image—the vera icon—the perfect match between image and model, sign and thing.[52] Once again, Christian iconography is in play and de-sacralized. By way of the life mask, Hitchcock records Hedren's face at the moment of its imprinting, creating an indexical image, like the photograph. A Pygmalion in reverse here, Hitchcock captures Hedren in an act of perfect mimesis, both "killing her off" and preserving her as material image and effigy. Surely *Psycho*'s Norman is not far to seek in this scenario, the son who rendered his Mummy both corpse and sculpture, psychotically collapsing sign and thing. Hitchcock's appetite for representational strategies that literalize metaphor, that collapse the distinctions between word and referent, art and the body, corpse and food (impure and pure), is precariously close to that of the psychotic, to whom such distinctions are unavailable.

Literal Cannibalism: Psychotic Appetites and Representation

Taste—and distaste—have a central role to play in horror involving cannibalism. Because horror is in all senses a limit case of taste, it is not surprising that, as Julia Kristeva and others have argued, one of the central affects attached to the experience of horror is disgust.[53] Spectatorial disgust is deliberately intensified in cannibalistic horror, which strives to evoke nausea, its physiological aspect. As one of the affective operators behind such basic taboos as cannibalism and incest, for Freud disgust motivates humankind's entry into culture. In the horror film, the taboos against cannibalism and incest are often featured in tandem and jointly undermined: cannibalism, as Lévi-Strauss has put it, is the "alimentary form of incest."[54] The superego takes shape at the moment the sons of the primal horde experience guilt at the killing and eating of the father, Freud famously suggests in *Totem and Taboo*. But in the psychotic cannibals with whom we are concerned, the superego is missing. In these instances of cannibalism, symbolic transactions between self and other are recast in the register of literal taste: communication is eating. Once the ingestion of the other has taken place, for the cannibal the despised gap between subject and object collapses.[55]

With disgust—dégoût—the literal and figurative meanings of "goût" or taste are violently brought together. We noted above that pre-Kantian aestheticians such as Lessing categorized disgust as a response to the ugly. As Winfried Menninghaus has pointed out, disgust has been the Other of aesthetic pleasure since the middle of the eighteenth century.[56] But while disgust may be the opposite of aesthetic *pleasure*, it is nevertheless a response to aesthetic experience. It is only with Kant, says Menninghaus, that disgust as a response separates the real from the imagined: if something disgusts the spectator—if the body is involved—for Kant it is experienced as real—not as art. The aesthetic field thus excludes the subject, or, as Joan Copjec puts it, "Kant thus made the beautiful the signifier of a limit, a barrier against the real."[57] With respect to film, to which an embodied spectator is integral, Kant's distinction is necessarily called into question. For the variety of reasons that this book has suggested, the border between the represented and the real is often deliberately blurred in film, and the nature and intensity of spectatorial response

Images of Horror: Taste, Cannabalism, and Visual Display   177

plays a part in this blurring. By way of horror's intensification of affect—particularly of disgust—spectators find themselves at a liminal point between the represented and the reality of their response, a point at which the two are merged in experience. In the films under review, the collapse of the real and the represented is reified in the psychotic "works of art," in the tableaux and artifacts with which the cannibals of horror surround themselves. Literalists par excellence, like Norman Bates these cannibals psychotically collapse the figurative into the literal—such as when an armchair in *Texas Chainsaw Massacre* is just that, a chair made of human arms. Launched by the descriptions of the historical Ed Gein's practices in Robert Bloch's novel *Psycho*,[58] visual display and psychotic tableaux in the *Texas Chainsaw Massacre* films (1974, 1986) and in the films based on the Thomas Harris novels always exceed their origins in the Gein case. From a representational standpoint, the material images that accompany cannibal horror blur the boundaries between art and the real in the manner of trompe l'oeil painting and of waxworks. Using the materials of the human body, these works are the products of psychosis.

As will become evident in the reading to follow, Hooper's *Texas Chainsaw Massacre* is a perverse film, a film of abjection. Although the film is often screened at film festivals and resides in the Museum of Modern Art's permanent collection, the extreme ambivalence spectators express about it is widespread and unsurprising. For Robin Wood, Hooper's film "achieves the force of authentic art, profoundly disturbing, intensely personal" even as it "brings to a focus a spirit of negativity" and an "undifferentiated lust for destruction."[59] Janet Staiger, calling herself a "perverted reader," feels compelled to justify her interest in its "sado-masochistic fantasies" by way of its indebtedness to *Psycho*,[60] and both Staiger and Wood distance themselves from their strong reactions by reading the film as a comedy.[61] Although *Texas Chainsaw Massacre* is indeed "over the top," eliciting a disbelief that may lead its spectators to find refuge in laughter, that is not the film's objective. The utter degradation of the human body as material is at its center. One might easily seek the reasons for this preoccupation in, say, the psychosexual dispositions of Hooper and the other young people who made the film,[62] or one might ascribe its attitude toward the body to the problems—familial, ideological, economic—manifest in American society of the 1970s.[63] There is textual evidence to support both of these approaches. No special dispensation should be required to take Hooper's films seriously, then, and Carol Clover's fine work has notably paved the way.[64] A high degree of filmic self-consciousness in the production of *Texas Chainsaw Massacre* can be assumed:

as former graduate students in the drama and film departments of the University of Texas and as art students at Rice, the participants in this low-budget Indie film were schooled in matters of genre and plotting, interested in all aspects of mise en-scène and sound, as well as in cinéma verité.[65] Why my disclaimers, then? The ensuing description should make that abundantly clear.

The film opens with a black frame, followed by a series of flashes. Flash after flash lights up body parts in close-up, with the spectator—typically in horror films—sharing the point of view of the camera. After we have seen them at night, fragmented in photographic close-up, the film camera pulls up in daylight to reveal two decayed cadavers in tableau, arranged in sodomitic sculptural display atop a phallic grave monument. This "sculpture" is produced by Hitchhiker, a feeble-minded member of the cannibal family of this film, and we can't miss the reference to Hitchcock in his name. Hitchhiker as grave robber may or may not eat of the graves' contents, but he certainly makes a sculpture of them, in this case a synthetic, pornographic work whose separate parts—a hand, a head—he first records with his Polaroid. (Both his camera's sound and the flashes of light that separate the images we see illuminated by its flash attachment connect this opening sequence filmically with the famous scene in *Rear Window* in which Jeff uses his flash attachment to defend himself.) It is with loathing and disgust that we learn with whom we have looked through the lens of the camera.[66] Given to self-mutilation as well as to gratuitous acts of cruelty, Hitchhiker lives with an older brother—a cook who produces and sells barbecue made of human bodies. He also has a younger brother, Leatherface, who wears masks of human skin to replace his missing features. It is Leatherface, the cross-dressing butcher (one of his masks is called "Pretty Woman") who wields the chainsaw of the title. The most deeply regressive of the brothers, he cannot speak, communicating only by way of grunts and the phallic instrument of his aggression. Rounding out the family is Grandma—a mummy in the mode of Mrs. Bates—and Granddaddy, almost a sculpture, kept barely alive on a "liquid diet" of drops of blood. Their dwelling place is furnished with trophies from the dead, with ornamental still lifes and decorative mobiles made of bones. And, we should add, with lamps made of bone and human skin in a chilling and even more deeply transgressive allusion to Buchenwald. It would seem that Hitchhiker is the artisan who produced these *objets*—literal body art—just as he has produced fetishistic snapshots as trophies of the body parts he digs up.

The eye that most notably views Hitchhiker and his brothers—Clover's "eye of horror"[67]—belongs to Sally, one of the young people who enter a deserted family house to become the victims of the cannibal family who lives nearby. Depicted in a montage of almost unbearably extreme close-ups, the eye is rendered as tissue laced with blood vessels, as an organ of vision rather than as the window on the soul. The moans and screams of cattle that accompany this montage mark it as yet another homage to Buñuel's *Un Chien Andalou* (1930) and its representation of a razor cutting the eye. Like the cattle of the nearby slaughterhouse, Sally is readied for the kill. Ruthlessly attacked by the cannibal family, the young people of Hooper's film are hung from meat hooks, butchered, served up for dinner—and, in the case of Sally, the "final girl" who will survive—chased indefatigably with a chainsaw. Sally endures a series of harrowing encounters during which she is also made to assume the "maternal" position in the family, feeding Granddaddy with blood from her finger: the film's investment in cruel orality is not far to seek, and has a number of permutations. As tales from the film's reception history make clear, spectators of *Texas Chainsaw Massacre* were physically affected by what they saw, with vomiting in the movie theater a common occurrence.[68] Although the sadistic torture of Sally and the relentless screaming that attests to it no doubt occasioned fear and screams in the spectator as well, it is the disgust generated by the blood and guts that mark the family's cannibalism and by the film's "body art" that makes *Texas Chainsaw Massacre* a prime example of what has been called *cinéma vomitif*.[69] Boundaries are crossed here that are not normally crossed. Cannibalizing Hitchcock, Hooper's films everywhere suggest the coextensiveness of vision, touch, and taste and—for their more imaginative spectators—Bal's "putrifying smell" is no doubt present, as well.

The film students involved in the film's production had done their homework. Hitchhiker's cadaver sculptures trope the idea of literalness in art: we are reminded of the mummy in *Psycho* and, in a minor key, of the relation of Miss Gravely to the figurehead in *The Trouble with Harry*. With the help of his Polaroid, Hitchhiker produces horrific photographs without a negative—and hence fetishistic objects that are at once image and thing. Like Hitchcock, Hitchhiker sells his images for profit and, just as his brother's barbecue collapses the eater with the eaten, Hitchhiker's abject "art" is inadequately symbolized. By burning a Polaroid photo of Sally's brother, for example, Hitchhiker communicates his desire to do the same to its model—he does not see a difference between the boy and his image. In Hitchhiker's brother the cook, we likewise see an intensified figuration of Hitchcock, in whose films food is so often tainted by its figured juxtaposition with the body. Also resembling Hitchcock in this, the third brother, Leatherface, "cuts" and fragments the human body—not photographically, however, but literally. The aproned Leatherface is faceless, undefined, fixed within a prelinguistic orality that precedes all binarisms. For him, communication with the other takes place primarily through consumption. Arguably, oral-stage fixation is responsible for the general collapse of binarisms here, as evidenced in the film's cannibalism, its reference to cross-dressing (Leatherface) and homosexuality (Hitchhiker's sculpture), in the blurred boundary between life and death embodied by Granddaddy—and perhaps even in the typical conflation of character and spectator in point-of-view shots. This is the terrain of Kristeva's abject with its fragile boundaries: here is the place where meaning collapses—a collapse reified in the merger of representation with the real that characterizes "cannibal art."

At the end of the film, having implausibly outrun Leatherface, the film's heroine Sally encounters a red cattle truck called "Black Maria." This truck is seen hurtling by at breakneck speed in an earlier scene, putting Sally and her friends in danger. Now its driver stops to help the desperate Sally, although the cattle truck is not ultimately her means of escape. What can this reference to Edison's "Black Maria" mean? Is it merely a homage to Edison, a reminder to us that what we have experienced is "just a film?" Sally does *not* escape in the truck called Black Maria—in Edison's box in which moving images are both produced and screened—her body does not in some sense become an image. In refusing to promote Sally's incorporation by the "Black Maria," the film refuses to extend the figured collapse of the real with representation that characterizes Hitchhiker's art to its own filmic image. The "Black Maria" as cattle truck carries animals to the slaughterhouse, and Sally's companions have been slaughtered like cattle by the cannibal family, it is true. But Sally's body, it is metaphorically suggested in this scene, must not enter the cinema machine at the level of the real. *The Texas Chainsaw Massacre*'s images, the film proclaims, are *not* "cannibal art." Or are they? Because the driver of the truck is African American, "Black Maria" suggests not only the name of the truck, but may also be the name of this black man. Once again words do not completely hit their mark.

Hooper's sequel to this film, *Texas Chainsaw Massacre II*, likewise takes up the figured merger of representation with the real. Here tableaux that support cultural fantasies are in the form of gigantic cowboy figures in a "Texas Battleland" theme park, images that support a degraded mythical history. In their psychotic form, tableaux as the props for fantasy exist in the subter-

Images of Horror: Taste, Cannabalism, and Visual Display 181

ranean "house of horrors" below the theme park, a space the cannibal family shares with skeleton sculptures seated in armchairs. In this film, the cannibals' home is a series of underground rooms and tunnels recalling both ancient catacombs and Gothic houses modeled on the body. In a particularly grotesque example of "cannibal art," blood and guts pour out of the mouth of a portraitized head on one of the murals that decorates an entire wall. Not only is the continuity of the real with representation emphasized by these means, but this image expresses visually the response that it hopes to evoke in its spectator, suggesting a disgust so strong that it is eviscerating. When Lefty, the Dennis Hopper character, comes to avenge the murder of his nephew (in *Texas Chainsaw Massacre I*), he puts his fist through the mural and is deluged by a veritable flood of the same substances. Stressing the continuity of looking and touching featured in horror films, this moment promotes a tactile encounter with viscera that the spectator experiences viscerally. More importantly, representation in the form of the mural collapses in upon itself: it is revealed simply to be a "curtain" that doesn't quite contain the real. This attitude is both the reverse of—as well as essentially identical to—the situation suggested in Hitchcock's direction for the shower scene in *Psycho* to the effect that Norman's knife should slash through the shower curtain "as if tearing at the very film, ripping the screen."[70]

In Hooper's sequel, the chambers of the subterranean house *are* the interior of a body, complete with blood vessels and intestines. It is the mother's body, in which the cannibal family is entombed in an intrauterine existence. When Stretch, the feisty heroine of *Texas Chainsaw Massacre II*, finally escapes two of the brothers and climbs out of their corporeal retreat, she makes her way to a tower chamber atop the theme park's fort, chased by Hitchhiker (called Chop Top in the sequel) to music eerily reminiscent of *Vertigo*. As suggested in Chapters 4 and 5, in Hitchcock's film male myths about women are usually expressed by means of the Pygmalion theme, often involving the animation of a statue. In Hooper's film, it is intimated that Mother may have met her end—is both rendered inanimate and contained in a tableau—so that she may live on in myth. Making her way toward the top of the tower in Hooper's film, Stretch the heroine discovers a shrine to the mother—she is Big Mama in the film's parlance—containing her mummified body covered over in spiderwebs and silvery hair, complete with huge, pendulous breasts. In death, the ancestress of the cannibal family becomes a devotional mummy-statue, an inversion of the Virgin Mary, her breasts a reminder of a different kind of communion, a literal eating of the body. Enthroned and illuminated, she is surrounded by candelabra, skeleton angel "sculptures," and "putti" mobiles made of skulls, works of art that do double duty as cultic objects and saints' relics. In this film's transgressive plot, the shrine and its sculpture function ambiguously: the tableau represented here overtly speaks of death.[71] Yet the shrine is also a work of commemoration produced by the "artist" of horror, Hitchhiker/Chop Top. He has been able to escape the family's corporeal residence—the mythic mother's subterranean "body"—long enough to create a sanctuary for Big Mama's real body. But placing the mummy/sculpture in its enthroned position is only partially an act of separation, for the commemorative statue is not separable from its model. It is identical with itself, its grotesque literalism only partly relativized by its ornamentation. As a (perverted, inverted) "religious" image, the mother's body as sculpture invites participation rather than mere spectatorship from her sons: Mother as icon becomes "part of a process, is treated like a doll, as the principal of a cast of dramatis personae in an unfolding game of make-believe."[72] Participation also takes the form of the literalism that is cannibalism—it takes the form of the cannibal meal.

Games of make believe and their tableaux also proliferate among the psychotic cannibals featured in the novels of Thomas Harris and the films based upon them, each film taking its own attitude toward the role played by nonfilmic visual representations in the novels.[73] Like *Psycho* and the *Texas Chainsaw Massacre* films, Harris's novels draw on the Ed Gein case, with the last novel, *Hannibal*, (1999) taking another real-life cannibal into account—Jeffrey Dahmer, whose crimes came to light in 1991. As examples of mainstream horror featuring well-known actors, the Lecter films could be expected to produce high box office returns, so it is not wholly surprising that well-known directors took on these projects. Michael Mann's *Manhunter* (1986, based on Harris's *Red Dragon*, 1981, the first of his cannibal novels), is the least involved with the tableaux in which transactions between the real and representation are enacted, and I will only briefly touch on it. Indeed, I'd like to suggest that its cool, detached modernist style goes out of its way to preserve the film image from a (figured) collapse with the real—that it resists an infection by horror at the level of filmic style. Mann's film, in other words, may deliberately protect itself from literalism, from "material images." At the level of style it represses affinities expressed in its plot, affinities such as those that make the detective of *Manhunter* an intuitive analyst of psychotic murderers. Demme's *The Silence of the Lambs* (1991) is the first of the films to give the Hannibal Lecter character—so memorably embodied here by Anthony Hopkins—a more prominent role. In the films by Demme and Ridley Scott (*Hannibal*, 2001), Lecter as aesthete, artist, psychiatrist, and cannibal is a disturbingly seductive counterpart to the more overtly psychotic cannibal whom he helps to capture. Ratner's film (*Red Dragon*, 2003), based like *Manhunter* on the first Harris novel, is the last of the films to appear. It adheres most closely to its literary model, finding its occasion not only in the audience demand for another Hopkins appearance as Lecter, but also in the representational possibilities that Michael Mann deliberately chose to downplay.

Following Harris's novel, Demme's film stresses Hannibal Lector's hypersensuality and his refined taste in all things save one—the taste for human flesh that locates him outside culture. Lecter's olfactory sense is as acute as that of an animal, allowing him to detect the Evian skin cream Clarice Starling—fledgling FBI agent—is wearing along with the traces of L'Air du Temps she applied several days before. Hearing is intensified in Lecter as well: its aesthetic manifestation is in his connoisseurship of classical music—he favors Bach—and in his own musical performances. A practitioner also of the visual arts, Lecter's remarkable visual memory enables him painstakingly to recreate Florence's Duomo as seen from the Belvedere. But in some sense his memory is so detailed and so accurate because it is photographic, simply recorded by the eye and transmitted to the hand unprocessed. Tacked up on the wall, the cityscape of Florence *is* Lecter's window on the world, his beautiful view—his belvedere. Not surprisingly, in Lecter the ritual aspects of cannibalism are expressed in gourmet practices—recall the famous fava beans and Chianti, for instance, that accompany his meal of human body parts. Like all cannibals, however, Lecter is ever the literalist: when he speaks of having an old friend for dinner, we can take him at his word.

Too literal also are Lecter's artistic practices. Again works of art are sites of psychotic expression, producing synesthetic effects that promote the simulation of embodiment. After drawing Clarice in Renaissance robes holding the lamb that provides the clue to her psychological fragility, Lecter requests a meal of extra rare lamb chops. Lecter's associative processes here are at once complexly figurative and simply literal. Metaphorically a wounded lamb, Clarice herself is materialized in the lamb chops and Lecter materializes his pencil drawing of Clarice by way of the lamb chops he orders. But Lecter's drawing also depicts Clarice as the Madonna figure who holds the lamb of God in her arms. The connections that promote the collapse of the sketch with the chops are several, then, including references to Christ as the Paschal Lamb held by his Virgin Mother—here Clarice. Further, the film suggests that the drawing also refers to Lecter himself as the "lamb of God," as Christ. It is precisely this multiplicity of associations, it is implied, that may have lead to Lecter's confusion of communion with cannibalism.[74] It is as a material token of a perverse love feast that Lecter orders his meal. That such confusion is intimately connected to the maternal breast and a fixation at the oral stage is likewise implied by Demme's film when it includes a conversation—not present in Harris's novel—in which Lecter asks a mother whose daughter has been kidnapped whether she will feel pain in her nipples when the child she has breast-fed is dead. Linking feeding with pain that is not simply emotional but physical, Lecter's question serves as an instrument of his sadism. It posits a sense of connection between mother and child so deep that it is experienced as bodily sensation, linking the two at the neuronal level. The lamb chops of Lecter's drawing materialize both mother *and* child, Clarice and Lecter.

Not surprisingly, then, it is the meal of rare lamb chops that signals the cataclysmic violence of the escape that follows. In this scene Demme again significantly diverges from Harris's novel, in which the sculptural tableau that theatricalizes the murder scene in the film does not exist. In Demme's film, the synesthetic effects of theater preside over the perverse tableau in which Lecter arranges human material, with Bach's Goldberg Variations functioning as background music. Here the murder scene as tableau is a crucifixion of sorts, perversely literal, including the body of one of the prison guards whom Lecter has eviscerated and suspended from the bars of the cell, with red, white and blue bunting forming outspread wings behind him. Lecter's politicized arrangement suggests that the *Texas Chainsaw Massacre* films are not far to seek in this scene. The allusion is confirmed by another grotesque detail that aids Lecter in his escape: he evades detection by participating in the tableau, wearing a mask fashioned from the second policemen's face. Appropriately, perhaps, in Demme's film the design of Lecter's tableau was inspired by the work of Francis Bacon, an artist whose paintings are also sites of sadomasochistic pleasure and abjection.[75] Here is yet another moment of intermediality in cinema that resorts to tableau vivant—tableau vivant in its most horrifying aspect: in Lecter's highly perverse tableau, a sadomasochistic performance produces sculptural arrangements inspired by painting and representing crucifixion. But this crucifixion can never promote the transformation of the material to the spiritual. The artistry of his tableau does not mask Lecter's perversions—rather, they come to light within it.[76] The high-cultural practices that are here called into play make

Lecter's tableau all the more shocking, much as when the cooking of human body parts is rendered even more offensive when the culinary arts come into play. Because the raw material Lecter uses in his perverted practices is taboo—they involve the degradation of the human body as material—the aestheticization of this composed scene simply points to the gap between material and form. In Lecter, metaphorical taste is not collapsed with its literal version, but rather exists to keep the two in a state of extreme tension.

Lecter is a reader—lector—of the human body as well as of the mind, at once an analyst and a literalist who sniffs out neuroses by way of body odors and fulfills his passions by licking: his name must also derive from the German *lecken*, to lick. What Lecter understands about the cannibalistic psychotics whose behavior he anticipates is at the crux of his own behavior: transformation is the point of the deep transactions in which these psychotic murderers are involved. Like Lecter a serial killer and cannibal, Buffalo Bill is also an artist of the real. This "fledgling killer's first effort of transformation," as Lecter puts it, is likewise expressed in a tableau, as Clarice discovers when she enters the Yourself Storage garage that contains Buffalo Bill's first victim and lover. In predictable homage to Hitchcock, the garage includes a bronze bird of prey with outstretched wings familiar from *Psycho*, and there is more. Here a headless female manikin in women's evening dress sits in a car, cigarette in gloved hand, while a decaying male head in makeup sits in a Bell jar beside it. This is another theatrical scene, a psychotic fantasy involving transactions that do *not* have their origins in mere transvestism, Lecter hastens to inform Clarice—but in "something worse." Later on, in his basement work room, surrounded by the manikins and mirrors that support his fantasy, Buffalo Bill will skin the young women he captures and kills in search of more material for the "woman suit" he is creating.[77]

But Buffalo Bill's aim is not merely to dress as a woman, we learn, nor even exactly to be one, but to be contained once again by way of the "woman suit" within the body of his mother, a scenario that also vividly recalls *Psycho* to mind. In a scene omitted by Demme's film, Harris's novel explains Buffalo Bill's psychotic drive by way of a videotape comprised of spliced-together film footage including images of his mother, a montage the serial killer watches as he sews his suit. Buffalo Bill's response to the tape is participatory, interactive: when his mother's image smiles out of the frame, he smiles back.[78] By suggesting an exchange, a permeability between these images and the psychotic's "reality," Harris's novel is also referring to that other famous slasher film of 1960: Powell's *Peeping Tom* in which, for its central character, reality and image are nearly impossible to unstitch. But Demme chose to omit this potentially self-referential scene from his film, and to substitute Lecter's tableau for it instead, a choice that is in keeping with scenes from other Harris novels.

The interest in nonfilmic visual representation that pervades the Lecter films derives from Harris's novels themselves, which seem particularly to have been inspired by the artifacts Ed Gein produced from the bodies of his victims.[79] References to Géricault's *Raft of the Medusa* and to Titian's *Flaying of Marsyas*, for instance, are not surprising in stories about cannibalism, but as we have suggested, Harris's interest in visual representation extends beyond mere references to specific paintings. Although the set designer for *Silence of the Lambs* seems right on the mark in basing Lecter's tableau on paintings by Francis Bacon, it is the tableau form *itself* that is of central importance to the Harris novels, where the tableau is a "fleshing out" of the perverse mimetic regression that characterizes the cannibals who populate them. In Brett Ratner's *Red Dragon*, which stays much closer to the plot of Harris's novel of that title than *Manhunter* (Mann's earlier adaptation of the same novel), the serial killer Dolarhyde not only makes videotapes of his crime scenes, propping up his dead victims to "watch" the scenarios he enacts with others, but films himself as well, later cutting images of the victims with images of himself to create a synthetic "reality" that supports his fantasy. William Blake's watercolor, pen, and pastel rendering of "The Great Red Dragon and the Woman Clothed with the Sun" provides the visual stimulus for Dolarhyde's fantasy, and his perverse enactment of "becoming" (transformation) in the form of a psychotic tableau is suggestive in this regard. Standing naked in front of his home movie screen, back to the projector, his body covered with tattoos that simulate the dragon's markings, Dolarhyde clicks on slides of Blake's "Great Red Dragon" in alternation with those of his dead female victims. Thus Dolarhyde's body enters the space of representation by appearing between projector and screen, his tattooed back also serving as a fleshly ground for the projected images: "I am the dragon—look at me," says Dolarhyde. This scene evokes a similar one in *Peeping Tom*, in which the central character's body also serves as a screen for images. Like Lecter's, Dolarhyde's performance "art" is intermedial: by way of the body art that contains him within representation, standing at the interface between photographic images of the dead women and images of the Blake watercolor, Dolarhyde imagines himself "reborn" and "changing." Transformation is enacted by "entering the screen," by enacting a collapse between representation and the real. Later, when Dolarhyde journeys to the Brooklyn Museum to see Blake's original watercolor, he promptly eats it in another literalist and cannibalistic effort to contain the dragon's power within his body, much as when, in mortuary cannibalism, the cannibal eats the body of his father.[80] In Dolarhyde's scenarios, transformation is simulated by way of props, and embodiment is ultimately reduced to containment.

Harris's novel *Hannibal* and Ridley Scott's filmic adaptation of it both feature the escaped Lecter living the life of an Italian cultural historian and museum curator in Florence, so it comes as no surprise that the visual arts are again at the crux of psychopathology and aestheticism here. Not that the opera based on Dante's *Divine Comedy* doesn't round out the synesthetic delights in which Lecter indulges with "Vide cor meum" playing on a literalization that one hopes will not take place. Like all good detectives in the Harris novels, Inspector Pazzi (Giancarlo Giannini) shares Lecter's hypersensuality, hence is able to "sniff him out," hoping to turn him in for a reward. Once again it is a painting that provides the scenario for the transactions that bridge the gap between psychotic reality and representation. Trapping Pazzi by way of his own superior intellect, Lecter decides to execute him as a Judas figure (another instance of Lecter's self-figuration as Christ) in a tableau vivant (or meurant?) of a painting in the Palazzo Vecchio that represents one of Pazzi's dead ancestors. With references to the Judas story and to the scenario recorded in the painting, death by hanging is the order of the day. Figuring the synthesis of the real with the image, the intended victim's back serves as a screen for the projected image of the painting, with Lecter's shadow diabolically obliterating this image. Although Pazzi is sadistically asked whether he would prefer to be represented with bowels in or out, Pazzi has no true choice since the manner of his death is preordained by the painting. Pazzi must figure in Lecter's snuff tableau with bowels out, like Judas, just as his ancestor was executed and painted centuries before. Like the punishment the painting illustrates, the inspector's murder is in the form of a public spectacle, first perceived by the crowd below as a theatrical event.

Once again Lecter's murderous tableau involves "deep transactions," his rendition of the Judas story suggesting anew that Lecter's psychoses are expressed in perversions of Christian scenarios, specifically with himself as Christ. Once again Lecter's tableau illustrates the extreme endpoint of the realist impulse in representation: in this film Lecter's "art" is "snuff art." This will likewise be the case when, in what I take to be a reference to Montaigne,[81] Lecter serves his lobotomized FBI enemy his own brain, elegantly sautéed. Aestheticism in its decadent phase: here, too, is the presence of Thomas de Quincey's "Murder as One of the Fine Arts," mediated by Hitchcock, grotesquely exaggerated by Harris, and illustrated with Ridley Scott's sure sense of mise-en-scène. Lecter's "evil eye" and his cannibalism are deeply related as introjective vision finds expression in the act of eating and incorporation that is cannibalism. Unlike the spare, objective look of Demme's film, *Hannibal*'s style is flamboyant. Visual interest is heightened in Scott's film, taking the form of special effects such as the appearance of Lector's face in a flock of flying pigeons. Scott's interest in the varieties of visual representation is one center of the film's attention, with the opera as spectacle par excellence continuing to permeate the film musically long after the scene is over. Indeed, all forms of image production are cannibalized by Scott's film. X-ray images and photographs abound, as do black-and-white video images generated by a security camera; we see images on computers and TV screens, not to mention the projection of paintings as slides. Special lighting effects—painterly effects—intensify Scott's aestheticized images. Small wonder that the final frame of Scott's film is an iris-in on Lecter's eye—his direct look out of the camera that recalls Hitchcock. Scott's conflation of the camera eye with Lecter's here promotes their identification. Scott happily figures his film as "cannibal art."

The Eye as Mouth

In addition to the obvious pleasures involved in flaunting taboos, what is it about cannibal horror that makes it a compelling subject for film? Perhaps it is that cannibalism in film marks the endpoint of an incorporating gaze, its literal expression. The notion of sight and ingestion as similar physiological processes suggested itself to us earlier with Metz's introjective gaze, a gaze that incorporates the world viewed into the body, its antecedents in Locke's notion of the image as imprinted upon the retina. Carol Clover's "Eye of Horror" similarly posits a gaze that "takes in." Opposing it to the "assaultive" and sadistic gaze (Lecter's, for instance), Clover reads the "reactive," introjective gaze as the central gaze of horror. This reactive gaze is the gaze of the victim, it is feminine (though not necessarily female), it is penetrated by the image, and its pleasure is masochistic. In defining her categories, Clover deliberately revises and expands Metz's introjective gaze, pointing out that while Metz and subsequent film theorists elaborate on the connection of the projective gaze to sadism, the introjective gaze is dropped from theoretical discourse—never pursued, never connected with masochism.[82] Because I briefly take up the tableau in relation to masochism in Chapter 5, I will not focus on that aspect here, choosing instead to elaborate on the idea of vision as a taking in—that is, on the idea of the reactive eye in cannibal horror as material, rather than as gaze. As we recall, the connection of the eye with the mouth is present in Baudry's insistence on the regressive orality—on the desire for incorporation—which he posits in relation to all film experience. An equation between seeing and eating is forged also in the affect that is disgust, a response to horror that is at once physiological and emotional. Arguing on behalf of a hybrid reaction to the monsters of horror—fear is not enough, we must also feel disgust—Noël Carroll, for instance, asks his readers to imagine how we would feel were we to *eat* the loathsome substances that constitute the monsters we *see* in horror film: "Were a part of their anatomy to find its way into our mouth, like the tentacles of so many slimy aliens, we would want to gag and spit it out."[83] We might put it somewhat differently, however: when we visually ingest disgusting substances—substances that remind us of our own materiality—we experience at once disgust, displeasure, and fascination as we seek also to take in the implication of that materiality. In cannibal horror, the eye functions as a mouth.

To cite another example, Dolarhyde, the psychotic killer of *Red Dragon*, is known as the Tooth Fairy because of the characteristic bite marks he leaves on victims. Ratner's film, following Harris in this, calls attention to the set of teeth Dolarhyde inserts into his mouth when he bites and kills his victims—the modernist, visual *Manhunter* omits this perversion. A sequence in a Hitchcock film again serves as a model for horror: it is our last glimpse of Norman in *Psycho*, the point at which the mother's skull complete with teeth is superimposed upon Norman's face. For a brief moment, Norman's psychotic eyes are replaced as the focal point of our look by the macabre, grinning teeth briefly prominent on Norman's face. Similarly, in *Red Dragon* Dolarhyde's flesh-eating teeth are modeled on those of the grandmother who functions as the vagina dentata of Dolarhyde's childhood, the authority figure who keeps him under constant, demeaning surveillance, delivering harsh punishments for the transgressions she views. After her death, Dolarhyde transforms his grandmother into the man-eating tiger he himself aspires to be. She is, therefore, metaphorically joined with Dolarhyde in the transactions with the Blake engraving and the film footage of his crime scenes mentioned above, crimes during which he notably chews upon his victims. In Dolarhyde's perverse scenarios, biting is an extension of looking: the grandmother's acts of surveillance followed by her physical aggression against Dolarhyde as a child are given oral expression by Dolarhyde as a psychotic adult. Antithetically, biting also stands in for the hoped-for affection the child never received, an affection that might also have been expressed orally, by way of the mouth, as nourishment or as a kiss. In Dolarhyde's performance, the eye becomes mouth in a horrifying psychotic synthesis.

In *Texas Chainsaw Massacre*, two scenes of looking—the opening sequence in which we see through the lens of a Polaroid and the later shots of Sally's eye in extreme close-up—also have something to say on this topic. With the self-consciousness typical of horror, the film's opening shots allude both to Hitchcock and Michael Powell. The staccato series of flashes and images seen through the lens of a camera recalls the exchange between Jeff and Thorwald in *Rear Window*, which likewise features vision in its visceral form, as I argued earlier (Chapter 5), outrageously troped here by Hooper. Looking at body parts lit up by flash bulbs, our point of view merged with that of a psychotic cannibal presented as artist, our look is rendered too uncomfortably material. Hitchhiker's Polaroids record fetishized body parts *and* are themselves fetishes and trophies. We are also led to read Hooper's opening sequence as follows: having entered the film by way of Hitchhiker's eye—inside the body of a cannibal, as we retrospectively learn—as the film's spectators, we have already been ingested, cannibalized, rendered wholly material. Hooper's other model for the Polaroid sequence is the final scene of Powell's *Peeping Tom*, in which a myriad of flash bulbs illuminates the murderer's suicide by means of his own camera—a camera whose projective gaze is tactile, material, and death-bringing, literalized in its deadly spike. When we are served up the eye as a body part, what we see is too close to what we are. Cannibal horror promotes the material look.

In keeping with the materialism of cannibal "art," the eye that views it later on in the film—Sally's eye—is seen in extreme close-up à la Buñuel, recalling the surrealist, sadistic slashing of the woman's eye in *Un Chien Andalou*. But Powell and Hitchcock are present here as well. On the one hand, the close-up of Sally's eye echoes the female eye in similar close-up that forms a backdrop for *Vertigo*'s credit sequence (Chapter 5), an eye whose blinking is portrayed as an involuntary action that keeps it moist, rather than as an emotional response. Sally's eye widens in horror, it is true, but it is its visceral aspect that is stressed. Her eye alludes to the eye in extreme close-up in the credit sequence of *Peeping Tom*, where the eye opens, blinks, then widens in fear. As Clover points out in "The Eye of Horror," the reactive eye belongs to the standard iconography of the horror film, usually in its function of suggesting painful looking.[84] Yet when, for instance, the murderer of *Peeping Tom* tries to photograph the fear in his victims' eyes, it is not only because the eye is a "window on the soul," it is also because he hopes that the camera as optical instrument can record something like fear's objective correlative, its physiological aspect. What is revealed in medical close-up in Hooper's film, in *Vertigo*'s credit sequence, and in *Peeping Tom* is the eye as eyeball, as a web of living tissue, complete with blood vessels and tear glands. Our response to its physicality is likewise somatic.

But what of the eyes that don't see? The presence of the blind in horror heightens the spectator's visual experience by contrast. Because blindness creates vulnerability, it plays to spectatorial pleasure in its masochistic form. When Clarice enters Buffalo Bill's basement workshop in *Silence of the Lambs*, she is temporarily blinded when he turns out the lights, but the spectator is not blinded, at times even made to share the psychotic's point of view through infrared goggles. In *The Village* (2004), the blind girl played by Bryce Dallas Howard is the only one who can undertake the horrifying journey through the forest. She does not see the "creatures" who populate it, although she does fall into their grasp. In the spectator, her blindness promotes an analogous fear of touching threatening or disgusting beings, emphasizing horror's tactile dimension. Why do the blind populate horror, if not also to suggest an alternative avenue to perception—not the romantic connection between blindness and insight, but rather a tactile path to understanding? In *Manhunter* and in Ratner's *Red Dragon*, Dolarhyde's love interest can only be a blind woman, since she cannot see the deformity that cripples him both physically and psychologically, reading his face as she does only with her hands. For this woman, images are of necessity material, experienced through touch. Her apprehension of the drugged tiger—at once aural, tactile, and deeply erotic—allows the killer to hope that her touch might also engulf him in sensuality. Her blindness renders her temporarily inviolable, much as it does the blind mother of *Peeping Tom*. While the blind mother in Powell's film is the only one who suspects the identity of the murderer, she will never be the victim of his camera. Since fear does not come to her by way of sight, she is not a fitting subject for the murderer's "experiment" and hence escapes the camera's tactile look.

As Clover realizes, horror films in their self-reflexiveness often locate responsibility for physical harm in the image maker: "Film after film presents us with stories in which audiences are assaulted by cameras, invaded by video signals or film images, attacked from screens."[85] But, as I have argued in earlier chapters (especially in Chapter 5), these preoccupations are not merely thematic or ideological. They go beyond the fear that images are colonizing our unconscious—translated into "our bodies" by the material idiom of horror—to figure a more abstract concern with the mutual permeability of representation and the real. Its pornographic overlay aside, a transgressive sequence from Cronenberg's *Videodrome* (1982) may say it all. Here the film camera tracks in on a woman's face in extreme close-up looking directly out of a TV screen. When she calls the male spectator of her image to "come to her," he places his mouth upon the TV screen, which now no longer contains the woman's entire face, but simply her huge, magnified lips. This moment of what we might call "representation horror" comes to fruition as her lips bulge out of the screen to envelope his entire head. Such are the looks that collapse the distance between spectator and screen—here rendered grotesquely as ingestion (and something more sexual)—looks that figuratively include the spectator within the space of representation. In its more commonplace manifestation as the direct look out of the camera and at the spectator, this look is notoriously featured in Hitchcock's films and is a hallmark of his style. It is an incorporating look, a look that figures the collapse of the image with the real. In repeatedly extending the direct look out of the frame to Hannibal Lecter, Demme's *Silence of the Lambs* brilliantly chooses an incorporating look for the look of his cannibalistic aesthete. This look—a look that both penetrates spectatorial space *and* draws the spectator into the space of representation—effectively collapses the two. As the producer of tableaux in which human bodies, dead and living, are arranged in painterly compositions, Hannibal Lecter knows a great deal about the transgressive collapse of the image with the real.

Notes

INTRODUCTION

1. For an excellent overview of realism in cinema, see Julia Hallam and Margaret Marshment, *Realism and Popular Cinema* (Manchester, UK: Manchester University Press, 2000). See also *Realism and 'Reality' in Film and Media*, ed. Anne Jerslev (Copenhagen: Museum Tusculanum Press, 2002), an anthology of essays on cognitive approaches to the topic, and Joseph D. Anderson, *The Reality of Illusion: An Ecological Approach to Cognitive Film Theory* (Carbondale: Southern Illinois University Press, 1996). The introduction to Joel Black's *The Reality Effect: Film Culture and the Graphic Imperative* (New York: Routledge, 2002) has influenced my thinking.

2. Siegfried Kracauer, *Theory of Film: The Redemption of Physical Reality* (London: Oxford University Press, 1960), ix.

3. As Dudley Andrew points out, the similarities between Kracauer and Bazin have primarily to do with their belief in the "essential realism of the film image," although Bazin and Kracauer differ on the issue of cinematic form. Interestingly, as Andrew notes, there is no reference to Bazin in Kracauer's bibliography. Dudley Andrew, *The Major Film Theories: An Introduction* (London: Oxford University Press, 1976), 131–33. Indeed, there are (uncited) allusions to Bazin all over *Theory of Film*. It does, however, acknowledge "Henri Langlois and his associates at the Cinémathek Française, old friends from my years in Paris," xiii. Another reason for the lack of reference to Bazin may lie in the fact that Kracauer had been developing his ideas from the time of his essay on photography ("Die Photographie"), first published in 1927. In this early essay, however, indexicality is not an issue.

4. Ivone Margulies, "Introduction," *Rites of Realism: Essays on Corporeal Cinema*, ed. Margulies (Durham, NC: Duke University Press, 2002), 3.

5. Kracauer, xi.

6. There is no doubt a political concern expressed here as well. As Sabine Hake points out: "Above all, *surface* evokes the things in *statu nascendi*, that is, the moment of emergence and least ossification; it is also the state in which ideological determinations are most evident." *The Cinema's Third Machine: Writing on Film in Germany, 1907–1933* (Lincoln: University of Nebraska Press, 1993), 260. And, as Miriam Bratu Hansen points out in her introduction to the Princeton paperback

edition, "photographic representation has the perplexing ability not only to resemble the world it depicts but also to render it strange, to destroy habitual fictions of self-identity and familiarity." *Theory of Film* (Princeton, NJ: Princeton University Press, 1997), xxv.

7. For a discussion of related issues, see Peter Wollen, "'Ontology' and 'Materialism' in Film," *Readings and Writings: Semiotic Counter-Strategies* (London: Verso, 1982), 191ff. Wollen asserts that—like Kracauer's—Bazin's "vision of cinema privileges the pro-filmic event and that, for Bazin, photographic registration in effect "effaces language."

8. André Bazin, "Cinema and Exploration," *What Is Cinema?*, Vol. I, ed. Hugh Gray (Berkeley: University of California Press, 1967), 163. See also Bazin's note to "The Ontology of the Photographic Image" in this same volume, in which he writes: "Let us merely note in passing that the Holy Shroud of Turin combines the features alike of relic and photograph," 14.

9. See Brigitte Peucker, "The Material Image in Goethe's *Wahlverwandtschaften*," *The Germanic Review* 74:3 (Summer, 1999), 205; and Joseph Koerner, *The Moment of Portraiture in German Renaissance Art* (Chicago: University of Chicago Press, 1993), 86.

10. Kracauer, 245–56.

11. Theodor W. Adorno, "Der wunderliche Realist," *Noten zur Literatur III* (Frankfurt: Suhrkamp, 1965), 96.

12. Kracauer, 51.

13. Kracauer, 16.

14. *Ibid.*

15. Kracauer, 68–9; 71; 122; 131. As Kracauer puts it: "The generic term 'psychophysical correspondences' covers all these more or less fluid interrelations between the physical world and the psychological dimension in the broadest sense of the word—a dimension that borders on that physical universe and is still intimately connected with it," 69.

16. Kracauer, 158; 159.

17. Kracauer, 165. Gertrud Koch sees the origin of this formulation in Kracauer's indebtedness to existential philosophy. Koch, *Kracauer zur Einführung* (Hamburg: Junius Verlag, 1996), 165. The "Ding-an-sich" also hovers in the background: Heide Schlüpmann points out that Kracauer studied Kant with Adorno. Schlüpmann, *Ein Detektiv des Kinos: Studien zu Siegfried Kracauers Filmtheorie* (Basel: Stroemfeld/Nexus, 1998), 23.

18. *Siegfried Kracauer-Erwin Panofsky Briefwechsel, 1941–1966*, ed. Volker Breidecker (Berlin: Akademie Verlag, 1996), 85.

19. Both Kracauer and Merleau-Ponty were influenced by German phenomenology, especially by the *Lebenswelt* of Edmund Husserl. The role of vision is central in Husserl. Martin Jay traces Merleau-Ponty's indebtedness to Husserl and Martin Heiddeger in *Downcast Eyes: The Denigration of Vision in Twentieth-Century French Thought* (Berkeley: University of California Press, 1993), 265–75. On Husserl's in-

fluence on Kracauer, see D. N. Rodowick, "The last things before the last: Kracauer and history," *New German Critique* 41 (Spring-Summer 1987), 109–39.

20. Vivian Sobchack, *The Address of the Eye: A Phenomenology of Film Experience* (Princeton, NJ: Princeton University Press, 1992), 3.

21. Kracauer, 165. As Hansen points out, the spectator can also meander away from [one might, perhaps, say *through*?] the images of films—"into the labyrinths of our own imaginations, memories, and dreams . . . into the slippery realms of experience, the heterogeneity of social space, the unpredictable dynamics of public life." It is in this aspect of film experience that "we hear an echo, albeit a distant one, of his earlier vision of cinema as an alternative public sphere." Hansen, "Introduction," xxxiii–xxxiv.

22. Kracauer, 165.

23. Walter Benjamin, "The Work of Art in the Age of Its Technological Reproducibility," *Selected Writings*, Vol. 3, eds. Marcus Bullock and Michael W. Jennings (Cambridge, MA: Belknap Press), 120.

24. No doubt ideology enters the discussion again here, as it is the peace suggested by his represented landscape that draws the Chinese painter.

25. Michael Fried, *Courbet's Realism* (Chicago: University of Chicago Press, 1990), 141.

26. *Courbet's Realism*, 49–50.

27. Jean-Louis Baudry, "The Apparatus: Metapsychological Approaches to the Impression of Reality in the Cinema," *Narrative, Apparatus, Ideology: A Film Theory Reader*, ed. Philip Rosen (New York: Columbia University Press, 1986), 302.

28. Baudry, 303.

29. Baudry, 314.

30. Baudry, 306.

31. André Bazin, "The Ontology of the Photographic Image," *What Is Cinema?*, Vol. I, ed. Hugh Gray (Berkeley: University of California Press, 1967), 10.

32. Richard Allen, "Representation, Illusion, and the Cinema," *Projecting Illusion: Film Spectatorship and the Illusion of Reality* (Cambridge, UK: Cambridge University Press, 1995), 81.

33. Mary Ann Doane, *The Emergence of Cinematic Time: Modernity, Contingency, and the Archive* (Cambridge, MA: Harvard University Press, 2002), 70; Murray Krieger, *Ekphrasis: The Illusion of the Natural Sign* (Baltimore, MD: Johns Hopkins University Press, 1992); Ivone Margulies, ed., *Rites of Realism: Essays on Corporeal Cinema* (Durham, NC: Duke University Press, 2003), 3.

34. Jacques Aumont, *The Image*, trans. Claire Pajackowska (London: BFI, 1997), 73.

35. Jacques Lacan, *The Four Fundamental Concepts of Psycho-Analysis*, ed. Jacques-Alain Miller, trans. Alan Sheridan (New York: W. W. Norton, 1978); Jean Buadrillard, "The Trompe-l'oeil," *Calligram: Essays in New Art History from France*, ed. Norman Bryson (Cambridge, UK: Cambridge University Press, 1988) and "Trompe l'oeil or Enchanted Simulation," *Seduction*, trans. Brian Singer (New York: St, Martin's Press, 1990), 60–66.

36. To name just a few: Roland Barthes, "The World as Object," *A Barthes Reader*, ed. Susan Sontag (New York: Hill and Wang, 1982), 62–73; John Berger, "Hals and Bankruptcy," *About Looking* (New York: Vintage, 1991), 169–77; Richard Wohlheim, "The Spectator in the Picture: Friedrich, Manet, Hals," *Painting as an Art* (London: Thames and Hudson, 1987), 101–86; Simon Schama, *The Embarrassment of Riches: An Interpretation of Dutch Culture in the Golden Age* (New York: Vintage Books, 1997).

37. Schama, 11.

38. See Michael Fried on Diderot's "physical entry" into the space of painting, *Absorption and Theatricality: Painting and Beholder in the Age of Diderot* (Chicago: University of Chicago Press, 1980), 118.

39. See David Marshall on this topic. Marshall, *The Surprising Effects of Sympathy: Marivaux, Diderot, Rousseau, and Mary Shelley* (Chicago: University of Chicago Press, 1988).

40. Johann Wolfgang von Goethe, "The Collector and His Circle," *Essays on Art and Literature*, ed. John Gearey (New York: Suhrkamp, 1986), 121–59.

41. Susan Stewart, "Death and Life, in that order, in the Works of Charles Willson Peale," *Visual Display: Culture Beyond Appearances*, eds. Lynne Cooke and Peter Wollen (Seattle, WA: Bay Press, 1995), 44.

42. See Peucker, "The Material Image in Goethe's *Wahlverwandtschaften*."

43. Edward Schwarzschild, "From Physiognotrace to the Kinematoscope: Visual Technology and the Preservation of the Peale Family," *Yale Journal of Criticism* 12:1 (Spring 1999), 60.

44. Serge Daney, "The Screen of Fantasy (Bazin and Animals)," trans. Mark A. Cohen, in Margulies, ed. *Rites of Realism*, 35.

45. Fredric Jameson, "The Cultural Logic of Late Capitalism," *Postmodernism or, The Cultural Logic of Late Capitalism* (Durham, NC: Duke University Press, 1991), 11.

46. Jameson, 6; 4.

47. Jacques Aumont, "The Variable Eye, or the Mobilization of the Gaze," trans. Charles O'Brien and Sally Shafto, in *The Image in Dispute: Art and Cinema in the Age of Photography*, ed. Dudley Andrew (Austin: University of Texas Press, 1997), 238.

48. Susan Sontag, *The Volcano Lover: A Romance* (New York: Farrar, Straus, and Giroux, 1992), 153–54.

49. Sontag, 155.

50. Slavoj Zizek, "How Real is Reality?" *Looking Awry: An Introduction to Jacques Lacan Through Popular Culture* (Cambridge, MA: MIT Press, 1992), 33.

51. Zizek, "How Real is Reality?," 34.

52. Hal Foster, "The Return of the Real," *The Return of the Real: The Avant-Garde at the End of the Century* (Cambridge, MA: MIT Press, 1996), 128.

53. Foster, 136.

54. Foster, 152.

55. Stewart, 314.

56. "Eines der Modelle von Kunst wäre die Leiche in ihrer gebannten, unverweslichen Gestalt." Theodor W. Adorno, *Ästhetische Theorie, Gesammelte Schriften in zwanzig Bänden*, ed. Rolf Tiedemann, vol 7 (Berlin: Directmedia, 2003), 417.

57. Among those originally published in English, I have in mind Angela Dalle Vacche's *Cinema and Painting: How Art Is Used in Film* (Austin: University of Texas Press, 1996); Garrett Stewart's, *Between Film and Screen: Modernism's Photo Synthesis* (Chicago: University of Chicago Press, 1999); Susan Felleman's *Art and the Cinematic Imagination* (Austin: University of Texas Press, 2006); my own *Incorporating Images: Film and the Rival Arts* (Princeton, NJ: Princeton University Press, 1995), as well as several edited anthologies of essays: Dudley Andrew's *The Image in Dispute: Art and Cinema in the Age of Photography* (Austin: University of Texas Press, 1997), Linda Ehrlich and David Desser's *Cinematic Landscapes: Observations on the Visual Arts and Cinema in China and Japan* (Austin: University of Texas Press, 1994); Patrice Petro's *Fugitive Images: From Photography to Video* (Bloomington: University of Indiana Press, 1995), and Angela Dalle Vacche's *The Visual Turn: Classical Film Theory and Art History* (New Brunswick, NJ: Rutgers University Press, 2003).

CHAPTER I

1. Wharton, Edith. *Summer* (New York: Bantam, 1993), (731–51). See Scott Marshall's excellent compendium, "Edith Wharton on Film and Television: A History and Filmography," *Edith Wharton Review* 13 (Spring 1995), 15–26.

2. Wharton, *Summer*, 97.

3. From "A Little Girl's New York," quoted from Scott Marshall, 16. Walter Benjamin's "The Work of Art in the Age of Mechanical Reproduction," 1935, later famously theorized this attitude. Benjamin's essay is anthologized in *Film Theory and Criticism: Introductory Readings*, Leo Braudy and Marshall Cohen (Eds.). (New York: Oxford University Press, 1999).

4. For that matter, she did not see the stage version starring Katharine Cornell, either. *The Age of Innocence* was first filmed in 1924 by Wesley Ruggles, with Beverly Bayne as the Countess Olenska and Eliot Dexter as Newland Archer. Unfortunately, this silent film was lost. In 1934, Wharton's novel was filmed again, this time by Philip Moeller, with Irene Dunne as the Countess and John Boles as Archer. For further information, see Scott Marshall, 17; 22.

5. Smith, Gavin. "Martin Scorsese Interviewed by Gavin Smith." *Film Comment* 29:6 (1993), 15–26:22.

6. I make this argument about film at greater length in *Incorporating Images: Film and the Rival Arts*. (Princeton, NJ: Princeton University Press, 1995).

7. R. W. B. Lewis, Introduction, xi. Wharton, Edith. *The Age of Innocence*. (New York: Scribner's, 1968). All subsequent references to this edition will be parenthetical.

8. Smith, 16.

9. Ibid.

10. Smith, 18.

11. The landscape painting chosen by Scorsese is a divergence from Wharton's novel, in which "a couple of Italian-looking pictures in old frames" (69), mounted on red damask, take center stage in the Countess' drawing room. Scorsese relinquishes the erotic resonance of these paintings in favor of the long landscape painting that allows a "brushstroke" tracking shot.

12. Taubin, Amy. "Dread and Desire." *Sight and Sound* 3:12 (1993), 6, and see also Cook, Pam. "Review of *The Age of Innocence* by Martin Scorsese." *Sight and Sound* 4:2, (1994) 45.

13. Benjamin, Walter. *The Origin of the German Tragic Drama*, 200. (Verso: London and New York, 1977).

14. Smith, 21. It should be noted, further, that Scorsese made one major visual change in his film: May Welland, as played by Winona Ryder, is not a blonde and blue-eyed athlete, just as the Countess Olenska as played by Michelle Pfeiffer is not dark and frail. Scorsese does not code these women as convention would dictate with the "dark lady" (the Countess) as literally dark haired, as well as dangerously alluring.

15. Smith, 18.

16. Although I am usually a great admirer of Joanne Woodward, her accent and inflection do not seem appropriate to Wharton's narrator.

17. This is a balancing act familiar to us from the films of R. W. Fassbinder, to whom we shall recur below.

18. It is interesting that the *New York Times* critic of Philip Moeller's earlier film adaptation also makes the point that his "photoplay" "leaves the spectator curiously cold and detached from the raging emotions of the story." *New York Times Film Reviews, 1932–38*, vol. 2, 1105. (New York: New York Times Press, 1970).

19. Taubin, Amy. (1993). "Dread and Desire." *Sight and Sound* 3:12, 6–9:8.

20. Wolff, Cynthia Griffin. *A Feast of Words: The Triumph of Edith Wharton*, 312. (New York: Oxford University Press, 1977).

21. Waid, Candace. (1991). *Edith Wharton's Letters from the Underworld: Fictions of Women and Writing*, 29. (Chapel Hill: University of North Carolina Press, 1991).

22. Among these are New York City films, including some very early Otoscope rolls whose images are reminiscent of the pages of a flipbook; Dreyer's *Gertrud*; Max Ophuls's *Lola Montes* and *Letter from an Unknown Woman*; William Wyler's *The Heiress* (based on *Washington Square* by Henry James). See Christie, Ian. "The Scorsese Interview." *Sight and Sound* 4:2 (1994) 10–15.

23. Rohmer, Eric. *L'organisation de l'espace dans le "Faust" de Murnau*. (Paris: Union Générale d'Editions, 1977).

24. Pygmalion, the sculptor of classical antiquity, fell in love with his own work of art and, as Ovid tells us, took the sculpture to bed with him.

25. The tableau vivant scene in Wharton's *House of Mirth* closely recalls that of Goethe's novel, *Elective Affinities* (1808), which established the real-life fashion

for such entertainments in the nineteenth century. Wharton herself was a reader of Goethe.

26. Waid, 27–31.

27. Kracauer, Siegfried. *Theory of Film: The Redemption of Physical Reality,* ix. (Oxford: Oxford University Press, 1960).

28. Most notably it occurs in Fritz Lang films, but it is generally a self-conscious reference to another lens, that of the camera.

29. The novel refers to the "vista of mummies and sarcophagi" through which the museum guard wanders "like a ghost stalking through a necropolis" (311).

30. Bazin, André. "The Ontology of the Photographic Image," *What is Cinema?* vol. 1, 9-11. (Berkeley and Los Angeles: University of California Press, 1967).

31. Waid, 38.

32. As we recall, Saul Bass designed the famous credit sequence for *Vertigo,* as well as for many other Hitchcock films.

33. Lindsay, Vachel. "Hieroglyphics." *The Art of the Moving Picture,* 203. (New York: Liveright, 1970).

34. For a thought-provoking reading of film's various forms of "Egyptomania" see Lant, Antonia. "The Curse of the Pharaoh, or How Cinema Contracted Egyptomania." *October* 59: (1992) 87–112.

35. Wolff, 333–4.

CHAPTER 2

1. Noël Burch, "Building a Haptic Space," *Life to Those Shadows,* ed. and trans., Ben Brewster (London: BFI, 1990), 167. See also Ben Brewster and Leah Jacobs, *Theater to Cinema: Stage Pictorialism and the Early Feature Film* (Oxford and New York: Oxford University Press, 1997).

2. Susan Sontag, *The Volcano Lover, a Romance* (New York: Farrar, Straus, and Giroux, 1992), 179.

3. Jean-François Lyotard, "Acinéma," *Narrative, Apparatus, Ideology: A Film Theory Reader,* ed. Philip Rosen (New York: Columbia University Press, 1986), 356.

4. Burch, 170.

5. Burch, 183.

6. Burch, 176.

7. It is typical of Burch that he would see in such effects a "striking anticipation of Magritte's 'visual puns.'" Burch, 168.

8. Pascal Bonitzer, *Décadrages: Peinture et cinéma* (Paris: Câhiers du Cinéma, 1985), 31.

9. See my discussion of this in *Incorporating Images: Film and the Rival Arts* (Princeton, NJ: Princeton University Press, 1995), 143–56.

10. Ian Haywood, "Crusaders Against the Art Market: Hans van Meegeren and Tom Keating," *Art and the Politics of Forgery* (New York: St. Martin's Press, 1987), 105–30.

11. Peucker, *Incorporating Images*, 157–179.
12. Svetlana Alpers, *The Art of Describing: Dutch Art in the Seventeenth Century* (Chicago: University of Chicago Press, 1983), 167.
13. Internet: Peter Greenaway website; December, 1998. "Cinema begint bij Vermeer," Interview by René Kurpershoek, trans. Bruno Bollaert.
14. Here Alpers departs from the readings of Dutch art that view it as emblematic and didactic.
15. Alpers, xxi.
16. Alpers, xxiv.
17. Alpers, xxvii.
18. Lawrence Gowing, *Vermeer* (London: Faber and Faber, 1970), 54.
19. Edward Snow, *A Study of Vermeer*, rev. ed. (Berkeley: University of California Press, 1994), 101.
20. Kurpershoek, "Cinema begint bij Vermeer."
21. These include "The Concert," "Couple Standing at a Virginal," "Young Woman with a Water Pitcher," "Soldier and Young Girl Smiling"—in all four of which the woman is wearing the yellow bodice—and "Woman in Blue Reading a Letter."
22. Mary Ann Doane, "The Moving Image," *Femmes Fatales: Feminism, Film Theory, Psychoanalysis* (New York and London: Routledge, 1991), 194.
23. Leonard Slatkes, "Utrecht and Vermeer," *Vermeer Studies*, eds. Ivan Gaskell and Michiel Jonker (New Haven and London: Yale University Press, 1998), 81–88.
24. Michael Fried, *Realism, Writing, Disfiguration: On Thomas Eakins and Stephen Crane* (Chicago: University of Chicago Press, 1987), 64.
25. Eric Jan Sluijter, "Vermeer, Fame, and Female Beauty: The *Art of Painting*," *Vermeer Studies*, 265–83.
26. Alpers, 167.
27. See Albrecht Dürer, *Unterweisung der Messung*, 1538.
28. Irene Netta, "The Phenomenon of Time in the Art of Vermeer," *Vermeer Studies*, 262.
29. Ben Broos, "Un celebre Peijntre nommé Verme[e]r," *Johannes Vermeer*, ed. Arthur K. Wheelock, Jr. (New Haven and London: Yale University Press, 1995), 57.
30. Wheelock, ed., *Johannes Vermeer*, 172.
31. The black-and-white doublet might very well have been worn by an artist during this period. See Marieke de Winkel, "The Interpretation of Dress in Vermeer's Paintings," *Vermeer Studies*, 332.
32. Stephen Heath, "Narrative Space," *Questions of Cinema* (Bloomington: Indiana University Press, 1981), 27ff.
33. Brigitte Peucker, "Wim Wenders' Berlin: Images and the Real," *Berlin in Focus: Cultural Transformations in Germany*, ed. Barbara Becker-Cantarino (Westport, CT: Praeger, 1996), 125–38.
34. Tony Rayns, "Forms of Address: Interviews with Three German Filmmakers," *Sight and Sound* 44 (Winter 1974–75): 6.

35. André Bazin, "The Ontology of the Photographic Image," *What is Cinema?*, vol. 1, ed. and trans., Hugh Gray (Berkeley: University of California Press, 1967), 14.
36. Jan Dawson, "An Interview with Wim Wenders," *Wim Wenders*, trans. Carla Wartenberg (New York: Zoetrope, 1976), 10–11.
37. Walter Donohue, "Revelations: An Interview with Wim Wenders," *Sight and Sound* 12 (May 1992), 10. See also Charles Hagen, "From the End of the World to Smack Dab in the Middle: An Interview with Wim Wenders," *Aperture* 123 (Spring 1991), 90.
38. Walter Benjamin, "A Small History of Photography," *One-Way Street and Other Writings*, trans. Edmund Jephcott (London: NLB, 1979), 251ff. Wenders makes use of Sander photo portraits in *Wings of Desire*.
39. Siegfried Kracauer, *Theory of Film: The Redemption of Physical Reality* (London: Oxford University Press, 1960), ix.
40. Jan Dawson, *Wim Wenders*, trans. Carla Wartenberg (New York: Zoetrope, 1976), 10–11.
41. Walter Benjamin, *Charles Baudelaire, a Lyric Poet in the Age of High Capitalism*, trans. Harry Zohn (London: Verso, 1983), 243.
42. Siegfried Kracauer, "Die Photographie," *Das Ornament der Masse* (Frankfurt am Main: Suhrkamp, 1963), 21–39.
43. Roland Barthes, "The Photographic Message," *Image, Music, Text*, trans. Stephen Heath (New York: Hill and Wang, 1977), 16–17.
44. Barthes, "The Third Meaning," *Image, Music, Text*, 64–65.
45. Roland Barthes, *Camera Lucida: Reflections on Photography*, trans. Richard Howard (New York: Hill and Wang, 1981), 80.
46. Bazin, "The Ontology of the Photographic Image," *What is Cinema?*, 15. See also Hugh Gray's introduction to this volume: "Bazin holds that the cinematic image is more than a reproduction, rather it is a thing in nature, a mold or masque," 6.
47. Wim Wenders, "Tokyo-Ga," *The Logic of Images: Essays and Conversations*, trans., Michael Hofmann (London and Boston: Faber and Faber, 1992), 65.
48. Nora M. Alter, "Documentary as Simulacrum: *Tokyo-Ga*," *The Cinema of Wim Wenders: Image, Narrative, and the Postmodern Condition*, ed. Roger F. Cook and Gerd Gemünden (Detroit, MI: Wayne State University Press, 1997), 143.
49. Bazin, 96.
50. Jean Baudrillard, *America*, trans. Chris Turner (London and New York: Verso, 1989), 37.
51. Charles Baudelaire, "The Painter of Modern Life," *Selected Writings in Art and Literature*, trans. P. E. Charvet (London: Penguin Books, 1992), 309–435.
52. See in particular Nora M. Alter, "Documentary as Simulacrum: *Tokyo-Ga*" and Alice Kuzniar, "Wenders' Windshields," *The Cinema of Wim Wenders*, 222–39.
53. Gowing, 18; 19.
54. Gowing, 22; 56; 65; 61.

55. In a recent essay, Jean-Luc Delsaute claims, however, that "it seems rash to continue to believe that the camera obscura was one of the tools with which he worked." Jean-Luc Delsaute, "The Camera Obscura and Painting in the Sixteenth and Seventeenth Centuries," *Vermeer Studies*, 120.

56. Dawson, 23.

57. This garden is mentioned in Jacques Aumont, "The Variable Eye or the Mobilization of the Gaze," *The Image in Dispute: Art and Cinema in the Age of Photography*, ed. Dudley Andrew (Austin: University of Texas Press, 1997), 238. It should be noted that in the German title, *Bis ans Ende der Welt*, the word *bis* can take on either a spatial or a temporal meaning.

58. Thomas Elsaesser, "Spectators of Life: Time, Place, and Self in the Films of Wim Wenders," *The Cinema of Wim Wenders*, 254.

59. Kuzniar, 230.

60. Here I part company with Alice Kuzniar, who claims that "Wenders' other films likewise invite an antioedipal reading," note #38, p. 239, and side with Elsaesser's reading in "Spectators of Life." Much as we might like to see Wenders as an advocate of the postmodern, his films bear traces of a nostalgia for the real.

61. Alpers, 223.

62. Elsaesser, 255.

63. This contention leaves aside the situation of the lesbian spectator.

64. Norman Bryson, "The Gaze and the Glance," *Vision and Painting: The Logic of the Gaze* (New Haven: Yale University Press, 1983), 112.

65. Bryson, 114.

66. Bryson, 117.

67. Jean Baudrillard, "Simulacra and Simulations," *Selected Writings*, ed. and introd., Mark Poster (Cambridge: Polity Press, 1988), 180.

68. Bryson, 115; 116.

69. I am indebted to Catriona MacLeod for the reminder that Richter's work is pertinent here.

70. Roberta Bernstein, "Warhol as Printmaker, 14–15.

71. Wim Wenders, "High Definition," *The Act of Seeing: Essays and Conversations*, trans. Michael Hofmann (London: Faber and Faber, 1996), 77–78.

72. Shawn Levy, "*Until the End of the World: Wim Wenders' Dance Around the Planet*," *American Film* 17:1 (January/February 1992), 52.

73. Yvonne Spielmann, "Intermedia and the Organization of the Image: Some Reflections on Film, Electronic, and Digital Media," *Iris* 25 (Spring, 1998), 65.

CHAPTER 3

1. Sarah Mower, "The King of Kink Made Naughty Fashionable," *New York Times*, 21, September 2003, Section 9:1.

2. Susan Sontag, "Fascinating Fascism," *Movies and Methods*, ed. Bill Nichols (Berkeley: University of California Press, 1976), 31–43. Sontag first published this frequently anthologized piece in *The New York Review of Books* on February 6, 1975.

3. Sontag, 40.
4. Sontag, 41; 40.
5. Wilhelm Reich, "The Race Theory," *The Mass Psychology of Fascism*, trans. Vincent R. Carfagno (New York: Farrar, Straus, and Giroux, 1970), 87.
6. Theodor W. Adorno, "Freudian Theory and the Pattern of Fascist Propaganda," *The Essential Frankfurt School Reader*, eds. Andrew Arato and Eike Gebhardt (New York: Urizen Books, 1978), 132.
7. Sontag, 41.
8. Saul Friedländer, *Reflections of Nazism: An Essay on Kitsch and Death*, trans. Thomas Weyr (Bloomington: Indiana University Press, 1993), 78.
9. Sontag, 40.
10. See Gaylyn Studlar's exemplary analysis of masochism in film, *In the Realm of Pleasure: Von Sternberg, Dietrich, and the Masochistic Aesthetic* (New York: Columbia University Press, 1988), 124.
11. Siegfried Kracauer, *From Caligari to Hitler: A Psychological History of the German Film* (Princeton, NJ: Princeton University Press, 1947), 300; 302. As Thomas Elsaesser notes in, "Leni Riefenstahl: The Body Beautiful, Art Cinema and Fascist Aesthetics," *Women and Film. A Sight and Sound Reader*, ed. P. Cook and P. Dodd (London: Scarlet Press, 1994), 192: Riefenstahl "did something original" by "putting staged tableaux to movement, music and vocals."
12. Russell Berman, "Written Right Across Their Faces: Leni Riefenstahl, Ernst Jünger, and Fascist Modernism," *Modern Culture and Critical Theory: Art, Politics, and the Legacy of the Frankfurt School* (Madison: University of Wisconsin Press, 1989), 99.
13. Berman, 110.
14. Berman, 109, 116.
15. Berman, 115.
16. See Enrico Vicentini, "The Venetian *Soleri* from Portable Platforms to Tableaux Vivants," *Petrarch's Triumphs*, ed. Konrad Eisenbichler and Amilcare A. Iannucci (Ottawa: Dovehouse, 1990), 383–94; and George R. Kernodle, *From Art to Theatre: From Art to Convention in the Renaissance* (Chicago: University of Chicago Press, 1944). I am indebted to Peter Eleey for these references.
17. Walter Benjamin, *The Origin of German Tragic Drama*, trans. John Osborne, introd. George Steiner (London: Verso, 1977), 195. The trionfi created the fashion for allegorical tableaux in baroque drama, where they occur as allegorical pictures performed by living actors whose spoken words function only as "a commentary on the images, spoken by the images themselves."
18. Benjamin, 119.
19. Hilmar Hoffmann, *The Triumph of Propaganda: Film and National Socialism, 1933–1945*, trans. John A. Broadwin and V. R. Berghahn (Providence and Oxford: Berghahn Books, 1996), 30.
20. Benjamin, 197.
21. The problematic of looking and the look is naturally implicated in the "fascist privileging of sight and visual representation," mentioned in passing by

Berman, 100. For a discussion of the topic with regard specifically to this film, see Steve Neale, "*Triumph of the Will: Notes on Documentary and Spectacle,*" *Screen* 20:1 (November–December 1983), 63–86.

22. Neale, 68.
23. Benjamin, 196.
24. Benjamin, 196.
25. Benjamin, 192.
26. Berman, 101.
27. Benjamin, 177.
28. See Leopold von Sacher-Masoch, *Venus in Furs*, 143–271, in Gilles Deleuze, *Masochism: An Interpretation of Coldness and Cruelty*, trans. Jean McNeil (New York: George Braziller, 1971). See Deleuze, 33.
29. These forms of "body art" suggest a special kind of pornographic effect: they are not simply nude male figures, they are simulacra, representations not of bodies, but of other statuary.
30. Siegfried Kracauer, "The Mass Ornament," trans. B. Lovell and J. Zipes *New German Critique* 5 (Spring 1975), 67–76; references to *Triumph of the Will* in *From Caligari to Hitler*, 301.
31. Sontag, 40.
32. Benjamin, 95.
33. See Brigitte Peucker, "Looking and Touching: Spectacle and Collection in Sontag's *Volcano Lover*," *Yale Journal of Criticism* 11:1 (1998), 159–65.
34. Benjamin, 177.
35. *Laocoön, or the Boundaries Between Poetry and Painting*, G. E. Lessing's seminal mid-eighteenth-century aesthetic treatise distinguishing the visual from the verbal arts, uses a Greek sculptural group representing the priest Laocoön and his sons as well as the dramatic narrative in the *Aeneid* in which it originates as the points of departure for a disquisition on the boundaries between poetry and painting. Like Lessing, Berman privileges writing's temporal dimension and its concomitant ability to render narrative and history (both are *Geschichte* in German), whereas the visual—often tied to bodies in these readings—is merely imbued with a nonlinguistic expressive force. Also like Lessing, Berman is opposed to the generic boundary crossings that descriptive poetry (Lessing) or ekphrasis (Berman) entail.
36. Benjamin, 216.
37. Neale, 77.
38. Philippe Lacoue-Labarthe and Jean-Luc Nancy, "The Nazi Myth," trans. Brian Holmes, *Critical Inquiry* 16 (Winter 1990), 302.
39. See Simon Richter, *Laocöon's Body and the Aesthetics of Pain: Winckelmann, Lessing, Herder, Moritz, Goethe* (Detroit, MI: Wayne State University Press, 1992), 10.
40. It was Riefenstahl's dancing that won her this role. Riefenstahl studied at the Jutta Klamt School for expressive dance as well as with Eugenie Eduardova and

Mary Wigman. In 1923, at the age of twenty-one, she performed publicly in Berlin, Munich, and other cities until a knee injury terminated her short career in May 1924. See Rainer Rother, *Leni Riefenstahl: The Seduction of Genius*, trans. Martin H. Bott (London: Continuum, 2002), 13–22, for an account of her career as a dancer. Reviews of Riefenstahl's performances during her brief career tend to read her dances as derivative, but praise her body for its beautiful form, sometimes read in explicitly sculptural terms. As one writer puts it, her body seemed to be "chiselled from marble, perfectly proportioned, beautifully groomed and evenly honed." *Züricher Post*, February 22, 1924; quoted from Rother, *Leni Riefenstahl*, 20.

41. *The Blue Light* (1932) and the much-disputed *Tiefland* (1940/54), likewise juxtapose fluidity of movement with static poses. In this regard, *The Blue Light* has much in common with *The Holy Mountain*, as it also features Riefenstahl's lithe movements and poses against natural scenes. Similarly, her dance in *Tiefland*, set in Spain, draws on the erotic rhythm of movement and its abrupt cessation that characterizes flamenco.

42. Zielke, who had been interned in an insane asylum after directing *Das Stahltier* for the German railroad, was released at Riefenstahl's insistence to shoot her film. See Cooper Graham, *Leni Riefenstahl and Olympia* (Metuchen, NJ: Scarecrow Press, 1986), 42, 45, and Elsaesser, 195.

43. Ibid.

44. Graham, 157.

45. See Berman, 113–14.

46. Linda Schulte-Sasse refers to the "illusory reconciliation of oppositional experiences in modernity: of the rational and beautiful, difference and sameness, the mechanized and the organic" in her excellent study of Nazi film, *Entertaining the Third Reich: Illusions of Wholeness in Nazi Culture* (Durham, NC: Duke University Press, 1996), 23.

47. Graham, 157.

48. Viz. Riefenstahl's "regenerative aesthetics," see Berman, 114.

49. Pierre de Coupertin revived the Olympic games at the end of the nineteenth century in a humanistic intellectual climate that believed in the importance of the parallel development of the mind and the body, the importance of physical exercise. Coupertin's undertaking, interestingly, occurred virtually simultaneously with the successful excavation of important archeological sites in Greece that included the Acropolis and Olympia itself. See John J. MacAloon, *This Great Symbol: Pierre de Coupertin and the Origins of the Modern Olympic Games* (Chicago: University of Chicago Press, 1981), 188.

50. Lacoue-Labarthe and Nancy, 309.

51. Lacoue-Labarthe and Nancy, 297.

52. Zielke is said to have used great quantities of smoke powder in a short time, see Graham, 44, and the sculptures were covered in Vaseline to "bring the sculptures to life." Audrey Salkeld, *A Portrait of Leni Riefenstahl* (London: Pimlico, 1997), 182.

53. Kirsten Gram Holmström, *Monodrama, Attitudes, Tableaux Vivants: Studies in Some Trends of Theatrical Fashion, 1770–1815*, (Stockholm: Almquist and Wiksell, 1967), 93.

54. The discus thrower was the German decathlete Erwin Huber. See Salkeld, 182.

55. Jean-Luc Nancy and Lacoue-Labarthe, "The Nazi Myth," 309.

56. Riefenstahl writes that the study and practice of dance inflected her understanding of painting as well. Leni Riefenstahl, "Dance and Film," *A Memoir* (New York: St. Martin's Press, 1992), 34–35.

57. Because my aim is primarily to contextualize and examine interarts questions in Riefenstahl's work, I will not focus on the entire prologue, although its interest is evident. Following the sequences of single male athlete and women dancers in groups, the torchbearer sequence is significant for any ideological analysis. First filmed in slow motion—effecting a temporal elision—the torchbearer runs through ruins, then through a scene with intact buildings, a reconstructed world. The torch is shown to travel first through time and then through space, its route traced on a map until finally torch—and tradition—descending like Hitler through the clouds, arrive at Hitler's Olympic Stadium in Berlin, in Nazi Germany.

58. As Graham tells us, Stowitts was particularly interested in the male physique, and painted a series of nude figures of UCLA and USC athletes, which he called "The American Champions." These homoerotic portraits shocked the American art committee and they refused to include them in the American art exhibition in Berlin, causing Stowitts to exhibit them in Berlin at his own expense. Apparently the paintings were well received by critics, but because the portraits included some Black and Jewish athletes, Alfred Rosenberg closed the show (136–7).

59. Interestingly, the dance sequences of the prologue were shot later, on the Baltic Sea, not on location in Greece, and Riefenstahl herself is said to be among the performers. See Audrey Salkeld, *A Portrait of Leni Riefenstahl* (London: Pimlico, 1997), 182; 289.

60. Graham, 136.

61. Walter Sorell, *Dance in its Time* (Garden City, NJ: Anchor Books, 1981), 321. I am indebted to Kristen Hylenski for this reference.

62. The writer Hugo von Hofmannsthal also shares this conception of dance as the movement of the soul. See Assenka Oksiloff, "Archaic Modernism: Hofmannsthal's Cinematic Aesthetics," *The Germanic Review* 73:1, 78.

63. Leni Riefenstahl, *A Memoir* (New York: St. Martin's Press, 1992), 34. See also Mary Wigman, "Dance and Gymnastics" and Felix Hollaender, "Ways to Strength and Beauty," in *The Weimar Republic Sourcebook*, ed. Anton Kaes, Martin Jay, and Edward Dimendberg (Berkeley: University of California Press, 1994), 685–7; 677. See also Karl Toepfer, *Empire of Ecstasy: Nudity and Movement in German Body Culture 1910–35* (Berkeley: University of California Press, 1997) and George Mosse, *The Nationalization of the Masses: Political Symbolism and Mass Movements in Germany from the Napoleonic Wars to the Third Reich* (Ithaca, NY: Cornell University Press, 1975), 127–60.

64. Peter Wollen, "Tales of Total Art and Dreams of the Total Museum," *Visual Display: Culture Beyond Appearances* (Seattle, WA: Bay Press, 1995), 154–77.

65. Wigman did contribute to the opening ceremony. Laban later fled to England in 1937. See Karl Toepfer, *Empire of Ecstasy: Nudity and Movement in German Body Culture 1910–35* (Berkeley: University of California Press, 1997), 65.

66. Wollen, 168.

67. Arnd Krüger, "There Goes This Art of Manliness: Naturism and Racial Hygiene in Germany," *Journal of Sports History*, 18:1 (Spring 1991), 139.

68. David Welch, *Propaganda and the German Cinema, 1933–45* (Oxford: Clarendon Press, 1983), 114–15.

69. Lacoue-Labarthe and Nancy refer to myth as "the mimetic instrument par excellence" in fascism, 298.

70. Michel Foucault, *Discipline and Punish: The Birth of the Prison*, trans. Alan Sheridan (New York: Vintage Books, 1979), 136.

71. See Brigitte Peucker, "The Material Image in Goethe's *Wahlverwandtschaften*," *The Germanic Review* 74:3 (Summer 1999), 195–213.

72. Hart's earliest tableaux in London were in fact pornographic, supposedly to encourage performance in a "celestial bed." See Brigitte Peucker, "Looking and Touching: Spectacle and Collection in Sontag's *Volcano Lover*," *Yale Journal of Criticism*, 11:1 (1998), 159–65.

73. Angela Dalle Vacche, *The Body in the Mirror: Shapes of History in Italian Cinema* (Princeton, NJ: Princeton University Press, 1992), 69.

74. Roland Barthes, *Camera Lucida: Reflections on Photography*, trans. Richard Howard (New York: Hill and Wang, 1981), 32.

75. Among these are *The Land of the Nuba* (*Die Nuba. Menschen wie von einem anderen Stern*, 1973); *The People of Kau* (*Die Nuba von Kau*, 1976); *Coral Gardens* (*Korallengärten*, 1978); *My Africa* (*Mein Afrika*, 1982); *Underwater Wonders* (*Wunder unter Wasser*, 1990); and *Olympia* (1994).

76. Sontag, 38.

77. Kracauer, Benjamin, and Bazin all preceded him in making this connection. See Siegfried Kracauer, "Die Photographie," *Das Ornament der Masse* (Frankfurt am Main: Suhrkamp, 1963), 21–39; Walter Benjamin, "The "Little History of Photography," translated by Edmund Jephcott and Kingsley Shorter, *Selected Writings, vol. 2, 1927–34*, ed. Michael W. Jennings, Howard Eiland, and Gary Smith University Press (Cambridge: Belknap, Harvard Press 1999), 507–28; André Bazin, "The Ontology of the Photographic Image," *What is Cinema? vol. I*, ed. and trans. Hugh Gray (Berkeley: University of California Press, 1967), 9–16.

78. Barthes, 31.

79. Sontag, 38.

80. Friedländer, *Reflections of Nazism: An Essay on Kitsch and Death*. (Bloomington: Indiana University Press, 1993).

81. Leni Riefenstahl, *The Last of the Nuba*, trans. Fitzburg and Whiteside (Verona: Arnoldo Mondadori, 1973), 171.

82. Russell Berman, "German Primitism/Primitive Germany," *Fascism, Aesthetics and Culture* ed. Richard Goslan (Hanover, NH: University Press of New England, 1992), 63.

83. Elsaesser, 190.

84. Ibid.

85. Kracauer refers to them as "statues of saints," 259.

86. Bazin, 14–15. See also "Cinema and Exploration," 162–63.

87. The camera's intense physiognomic interest in the faces of the villagers in this film no doubt derive from Riefenstahl's collaboration with Béla Balázs, who wrote the screenplay for *The Blue Light*. For Balázs, the significance of the photographic apparatus resides in its ability to reveal the expressive power of the human face and of objects. As Balázs puts it "the mute soliloquy of the face speaks": meaning, that it—to recur to Berman's phrase—is "written right across their faces." It is the close-up, according to Balázs, that allows us to "see to the bottom of the soul by means of . . . tiny movements of facial muscles." Although at some remove from Benjamin's optical unconscious, Balázs's interest in the photographic dimension of film is likewise optical, lodged in the revelatory capacity of the camera. And although it contradicted his leftist political leanings, Balázs's belief in optically rendered expressiveness was easily assimilable to a fascist concern with physiognomy and racial typology. Béla Balázs, *Theory of the Film: Character and Growth of a New Art* (New York: Dover, 1970), 63.

88. Eric Rentschler, "Mountains and Modernity: Relocating the *Bergfilm*," *New German Critique* 51 (1990), 156.

89. The framed photograph of Junta is not the final image of *The Blue Light*, of course, that is the image of writing, the ornamental typeface of the book that tells her story. And this was not originally the final image of film, which we now know only from outtakes compiled and released in 1952, in any case. Schulte-Sasse, 142.

90. It is totally consistent then, that in 1973 Riefenstahl hoped to release a film on the Nuba in which still and moving images were to be interspersed. See Barsam, 37.

91. Raymond Bellour, "The Film Stilled," *Camera Obscura* 24 (1990), 108.

92. Bellour, 108.

93. Quentin Bajac, *Tableaux Vivants: Fantaisies photographiques victoriennes (1840–1880)* (Paris: Réunions des musées nationaux: 1999), 16. My thanks to Peter Eeley for this reference. See also Ellen Handy, *Pictorial Effect, Naturalist Vision: The Photographs and Theories of Henry Peach Robinson and Peter Henry Emerson* (Norfolk, VA: Chrysler Museum, 1994).

94. Carol Christ, "Painting the Dead: Portraiture and Necrophilia in Victorian Art and Poetry," *Death and Representation*, ed. Sarah Webster Goodwin and Elizabeth Bronfen (Baltimore, MD: Johns Hopkins University Press, 1993), 133.

95. Christ, 149.

96. Deleuze, 33.

CHAPTER 4

1. See Kerry Brougher and Michael Trantino, *Notorious: Alfred Hitchcock and Contemporary Art* (Oxford: Museum of Modern Art, 1999), and Dominque Païni and Guy Cogeval, *Hitchcock et l'art: coïncidences fatale*, Musée des Beaux-Arts Montréal (Milan: Mazzotta, 2000). For information on the Hitchcock's art collection, see Nathalie Bondil-Poupard, "Hitchcock, artiste malgré lui," *Hitchcock et l'art*, 179–88. Although characters in Hitchcock's film are often sceptical about modern art, the Hitchcocks' collection was comprised primarily of twentieth-century paintings. They owned several Dufys; two Vlamincks; two Utrillos; and works by Rouault, Soutine, Gaudies-Brzeska, Soulages, Braque, Klee, and Avery—as well as a painting by Walter Richard Sickert, "The Camden Town Murder." Interestingly, in a recent book, the crime writer Patricia Cornwell has argued that Sickert was the actual Jack the Ripper. Cornwell, *Portrait of a Killer: Jack the Ripper Case Closed* (New York: Berkley Books, 2003).

2. Drawing on the work of Hélène Cixous, Tania Modeleski suggests that "decapitation" as opposed to castration, is what is at stake for the female—in cinema, as elsewhere." *The Women Who Knew Too Much: Hitchcock and Feminist Theory* (New York: Routledge, 1988), 20.

3. Marshall Deutelbaum and Leland Poague, "Hitchcock in Britain," *A Hitchcock Reader*, ed. Deutelbaum and Poague (Ames: Iowa State University Press, 1986), 64.

4. Louis Marin, "Et in Arcana hoc," *To Destroy Painting*, trans. Mette Hjort (Chicago: University of Chicago Press, 1995), pp. 95–169. Although my work draws directly on that of Marin, I have also read with interest an essay by Catriona MacLeod called "Floating Heads: Portrait Busts in Classical Weimar," in *Unwrapping Goethe's Weimar*, ed. Burhard Henke, Susanne Kord, and Simon Richter (Rochester, NY: Camden House, 1999), and her references to Medusa in *Embodying Ambiguity: Androgeny and Aesthetics from Winckelmann to Keller* (Detroit: Wayne State University Press, 1998). J. Bertolini also mentions the Medusa figure in connection with *Rear Window* in "*Rear Window* or the Reciprocated Gaze," republished in *Framing Hitchcock*, ed. Sidney Gottlieb and Christopher Brookhouse (Detroit: Wayne State University Press, 2002), 234–50.

5. Marin, 145–49. Here Marin refers to and elaborates on Freud's work on Medusa's head, in which he famously links decapitation to castration and connects the terror produced by the sight of Medusa to that produced by the sight of the mother's (castrated) genitals.

6. Marin, 112.

7. Stephen Heath, "Narrative Space," *Questions of Cinema* (Bloomington: Indiana University Press, 1981), 23–24. See also Diane Waldman's reading of this still life in "The Childish, the Insane, the Ugly: The Representation of Modern Art in Popular Films and Fictions of the Forties," *Wide Angle* 5:2 (1982), 55.

8. Its fruits and flowers suggest that this is a female space. This particular painting, with its fragmentation of space, serves to double the connotative value of the still life.

9. Tania Modleski refers to the theme of cannibalism in Hitchcock, especially in *Frenzy*, with reference to an oral-stage fixation. *The Women Who Knew Too Much*, 106.

10. See Chapter 9 for a discussion of *The Trouble with Harry*, the Hitchcock film in which this is most obviously the case.

11. James Lastra, "From the Captured Moment to the Cinematic Image: A Transformation in Pictorial Order," *The Image in Dispute: Art and Cinema in the Age of Photography*, ed. Dudley Andrew (Austin: University of Texas Press, 1997), 276.

12. As Rothman points out, Norman's hobby is "analogous to Hitchcock's hobby, fixing the human subject with a camera." William Rothman, *Hitchcock— The Murderous Gaze* (Cambridge, MA: Harvard University Press, 1982), 279.

13. In the nineteenth century, women with particularly beautiful hands often had them modeled. In Edith Wharton's *Age of Innocence*, for instance, May Welland's hands are sculpted during her wedding trip to Paris.

14. André Bazin, "The Ontology of the Photographic Image," *What is Cinema?*, vol. 1, ed. and trans. Hugh Gray (Berkeley and Los Angeles: University of California Press, 1967), 9.

15. Richard Allen, "Avian Metaphor in *The Birds*," *Hitchcock Annual* (1997–98), 58–59, makes the following connection between the birds and Bates's mummy: "this 'stuffed bird' was created by the act of 'stuffing a bird' in the sense that combines both a sexual act—the implied incest between Norman and his mother—and the act of killing."

16. Ibid.

17. Kenneth Gross, *The Dream of the Moving Statue*, (Ithaca, NY: Cornell University Press, 1992), 19.

18. Ibid., 23.

19. François Truffaut, *Hitchcock*, (New York: Simon and Schuster, 1984), 165.

20. Stanley Cavell, "North by Northwest," *A Hitchcock Reader*, 263.

21. The heroine's father in Hitchcock's *Rebecca* is referred to as a painter who painted the same tree over and over again.

22. When portraits of men are featured, they function quite obviously as reminders of the law of the father and of the oedipal power that he exerts.

23. Slavoj Zizek, "The Hitchcockian Blot," *Looking Awry: An Introduction to Jacques Lacan Through Popular Culture* (Cambridge, MA: MIT Press, 1998), 91.

24. Michael Fried, *Absorption and Theatricality: Painting and the Beholder in the Age of Diderot* (Berkeley and Los Angeles: University of California Press, 1980), 100–3.

25. For an overview of the "look back" in cinema, see Wheeler Winston Dixon, *It Looks at You: The Returned Gaze of Cinema* (Albany: State University of New York Press, 1995).

26. Maurice Yacowar, *Hitchcock's British Films* (Hamden, CT: Archon, 1977), 111.

27. One critic suggests that Hitchcock's interest in the double may have been influenced by Murnau's *Der Januskopf* (1920). See Theodore Price, *Hitchcock and Homosexuality* (Metuchen, NJ, and London: The Scarecrow Press, 1992), 202; 220.

28. Sir William Smith, *Smaller Classical Dictionary*, rev. ed. (New York: E. P. Dutton, 1958), 163.

29. Raymond Bellour, "Psychosis, Neurosis, Perversion," *A Hitchcock Reader*, 328–9. See also George Toles, who notes of Marion and Norman that "the profile views of the two facing figures are perfectly symmetrical." Toles, "If Thine Eyes Offend Thee . . .": *Psycho* and the Art of Infection," in *Centenary Essays*, 169.

30. Marin, *To Destroy Painting*, 143.

31. In her seminal article on visual pleasure, Laura Mulvey refers to the focus on one body part or fragment in a film as endowing it with the visual quality of a "cutout." See "Visual Pleasure and Narrative Cinema," *Narrative, Apparatus, Ideology: A Film Theory Reader*, ed. Philip Rosen (New York: Columbia University Press, 1986), 203.

32. As Modleski put its, "if castration is, as Laura Mulvey has persuasively argued, always at stake for the male in classical narrative cinema, then decapitation is at stake for the female—in the cinema as elsewhere." Modleski, *The Women Who Knew Too Much*, 20.

33. Donald Spoto, *The Dark Side of Genius: The Life of Alfred Hitchcock* (New York: Ballantine Books, 1983), 38ff.

34. Modleski suggests that it is as if Scottie were continually confronted with the fact that "he resembles her in ways intolerable to contemplate." *The Women Who Knew Too Much*, 92.

35. J. Hillis Miller, *Versions of Pygmalion* (Cambridge, MA: Harvard University Press, 1990), 11.

36. Robin Wood, "Male Desire, Male Anxiety: The Essential Hitchcock," *A Hitchcock Reader*, 228.

37. Païni and Cogeval, 153.

38. Marin, 117.

39. Marin, 126.

40. Marin, 133.

41. Bruno Villien, *Hitchcock* (Marseille: Rivages, 1985), 7.

42. Marian E. Keane, "A Closer Look at Scopophilia: Mulvey, Hitchcock, and *Vertigo*," *A Hitchcock Reader*, 234.

43. Rothman, influenced by Cavell, suggests that some of Hitchcock's characters "seem to possess the power to confront—hence also to avoid—the camera's gaze." Rothman, 60.

44. Ibid.

45. Keane, 235.

46. Marin, 143.

47. Gross sees the "statue as an archaic double for the cadaver." Gross, 19.

CHAPTER 5

1. Marin, "Et in Arcana hoc," *To Destroy Painting*, 119.
2. Francesco Casetti, "Face to Face," *The Film Spectator: From Sign to Mind*, ed. Warren Buckland (Amsterdam: Amsterdam University Press, 1995), 118–39. (First published as "Les yeux dans les yeux" in 1983). Marc Vernet contextualizes Casetti's insights in his reading of a number of generically different films, including Hitchcock's *Spellbound*. See "The Look at the Camera," *Cinema Journal* 28:2 (Winter 1989), 48–63; 57. For an analysis of the look into the camera, also see Casetti, *Inside the Gaze: The Fiction Film and Its Spectator*, trans. Nell Andrew with Charles O'Brien, introd. Christian Metz (Bloomington: Indiana University Press, 1998), 1–44. See also Paul Willemen, "The Fourth Look," *Looks and Frictions: Essays in Cultural Studies and Film Theory* (Bloomington: Indiana University Press, 1994), 99–110; and Wheeler Winston Dixon, *It Looks At You: The Returned Gaze of Cinema* (Albany: State University of New York Press, 1995). Dixon adapts Lacan to his purposes; for Dixon, "the look back" is "not only a function of the gaze of the performers, or of the setting they use. Rather, it is the result of the power of the screen, which reflects its gaze upon the spectator. For an analysis of the look into the camera in early cinema, see Elena Dagrada, "Through the Keyhole: Spectators and Matte Shots in Early Cinema," *Iris* 11 (Summer 1990), 95–106.
3. Casetti, 124; 119.
4. Stanley Cavell, "The Camera's Implication," *The World Viewed: Reflections on the Ontology of Film* (Cambridge, MA: Harvard University Press, 1979), 128–9.
5. Stanley Cavell, "North by Northwest," *Hitchcock Reader*, 259. This essay is reprinted from *Critical Inquiry*, 7:4 (1981). Godard made this observation in 1988. See Serge Daney, "Godard Makes [His]tories, Interview with Serge Daney," *Jean-Luc Godard: Son + Image*, ed. Raymond Bellour and Mary Lea Bandy (New York: The Museum of Modern Art, 1992), 164. Cited by Joe McElheny, "Touching the Surface," *Centenary Essays*, 103.
6. Slavoj Zizek, "The Hitchcockian Blot," *Looking Awry: An Introduction to Jacques Lacan Through Popular Culture* (Cambridge, MA: MIT Press, 1998), 91. As Zizek points out elsewhere, it is important to recall that the Lacanian gaze reverses the relationship between subject and object—"the gaze is on the side of the object, it stands in for the blind spot in the field of the visible from which the picture itself photographs the spectator." "Why is Reality Always Multiple?" *Enjoy Your Symptom!: Jacques Lacan in Hollywood and Out* (New York: Routledge, 2001, 2nd ed.), 201. In a recent article, Todd McGowan seeks to rehabilitate the reputation of Lacanian film theory by correcting the misapprehension among film theorists who do not take precisely this reversal (mentioned by Zizek above) into account. Todd McGowan, "Looking for the Gaze: Lacanian Film Theory and its Vicissitudes," *Cinema Journal* 42:3 (2003), 27–47.
7. Vernet, 48.

8. Tom Gunning, "Final Figure: The Look at the Camera," *The Films of Fritz Lang: Allegories of Vision and Modernity* (London: BFI, 2000), 30–33.

9. Michael Fried, *Absorption and Theatricality: Painting and Beholder in the Age of Diderot* (Berkeley: University of California Press, 1980). Martin Jay has interestingly pointed out that Fried's dialectic of absorption and theatricality (distanciation) is inflected by the work of Merleau-Ponty. See Martin Jay, *Downcast Eyes: The Denigration of Vision in Twentieth-Century French Thought* (Berkeley: University of California Press, 1994), 56.

10. See Brigitte Peucker, *Incorporating Images: Film and the Rival Arts* (Princeton, NJ: Princeton University Press, 1995), 24–25. Fried's interest in spectatorship—or "beholding," as he terms it—is already coming to the fore in his seminal essay, "Art and Objecthood," originally printed in *Artforum*, June 1967. In this response to Clement Greenberg's work on Abstract Expressionism, Fried writes about the literalist movement in art (his term for minimalism) and its "espousal of objecthood" that "it amounts to nothing more than a plea for a new genre of theatre; and theatre is now the negation of art since the experience of literalist art is of an object in a situation—one that, virtually by definition, *includes the beholder*" (italics his). In contradistinction to modernism in painting, that seeks to undermine objecthood, Fried argues, the literalist sensibility is theatrical. "Art and Objecthood," *Minimal Art: A Critical Anthology*, ed. Gregory Battcock (New York: E. P. Dutton, 1968), 125; 137. For another significant approach to the place of the spectator with respect to painting, see Richard Wollheim, *Painting as an Art* (London: Thames and Hudson, 1987). With regard especially to C. D. Friedrich, Manet, and Frans Hals, Wollheim analyzes the way in which pictorial codes particular to these artists construct the relation of the spectator to the painting, arguing that they create a spectator internal to the painting, a spectator in the text.

11. Michael Fried, *Courbet's Realism* (Chicago: University of Chicago Press, 1990). It is important to note here that the realism Fried sees in Courbet is not the Bazinian realism that tends to predominate in discussions of film. The idea that the spectator is determined by the spatial structure of a painting becomes a topic of interest with Foucault's analysis of Velasquez's *Las Meninas* in *The Order of Things* and, in the area of film studies, produced important work on spectatorship that have influenced this chapter: Jean-Pierrre Oudart on suture and on the "reality effect," ("La Suture," *Câhiers du Cinéma* 211; 212, April, May 1969; "L'effet de réel," *Câhiers du Cinéma* 228, March–April, 1971) See also Daniel Dayan, "The Tutor Code of Classical Cinema," anthologized in *Movies and Methods*, ed. Bill Nichols (Berkeley: University of California Press, 1976), 438–51, and Pascal Bonitzer on the "reality" of denotation, and on off-screen space ("'Réalité' de la dénotation," *Câhiers du Cinéma* 229, May–June 1971; "Hors-champ: un espace en défaut," *Câhiers du Cinéma* 229, May–June 1971).

12. Fried, *Courbet's Realism*, 287. Of course the direct look out of the canvas is featured in painting before Manet—in the work of Velasquez, for instance, and in

that of Franz Hals, to name just two earlier painters from different traditions who frequently resorted to this strategy. There will be other explanations for the use of this technique at these moments in the history of painting. Fried reads Manet's work against the backdrop of opposing strategies developed in French painting of the eighteenth and early nineteenth centuries. See Fried, *Manet's Modernism or, The Face of Painting in the 1860s* (Chicago: University of Chicago Press, 1996).

13. We should note, of course, that the direct look out of the painting is not new to the nineteenth century: it occurs considerably earlier, and has been analyzed in the work of Velasquez and Frans Hals, among others.

14. Fried writes of the "corporeal realism" of Courbet, who attempts (metaphorically) to enter his own paintings. See *Courbet's Realism*, 286–7. For an interesting approach to the coexistence of realist and modernist strategies in Hitchcock's films, see Joe McElheney, "Touching the Surface: *Marnie*, Melodrama, Modernism," *Centenary Essays*, 87–106.

15. Gilles Deleuze, *Cinema I: The Movement Image*, trans. Hugh Tomlinson and Barbara Habberjam (Minneapolis: University of Minnesota Press, 1986), 203–5.

16. Christian Metz, *The Imaginary Signifier: Psychoanalysis and the Cinema*, trans. Celia Britton, Annwyl Williams, Ben Brewster, and Alfred Guzzetti (Bloomington: Indiana University Press, 1977), 45.

17. Slavoj Zizek, *Enjoy Your Symptom! Jacques Lacan in Hollywood and Out*, rev. ed. (New York and London: Routledge, 2001), 15.

18. Rothman, *Hitchcock: The Murderous Gaze*, 19.

19. It is not my aim here to discuss the female portrait as the lodger's double, or the ambiguous gendering that this suggests.

20. There is much about the rendering of the lodger that recalls Murnau's vampire, Nosferatu—the lodger's entrance through the door, his femininity—and certainly this shot of the lodger behind windowpanes echoes a similar composition in *Nosferatu* when the vampire is shot behind a window with cross-shaped dividers. Early in his career—1924–25—Hitchcock spent time in Germany, where he is said to have worked with Fritz Lang and admired Murnau's work a great deal. The direct look out of the frame is a strategy to which Lang often resorts in his films, where it has the same uncanny effect as it does in Hitchcock's films—one notable example is Death's direct look out of the frame in Lang's *Destiny* (*Der müde Tod*, 1921). For a discussion of the direct look out in Lang's work, see Gunning, "Final Figure," 30–33.

21. Zizek, "The Hitchcockian Blot" *Looking Awry*, 91.

22. Miran Bozovic, "The Man Behind His Own Retina," *Everything You Always Wanted to Know About Lacan (But Were Afraid to Ask Hitchcock)*, ed. Slavoj Zizek (London: Verso, 1992), 167.

23. Zizek, "The Hitchcockian Blot," 96.

24. As Michel Chion puts it, "tennis is the acoustic sport par excellence." *Audio-Vision: Sound on Screen*, ed. and trans. Claudia Gorbman (New York: Columbia University Press, 1990), 159.

25. Zizek, "Pornography, Nostalgia, Montage," *Looking Awry*, 116.
26. Zizek, "Why is Reality Always Multiple?" *Enjoy Your Symptom!*, 201.
27. Zizek, "Pornography, Nostalgia, Montage," 116.
28. These shots may be found in the British version of this film, the version without the appended Hollywood ending.
29. I mention "Uncle Josh" in the context of a discussion of "Cinema and the Real" in *Incorporating Images*, 118.
30. As Jacqueline Rose puts it, "The gull releases the aggressivity latent to the miming of looks between the protagonists, and takes the place of the persecutory object." See Jacqueline Rose, "Paranoia and the Film System," *Feminism and Film Theory*, ed. Constance Penley (New York: Routledge, 1988), 148.
31. The story of Zeuxis and Parrhasios comes from Pliny's *Natural History*. Norman Bryson considers this anecdote to have launched "the natural attitude" in the visual arts as well as in writing about them. Bryson, *Vision and Painting: The Logic of the Gaze* (New Haven: Yale University Press, 1983), 3. See also Jacques Lacan, "What is a Picture?" in *The Four Fundamental Concepts of Psycho-Analysis*, ed. Jacques-Alain Miller, trans. Alan Sheridan (New York: W. W. Norton, 1978), 111–12. Of importance to Lacan is his observation that "if one wishes to deceive a man, what one presents to him is a veil, that is to say, something that incites him to ask what is behind it."
32. For an account of the theatrical space in which the contest takes place, see Norman Bryson, *Looking at the Overlooked: Four Essays on Still Life Painting* (Cambridge, MA: Harvard University Press, 1990), 31–32. For Lacan, the tompe l'oeil picture does not compete with appearance, but rather with something beyond appearance "which Plato designates as the Idea" (112).
33. John Belton, "The Space of *Rear Window*," *Hitchcock's Re-Released Films: From Rope to Vertigo*, ed. Walter Raubicheck and Walter Srebnick (Detroit: Wayne State University Press, 1991), 79.
34. Belton, 80.
35. Belton, note #8, 92.
36. Michel Chion, "The Fourth Side," *Everything You Always Wanted to Know About Lacan*, 155–60.
37. Chion, "The Fourth Side," 175.
38. On the two other occasions when the film shows Jeff with his back to the window for any sustained period of time, he is asleep.
39. William Egginton, "Reality is Bleeding: A Brief History of Film from the Sixteenth Century," *Configurations* 9 (2001), 208. I am indebted to Genie Brinkema for this reference. In an unpublished paper, Vineet Dewan applies the term "bleeding" to similar moments in *The Birds*.
40. Egginton, 210. Egginton calls the first mode "illusionism" and the second "realism," but because his terms conflict with what is usually referred to as realism in film, and confuse distinctions with which we have been working, I will not refer to his categories by name.
41. Egginton, 215.

42. The shooting of a gun directly into the space of the audience is a ploy familiar from the films of Fritz Lang. One such instance involves the character Kent in *The Testament of Dr. Mabuse.*

43. The use of red flashes is central to *Marnie* (1964), where their function is to intensify the subjectivity of the shots in which they occur—and to indicate that the images we see are connected with the trauma in which Marnie's illness originates. Here, psychological disturbance is registered in the domain of sight: the flashes of red that disturb Marnie's sight indicate a recursion of memory fragments and delusion. Yet here, too, the film reveals that the origin of psychological trauma is in the blood of the inaugural crime scene.

44. "Courbet," writes Fried, "is a painter seeking to express by all the means at his disposal his own embodiedness." *Courbet's Realism,* 78.

45. Rothman, 251.

46. Stephen Rebello, *Alfred Hitchcock and the Making of Psycho* (New York: St. Martin's Griffin, 1990), 153–4.

47. Spoto, 455.

48. Zizek, "The Hitchcockian Blot," *Looking Awry,* 98–99.

49. Zizek, "How the Non-duped Err," *Looking Awry,* 81.

50. Fred Jameson, "Spatial Systems in *North by Northwest,*" *Everything You Always Wanted to Know About Lacan,* 50.

51. Jameson, "Spatial Systems," 60.

52. Ibid.

53. Michael Kerbel, "3-D or Not 3-D," *Film Comment,* 16:6 (November–December 1980), 15.

54. Jameson, "Spatial Systems," 63. Jameson does not remain content to juxtapose these two movements described, however. Instead, he proposes that we contrast the movement into the screen (Courbet's figured entry into the text) as he puts it, "*not* with its logical 3-D opposite, but rather with a movement *on to* the great sheet of space with which the Grant figure is associated, and away from it again" (61).

55. Jameson, "Spatial Systems," 63.

56. Cavell, "North by Northwest," *Hitchcock Reader,* 259.

57. Quoted from an unpublished lecture, "Pretexts of Occasion: Representing Representation Anxiety in Still Lifes and Group Portraits," delivered at a conference on "Visual Culture in Early Modern Europe: The Dutch Experience," at the Whitney Humanities Center, Yale University, February 1–2, 2002.

58. Jean Baudrillard, "The Trompe-l'oeil," *Calligram: Essays in New Art History from France,* ed. Norman Bryson (Cambridge: Cambridge University Press, 1988), 53.

59. Baudrillard, 57.

60. Baudrillard, "The Trompe l'Oeil," 59.

CHAPTER 6

1. The phrasing of this exchange is taken from the English translation of Roland Barthes's *Camera Lucida,* probably the version read by Kubrick (*Camera Lucida: Re-*

flections on Photography, trans. Richard Howard [New York: Hill and Wang, 1981], 53). Gustav Janouch's original—and perhaps fictitious—account is as follows: "Die Vorbedingung des Bildes ist das Sehen." Kafka lächelte. "Man photographiert Dinge, um sie aus dem Sinn zu verscheuchen. Meine Geschichten sind eine Art von Augenschliessen" (*Gespräche mit Kafka: Aufzeichnungen und Erinnerungen* [Frankfurt am Main: S. Fischer, 1968], 54). The English translation of *Conversations with Kafka* is as follows: "The condition of an image is vision." Kafka smiled. "One photographs things in order to get them out of one's mind. My stories are a kind of closing one's eyes" (*Conversations With Kafka*, trans. Goronwy Rees [London: Quartet Books, 1985]), 31.

2. Indeed, Kubrick's reported interest is in filming things that "the mind could see but the eye could not." (Alexander Walker, Sybil Taylor, Ulrich Ruchti, *Stanley Kubrick, Director: A Visual Analysis* [New York and London: W. W. Norton], 344–45.)

3. In the title of his memoir of Stanley Kubrick, *Eyes Wide Open*, Frederic Raphael, who wrote the screenplay for Kubrick's last film, excises the paradox from Kubrick's title, which he neither liked nor understood. (*Eyes Wide Open: A Memoir of Stanley Kubrick* [New York: Ballantine, 1999], 136.)

4. Barthes, *Camera Lucida*, 55.

5. Barthes, *Camera Lucida*, 26.

6. Barthes, *Camera Lucida*, 27; 40.

7. Michel Ciment, *Kubrick*, trans. Gilbert Adair (New York: Holt, Rinehart, Winston, 1983), 66; 146; 154; 156; 186.

8. Ciment, 154; 156.

9. Raphael, *Eyes Wide Open*, 112.

10. See Dennis Bingham, "The Displaced Auteur: A Reception History of *The Shining*," 290, in *Perspectives on Stanley Kubrick*, ed. Mario Falsetto (New York: G. K. Hall, 1996).

11. Ciment, 186.

12. Ciment, 144.

13. See Ciment, 186.

14. Bingham, "The Displaced Auteur," 301.

15. Bingham, "The Displaced Auteur," 291.

16. Winfried Menninghaus, *Ekel: Theorie und Geschichte einer starken Empfindung* (Frankfurt am Main: Suhrkamp, 1999), 133.

17. Frederic Raphael claims that "the still—or *almost* still—image was fundamental to Kubrick's vision of cinema. The density and care with which the frame was so often composed in his work showed very little to any appetite for motion," *Eyes Wide Open*, 134.

18. Annette Michelson, "Bodies in Space: Film As Carnal Knowledge," *Artforum* 7:6 (1969), 59.

19. Siegfried Kracauer, "Die Photographie," *Das Ornament der Masse* (Frankfurt am Main: Suhrkamp, 1963), 31.

20. Barthes, *Camera Lucida*, 15.

21. See Brigitte Peucker, *Incorporating Images: Film and the Rival Arts* (Princeton, NJ: Princeton University Press, 1995), 10–15.

22. Barthes, *Camera Lucida*, 9. In essay form, this reading was completed before I had read *Between Film and Screen*, Garrett Stewart's comprehensive study of—among other things—the presence of photography in film, yet it is clear that Stewart preempts my reading of *The Shining* here in a some ways. Nevertheless, my emphasis is rather different from his. See Garrett Stewart, *Between Film and Screen: Modernism's Photo Synthesis* (Chicago: The University of Chicago Press, 1999), 176–87.

23. Indiscriminately combining the different temporal moments of the photographs—Grady's stewardship of the Overlook in the 1970s is merged with the 1920s during which the hotel flourished—Jack's visions deemphasize temporality in favor of the space of their setting, the hotel. But it is not "nostalgia" for the past—for *which* past? we might well ask—that animates Kubrick to bring them to life, as Fred Jameson has suggested. (See Fredric Jameson, "Historicism in *The Shining*," *Signatures of the Visible* [New York: Routledge, 1992], 82–98.) Rather, it is the temporality of the photograph, its unique moment in time, that these sequences undermine as they conflate and subvert their several temporalities by introducing narrative—or cinematic time—into their frames.

24. See Jameson, 94.

25. See *Faust I*, "Auerbach's Cellar."

26. Linda Williams, *Hardcore: Power, Pleasure, and the "Frenzy of the Visible"* (Berkeley: University of California Press, 1989), 191.

27. Barthes, *Camera Lucida*, 92.

28. See Michelson, 60.

29. See my reading of *Day of Wrath* in *Incorporating Images*, 94–101.

30. Another example of this occurs as the camera, having peered from behind a pillar in the "8 A.M." sequence, then reveals Jack also to be peering.

31. In this it resembles *2001*, where science fiction's "denial of sexuality, mortality, fleshy bodies" (See Scott Bukatman, "The Artificial Infinite: On Special Effects and the Sublime," in *Visual Display: Culture Beyond Appearances*, ed. Lynne Cooke and Peter Wollen [Seattle: Bay Press, 1995, 289]) finds its counterpart, too, in an address of the spectatorial body. As Annette Michelson has brilliantly argued with regard to *2001*, "Things happen between the screen and the spectator" that "dissolve the opposition of body and mind" (57).

32. Kubrick's visual allusion to Lewis Carroll is a complex one, perhaps referring less directly to *Through the Looking Glass* than to Carroll's staged photographs, whose transparent dream figures and ghosts seem to speculate on the nature of the photographic medium. Kubrick also alludes to sequences in Expressionist film in which the mirror image takes on a life of its own. See especially Paul Wegener's *The Student of Prague* (1913), on which Otto Rank based his study of the double.

33. Menninghaus, *Ekel*, 336; my translation.

34. Gilles Deleuze, *Cinema 2: The Time-Image*, trans. Hugh Tomlinson and Robert Galeta (Minneapolis: University of Minnesota Press, 1994), 205–6.

35. Ciment, *Kubrick*, 144.
36. Pietro Santarcangeli, quoted in Ciment, 146.
37. Walker, Taylor, and Ruchti, 233.
38. See, for example, Barbara Creed, *The Monstrous-Feminine: Film, Feminism, Psychoanalysis* (London: Routledge, 1993).
39. Barthes, 40.
40. Ciment, 144.
41. See Julia Kristeva, *Powers of Horror: An Essay on Abjection*, trans. Leon S. Roudiez (New York: Columbia University Press, 1982), 16.
42. Kristeva, *Powers of Horror*, 55.
43. Kristeva, *Powers of Horror*, 13.
44. Arthur Schnitzler, *Traumnovelle* (Berlin: S. Fischer, 1926), 50.
45. Raphael, *Eyes Wide Open*, 59.
46. Ibid.
47. Raphael, *Eyes Wide Open*, 108. Nevertheless, as Raphael puts it, "my glib suspicion is that the only serious scandal for him is the Holocaust, which is why he will not, or cannot, deal with it," 151.
48. Frederic Raphael asserts: "It is, however, absurd to try to understand Stanley Kubrick without reckoning on Jewishness as a fundamental aspect of his mentality, if not of his work in general" even though "he himself was known to have said that he was not really a Jew, he just happened to have two Jewish parents. Jews are not featured in any of his films; he seemed to expose, or at least to dwell on, many ugly aspects of human behavior, but he never confronted anti-Semitism. Is it unduly fanciful to see fear and horror driving him to face in art the malice that he feared in life?" (107–8).
49. It is not known whether Schnitzler ever read Kafka's *The Trial*. He seems to have read *The Castle* in 1928, two years after the publication of *Traumnovelle*. But the actual presence of "Kafkaesque" material in Schnitzler's text is not at issue. What matters is how Kubrick—who did read Kafka—may have read the Schnitzler novella, one of the literary texts that most fascinated him. One might add that turning the *Traumnovelle* into a film was also a long-standing wish of Schnitzler's, who began to work on a screenplay for this novella shortly before his death. My thanks to Leo Lensing, who steered me to his article "Schnitzler's alphabet of love: Sex, music and dreams in *fin-de-siècle* Vienna," *TLS* October 13, 2000, 5–6, in which he writes: "Did Schnitzler read Kafka? In Hohenschwangau, of all places, where he stayed while touring what he called the 'regal kitsch' of Neuschwanstein, he records reading Kafka's very different *Castle* on the evenings of August 19 and 21, 1928; on each of the following mornings he begins his journal entry with the text of a dream. Schnitzler dreaming of Kafka? Psychoanalysts will want to read carefully" (6).
50. Slavoj Zizek, *Looking Awry: An Introduction to Jacques Lacan Through Popular Culture* (Boston: MIT Press, 1991), 147.
51. Zizek, *Looking Awry*, 147.
52. Zizek, *Looking Awry*, 149.

53. Zizek, *Looking Awry*, 150.
54. Ibid.
55. Kevin Stoehr, "Kubrick and Ricoeur on Nihilistic Horror and the Symbolism of Evil," *Film and Philosophy*, special ed. (2001), 98.
56. Schnitzler uses the term "Femrichter," judges of the "Feme," which, from the fourteenth through the eighteenth centuries, referred to a secret court to which only the initiated had access.
57. Zizek, *Looking Awry*, 151.
58. Michelson, 58.

CHAPTER 7

1. Roland Barthes, *S/Z*, trans. Richard Miller (New York: Hill and Wang, 1975), 20.
2. Barthes, 39.
3. Barthes, 200.
4. Barthes, 202. The significant chain of textualities in *Sarrasine* involves a (fictional) plaster sculpture of the castrato Zambinella, later executed in marble and copied by Vien for his painting of Adonis, in its turn imitated by Girodet for his *Endymion*—from which the narrator's story proceeds. Moving from fictional "life" to sculpture to painting and then back to narrative, *Sarrasine* embraces the movement through various mediums and genders, always with the ironic awareness that the "real" body of Zambinella is ambiguously gendered, that of a castrato.
5. Timothy Corrigan, *A Cinema Without Walls: Movies and Culture After Vietnam* (New Brunswick, NJ: Rutgers University Press, 1991), 69.
6. Julia Kristeva, "Approaching Abjection," *Powers of Horror: An Essay on Abjection* (New York: Columbia University Press, 1982), 18.
7. Thomas Elsaesser, *Fassbinder's Germany: History Identity Subject* (Amsterdam: Amsterdam University Press, 1996), 191.
8. Roland Barthes, *The Pleasure of the Text*, trans. Richard Miller (New York: Hill and Wang, 1975), 67.
9. Roland Barthes, "The Grain of the Voice," *Image, Music, Text*, trans. Stephen Heath (New York: Hill and Wang, 1977), 182.
10. As John Belton points out, "sound recorded at the same time as the image is recorded locks the sound indexically into the profilmic event." "Technology and the Aesthetics of Film Sound," *Film Sound: Theory and Practice*, ed. Elisabeth Weis and John Belton (New York: Columbia University Press, 1985), 70.
11. Robert Burgoyne, "Narrative and Sexual Excess," *October* 21 (1982), 59.
12. Kaja Silverman, *The Acoustic Mirror: The Female Voice in Psychoanalysis and Cinema* (Bloomington: Indiana University Press, 1988), 18.
13. Kaja Silverman, *Male Subjectivity at the Margins* (New York: Routledge, 1992), 258.

14. Fassbinder credits himself with virtually all of the authorial functions in this film. For details about the autobiographical significance of this film for Fassbinder, see Elsaesser (197–8) and Silverman (*Male Subjectivity at the Margins*, 214–15). In her suggestive chapter, Silverman discusses the relay from Erwin to Tasso and Fassbinder, reading this structure under the sign of sadomasochistic excorporation (257).

15. Although the film was not shown in its entirety in Germany after the war, from the 1960s on the abbatoir scene was often included in documentary film and television programs, and Fassbinder is very likely to have seen it. See Stig Hornsøj-Møller and David Cuthbert, "*Der ewige Jude* (1940): Joseph Goebbels Unequaled Monument to Anti-Semitism," *Historical Journal of Film, Radio, and Television* 12:1 (1992), 50.

16. See Andrei Markovits, Seyla Benhabib, and Moishe Postone, "Rainer Werner Fassbinder's Garbage, the City, and Death," *New German Critique* 38 (1986), 1–28, especially Gertrude Koch's discussion of Jewish characters in Fassbinder's work.

17. Elsaesser, 191; 207.

18. Alice A. Kuzniar, "Transgender Specularity in Leander and Fassbinder," *The Queer German Cinema* (Stanford, CA: Stanford University Press, 2000), 83.

19. See Kuzniar, 63; 66.

20. Kuzniar, 70.

21. As Sabine Hake points out, " From the conditions of production and reception to the filmic mise-en-scène of auditory relations and acoustic effects, music triumphs as the unifying force behind Sierck's conception of melodrama." "Detlef Sierck and *Schlussakkord (Final Chord*, 1936*)*: A Case Study of Film Authorship, *Popular Cinema of the Third Reich* (Austin: University of Texas Press, 2001), 114–15.

22. Silverman, *The Acoustic Mirror*, 85.

23. Mary Ann Doane, "The Voice in the Cinema: The Articulation of Body and Space," *Yale French Studies* 60 (1980), 44. See also Silverman, *The Acoustic Mirror*, 80ff.

24. Norbert Jürgen Schneider, *Handbuch Filmmusik: Musikdramaturgie im Neuen Deutschen Film* (München: Verlag Ölschläger, 1986), 109.

25. Silverman, *The Acoustic Mirror*, 85.

26. Kristeva, 3. For another reading of abjection in Fassbinder's films, see Steven Shaviro's discussion of abject identification in Fassbinder's *Querelle* in "Masculinity, Spectacle, and the Body of *Querelle*," *The Cinematic Body* (Minneapolis: University of Minnesota Press, 1993), 184–96.

27. Kristeva, 4.

28. Quoted in Neil Leach, *Re-Thinking Architecture: A Reader in Cultural Theory* (London: Routledge, 1997), 22.

29. Kristeva, 7.

30. Silverman, *Male Subjectivity*, 264.

31. Slavoj Zizek, *The Sublime Object of Ideology* (London: Verso, 1989), 116.

32. Zizek, 116.

33. Silverman, *Acoustic Mirror*, 218.
34. Elsaesser, 210.
35. Kristeva, 18.
36. Interesting here is that Armin Meier may have been a Lebensborn child, the product of Nazi eugenics experiments. See Al La Valley, "The Gay Liberation of Rainer Werner Fassbinder: Male Subjectivity, Male Bodies, Male Lovers," *New German Critique* 63 (1994), 123. As to Saitz, his transvestism (linking him with Elvire) is implied in the ritualist reenactment of a song-and-dance sequence from a televised Jerry Lewis film. The choice of Jerry Lewis as an object of identification is significant here, as well: the "affects of humiliation and embarrassment are central to his work," as Steven Shaviro has pointed out. Lewis's comedy "moves in the direction of abjection . . . shared in a kind of process of contagion" with the audience. Shaviro, *The Cinematic Body* (Minneapolis: University of Minnesota Press, 1993), 108.
37. My reading thus differs from the one put forward by Gertrude Koch, who points out that Fassbinder's suffering characters never include his Jewish characters among them.
38. Eric Santner, "Postmodernism's Jewish Question: Slavoj Zizek and the Monotheistic Perverse," *Discussions in Contemporary Culture: Visual Display*, eds. Lynne Cook and Peter Wollen (Seattle, WA: Bay Press, 1995), 253.
39. Hanns Eisler, *Composing for the Films* (New York: Oxford University Press, 1947), 77.
40. See Michel Chion for a different discussion of recorded or "on-the-air" sound. In *Audio-Vision: Sound on Screen*, trans. Claudia Gorbman (New York: Columbia University Press, 1999), 76ff.

CHAPTER 8

1. Peter Szondi, "*Tableau* and *Coup de Théâtre:* On the Social Psychology of Diderot's Bourgeois Tragedy," *On Textual Understanding and Other Essays, Theory and History of Literature*, vol. 15, trans. Harvey Mendelsohn, foreword Michael Hays (Minneapolis: University of Minnesota Press, 1986), 122–3.
2. Szondi, 123.
3. Szondi, 118.
4. Szondi, 132.
5. See David N. Rodowick, "Madness, Authority, and Ideology: The Domestic Melodrama of the 1950s," *Home is Where the Heart Is: Studies in Melodrama and the Woman's Film*, ed. Christine Gledhill (London: BFI, 1990, rpt), 273.
6. Stefan Grissemann, "'einen Film zu drehen, der zugleich komisch und scheusslich ist': Michael Haneke im Gespräch," *Haneke/Jelinek: Die Klavierspielerin: Drehbuch, Gespräche, Essays* (Vienna: Sonderzahl, 2001), 179.
7. Rodowick, 273. See also Thomas Elsaesser's influential essay, "Tales of Sound and Fury: Observations on the Family Melodrama," *Home is Where the Heart Is*, Gledhill, ed., 43–69.

8. Wolfgang Knorr, "Trilogie der Vereisung," *Kultur*, October 3, 1994, 116.

9. "Beyond Mainstream Film: An Interview with Michael Haneke," *After Postmodernism: Austrian Literature and Film in Transition*, ed. Willy Riemer (Riverside, CA: Ariadne Press, 2000), 162.

10. As Haneke remarked in an interview, he takes a Jansenist approach to beauty: "Um auf die Schönheit zurückzukommen. Ich glaube, sie ist immer ein Geschenk, nie das Resultat einer Absicht. Mit ihr verhält es sich ein bisschen wie mit dem Gott der Jansenisten: sie ist total verborgen and nähert sich nur im Gnadenakt." See Franz Graber, "Der Name der Erbsünde ist Verdrängung: Ein Interview mit Michael Haneke," *Utopie und Fragment: Michael Hanekes Filmwerk*, ed. Franz Grabner, Gerhard Larcher, and Christian Wessely (Thaur, Austria: Kulturverlag, 1996), 18.

11. Riemer, "Mainstream Film," 161.

12. Haneke, "*71 Fragments of a Chronology of Chance*: Notes to the Film," in Riemer, 175.

13. Haneke, "*71 Fragments*: Notes to the Film," 171.

14. As Amos Vogel was rightly prompted to note in response to Haneke's claim that his films encourage spectatorial participation, "cinema remains at all times a manipulative medium. All filmmaking inevitably entails control over the spectator; it is the degree and kind of control that will vary from filmmaker to filmmaker." Amos Vogel, "Of Nonexisting Continents: The Cinema of Michael Haneke," *Film Comment* 32:4 (July/August 1996), 75.

15. Haneke, "*71 Fragments*: Notes to the Film," 172.

16. Interview with Michael Haneke, *Pressemappe zu "71 Fragmente,"* 5. My thanks to Willy Riemer for providing me with this and a wealth of other Haneke material.

17. Haneke, "*71 Fragments*: Notes to the Film," 174.

18. Bresson sees ear and eye as providing different, disjunctive material or, as he puts it: "image and eye must not support each other, but must work each in turn." See Robert Bresson, *Notes on Cinematography*, trans. Jonathan Griffin (New York: Urizen Books, 1975), 28. This remark is no doubt what triggered Bazin's interest in the disjunction of image and sound in Bresson's filmmaking—"what the mind perceives is something that does not match." André Bazin, "'Le journal d'un Curé de Campagne' and the Stylistics of Robert Bresson," *What is Cinema?*, vol. 1 (Berkeley: University of California Press, 1967), 139. Further, Bresson believed in the greater realism of film sound, which he opposed to the stylization of the image. See Noël Burch, "On the Structural Use of Sound," *Film Sound*, ed. Elisabeth Weis and John Belton, 200. See also Fred Camper, "Sound and Silence in Narrative and Non-narrative Cinema" *Film Sound*, 374, on the spatial qualities of sound in Bresson's films: "Throughout these films, sound suggests dimensions to the image beyond what can be seen: both on a literal level, when the sound comes from off-screen, and metaphorically, as the sound adds a mysterious level of spatiality to images that are in themselves curiously despatialized."

19. Terry Eagleton, *The Ideology of the Aesthetic* (Oxford: Oxford University Press, 1990), 12.

20. For a stimulating discussion of corporeal cinema, see Ivone Margulies, "Toward a Corporeal Cinema," *Nothing Happens: Chantal Ackerman's Hyperrealist Everyday* (Durham, NC: Duke University Press, 1996), 48–64.

21. Fredric Jameson, "Introduction," *Signatures of the Visible* (New York: Routledge, 1992), 1.

22. Torben Grodal, *A New Theory of Film Genres, Feelings and Cognition* (Oxford: Clarendon Press, 1997).

23. Greg M. Smith, "Local Emotions, Global Moods, and Film Structure," *Passionate Views: Film, Cognition, and Emotion*, ed. Carl Plantinga and Greg M. Smith (Baltimore: Johns Hopkins University Press, 1999), 108.

24. Vivian Sobchack, *The Address of the Eye: A Phenomenology of Film Experience* (Princeton, NJ: Princeton University Press, 1992), 9.

25. From the trailer for *North by Northwest*. This conversation is also recorded in a slightly different formulation by Donald Spoto, *The Dark Side of Genius: The Life of Alfred Hitchcock* (New York: Ballantine Books, 1983), 440.

26. Peter Bogdanovich, *The Cinema of Alfred Hitchcock* (Garden City, NY: Museum of Modern Art, 1964), 4.

27. Linda Williams, *Hard Core: Power, Pleasure, and the "Frenzy of the Visible"* (Berkeley: University of California Press, 1989), 5.

28. On the temporality of video, see Timothy Corrigan "Immediate History: Videotape Interventions and Narrative Film," *The Image in Dispute: Art and Cinema in the Age of Photography*, ed. Dudley Andrew (Austin: University of Texas Press, 1997), 309–27.

29. See Joel Black's discussion of the reception of *The Blair Witch Project*, in *The Reality Effect: Film Culture and the Graphic Imperative* (New York: Routledge, 2002), 13–14.

30. Michael Fried, *Realism, Writing, Disfiguration: On Thomas Eakins and Stephen Crane* (Chicago: University of Chicago Press, 1987), 65.

31. An important source for *Benny's Video* is undoubtedly *Henry, Portrait of a Serial Killer* (John McNaughton, 1986), which for the first time features video replays by the perpetrators of acts of extreme violence, thus causing an uproar among critics and spectators alike.

32. Jean Baudrillard, "The Ecstasy of Communication" *The Anti-Aesthetic: Essays on Postmodern Culture*, ed. Hal Foster (Seattle, WA: Bay Press, 1983), 127.

33. The rejection of psychological acting is another feature of his filmmaking that Haneke has derived from Bresson. Paul Schrader, *The Transcendental Style in Film: Ozu, Bresson, Dreyer* (New York: Da Capo Press, 1972), 65.

34. Mary Ann Doane, "Information, Crisis, Catastrophe," *Logics of Television: Essays in Cultural Criticism*, ed. Patricia Mellencamp (Indianapolis: Indiana University Press, 1990), 225.

35. See the earlier version of this chapter for a reading of this sequence. "Fragmentation and the Real: Michael Haneke's Family Trilogy," *After Postmodernism:*

Austrian Literature and Film in Transition, ed. Willy Riemer (Riverside, CA: Ariadne Press), 176–88.

36. Another such auratic aural space seems intended partially to recuperate the death of the child in *The Seventh Continent*—or at least to offer some solace to the spectator. The only instance of nondiegetic sound in this film is the fragment of Alban Berg's requiem, "Dem Andenken eines Engels," which is heard at this moment. It is, however, abruptly cut.

37. In this film of fragments we find another form of indebtedness to Bressonian modernism. As Bresson puts it, fragmentation "is indispensable if one does not want to fall into REPRESENTATION [*sic*]. To see beings and things in their separate parts. Render them independent in order to give them a new dependence." Bresson, *Notes on Cinematography*, 46.

38. Haneke's films have motivated oral and written discussions by theologians. See especially the anthology *Utopie und Fragment: Michael Haneke's Filmwerk*.

39. See David Bordwell, *Narration and the Fiction Film* (New York: Routledge, 1988); Torben Grodal, "The Experience of Realism in Audiovisual Representation," *Realism and 'Reality' in Film and Media*, ed. Anne Jerslev (Copenhagen: Museum Tusculanum Press, 2002), 67–91; Julia Hallam with Margaret Marshment, "Discerning Viewers: Cognitive Theory and Identification," *Realism and Popular Cinema* (Manchester, UK: Manchester University Press, 2000), 122–42.

40. See Peucker, 176–88, and Margulies, 52.

41. Quoted from Georg Sesslen, "Strukturen der Vereisung," *Utopie und Fragment*, 47.

42. Hitchcock is not far to seek: here Haneke alludes to the tennis game sequence of *Strangers on a Train* (discussed in Chapters 4 and 5), appropriating what I call Hitchcock's "realist" strategy of expanding film's space by extending it into the space of the audience.

43. A videotape of one of his games will be similarly used by his trainer as a vehicle both for criticism and for the imposition of authority.

44. The concept of "emotional realism" comes from Ien Ang, *Watching 'Dallas': Soap Opera and the Melodramatic Imagination* (New York: Methuen, 1985).

45. Susan Sontag, "Film and Theater," *Film Theory and Criticism*, ed. Gerald Mast, Marshall Cohen, and Leo Braudy (New York: Oxford University Press, 1992), 374.

46. Stephen Prince, "Graphic Violence in the Cinema," *Screening Violence*, ed. Stephen Prince (New Brunswick, NJ: Rutgers University Press, 2000), 32.

47. See Joseph Frank's seminal essay, "Spatial Form in Modern Literature," anthologized in *Criticism: The Foundations of Modern Literary Judgment*, ed. Mark Schorer, Josephine Miles, and Gordon McKenzie (New York: Harcourt, Brace and World, 1948), 379–92.

48. See André Bresson, *The Cinema of Cruelty from Buñuel to Hitchcock*, ed. François Truffaut, trans. Sabine d'Estrée (New York: Seaver Books, 1982).

49. Theodor W. Adorno, "On the Fetish-Character in Music and the Regression of Listening," *The Essential Frankfurt School Reader*, ed. Andrew Arato and Eike Gebhardt (New York: Urizen Books, 1978), 287.

50. Indeed, Peter Handke's notorious play, *Publikumsbeschimpfung* (1966; poorly translated as *Offending the Audience*), which features the verbal assault of the spectator as a series of linguistic permutations or games, is surely a model for this film.

51. As characters, Peter and Paul no doubt derive from the two helpers in Kafka's *The Castle*; indeed, Frank Giering plays both Artur in Haneke's Kafka adaptation and Paul in *Funny Games*. Peter and Paul do not only play sadistic games with the family they murder, but have a sadomasochistic routine worked out between the two of them, as well.

52. Sesslen, 206.

53. This effect seems to extend beyond Leonard Berkovitz's contention that "the observation of aggression evokes aggression-related ideas and thought in the viewers." See "Some Effects of Thoughts on Anti- and Prosocial Influences of Media Events: A Cognitive-Neoassociation Analysis," *Screening Violence*, ed. Prince, 214.

54. Janet Staiger, "The Cultural Productions of *A Clockwork Orange*," *Perverse Spectators: The Practices of Film Reception* (New York: New York University Press, 2000), 94-95.

55. If one were to agree with Jeff Smith that a "central conceit" of Burgess's novel and Kubrick's film is that "Beethoven and other figures of Western culture might be implicated in Alex's 'ultraviolence'" then clearly Kubrick's film also has an influence on Haneke's *The Piano Teacher*. See J. Smith, "Movie Music as Moving Music: Emotion, Cognition, and the Film Score," *Passionate Views*, 147.

56. Susan Rice, 1973, quoted in Staiger, 93.

57. Bazin, *Cinema of Cruelty*, 132.

58. Bazin, *Cinema of Cruelty*, 122.

59. Translation from the German mine. Didier Peron,"Piano forté," *Libération*, 15 mai 2001. Quoted by Stefan Grissemann, "In zwei, drei feinen Linien die Badewanne entlang: Kunst, Utopie, und Selbstbeschmutzung: zu Michael Hanekes Jelinek Adaption," *Haneke/Jelinek: Die Klavierspielerin: Drehbuch Gespräche, Essays*, ed. Stefan Grissemann (Vienna: Sonderzahl, 2001), 7.

60. In the matter of adaptation, too, Haneke follows the example of Bresson who, in *The Diary of a Country Priest* uses Bernanos's novel, as Bazin has pointed out, as so much "material" from another art form. Bazin, 132. Haneke himself abjures adaptation as such in film, relegating faithful adaptations to the inferior medium of video. See Stefan Grissemann, "Österreich im Herbst," *Haneke/Jelinek, Die Klavierspielerin: Drehbuch, Gespräche, Essays* (Vienna: Sonderzahl, 2001), 170.

61. Although some readings of melodrama as a genre, such as Elsaesser's, seek to exclude psychology completely from its network of determinants, others acknowledge the interdependence of the psychological and the social (Rodowick), and others focus primarily on its psychoanalytic vectors (Nowell-Smith). Geof-

frey Nowell-Smith, "Minelli and Melodrama," *Home Is Where the Heart Is*, ed. Gledhill, 70–74.

62. Haneke says that his intention was "etwas Irreales als real auszugeben." Grissemann, "Österreich im Herbst," *Haneke/Jelinek*, 180.

63. Jameson, "The Existence of Italy," *Signatures of the Visible*, 211.

64. Peter Brooks, *The Melodramatic Imagination* (New Haven: Yale University Press, 1976), 57.

65. Nowell-Smith, 74.

66. The strategy of allowing the spectator little or no access to the face and hence to subjectivity is most pronounced in *The Seventh Continent*, where objects (again in keeping with Bresson's work) are the focus of attention.

67. When Erika moves among the cars in search of precisely the scene that she finds, one of the few traveling shots in this film allies our look with Erika's, thus effecting a notable break with the distanced objectivity of this film.

68. Joel Black, *The Reality Effect*, 51.

69. See another interview with Haneke: "einen Film zu drehen, der zugleich komisch und scheusslich ist: Stefan Grissemann im Gespräch mit Michael Haneke," *Haneke/Jelinek*, 179.

70. We should note that in masochism it is possible for a daughter to assume the position of son toward the beating mother "who possesses the ideal phallus." Deleuze, *Coldness and Cruelty*, 68. The female masochist occupies a lesbian position with regard to the mother; the articulation of this position is part of the emancipatory project in Jelinek's novel, in which gender is fluid.

71. He denies that his film is pornographic (by which he means commercial), but hopes that it is obscene. See Grissemann in *Haneke/Jelinek*, 190.

72. Susan Sontag, *Regarding the Pain of Others* (New York: Farrar, Straus, and Giroux, 2003).

73. Gaylyn Studlar, *In the Realm of Pleasure: Von Sternberg, Dietrich, and the Masochistic Aesthetic* (New York: Columbia University Press, 1988), 118.

74. Gilles Deleuze, *Masochism: Coldness and Cruelty* (New York: Zone Books, 1991), 109.

75. Translation mine. *Haneke/Jelinek*, 135.

76. Susan Sontag, "Spiritual Style in the Films of Robert Bresson," *Against Interpretation* (New York: Dell, 1966), 188. Paul Schrader's *Transcendental Style* derives a great many of its insights from Sontag's essay.

77. André Bazin, "*Le Journal d'un curé de campagne* and the Stylistics of Robert Bresson," *What is Cinema?*, vol. I, ed. Hugh Gray (Berkeley: University of California Press, 1967), 136.

78. Jelinek calls Huppert's acting "nearly sculptural," *Haneke/Jelinek*, 121. For the "woman of stone," see Leopold von Sacher-Masoch, *Venus in Furs*, reprinted in Deleuze, *Masochism*.

79. Grissemann, "In zwei, drei feinen Linien," *Haneke/Jelinek*, 31. Gaylyn Studlar, following Deleuze, emphasizes the theatricality of masochism. Theatricality—

and fetishistic behavior—are expressed simultaneously in the clothes Erika purchases in order to adorn her body for the roles she never plays.

80. Deleuze, 33.

81. Studlar, 153.

82. While Jelinek's novel represents sadomasochism, it sublates masochism by means of its feminism, precisely the dimension of *The Piano Teacher* that is de-emphasized by Haneke's film.

83. If the father as superego has been expelled from this universe—as in the case of *The Piano Teacher*—he lingers as the law that "defines a realm of transgression where one is already guilty, and where one oversteps the bounds of the laws without knowing what they are." This, as Deleuze puts it, is the world of Kafka. *Masochism*, 84.

84. Studlar, 152–3.

85. See Kaja Silverman, "The Ruination of Masculinity," *Male Subjectivity at the Margins* (New York: Routledge, 1992), 279, for a reading of a masochistic crucifixion scene in Fassbinder.

86. Klaus Nüchtern, "Schubert im Pornoladen," *Haneke/Jelinek*, 164.

87. "A Violent Streak in Austrian Film," *Austria Kultur* 8:2 (March/April 1998), 5.

88. Ed S. H. Tan and Nico Frijda, "Sentiment in Film Viewing," *Passionate Views: Film, Cognition, and Emotion*, ed. Carl Plantigna and Greg M. Smith (Baltimore: Johns Hopkins University Press, 1999), 52.

89. Tan and Frijda, 55.

90. Ibid.

91. Grodal, "Emotions and Narrative Patterns," *Passionate Views*, 136–7.

92. What this film is not about, asserts Haneke, is control in performance as an expression of a lingering fascism at the Vienna Conservatory. See Grissemann, "Gespräch mit Michael Haneke," 175.

93. Theodor W. Adorno, "Schubert," *Gesammelte Schriften*, vol 17, ed. Rolf Tiedemann (Frankfurt am Main: Suhrkamp, 1982), 23. My thanks to Leon Plantinga for helping me track down this essay.

94. Adorno, "Schubert," 25.

95. "Vor Schuberts Musik stürtzt die Träne aus dem Auge, ohne erst die Seele zu befangen: so unbildlich und real fällt sie in uns ein." Adorno, "Schubert," 33.

CHAPTER 9

1. Maurice Merleau-Ponty, *The Visible and the Invisible*, trans. Alphonso Lingis (Evanston: Northwestern University Press, 1968), 16.

2. Vivian Sobchack, *The Address of the Eye: A Phenomenology of Film Experience* (Princeton, NJ: Princeton University Press, 1992), 8ff.

3. Denis Diderot, *Thoughts on the Interpretation of Nature, and Other Philosophical Works*, introd. David Adams (Manchester, England: Clinamen Press, 1999); Johann Gottfried Herder, "Plastik," *Herders Sämtliche Werke*, vol. 8, ed. Bernhard Suphan (Berlin: Weidmann, 1892); Edmund Burke, *A Philosophical In-*

quiry into the Origin of Our Ideas of the Sublime and the Beautiful, The Works of Edmund Burke, vol I (Boston: Little, Brown and Co., 1871). First published in 1757 then, in an expanded version, in 1759.

4. Jonathan Crary, *Techniques of the Observer: On Vision and Modernity in the Nineteenth Century* (Cambridge, MA: MIT Press, 1990).

5. Walter Benjamin, "The Work of Art in the Age of Its Technological Reproducibility," *Selected Writings*, vol. 3, ed. Marcus Bullock and Michael W. Jennings (Cambridge, MA: Belknap Press), 119. Here Benjamin echoes Alois Riegl's interest in the spectator of visual representation, and deliberately (mis)appropriates Riegl's juxtaposition of the haptical and optical orientations to the representation of artistic space, categories that had preoccupied Benjamin from the writing of *The Origin of German Tragic Drama* onward (see ch. III).

6. Martin Jay, *Downcast Eyes: The Denigration of Vision in Twentieth-Century French Thought* (Berkeley: University of California Press, 1993), 362.

7. Jacques Lacan, *The Four Fundamental Concepts of Psycho-Analysis*, ed. Jacques-Alain Miller, trans. Alan Sheridan (New York: W. W. Norton, 1981), 123.

8. Gotthold Ephraim Lessing, *Laocoön: An Essay on the Limits of Painting and Poetry*, trans. Edward Allen McCormick (Baltimore: Johns Hopkins University Press, 1962), 131; Edmund Burke, *A Philosophical Inquiry into the Origin of Our Ideas of the Sublime and the Beautiful*, 239.

9. As Jocelyne Kolb points out, with the exception of Shakespeare's plays, references to actual food in literature before the late eighteenth century are confined to the lower genres of comedy and the novel. See Kolb, *The Ambiguity of Taste: Freedom and Food in European Romanticism* (Ann Arbor: The University of Michigan Press, 1995), 1.

10. Jacques Aumont, "The Variable Eye, or the Mobilization of the Gaze," trans. Charles O'Brien and Sally Shafto, *The Image in Dispute: Art and Cinema in the Age of Photography*, ed. Dudley Andrew (Austin: University of Texas Press, 1997), 244.

11. Jacques Lacan, *The Four Fundamental Concepts of Psycho-Analysis*, 115.

12. Bertram Lewin's "Sleep, Mouth and the Dream Screen," *Psychoanalytic Quarterly* (1946, 15:419–43 and his "Inferences from the Dream Screen," *International Journal of Psychoanalysis* (1948), 29:224–431. Cited by Jean-Louis Baudry, "The Apparatus: Metapsychological Approaches to the Impression of Reality in Film," *Narrative, Apparatus, Ideology: A Film Theory Reader*, ed. Philip Rosen (New York: Columbia University Press, 1986), 317.

13. Baudry, "The Apparatus," 310–11. It should be noted, however, that for Baudry the subject of film experience remains a transcendental subject.

14. Baudry, "The Apparatus," 316; 318.

15. Christian Metz, *The Imaginary Signifier: Psychoanalysis and the Cinema*, trans. Celia Britton et al. (Bloomington: University of Indiana Press, 1982), 50.

16. In her insightful study of the horror film, Carol Clover builds on Metz's double gaze, calling its two permutations in horror the "assaultive" and the "reactive"

gaze, thereby suggesting the connection to Freud's active and passive aims in looking. "The Eye of Horror," *Men, Women and Chainsaws: Gender in the Modern Horror Film* (Princeton, NJ: Princeton University Press, 1992), 199.

17. E. H. Gombrich, "Psycho-Analysis and the History of Art," *Meditations on a Hobby-Horse and other Essays on the Theory of Art* (Oxford: Phaidon, 1963), 39.

18. Ibid.

19. Ibid.

20. Ibid.

21. *British Journal of Medical Psychology* IV (1924), 152f. Cited by Gombrich in note #19, 165.

22. Gombrich, 43.

23. Noël Carroll, *The Philosophy of Horror, or Paradoxes of the Heart* (New York: Routledge, 1990), 14.

24. See Janet Staiger, "Hitchcock in Texas: Intertextuality in the Face of Blood and Gore," *Perverse Spectators: The Practices of Film Reception* (New York: New York University Press, 2000), 179–87.

25. Price's "Dialogue" is quoted in Christopher Hussey, *The Picturesque: Studies in a Point of View* (London: Frank and Cass, 1967), 77.

26. Mieke Bal, "Dead Flesh, or the Smell of Painting," *Visual Culture: Images and Interpretations*, ed. Norman Bryson, Michael Ann Holly, and Keith Moxey (Hanover, NH: University Press of New England, 1994), 373.

27. For a delineation of this subgenre, see Mikita Brottman, *Meat is Murder: An Illustrated Guide to Cannibal Culture* (London: Creation Books, 1998).

28. Gombrich, "On Physiognomic Perception," *Meditations on a Hobby-Horse*, 48.

29. Tania Modleski, *The Women Who Knew Too Much: Hitchcock and Feminist Theory* (London: Routledge, 1988), 107.

30. Citing Hitchcock's Catholicism, Modleski briefly pursues the question of the sacramental feast with regard to *Frenzy*. See *Women Who Knew*, 109. I have profited from reading Maggie Kilgour's suggestive study of cannibalism in literature, *From Communion to Cannibalism: An Anatomy of Metaphors of Incorporation* (Princeton, NJ: Princeton University Press, 1990); from Peggy Reeves Sanday's anthropological study of cannibalism, *Divine Hunger: Cannibalism as Cultural System* (Cambridge: Cambridge University Press, 1986); as well as from Mary Douglas's seminal study, *Purity and Danger* (London: Routledge and Kegan Paul, 1966).

31. Julia Kristeva, "From Filth to Defilement," *Powers of Horror: An Essay on Abjection* (New York: Columbia University Press, 1982), 75–76.

32. Raymond Bellour, "Psychosis, Neurosis, Perversion," *A Hitchcock Reader*, ed. Marshall Deutelbaum and Leland Poague (Ames: Iowa State University Press, 1986), 324.

33. Of particular interest, however, is Michel Chion, "The Voice That Seeks A Body," *The Voice in Cinema*, trans. Claudia Gorbman (New York: Columbia University Press, 1999), 125–61.

34. In his frequently anthologized essay, Robin Wood reads Mrs. Bates, Norman's mother, as a metaphorical cannibal "who swallows up her son." See "An Introduction to the American Horror Film," *Planks of Reason: Essays on the Horror Film*, ed. Barry Keith Grant (Metuchen, NJ: Scarecrow Press, 1984), 181–82.

35. George Toles, "'If Thine Eye Offend Thee . . .': *Psycho* and the Art of Infection," *Alfred Hitchcock Centenary Essays*, ed. Richard Allen and S. Ishii Gonzalès (London: BFI, 1999), 162.

36. Quoting Hitchcock, Pascal Bonitzer refers to the "stain" in Zizek's sense (see Chapters 4 and 5) as a "drop of blood" in the "clear waters" of a stream." See "Hitchcockian Suspense," *Everything You Always Wanted to Know About Lacan (But Were Afraid to Ask Hitchcock)* ed. Slavoj Zizek (London: Verso, 1992), 22.

37. Lesley Brill, *The Hitchcock Romance: Love and Irony in Hitchcock's Films* (Princeton, NJ: Princeton University Press, 1988), 285.

38. Slavoj Zizek, "The Hitchcockian Blot," *Looking Awry: An Introduction to Lacan Through Popular Culture* (Cambridge, MA: MIT Press, 1991), 90–93.

39. Zizek, "The Real and its Vicissitudes," *Looking Awry*, 26. This is a far cry from the prelapsarian innocence accorded to the characters of this film by Brill, *The Hitchcock Romance*, 284.

40. Brill, *The Hitchcock Romance*, 289.

41. Zizek, "The Real and its Vicissitudes," *Looking Awry*, 26.

42. Donald Spoto, *The Dark Side of Genius: The Life of Alfred Hitchcock* (New York: Ballantine Books, 1983), 563–4.

43. See D. A. Miller, "Anal *Rope*," *Representations* 32 (Fall 1990), 114–33; also, Thomas M. Bauso, "*Rope:* Hitchcock's Unkindest Cut," *Hitchcock's Re-Released Films*, ed. Walter Raubichek and Walter Skrebnick (Detroit, MI: Wayne State University Press, 1991), 226–39; Thomas Hemmeter, "Twisted Writing: *Rope* as an Experimental Film," *Hitchcock's Re-Released Films*, 253–65; Peter Wollen, "*Rope:* Three Theses," *Centenary Essays*, 75–85.

44. François Trauffaut, *Hitchcock*, rev. ed. (New York: Simon and Schuster, 1983), 184.

45. From a contemporary essay that Hitchcock called "My Most Exciting Picture" and published in *Popular Photography*, quoted from Bauso, "*Rope:* Hitchcock's Unkindest Cut," 228.

46. Spoto, *The Dark Side of Genius*, 371.

47. In "Anal *Rope*," D. A. Miller has evocatively pursued the manner in which gay themes motivate this film's fixation on technique, and I will not recount them here. See also Robin Wood, "Hitchcock's Homophobic Gays," and Amy Lawrence, "*Rope*, James Stewart, and the Postwar Crisis of American Masculinity," *Hitchcock's America*, ed. Jonathan Freedman and Richard Millington (New York: Oxford University Press, 1999), 55–76.

48. Zizek, "The Real and its Vicissitudes," *Looking Awry*, 43.

49. See Brigitte Peucker, *Incorporating Images: Film and the Rival Arts* (Princeton, NJ: Princeton University Press), 162–3.

50. Although Hitchcock is present in the more usual form of the cameo in this film, too—he is seen crossing the street right after the main title—this appearance does not undermine my argument.

51. Spoto, 495.

52. See Brigitte Peucker, "The Material Image in Goethe's *Wahlverwandtschaften*," *The Germanic Review* 74:3 (1999), 195–213. On the contact image, see Joseph Koerner, *The Moment of Portraiture in German Renaissance Art* (Chicago: University of Chicago Press, 1993).

53. Julia Kristeva, *Powers of Horror: An Essay on Abjection*, trans. Leon S. Roudiez (New York: Columbia University Press, 1982).

54. Claude Lévi-Strauss, *The Naked Man*, trans. J. Weightman and D. Weightman (London: Harper and Row, 1981), 141.

55. Seen from an anthropological perspective, cultural cannibalism is read as a symbolic system. As Peggy Reeves Sanday points out in her excellent study, dialectical opposition determines the symbolic ordering of ritual cannibalism, an ordering from which the construction of self and society proceeds, thus serving as a means of distinguishing the cultural self from the natural other. See *Divine Hunger: Cannibalism as a Cultural System*, 33.

56. Winfried Menninghaus, *Ekel: Theorie und Geschichte einer starken Empfindung* (Frankfurt am Main: Suhrkamp, 1999), 11.

57. Joan Copjec, "Vampires, Breast-Feeding, and Anxiety," *The Horror Reader*, ed. Ken Gelder (London: Routledge, 2000), 61.

58. Robert Bloch, *Psycho* (New York: Simon and Schuster, 1959). See also Mikita Brottman, *Meat is Murder: An Illustrated Guide to Cannibal Culture*. (London: Creation Books, 1998), 33–35.

59. Wood, "American Horror Film," 191.

60. Janet Staiger, "Hitchcock in Texas: Intertextuality in the Face of Blood and Gore," *Perverse Spectators: The Practices of Film Reception* (New York: New York University Press, 2000), 184. There are many more allusions to Hitchcock than Staiger mentions here, and they do not simply exist at the level of the plot. I will take up some of these in my reading, although it is not its object to be exhaustive.

61. Staiger, 185; Robin Wood, "The American Film Comedy from *Meet Me in St. Louis* to *The Texas Chainsaw Massacre*," *Wide Angle* 3:2 (1979), 5–11.

62. Material made available in Stefan Jaworzyn's *The Texas Chain Saw Massacre Companion* (London: Titan Books, 2003) might very well lead one in this direction.

63. See Reynold Humphries, *The American Horror Film: An Introduction* (Edinburgh: Edinburgh University Press, 2002), 123–4, and Christopher Sharrett, "The Idea of Apocalypse in *Texas Chainsaw Massacre*," *Planks of Reason*, ed. Barry Keith Grant (Metuchen, NJ: Scarecrow Press, 1984), 255–76.

64. Carol Clover first made it respectable to watch and study such films. See Carol J. Clover, *Men, Women and Chain Saws: Gender in the Modern Horror Film* (Princeton, NJ: Princeton University Press, 1992).

65. Jaworzyn, 31–32; 49.

66. The spectator's conflation with the subjective camera is one of the stock devices of horror, but does not begin with *Halloween* (1978), as claimed by Clover, 186.
67. See Clover, "The Eye of Horror," 166–230.
68. Staiger, 180.
69. Mikita Brottman, *Offensive Films: Towards an Anthropology of Cinéma Vomitif* (Westport, CT: Greenwood Press, 1997).
70. See Chapter 5. Spoto, 455.
71. Big Mama is rendered sculpture precisely because she is threatening. From her lap the heroine retrieves a chainsaw with which she finally puts an end to Hitchhiker/Chop Top. On the tower above the shrine flies the American flag, a fetish of another kind in a cultural comment that merges myths of the nation with the myth of the Mother. In the final images of the film, the heroine holds the chainsaw above her head in triumph, the living embodiment of the phallic Mother from whose lap she has wrested it. The mythologized heroes of Texas represented in the oversized plastic figures of cowboys, the film suggests, were not arrested in the oral stage, as were the cannibal brothers. At least in the cultural imagination that keeps them alive and sustains them, they derived their phallic power by triumphing over the death-bringing Mother, who must be killed off so that they may attain it. But the triumphant heroine with her chainsaw suggests that Big Mama lives on, after all. In some sense, then, this film seems finally to want to contradict Barbara Creed's contention—with which I agree—that the threatening mother figure of horror is the preoedipal mother. Barbara Creed, "Horror and the Monstrous-Feminine: An Imaginary Abjection," *Screen* 27:1 (January–February 1986), 44–70. Also see her essay "Kristeva, Femininity, Abjection," *The Horror Reader*, ed. Ken Gelder (London: Routledge, 2000), 64–70, republished from her book, *The Monstrous-Feminine* (Routledge, 1993).
72. Marina Warner, "Waxworks and Wonderlands," *Visual Display: Culture Beyond Appearances*, ed. Lynne Cooke and Peter Wollen (Seattle: Bay Press, 1995), 190. It should also be noted that Jeremy Bentham, the English philosopher, had himself displayed as corpse at the University of London, his body becoming an "auto-icon." Susan Stewart, "Death and Life, in That Order, in the Works of Charles Willson Peale," *Visual Display*, 314, note #20.
73. For a reading of Harris's fiction in the context of these films, see Philip L. Simpson, "The Psycho-Profilers and the Influence of Thomas Harris," *Psycho Paths: Tracking the Serial Killer Through Contemporary American Film and Fiction* (Carbondale: Southern Illinois University Press, 2000), 70–112.
74. Although it points out the association of the image with sacrifice and innocence, Yvonne Tasker's excellent book on *Silence of the Lambs* does not make the connection between cannibalism and communion. *The Silence of the Lambs* (London: British Film Institute, 2002), 16.
75. Yvonne Tasker mentions the indebtedness to Bacon (p. 32), and it is mentioned as well by Kristi Zea in the documentary concerning the making of Demme's film on its special edition DVD (2001).

76. See Kaja Silverman, "Masochistic Ecstasy and the Ruination of Masculinity in Fassbinder's Cinema," *Male Subjectivity at the Margins* (New York: Routledge, 1992), 279ff, for a reading of sadomasochistic pleasure in connection with scenes of crucifixion. See also Kristeva on Artaud's identification with the crucified Christ, 26–27.

77. The fact that transformation—metamorphosis—is at issue for Buffalo Bill is supported by the Death's Head moths that Bill places in the mouths of his female victims.

78. Thomas Harris, *The Silence of the Lambs* (New York: St. Martin's Press, 1988), 281–3.

79. In *The Hannibal Files*, Daniel O'Brien notes that the reclusive Harris, who has only produced four novels in twenty-four years, has a sculpture of a mutilated, headless woman in his garden in Sag Harbor. *The Hannibal Files* (London: Reynolds and Hearn, 2001), 9.

80. Peggy Reeves Sanday, 50.

81. Montaigne: "I think that there is more barbarity in eating a man alive than in eating him dead . . . in roasting a man bit by bit, in having him bitten and mangled by dogs and swine." The latter is to be the fate of Lecter through the agency of his enemy, Verger. "Of cannibals," *The Complete Essays of Montaigne*, trans. Donald M. Frame (Palo Alto, CA: Stanford University Press, 1958), 155.

82. Clover, "The Eye of Horror," 209. For an incisive study of masochism in its connection to film spectatorship, see Gaylyn Studlar's *In the Realm of Pleasure: Von Sternberg, Dietrich, and the Masochistic Aesthetic* (Urbana: University of Illinois Press, 1988).

83. Noël Carroll, "Film, Emotion, Genre," *Passionate Views: Film, Cognition, Emotion*, ed. Carl Plantinga and Greg M. Smith (Baltimore: Johns Hopkins University Press, 1999), 39. Carroll's *The Philosophy of Horror, or Paradoxes of the Heart* (London: Routledge, 1990) is not particularly relevant to my work on horror.

84. Clover, "The Eye of Horror," 166; 230.

85. Clover, "The Eye of Horror, 199.

INDEX

abjection, 177, 184, 221n26, 222n36; Kristeva on, 112, 115, 117, 122, 124, 125, 126, 168, 180
Addison, Joseph, 133
Adorno, Theodor: on the corpse as model for art, 13; "Freudian Theory and the Pattern of Fascist Propaganda," 49; and Kracauer, 4, 194n17; "On the Fetish-Character in Music and the Regression of Listening," 143; on Schubert's music, 157–58
aesthetics of affect, 129–31, 133, 147
Age of Innocence, The (Moeller film), 19–20, 23, 27–28, 197n4, 198n18
Age of Innocence, The (Reynolds painting), 22, 25
Age of Innocence, The (Ruggles film), 197n4
Age of Innocence, The (Scorsese film), 19–20, 21–26, 28–29, 198nn11,14,16
Age of Innocence, The (Wharton novel), 19–29, 163, 197n4, 198n11, 199n29, 210n13
Alberti, Leon Battista, 33, 38–39, 41, 45
Allen, Richard, 7–8, 210n15
Allen, Woody: *The Purple Rose of Cairo*, 95
Alpers, Svetlana: *The Art of Describing*, 33, 41–42, 200n14; on realism, 14, 33, 41–42, 43, 45

Andrew, Dudley, 193n3
Ang, Ien, 225n44
Antheil, George: *Ballet Mécanique*, 107
Antonioni, Michelangelo: *Blow-Up*, 145, 148
Arbus, Diane: "Identical Twins," 109
Ariosto, Ludovico: story of Angelica and Medora, 22
Aristotle, 12
Arnheim, Rudolf, 7
Astruc, Alexandre, 24
Aumont, Jacques, 8, 161, 202n57

Baburen, Dirck van: "The Procuress," 34, 35
Bacon, Francis, 184, 186, 233n75
Bakhtin, Mikhail, 115
Bal, Mieke, 164, 179
Balázs, Béla, 208n87
Ballet Mécanique, 107
Ballhaus, Michael, 26–27
Balzac, Honoré de: *Sarrasine*, 116, 120, 220n4
Barry Lyndon, 107
Barthes, Roland, 14, 117; on Balzac's *Sarrasine*, 116; *Camera Lucida*, 63, 105, 107, 111, 114; "The Photographic Message," 40; on photography, 40, 63, 105, 106, 107; on the realist text, 116; *S/Z*, 116

Bass, Elaine, 27
Bass, Saul, 27, 100–101, 199n32
Bataille, Georges, 123, 124
Baudelaire, Charles: *Painter of Modern Life*, 41
Baudrillard, Jean, 9, 11; and Haneke, 135, 146; on photographs, 40–41; on trompe l'oeil, 102
Baudry, Jean-Louis: "The Apparatus: Metapsychological Approaches to the Impression of Reality in Film," 161, 229n13; vs. Bazin, 7; on Plato's cave and film, 6–7; on the spectator, 161
Baumgarten, Alexander, 11
Baumgarten, Wilhelm Gottlieb, 160
Bazin, André, 100; on art as embalming time, 28, 39, 64–65, 72; vs. Baudry, 7; on Bresson, 132, 152, 226n60; *The Cinema of Cruelty*, 148; on film as showing reality, 1, 2, 3, 4, 40, 193n3, 194n7, 213n11; on Hitchcock, 148; on indexicality of film, 2, 4, 40, 201n46; on indexicality of photographs, 40, 64–65, 201n46; vs. Kracauer, 1, 2, 3, 4, 40, 193n3, 194n7; on off-screen space, 95; "The Ontology of the Photographic Image," 7, 194n8, 201n46; on photography, 40, 64–65, 72, 194n8, 201n46, 207n77; on psychological vs. aesthetic need, 7; on veil of Veronica, 4
Bellour, Raymond, 168; "The Film Stilled," 66; on Hitchcock, 77
Belton, John, 220n10; on theatrical vs. cinematic film space, 94–95
Belvedere Apollo, 56
Benjamin, Walter, 21, 51, 208n87; on film, 6, 160, 163; vs. Kracauer, 5–6, 39; *The Origin of German Tragic Drama*, 52–53, 54–55, 56, 58–59, 203n17, 229n5; on painting, 5–6; on photography, 39, 40; on triumphal processions, 52–53, 203n17; vs. Wenders, 39, 40; "The Work of Art in the Age of Its Technological Reproducibility," 5–6, 58, 160, 163, 197n3, 229n5
Benny's Video, 129, 130, 134–38, 139, 140, 141, 147, 154, 224n31
Bentham, Jeremy, 13, 233n72
Berg, Alban, 131, 225n36
Berger, Harry, 101–2
Bergson, Henri: *Matter and Memory*, 160
Berkovitz, Leonard, 226n53
Berlin Alexanderplatz, 124
Berman, Russell: "Written Right Across their Faces," 51, 53, 55, 58, 203n21, 204n35
Bernanos, Georges: *The Diary of a Country Priest*, 226n60
Bertolini, J., 209n4
binarisms: and Fassbinder, 116–17, 123, 125; and Greenaway, 38; and Hooper, 180; and modernity, 205n46
Birds, The, 74, 94, 134, 174–75, 210n15, 215n39
Black, Joel: *The Reality Effect*, 193n1
Blackmail, 28, 78, 80, 99, 166; portrait of jester in, 75–76, 77, 91–92
Blake, William: "The Great Red Dragon and the Woman Clothed with the Sun," 186–87, 189
Block, Robert: *Psycho*, 177
Blow-Up, 145, 148
Blue Angel, The: "Von Kopf bis Fuss," 118
Blue Light, The, 64–67, 205n41, 208nn87,89
body, the: decomposition of, 36, 38, 47; and the Eucharist, 123–24; as fragmented, 69–70, 71–72, 73, 77–78; in horror films, 108–9, 111; mummies,

27–28, 64, 72–73, 80, 168, 175–76, 178, 179, 181–82, 189, 199n29, 210n15; in pain, 15, 151; and pornography, 150–51; the senses and aesthetic response, 5, 159–65; smell, 164, 179; of the spectator, 1, 2, 15, 45–46, 110, 133–34, 139–40, 141–43, 144, 146–47, 156, 157–58, 159–65, 174, 176–77, 190–91, 229n5; taste, 159, 160–61, 162–63, 164, 165, 176, 179, 183, 185, 188, 189–90, 229n9; touch, 159, 160–61, 163–64, 165, 179, 191, 229n5; vision, 5, 160–63, 164–65, 179, 188–91, 194n19, 223n18, 229n5; voice, 15, 118–19, 126; of women, 32, 36–37, 38–39, 43–44, 69–70, 71, 73, 76, 77–78, 79–80, 110, 111, 115, 121–22. *See also* cannibalism
Bogdanovich, Peter, 134
Bonitzer, Pascal, 31
Bonitzer, Paul, 231n36
Bordwell, David, 146
Bouguereau, William-Adolphe, 162, 163
Brecht, Bertolt, 132, 142
Breker, Arno, 54
Bresson, Robert, 223n18; Bazin on, 132, 152, 226n60; *The Diary of a Country Priest*, 155, 226n60; vs. Haneke, 131, 132–33, 135, 136, 137, 138, 142, 149–50, 152, 154, 155, 224n33, 225n37, 226n60, 227n66; modernism of, 135, 225n37
Brill, Lesley, 169, 170, 231n39
Brinkema, Genie, 215n39
Broken Blossoms, 19
Brooks, Peter, 149
Bryson, Norman, 14, 215n31; "The Gaze and the Glance," 45
Buñuel, Luis: *Un Chien Andalou*, 73, 179, 190
Burch, Noël, 31, 199n7
Burgess, Anthony: *A Clockwork Orange*, 226n55

Burke, Edmund: *Philosophical Inquiry into the Origin of Our Ideas of the Sublime and the Beautiful*, 160, 161
Burne-Jones, Edward: "Pygmalion" series, 81

Cahiers du Cinéma, 134
camera obscura, 42, 202n55
Camper, Fred, 223n18
cannibalism, 71, 111–12, 123, 230n30, 232n55, 233n74, 234n81; cannibal horror film, 13–14, 15, 159, 165, 176–92; themes in Hitchcock, 71, 165–76, 210n9, 231n34
capitalism, 11, 129
Caravaggio, 35; "Head of Medusa," 69, 70, 77–78, 82–84, 87
Carpenter, John: *Halloween*, 233n66
Carroll, Lewis, 218n32
Carroll, Noël, 189
Casetti, Francesco, 87, 212n2
Castle, The (Haneke film), 153–55
Castle, The (Kafka novel), 153–55, 219n49, 226n51
castration, 70, 73, 76, 82, 116, 122, 209nn2,5, 211n32
Cavell, Stanley, 73, 83, 87, 99, 100, 211n43
Cézanne, Paul, 100, 150, 163
Chien Andalou, Un, 73, 179, 190
Chion, Michel, 95, 214n24
Christianity, 123–24, 125; Hitchcock and Catholicism, 167, 172, 230n30
Ciment, Michel, 106, 111
Civil War (Bürgerkrieg) trilogy, 129–42, 149, 153, 154
Cixous, Hélène, 209n2
Clockwork Orange, A, 145–46, 147, 148, 226n55
Close, Chuck, 46
Clover, Carol: "The Eye of Horror," 177, 178, 188, 190–91, 229n16, 233n66

collage effects, 31
commodity fetishism, 143
Cook, the Thief, His Wife and Her Lover, The, 32, 173
Copjec, Joan, 176
Cornwell, Patricia: *Portrait of a Killer: Jack the Ripper Case Closed*, 209n1
Corrigan, Tim, 116
Coupertin, Pierre de, 205n49
Courbet, Gustave: realism of, 6, 9, 69, 89, 96, 97, 99, 213n11, 214n14, 216nn44,54
Crary, Jonathan: *Techniques of the Observer*, 160
Creed, Barbara, 233n71
Cronenberg, David: *eXistenZ*, 96; *Videodrome*, 192

Dadaism, 142, 160
Dagrada, Elena, 212n2
Dahmer, Jeffrey, 182
Dali, Salvador: "Chevalier of Death," 68; "L'Oeil," 68; and *Spellbound*, 68, 73, 94
dance, 117, 206n62; and film, 14, 15, 50, 60–63, 206n56; and painting, 206n56; and sculpture, 61–63
Daney, Serge, 11
Dante Alighieri, 187
Da Vinci, Leonardo: "Mona Lisa," 71
Day of the Dead, 164–65
Day of Wrath, 109, 110
death: death masks, 10, 13, 40; and fascist aesthetics, 50; and film, 36, 63–64, 65–66, 67, 68, 69, 72, 74, 76, 77, 80–82, 107, 108, 122, 124–25, 134–35, 136, 182, 211n47; and Hitchcock, 68, 69, 72, 74, 76, 77, 80–82, 211n47; and photography, 36, 63–64, 65–66, 72, 107, 108, 207n77; Stewart on, 10; and tableaux vivants, 15, 26, 69; of women in art, 27–28, 33, 65, 77, 80–82
Death in Venice (Mann novel), 117
Death in Venice (Visconti film), 117
decapitation, 69, 70, 79, 209nn2,5, 211n32
Deleuze, Gilles: on Hitchcock, 89–90, 101; on Kubrick, 111; on masochism, 54, 151, 152, 153, 227n79, 228n83
Delsaute, Jean-Luc, 202n55
Demme, Jonathan: *The Silence of the Lambs*, 165, 177, 182–86, 188, 191, 192, 233nn74,75
De Quincey, Thomas: "Murder as One of the Fine Arts," 171, 187–88
Despair, 124
Destiny, 214n20
Dewan, Vineet, 215n39
Diary of a Country Priest, The (Bresson film), 155, 226n60
Diderot, Denis: and bourgeois melodrama, 30, 129–30, 141; "Letter on the Blind," 160; on painting and drama, 88; *Salons*, 9
Dietrich, Marlene, 118
digital images, 42–46, 47
Dixon, Wheeler Winston, 212n2
Doane, Mary Ann, 136
Dommartin, Solveig, 47
doubling in representation, 69, 70, 75, 76–78, 82–84, 211nn27,29
Douglas, Mary, 14; *Purity and Danger*, 230n30
drama: Benjamin on, 52–53, 54–55, 56, 58–59, 203n17, 229n5; bourgeois melodrama, 15, 30, 51, 129–31, 133, 144, 147–48, 149, 151, 152, 153, 155–56, 158, 226n61; and film, 14, 15, 26, 50, 52–53, 54–55, 94–95, 129–31, 133, 142, 144, 149, 151, 152, 153, 155–56; German tragic drama, 50, 52–53, 54–55, 203n17; Nietzsche on, 55–56; and painting, 88;

and tableaux vivants, 15, 26, 30–31, 50, 51, 52–53, 54–55, 130, 133, 152, 153, 155, 156
Draughtsman's Contract, The, 32
dreams, 7, 47–48
Dreyer, Carl Theodor: *Day of Wrath*, 109, 110; *Vampyr*, 110
Duchamp, Marcel, 12
Duncan, Isadora, 61
Dürer, Albrecht: "Draftsman Drawing a Reclining Nude," 36, 38–39, 44
Dutch Realism, 9, 101–2, 200n14; vs. Albertian perspective system, 33, 42; and optics, 42, 46; Vermeer, 15, 31–32, 33–39, 42, 43, 44, 47, 202n55

Eagleton, Terry, 133
Eakins, Thomas: "The Gross Clinic," 35
Edison, Thomas Alva: "Black Maria" of, 180
Eduardova, Eugenie, 204n40
Egginton, William, 102; on *Pleasantville*, 96; on the reality bleed, 96, 215n40
Eisenstein, Sergei, 55
ekphrasis, 51, 55, 56, 58, 67, 204n35
Elsaesser, Thomas, 43, 64, 124–25, 203n11, 226n61
Eternal Jew, The, 119–20, 125–26, 221n15
eXistenZ, 96
Expressionism, 218
Eyes Wide Shut, 105, 113–15, 217n3

Family Plot, 98
Fanck, Arnold, 64; *The Holy Mountain*, 57, 60, 65–66, 204n40, 205n41
fascist aesthetics, 15; and death, 50; and masochism, 50, 54, 66–67, 126; movement and stasis, 49, 50, 52, 54, 55–56, 57, 60, 62–63, 64, 65, 66–67, 208n90; prioritization of visual over verbal representation, 51, 52, 53, 54–55,

58, 203n21, 205n41; repetition, 50, 53–54, 58; Sontag on, 49–50, 52, 54, 63
Fassbinder, Rainer Werner, 15, 26, 198n17; and anti-Semitism, 117, 119–20, 124–26, 221n15, 222n37; *Berlin Alexanderplatz*, 124; and binary relations, 116–17, 123, 125; *Despair*, 124; *Garbage, the City, and Death*, 120; and Hippler's *Eternal Jew*, 119–20, 125–26, 221n15; *In a Year of Thirteen Moons*, 116–26, 135, 221n14; and masochism, 121, 124, 126, 221n14, 228n85, 234n76; and music, 118, 119, 121, 122, 126; *Querelle*, 124
Faust (Goethe drama), 27, 108
Faust (Gounod opera), 27
Faust (Murnau film), 23
fetishism, 143, 154
Foster, Hal, 14; on the mimesis of regression, 13; "Return of the Real," 13; on simulacral vs. referential representation, 13
Foucault, Michel: *The Order of Things*, 33, 213n11
fourth wall, 88–89, 91, 95, 97–98, 133, 144, 156
France: aesthetic practice in, 9; New Wave in, 23
Frank, Joseph: "Spatial Form in Modern Literature," 225n47
Frenzy, 71, 166–67, 168, 172, 174, 210n9, 230n30
Freud, Sigmund, 105, 110–11, 230n16; on children's games, 142; on disgust, 176; on Medusa's head, 209n5; on neurosis and art, 74; on primary process, 7; *Totem and Taboo*, 176; *The Uncanny*, 106, 107
Fried, Michael, 14, 75, 174; on absorption vs. theatricality in painting, 88–89, 91, 213n9; "Art and

Fried, Michael *(continued)*
Objecthood," 213n10; on Courbet, 6, 9, 69, 89, 96, 97, 213n11, 214n14, 216n44; on Eakins's "Gross Clinic," 35; vs. Kracauer, 6, 9; on Manet, 69, 89; on Merleau-Ponty, 6; on realism, 6, 69, 89, 96, 97, 102, 135, 213n11, 214n14, 216n44; on the spectator, 6, 88–89, 91, 213n10
Friedlander, Saul, 50, 64
Friedrich, Caspar David, 24–25, 213n10
Frijda, Nico, 156
Funny Games, 136, 142–45, 146–47, 149, 153, 155, 226nn50,51,53
futurism, 142

Gainsborough, Thomas G., 107
Garbage, the City, and Death, 120
Garreau, Louis, 37
gaze, the: Bryson on, 45; of characters out of film, 69, 74–75, 83–84, 87–94, 95, 96, 98, 102–3, 142, 144–45, 188, 192, 211n43, 212n2, 214n20; as introjective, 162, 188, 229n16; Lacan on, 87, 93, 94, 161, 212nn2,6; of Medusa, 69, 70, 76, 77–78, 80, 81, 82–84, 87, 209n4; Metz on, 161–62, 188, 229n16; as projective, 162, 188, 229n16; Sartre on, 161
Gein, Ed, 177, 182, 186
Géricault, Théodore: *Raft of the Medusa*, 186
Germany: aesthetic practice in, 9–10; rhythmic gymnastics in, 61–62
Glovers, Edward: "Significance of the Mouth in Psychoanalysis," 163
Godard, Jean-Luc, 32, 42, 87
Goebbels, Joseph, 53, 61
Goethe, Johann Wolfgang von: "The Collector and His Circle," 9–10, 175; *Elective Affinities*, 10–11, 12, 13–14, 51, 62, 198n25; *Faust*, 27, 108; and mimesis, 9–11, 13–14, 175; and Sontag, 12; *Torquato Tasso*, 119, 120, 221n14
Gombrich, E. H., 7, 14; on metaphors, 166; "Psycho-Analysis and the History of Art," 162
Gounod, Charles: *Faust*, 27
Gowing, Lawrence, 33, 42
Graham, Cooper, 206n58
Greenaway, Peter: *The Cook, the Thief, His Wife and Her Lover*, 32, 173; *The Draughtsman's Contract*, 32; vs. Wenders, 31–32, 42, 43, 44, 46–47; "Writing to Vermeer" project, 32; *A Zed and Two Noughts*, 31–39, 42, 43, 44, 46–47
Greenberg, Clement, 213n10
Griffith, D. W.: *Broken Blossoms*, 19
Grodal, Torben, 133, 157
Gross, Kenneth, 211n47
Gunning, Tom, 88

Habañera, La, 120–21, 221n21
Habermas, Jürgen, 129
Hake, Sabine, 193n6, 221n21
Hallam, Julia: *Realism and Popular Culture*, 193n1
Halloween, 233n66
Hals, Frans, 213n10, 214nn12,13
Hamlet, 74; Ophelia, 27, 65, 81
Handke, Peter, 143; *Publikumsbeschimpfung*, 226n50
Haneke, Michael, 15, 223n14, 225nn38,42, 227n69; and Baudrillard, 135, 146; on beauty, 223n10; *Benny's Video*, 129, 130, 134–38, 139, 140, 141, 147, 154, 224n31; and bourgeois melodrama, 129–31, 141, 144, 147–48, 149, 151, 152, 153, 155–56; vs. Bresson, 131, 132–33, 135, 136, 137, 138, 142, 149–50, 152, 154, 155, 224n33, 225n37, 226n60, 227n66; *The Castle*,

153–55; *Civil War (Bürgerkrieg)* trilogy, 129–42, 149, 153, 154; *Funny Games*, 136, 142–45, 146–47, 149, 153, 155, 226nn50,51,53; vs. Hitchcock, 143, 145; vs. Kubrick, 132, 143, 145–46, 147; modernism of, 131, 133, 135, 137, 139, 140, 142, 144, 145, 147, 149–50, 154, 156, 225n37; and music/sound, 131, 132–33, 137, 139–40, 143, 145, 146, 150, 153, 157–58, 225n36; *The Piano Teacher*, 130, 147, 148–53, 155, 157–58, 226n55, 227nn62,71,78, 228nn82,83,92; and realism, 131, 135–36, 141–42, 146–48; and sadomasochism, 130, 148–55, 157–58, 226n51, 228n82; *71 Fragments of a Chronology of Chance*, 129, 130–31, 132, 136, 138–41, 154–55; *The Seventh Continent*, 129, 130, 134–35, 138, 140, 150, 154, 225n36, 227n66; and violence, 15, 130–31, 132, 133, 134, 140–41, 142–48, 149, 153, 155–56
Hannibal (Harris novel), 165, 177, 182, 187–88
Hannibal (Scott film), 165, 177, 183, 187–88
Hansen, Miriam Bratu, 193n6, 195n21
Hanson, Duane, 13
Harnett, William, 103
Harris, Thomas, 234n79; *Hannibal*, 165, 177, 182, 187–88; *Red Dragon*, 165, 177, 182, 183, 186, 189; *Silence of the Lambs*, 165, 177, 182, 184, 185–86
Hart, Emma, 30, 62, 207n72
Heath, Stephen: on the camera, 38; on *Suspicion*, 70
Hedren, Tippi, 174–75
Henry, Portrait of a Serial Killer, 224n31
Herder, Johann Gottfried, 160
Herzog, Werner: *Nosferatu*, 64
Hess, Rudolf, 53

Hippler, Fritz: *The Eternal Jew*, 119–20, 125–26, 221n15
Hitchcock, Alfred, 15, 27, 109, 142, 161, 187–88; *The Birds*, 74, 94, 134, 174–75, 210n15, 215n39; *Blackmail*, 28, 75–76, 77, 78, 80, 91–92, 99, 166; cameo appearances, 98–99, 232n50; cannibalism themes, 71, 165–76, 210n9, 231n34; and Catholicism, 167, 172, 230n30; and death, 68, 69, 72, 74, 76, 77, 80–82, 211n47; Deleuze on, 89–90, 101; and De Quincey, 171, 187–88; the direct look out, 69, 74–75, 83–84, 87–94, 95, 98, 188, 192, 211n43, 214n20; dismemberment themes, 69–70, 71–72, 77–78, 79–80, 82, 180; doubling themes in, 69, 70, 75, 76–78, 82–84, 211nn27,29; *Family Plot*, 98; fragmentation themes, 69–70, 71–72, 73, 77–78, 79–80, 180; *Frenzy*, 71, 166–67, 168, 172, 174, 210n9, 230n30; vs. Haneke, 143, 145; vs. Hooper, 177, 178, 179–80, 181, 190–91, 232n60; *Lifeboat*, 166; *The Lodger*, 90–91; *The Man Who Knew Too Much*, 71–72; *Marnie*, 216n43; mirroring themes, 70, 75, 77–78, 80, 82, 83, 90–91, 95; modernism in, 79, 88, 89, 92, 93, 95, 97, 100–101, 102, 103, 214n14; museum sequences of, 28; *North by Northwest*, 73, 77, 78, 99–101, 166, 168, 224n25; *Notorious*, 174, 232n50; and painting, 68–71, 73–80, 81, 82–84, 88–94, 101–3, 170–71, 209n1, 210nn8,21,22; *Psycho*, 72, 76–77, 80, 97–98, 164–65, 166, 167–68, 171, 174, 175, 177, 179, 181, 185, 189, 210nn12,15, 231n34; and Pygmalion, 80, 81, 102, 170, 175, 181; realism in, 69, 89, 92–95, 96–99, 102–3, 169–70, 171–76, 192, 214n14, 225n42; and the reality bleed, 96–97;

Hitchcock, Alfred *(continued)*
   Rear Window, 71, 88, 91, 94–95, 96–97, 98, 165–66, 172, 178, 190, 209n4, 215n38; *Rebecca*, 78–79, 166, 210n21; relationship with Dali, 68, 73, 94; *Rope*, 103, 171–74, 231n47; on Rouault, 73–74; and sculpture, 68–69, 71–73, 74–75, 80–81, 165–66, 168, 170, 175, 181; on the spectator, 133–34, 142, 148; *Spellbound*, 68, 73, 94, 97, 212n2; *Strangers on a Train*, 74–75, 83, 92–94, 215n28, 225n42; *Suspicion*, 70–71; *The Thirty-nine Steps*, 77; *The Trouble with Harry*, 168–71, 174, 179, 210n10; *Vertigo*, 28, 77, 79–82, 83, 98, 101, 102, 170, 181, 190–91, 199n32, 211n34; Zizek on, 91, 92, 93, 98, 169, 170, 171, 173, 231n36
Hitler, Adolf, 52, 53, 54, 119, 125
Hockney, David, 42
Hofmannsthal, Hugo von, 206n62
Hogarth, William H., 107
Holbein, Hans: *The Ambassadors*, 88
Hölderlin, Friedrich: *Hyperion*, 57
Holy Mountain, The, 57, 60, 65–66, 204n40, 205n41
Hooper, Tobe: *The Texas Chainsaw Massacre* I and II, 163, 165, 177–82, 184, 190, 232n60, 233n71
horror films, 143, 163–65, 229n16, 233nn66,71; cannibal horror films, 13–14, 15, 159, 165, 176–92
Horst, Carl, 53, 54
Huillet, Danièlle, 131
Husserl, Edmund, 5, 194n19
Hylenski, Kristen, 206n61

illusion, 1–2, 6–14, 69, 93–94, 101–3; trompe l'oeil and film, 2, 8, 102–3; trompe l'oeil in painting, 8–9, 10, 33, 94, 102–3, 161, 175, 177, 215n32

Impressionism, 160, 163
In a Year of Thirteen Moons, 116–26, 135, 221n14
incest, 176
indexicality: of death masks, 10; of film, 1, 2, 4, 8, 39–41, 201n46, 220n10; of music, 158; of photographs, 10, 39–41, 64–65, 107–9, 115, 158, 175, 194n8, 201n46
intermediality, 19–26, 206n57; film and dance, 14, 15, 50, 60–63, 88; film and drama, 14, 15, 26, 50, 52–53, 54–55, 94–95, 129–30, 133, 142, 144, 149, 151, 152, 153, 155–56; film and literature, 14–15, 19–20, 21–23, 27, 28, 105–6, 111–12, 113–15, 148–49; film and painting, 5–6, 8, 14–15, 20, 21, 22–26, 27, 28–29, 30, 31–39, 45, 46–48, 60–61, 65, 66–67, 68–71, 74–80, 81, 82–84, 88–94, 101–3, 106, 107, 118, 150, 170–71, 184–85, 186–87, 188, 192, 198n11, 209n1, 210nn8,21,22; film and photography, 14, 15, 36, 38, 39, 40, 46, 47, 50, 63–67, 106–9, 186, 208nn87,89, 217n17, 218nn22,23,32; film and sculpture, 14, 15, 26, 27–28, 50, 57–63, 64–65, 66–67, 68–70, 71–73, 74, 80–81, 152–53, 165–66, 168, 170, 175, 181–82, 184–85; literature and photography, 104–5; painting and drama, 88; painting and literature, 21, 25, 220n4; painting and photography, 33, 46, 47; sculpture and dance, 61–63; sculpture and literature, 220n4

James, Henry, 28; *Portrait of a Lady*, 22, 25
Jameson, Fred, 11, 108, 133, 149, 218n23; "Spatial Systems in *North by Northwest*," 99–100, 216n54
Janouch, Gustav, 104–5, 107, 216n1

Janus-face, the, 69, 76, 77–78, 80, 211nn27,29
Januskopf, Der, 211n27
Jaworzyn, Stefan: *The Texas Chain Saw Massacre Companion*, 232n62
Jay, Martin, 160–61, 213n9
Jelinek, Elfriede: on Haneke, 151, 227n78; *The Piano Teacher*, 148–49, 155, 227n70, 228n82
Jesus Christ, 123–24, 125, 175, 187, 234n76
Jews and Judaism: Fassbinder and anti-Semitism, 117, 119–20, 124–26, 221n15, 222n37; Kubrick and Judaism, 113–14, 115, 219nn47,48
Johnson, Diane, 106
Joyce, James, 131
Jünger, Ernst, 51

Kafka, Franz, 131, 228n83; and the body, 111; *The Castle*, 153–55, 219n49, 226n51; conversation with Janouch, 104–5, 107, 216n1; and Kubrick, 105, 106, 111–12, 113–14, 115, 219n49; on narrative, 104–5; *The Penal Colony*, 115; on photography, 104–5; *The Trial*, 106, 114, 155, 219n49; Zizek on Kafka, 114, 115
Kant, Immanuel, 176, 194n17
Keane, Marian, 83
Keaton, Buster: *Sherlock, Jr.*, 95
Kerbel, Michael, 99
Kilgour, Maggie, 230n30
Kleist, Heinrich von: *The Marquise of O.*, 23, 121
Klimt, Gustav, 106
Koch, Gertrude, 194n17, 222n37
Koerner, Joseph, 4
Kolb, Jocelyne, 229n9
Kracauer, Siegfried, 63, 194n19; and Adorno, 194n17, 4; vs. Bazin, 1, 2, 3, 4, 40, 193n3, 194n7; vs. Benjamin, 5–6, 39; on camera work, 26; on film as showing reality, 1, 2–6, 39–40, 193nn3,6, 194n7; on "Film as the Discoverer of the Marvels of Everyday Life," 2–4; on the found story, 4; vs. Fried, 6, 9; on indexicality of film, 2, 4; "The Mass Ornament," 54; on movement in film, 4, 5; on the photographer/cinematographer, 4–5; on photography, 107, 207n77; on Riefenstahl, 50; as spectator, 4–6; on the spectator, 4–5, 194n15, 195n21; *Theory of Film*, 2–6, 39–40, 193nn3,6; vs. Wenders, 39–40
Kristeva, Julia, 234n76; on abjection, 112, 115, 117, 122, 124, 125, 126, 168, 180; on disgust, 176
Kubrick, Stanley, 15; *Barry Lyndon*, 107; *A Clockwork Orange*, 145–46, 147, 148, 226n55; *Eyes Wide Shut*, 105, 113–15, 217n3; vs. Haneke, 132, 143, 145–46, 147; and Judaism, 113–14, 115, 219nn47,48; and Kafka, 105, 106, 111–12, 113–14, 115, 219n49; and photography, 106–9, 217n17, 218nn22,23,32; and Schnitzler, 105–6, 113–14, 115, 219n49, 220n56; *The Shining*, 106, 107–10, 111, 115, 143, 145, 218nn22,23,30,31; *2001*, 105, 107, 109, 115, 218n31
Kuzniar, Alice, 120–21, 202n60

Laban, Rudolf von, 61
Lacan, Jacques, 9, 69, 88, 151, 215n31; on the gaze, 87, 93, 94, 161, 212nn2,6; on trompe l'oeil painting, 215n32
Lacoue-Labarthe, Philippe: "The Nazi Myth," 56, 58, 59, 207n69
Lang, Fritz, 88, 101, 199n28; *Destiny*, 214n20; *Metropolis*, 111; *The Testament of Dr. Mabuse*, 216n42
Laocoön sculptural group, 56, 204n35

Last of the Nuba, 49, 63
Leander, Zarah, 120
Leeuwenhoek, Anthony van, 37, 38
Lehman, Ernest, 134
Lensing, Leo, 219n49
Lessing, Gotthold Ephraim, 51, 55, 176; and bourgeois melodrama, 130; *Laocoön, or the Boundaries Between Poetry and Painting,* 161, 204n35; *Nathan the Wise,* 141
Lévi-Strauss, Claude, 168, 176
Lewin, Bertram: "Sleep, Mouth and the Dream Screen," 161
Lewis, Jerry, 222n36
Lifeboat, 166
Lindsay, Vachel, 28
literalism, 1, 2, 174; and cannibal horror films, 13–14, 15, 159, 165, 177, 179–82, 180–81, 183, 186–87; Fried on, 213n10
literature: ekphrasis, 51, 55, 56, 58, 67, 204n35; and film, 14–15, 19–20, 21–23, 27, 28, 105–6, 111–12, 113–15, 148–49; and painting, 21, 25, 220n4; and photography, 104–5; and sculpture, 220n4; and tableaux vivants, 10, 22, 25, 62, 198n25
Locke, John, 160, 188
Lodger, The, 90–91
Loos, Adolf, 131–32
Lyotard, Jean-François: *Acinéma,* 30

MacLeod, Catriona, 202n69, 209n4
Magritte, René, 199n7
Mahler, Gustav: Fifth Symphony, 117
Manet, Édouard, 69, 89, 93, 213n10
Mann, Michael: *Manhunter,* 182, 183, 186, 189, 191
Mann, Thomas: *Death in Venice,* 117
Mantegna, Andrea, 170
Man Who Knew Too Much, The, 71–72

Marin, Louis, 14, 209nn4,5; on Caravaggio's "Head of Medusa," 69, 70, 78, 82, 83, 87
Marquise of O., The (Kleist novella), 23, 121
Marquise of O., The (Rohmer film), 23
Marshment, Margaret: *Realism and Popular Culture,* 193n1
masochism, 15, 115; and arrested actions/sculptural display, 152–55, 157; and control, 151–52; Deleuze on, 54, 151, 152, 153, 227n79, 228n83; in fascist aesthetics, 50, 54, 66–67, 126; in Fassbinder's films, 121, 124, 126, 221n14, 228n85, 234n76; in Haneke's films, 130, 148–55, 157–58, 226n51, 227n70, 228n82; and horror films, 184, 188–89, 191; and iconicity, 153, 157–58; Sacher-Masoch, 54, 151, 152, 153, 227n78; Studlar on, 151, 153, 154, 203n10, 227n79, 234n82
McElheney, Joe, 214n14
McGowan, Todd, 212n6
McNaughton, John: *Henry, Portrait of a Serial Killer,* 224n31
Medusa, 76, 80, 81, 209nn4,5; Caravaggio's "Head of Medusa," 69, 70, 77–78, 82–84, 87; in Ovid, 70
Meegeren, Hans van, 31, 33
Meier, Armin, 124–25, 222n36
Méliès, Georges, 30
Menninghaus, Winfried, 110–11, 176
Merleau-Ponty, Maurice, 5, 6, 159, 160, 194n19, 213n9
metaphors, 1, 166
Metropolis, 111
Metz, Christian: on the gaze, 161–62, 188, 229n16; on the spectator, 90
Michelson, Annette, 107, 109, 115, 218n31
Mies van der Rohe, Ludwig, 100

Miller, D. A.: "Anal *Rope*," 231n47
mimesis, 3, 7, 62, 172, 207n69; and
   Dutch Realism, 33, 101–2; Foster on,
   13; and Goethe, 9–11, 13–14, 175;
   simulation, 13, 40–41, 42, 45, 47–48
modernism, 94, 189, 205n46; of Bresson,
   135, 225n37; direct look out as expression of, 69, 88, 89, 92, 93, 95, 97, 102;
   of Haneke, 131, 133, 135, 137, 139, 140,
   142, 144, 145, 147, 149–50, 154, 156,
   225n37; of Hitchcock, 79, 88, 89, 92,
   93, 95, 97, 100–101, 102, 103, 214n14;
   modernist aesthetics, 15, 115; in
   painting, 15, 79, 89, 100, 103, 213n10
Modleski, Tania, 166–67, 209n2, 210n9,
   211nn32,34, 230n30
Moeller, Philip: *The Age of Innocence*,
   19–20, 23, 27–28, 197n4, 198n18
Molière, 12
Montaigne, Michel de, 187, 234n81
movement in film, 3, 4, 5, 24, 26, 29, 36,
   47, 106–7, 108–9, 217n17; and stasis in
   fascist aesthetics, 49, 50, 52, 54, 55–56,
   57, 60, 62–63, 64, 65, 66–67, 208n90
Mozart, Wolfgang Amadeus, 12
Mulvey, Laura, 211nn31,32
Murnau, F. W., 107; *Faust*, 23; *Der
   Januskopf*, 211n27; *Nosferatu*, 24, 25,
   214n20; and Rohmer, 23, 24; and
   Scorsese's *Age of Innocence*, 23, 24, 25
music, 34, 105, 221n21; Bach, 184; Berg,
   131, 225n36; and Fassbinder, 118, 119,
   121, 122, 126; and Haneke, 132–33, 137,
   143, 145, 146, 150, 153, 157–58, 225n36;
   indexicality of, 158; Mahler, 117;
   Nietzsche on, 56, 62–63; Schubert,
   151, 157–58

Nancy, Jean-Luc: "The Nazi Myth," 56,
   58, 59, 207n69

Neale, Steve, 52–53, 55
Newton, Helmut, 49
Nietzsche, Friedrich, 173; *Birth of
   Tragedy*, 55–56, 61, 62–63, 117; *Thus
   Spoke Zarathustra*, 61
North by Northwest, 73, 77, 78, 99–101,
   166, 168, 224n25
Nosferatu (Herzog film), 64
Nosferatu (Murnau film), 24, 25, 214n20
Notebook on Cities and Clothes, 41
Notorious, 174, 232n50
Nowell-Smith, Geoffrey, 149, 226n61

O'Brien, Daniel: *The Hannibal Files*,
   234n79
Oedipus the King, 74
Olympia, Part I, 57–63, 205nn42,52,
   206nn57,59
oral stage and film, 7, 49–50, 69, 122,
   154, 161, 167–68, 180, 184, 190, 210n9,
   233n71
Ovid's *Metamorphoses*: Medusa, 70;
   Pygmalion and Galatea, 13, 23, 25, 27,
   28, 29, 33, 59, 80, 81, 102, 170, 175, 181,
   198n24
Ozu, Yasujiro: *Tokyo Story*, 41

painting: absorption vs. theatricality in,
   88–89, 91–92, 213n9; Benjamin on,
   5–6; direct look out in, 88–89, 213n12,
   214n13; and drama, 88; Dutch
   Realism, 9, 15, 31–32, 33–39, 42, 43, 44,
   46, 47, 101–2, 200n14, 202n55; and
   film, 5–6, 8, 14–15, 20, 21, 22–26, 27,
   28–29, 30, 31, 32–39, 45, 46–48, 60–61,
   65, 66–67, 68–71, 74–80, 81, 82–84,
   88–94, 101–3, 106, 107, 118, 150,
   170–71, 184–85, 186–87, 188, 192,
   198n11, 209n1, 210nn8,21,22; fourth
   wall in, 88–89, 91; and Hitchcock,

painting (continued)
68–71, 73–80, 81, 82–84, 88–94, 101–3, 170–71, 209n1, 210nn8,21,22; Impressionism, 160, 163; and literature, 21, 25; metaphorical absorption by, 5–6; modernism in, 15, 79, 89, 100, 103, 213n10; and oral gratification, 162–63; and photography, 33, 46, 47; and poetry, 204n35; Pre-Raphaelites, 65, 66, 81; realism in, 6, 9, 15, 31–32, 33–39, 42, 43, 44, 46, 47, 101–2, 200n14, 202n55; and tableaux vivants, 26, 30–31; trompe l'oeil in, 8–9, 10, 33, 94, 102–3, 161, 175, 177, 215nn32,36

Panofsky, Erwin, 5

Pater, Walter, 20

Peale, Charles Willson, 10–11; "Staircase Group," 10

Peckinpah, Sam, 132

Peeping Tom, 185, 186, 190–91

Perseus, 70, 78, 82. *See also* Medusa

phenomenology, 5, 6, 159, 160, 194n19, 213n9

photography: Barthes on, 40, 63, 105, 106, 107; Baudrillard on, 40–41; Bazin on, 40, 64–65, 72, 194n8, 201n46, 207n77; Benjamin on, 39, 40; and death, 36, 63–64, 65–66, 72, 107, 108, 207n77; and film, 14, 15, 36, 38, 39, 40, 46, 47, 50, 63–67, 106–9, 186, 208nn87,89, 217n17, 218nn22,23,32; indexicality of, 10, 39–41, 64–65, 107–9, 115, 158, 175, 194n8; Kafka on, 104–5; Kracauer on, 107, 207n77; and literature, 104–5; and painting, 33, 46, 47; polaroids, 39, 40–41, 179, 190; Wenders on, 39

Piano Teacher, The (Haneke film), 130, 147, 148–53, 155, 157–58, 226n55, 227nn62,71,78, 228nn82,83,92

Piano Teacher, The (Jelinek novel), 148–49, 155, 227n70, 228n82

Picasso, Pablo, 163

picturesque, the, 164

Plantinga, Leon, 228n93

Plato, 215n32; cave analogy, 6–7, 11; *Symposium*, 57

Pleasantville, 96

Pliny the Elder: on Zeuxis and Parrhasios, 8–9, 94, 215n31

pornography, 150–51, 152, 153, 157, 204n29, 207n72, 227n71; and tableau vivants, 30, 32, 62

Porter, Edwin: "Uncle Josh at the Moving Picture Show," 94

postmodernity: and Fassbinder, 116, 118; and Greenaway, 31, 37; and Haneke, 129, 131, 135, 137, 149; and Wenders, 11–12, 31, 41, 45

Powell, Michael: *Peeping Tom*, 185, 186, 190–91

Pre-Raphaelites, 65, 66, 81

Price, Theodore, 211n27

Price, Uvedale: *Dialogue*, 164

Psycho, 166, 167–68, 171, 174, 210n12, 231n34; vs. *Day of the Dead*, 164–65; doubling in, 76–77; mother as mummy in, 72, 80, 168, 175–76, 179, 189, 210n15; realism in, 97–98, 181; vs. *Red Dragon*, 189; shower scene, 97–98, 181; vs. *Silence of the Lambs*, 185; vs. *Texas Chainsaw Massacre*, 177, 179, 181

psychoanalysis, 14, 88, 90, 102, 161–63, 169, 226n61; infantile regression, 34, 49–50, 143, 150–51, 161, 163, 178, 189; oral stage, 7, 49–50, 69, 122, 154, 161, 167–68, 180, 184, 189, 190, 210n9, 233n71. *See also* Freud, Sigmund; Lacan, Jacques

Purple Rose of Cairo, The, 95

Pygmalion and Galatea, 13, 33, 198n24; and Hitchcock, 80, 81, 102, 170, 175, 181; and Riefenstahl, 57, 59; and Scorsese, 23, 25, 27, 28, 29
Querelle, 124

Raben, Peer, 122
Rank, Otto, 112, 218n32
Raphael, Frederic, 105, 106, 113, 217nn3,17, 219nn47,48
Ratner, Brett: *Red Dragon*, 165, 177, 183, 186–87, 189–90, 191
realism, 193n1, 223n18, 225n44; Alpers on, 14, 33, 41–42, 43, 45; in cannibal horror films, 13–14, 15, 165, 177, 179–82, 183, 186–87; of Courbet, 6, 9, 69, 89, 96, 97, 99, 213n11, 214n14, 216nn44,54; Dutch Realism, 9, 15, 31–32, 33–39, 42, 43, 44, 46, 47, 101–2, 200n14, 202n55; Fried on, 6, 69, 89, 96, 97, 102, 135, 213n11, 214n14, 216n44; and Haneke, 131, 135–36, 141–42, 146–48; in Hitchcock's films, 69, 89, 92–95, 96–99, 102–3, 169–70, 171–76, 192, 214n14, 225n42; literalism, 1, 2, 13–14, 15, 159, 165, 174, 177, 179, 180–82, 183, 186–87, 213n10; in painting, 6, 9, 15, 31–32, 33–39, 42, 43, 44, 46, 47, 101–2, 200n14, 202n55. *See also* indexicality; mimesis
reality bleed, 1, 96–97, 215nn39,40
Rear Window, 71, 165–66, 172, 209n4, 215n38; frontality in, 88, 91, 94–95; Thorwald-Jeff scene, 96–97, 98, 178, 190
Rebecca, 78–79, 166, 210n21
Red Dragon (Harris novel), 165, 177, 182, 183, 186, 189
Red Dragon (Ratner film), 165, 177, 183, 186–87, 189–90, 191

Reich, Wilhelm: *Mass Psychology of Fascism*, 49
Rembrandt: "Anatomy Lesson of Dr. Tulp," 35; "Slaughtered Ox," 118, 164
Renoir, Jean, 144
Rentschler, Eric, 65
repetition, 50, 53–54, 58
representational layering, 46–48
Reville, Alma, 68
Reynolds, Joshua R., 107; *The Age of Innocence*, 22, 25
Richardson, Samuel, 129
Richter, Gerhard, 46; *Stag*, 100
Riefenstahl, Leni, 15, 49–67; *The Blue Light*, 64–67, 205n41, 208nn87,89; and dance, 50, 60–63, 206n56; *Last of the Nuba*, 49, 63; *Olympia, Part I*, 57–63, 205nn42,52, 206nn57,59; photographs of, 49, 63–64, 208n90; and Pygmalion, 57, 59; role in Fanck's *Holy Mountain*, 57, 60, 65–66, 204n40, 205n41; *Tiefland*, 205n41; *Triumph of the Will*, 51–56, 58, 64, 65; use of tableau vivant moments by, 50, 203n11
Riegl, Alois, 163, 229n5
Riemer, Willy, 223n16
Robinson, Henry Peach: "The Lady of Shalott," 66
Rodowick, David N., 226n61
Rohmer, Eric: *The Marquise of O.*, 23; and Murnau, 23, 24; and Scorsese's *Age of Innocence*, 23, 24, 25; romantic theories of art in, 3
Romero, George: *Day of the Dead*, 164–65
Rope, 103, 171–74, 231n47
Rose, Jacqueline, 215n30
Rosenberg, Alfred, 51, 59, 60, 206n58
Rosolato, Guy, 122
Ross, Gary: *Pleasantville*, 96

Rossetti, Dante Gabriel, 66
Rother, Rainer, 205n40
Rothman, William, 83, 87, 90, 97, 210n12, 211n43
Rouault, Georges, 73–74
Ruggles, Wesley: *The Age of Innocence*, 197n4
Rumpelstiltskin, 118
Run, Lola, Run, 144
Ruskin, John, 20

Sacher-Masoch, Leopold von, 54, 151, 152; *Venus in Furs*, 153, 227n78
sadism, 142–43, 148–55, 179, 184, 188, 221n14, 226n51, 228n82, 234n76. *See also* masochism
Sanday, Peggy Reeves, 230n30, 232n55
Sander, August, 39
Santner, Eric, 125
Sartre, Jean-Paul: *Nausea*, 160–61
Schama, Simon, 9
Schiele, Egon, 106
Schiller, Friedrich: "The Ring of Polykrates," 118
Schlüpmann, Heide, 194n17
Schnitzler, Arthur: *Traumnovelle*, 105–6, 113–14, 115, 219n49, 220n56
Schrader, Paul: *Transcendental Style*, 227n76
Schubert, Franz, 151, 157–58
Schulte-Sasse, Linda, 205n46
science fiction films, 47–48, 147
Scorsese, Martin: *The Age of Innocence*, 19–20, 21–26, 198nn11,14,16
Scott, Ridley: *Hannibal*, 165, 177, 183, 187–88
sculpture, 66, 117, 175; and dance, 61–63; and film, 14, 15, 26, 27–28, 50, 57–63, 64–65, 66–67, 68–70, 71–73, 74, 80–81, 152–53, 165–66, 168, 170, 175, 181–82, 184–85; Herder on, 160; and Hitchcock, 68–69, 71–73, 74–75, 80–81, 165–66, 168, 170, 175, 181; Laocoön sculptural group, 56, 204n35; and literature, 220n4; and tableaux vivants, 26, 30–31, 54, 204n29; Winckelmann on, 56–57, 67

71 Fragments of a Chronology of Chance, 129, 130–31, 132, 136, 138–41, 154–55
Seventh Continent, The, 129, 130, 134–35, 138, 140, 150, 154, 225n36, 227n66
Shaviro, Steven: *The Cinematic Body*, 14, 221n26, 222n36
Sherlock, Jr., 95
Sherman, Cindy, 13
Shining, The, 106, 107–10, 111, 115, 143, 145, 218nn22,23,30,31
Shyamalan, M. Night: *The Village*, 191
Siddal, Elizabeth, 66
Sierck, Detlev: *La Habañera*, 120–21, 221n21
Silence of the Lambs, The (Demme film), 165, 177, 182–86, 188, 191, 192, 233nn74,75
Silence of the Lambs, The (Harris novel), 165, 177, 182, 184, 185–86
Silverman, Kaja, 118–19, 122, 124; *Male Subjectivity at the Margins*, 14, 221n14, 228n85, 234n76
Smith, Greg M., 133
Smith, Jeff, 226n55
Sobchack, Vivian, 5, 133–34, 159; *Address of the Eye*, 14
Sontag, Susan, 51; on art and audience, 142; "Fascinating Fascism," 49–50, 63, 202n2; on fascist aesthetics, 49–50, 52, 54, 63; and Goethe, 12; "Spiritual Style in the Films of Robert Bresson," 227n76; *The Volcano Lover*, 12; on watching the pain of others, 151; and Zizek, 12–13

sound, 36, 118, 131, 220n10, 223n18, 225n36. *See also* music
spectator, the, 14, 27, 34, 35, 94–99, 199n28, 223n14, 233n66; absorption vs. theatricality regarding, 88–89, 91; affective response of, 1, 5, 7–8, 9, 15, 129–31, 132–35, 139–40, 141–42, 146–48, 149, 156, 159, 163–64, 176–77, 179, 181, 189, 194n15; Albertian perspectival system, 33, 38–39, 45; body of, 1, 2, 15, 45–46, 110, 133–34, 139–40, 141–43, 144, 146–47, 156, 157–58, 159–65, 174, 176–77, 190–91, 229n5; cognitive response of, 132, 133, 138–39, 146, 159; and direct looks out in film, 69, 74–75, 83–84, 87–94, 95, 96, 98, 102–3, 142, 144–45, 188, 192, 211n43, 212n2, 214n20; and direct looks out in painting, 69, 88–89, 213n12, 214n13; Fried on, 6, 88–89, 91, 213n10; and gustatory experiences, 159; Hitchcock on, 133–34, 142, 148; Kracauer on, 4–5, 194n15, 195n21; Metz on, 90; and oral-stage fixation, 161; vs. photographer/cinematographer, 4–5; in Plato's cave, 6–7; psychological vs. aesthetic pleasure in, 7–8, 10–11; and the reality bleed, 1, 96–97, 215nn39,40; and tactile experiences, 159; Zizek on, 90
Spellbound, 68, 73, 94, 97, 212n2
Spoto, Donald, 174–75, 224n25
Stach, Reiner, 114
Stag, 100
Staiger, Janet, 177, 232n60
Sternberg, Josef von, 154
Stewart, Garrett: *Between Film and Screen*, 218n22
Stewart, Susan, 10, 14
Stowitts, Hubert, 60–61, 206n58
Strangers on a Train, 74–75, 83, 92–94, 215n28, 225n42

Straub, Jean-Marie, 131
structuralism, 88
Studlar, Gaylyn: *In the Realm of Pleasure*, 14, 234n82; on masochist aesthetic in film, 151, 153, 154, 203n10, 227n79, 234n82
sublimation of sexuality, 49–50
surrealism, 142
Suspicion, 70–71
Syberberg, Hans-Jürgen, 52
Szondi, Peter, 130, 155–56

tableaux vivants: and bourgeois melodrama, 15, 30, 51, 130, 133, 152, 153, 155, 156; and death, 15, 26, 69; and film, 2, 14, 15, 25–26, 28–29, 30, 31–32, 34–39, 42–45, 46–48, 50, 54, 55, 63, 64–66, 69, 80–82, 114, 184–85, 187–88, 192, 203n11; and German tragic drama, 50, 52–53, 54–55; and hybridity, 26, 30–31, 51; and literature, 10, 22, 25, 62, 198n25; origins of, 30, 51–52; and painting, 26, 30–31; and pornography, 30, 32, 62; and sculpture, 26, 30–31, 54, 204n29
Tan, Ed, 156
Tarantino, Quentin, 132
Tasker, Yvonne, 233nn74,75
Taubin, Amy, 22
taxidermy, 10, 72, 210n12
television, 136
Testament of Dr. Mabuse, The, 216n42
Texas Chainsaw Massacre, The I and II, 163, 165, 177–82, 184, 190, 232n60, 233n71
Thackeray, William Makepeace: *Vanity Fair*, 25
Thirty-nine Steps, The, 77
Thorak, Josef, 54
Tiefland, 205n41
Tiepolo, Giovanni Battista, 22

Tischbein, Johann Heinrich, 12
Titian: *Flaying of Marsyas*, 186
Tokyo-Ga, 40–41
Tokyo Story, 41
Toles, George, 168, 211n29
Torrance, Jack, 111
Trenker, Luis, 57
Trial, The, 106, 114, 155, 219n49
Triumph of the Will, 51–56, 58, 64, 65
trompe l'oeil: and film, 2, 8, 102–3; in painting, 8–9, 10, 33, 94, 102–3, 161, 175, 177, 215nn32,36; Zeuxis and Parrhasios, 8–9, 94, 215n36
Trouble with Harry, The, 168–71, 174, 179, 210n10
Truffaut, François, 73–74, 171–72
2001, 105, 107, 109, 115, 218n31
two- vs. three-dimensionality, 26, 30–31, 69, 81, 99–101, 216n54
Twyker, Tom: *Run, Lola, Run*, 144

uncanny, the, 88, 92–93, 107, 108, 110–11, 143, 169, 214n20
United States: aesthetic practice in, 9
Until the End of the World, 11–12, 31–32, 39, 41–48, 202nn57,60

Vampyr, 110
veil of Veronica, 4, 175
Velázquez, Diego, 213nn11,12, 214n13
Vermeer, Jan, 15, 31–39, 47; "The Artist in His Studio," 35–38, 44; "The Astronomer," 37, 38; and the camera obscura, 42, 202n55; "The Concert," 34; "Couple Standing at a Virginal," 34; "The Geographer," 37, 38; "Girl With a Pearl Earring," 43, 44; "The Girl with the Red Hair," 36; "A Lady Seated at a Virginal," 34; "Young Woman with a Water Pitcher," 43

Vernet, Marc, 88, 212n2
Vertigo, 79–82, 83, 98, 211n34; credit sequence for, 101, 190–91, 199n32; doubling in, 77; and female body, 28; fragmentation in, 79–80; vs. *Peeping Tom*, 190–91; and Pygmalion, 102, 170; vs. *Texas Chainsaw Massacre*, 181
Videodrome, 192
Village, The, 191
Visconti, Luchino: *Death in Venice*, 117
Vogel, Amos, 223
voyeurism, 33, 150

Wagner, Richard, 63
Waid, Candace, 22, 25
Warhol, Andy, 13; "Coca Cola Bottles," 12; silk screen photo portraits by, 46
Warner, Marina, 14
Wegener, Paul: *The Student of Prague*, 218n32
Wenders, Wim: vs. Benjamin, 39, 40; vs. Greenaway, 31–32, 42, 43, 44, 46–47; vs. Kracauer, 39–40; *Notebook on Cities and Clothes*, 41; on photography, 39, 40; on reality and film, 39–40; *Tokyo-Ga*, 40–41; *Until the End of the World*, 11–12, 31–32, 39, 41–48, 202nn57,60
Wharton, Edith: *The Age of Innocence*, 19–29, 163, 197n4, 198n11, 199n29, 210n13; attitudes toward film, 19–20; *The House of Mirth*, 22, 25, 28, 198n25; and Henry James, 22, 25, 28; *Summer*, 19; and visual sensations, 19, 20–21
Wigman, Mary, 61, 204n40
Williams, Linda, 108, 134; *Hard Core*, 14
Winckelmann, J. J., 59, 117; *Thoughts on the Imitation of Greek Art in Painting and Sculpture*, 56, 67
Wolff, Cynthia Griffin, 22, 25

Wollen, Peter, 194n7
Wollheim, Richard, 14, 213n10
women: bodies of, 32, 36–37, 38–39, 43–44, 69–70, 71, 73, 76, 77–78, 79–80, 110, 111, 115, 121–22; death in art, 27–28, 33, 65, 77, 80–82; and fruit, 168–69; the maternal body, 71, 110, 111, 112, 115, 121–22, 124; the maternal voice, 121–22; reality and the female body, 32, 36–37, 43–44; in Vermeer paintings, 33–36
Wood, Robin, 168, 177, 231n34
word and referent, 173–74, 175

Yamamoto, Yoji, 41

Zea, Kristi, 233n75
Zed and Two Noughts, A, 31–39, 42, 43, 44, 46–47
Zeuxis and Parrhasios, 8–9, 94, 215n36
Zielke, Willy, 57–58, 59, 61, 205nn42,52
Zizek, Slavoj, 14; on direct look out of the frame, 69, 74, 87–88, 91, 93; on Fassbinder, 124, 125; on Hitchcock, 91, 92, 93, 98, 169, 170, 171, 173, 231n36; on Kafka, 114, 115; and Lacan, 87, 212n6; on the real and the symbolic, 12–13; on the spectator, 90
Zorn, John, 143, 145, 146
Zweig, Stefan, 105

Cultural Memory in the Present

Brigitte Peucker, *The Material Image: Art and the Real in Film*
Natalie Melas, *All the Difference in the World*
Jonathan Culler, *The Literary in Theory*
Jennifer A. Jordan, *Structures of Memory*
Christoph Menke, *Reflections of Equality*
Marlène Zarader, *The Unthought Debt: Heidegger and the Hebraic Heritage*
Jan Assmann, *Religion and Cultural Memory: Ten Studies*
David Scott and Charles Hirschkind, *Powers of the Secular Modern: Talal Asad and His Interlocutors*
Gyanendra Pandey, *Routine Violence: Nations, Fragments, Histories*
James Siegel, *Naming the Witch*
J. M. Bernstein, *Against Voluptuous Bodies: Late Modernism and the Meaning of Painting*
Theodore W. Jennings, Jr., *Reading Derrida/Thinking Paul: On Justice*
Richard Rorty and Eduardo Mendieta, *Take Care of Freedom and Truth Will Take Care of Itself: Interviews with Richard Rorty*
Jacques Derrida, *Paper Machine*
Renaud Barbaras, *Desire and Distance: Introduction to a Phenomenology of Perception*
Jill Bennett, *Empathic Vision: Affect, Trauma, and Contemporary Art*
Ban Wang, *Illuminations from the Past: Trauma, Memory, and History in Modern China*
James Phillips, *Heidegger's Volk: Between National Socialism and Poetry*
Frank Ankersmit, *Sublime Historical Experience*
István Rév, *Retroactive Justice: Prehistory of Post-Communism*
Paola Marrati, *Genesis and Trace: Derrida Reading Husserl and Heidegger*

Krzysztof Ziarek, *The Force of Art*

Marie-José Mondzain, *Image, Icon, Economy: The Byzantine Origins of the Contemporary Imaginary*

Cecilia Sjöholm, *The Antigone Complex: Ethics and the Invention of Feminine Desire*

Jacques Derrida and Elisabeth Roudinesco, *For What Tomorrow . . . : A Dialogue*

Elisabeth Weber, *Questioning Judaism: Interviews by Elisabeth Weber*

Jacques Derrida and Catherine Malabou, *Counterpath: Traveling with Jacques Derrida*

Martin Seel, *Aesthetics of Appearing*

Nanette Salomon, *Shifting Priorities: Gender and Genre in Seventeenth-Century Dutch Painting*

Jacob Taubes, *The Political Theology of Paul*

Jean-Luc Marion, *The Crossing of the Visible*

Eric Michaud, *The Cult of Art in Nazi Germany*

Anne Freadman, *The Machinery of Talk: Charles Peirce and the Sign Hypothesis*

Stanley Cavell, *Emerson's Transcendental Etudes*

Stuart McLean, *The Event and its Terrors: Ireland, Famine, Modernity*

Beate Rössler, ed., *Privacies: Philosophical Evaluations*

Bernard Faure, *Double Exposure: Cutting Across Buddhist and Western Discourses*

Alessia Ricciardi, *The Ends Of Mourning: Psychoanalysis, Literature, Film*

Alain Badiou, *Saint Paul: The Foundation of Universalism*

Gil Anidjar, *The Jew, the Arab: A History of the Enemy*

Jonathan Culler and Kevin Lamb, eds., *Just Being Difficult? Academic Writing in the Public Arena*

Jean-Luc Nancy, *A Finite Thinking*, edited by Simon Sparks

Theodor W. Adorno, *Can One Live after Auschwitz? A Philosophical Reader*, edited by Rolf Tiedemann

Patricia Pisters, *The Matrix of Visual Culture: Working with Deleuze in Film Theory*

Andreas Huyssen, *Present Pasts: Urban Palimpsests and the Politics of Memory*

Talal Asad, *Formations of the Secular: Christianity, Islam, Modernity*

Dorothea von Mücke, *The Rise of the Fantastic Tale*

Marc Redfield, *The Politics of Aesthetics: Nationalism, Gender, Romanticism*

Emmanuel Levinas, *On Escape*

Dan Zahavi, *Husserl's Phenomenology*

Rodolphe Gasché, *The Idea of Form: Rethinking Kant's Aesthetics*

Michael Naas, *Taking on the Tradition: Jacques Derrida and the Legacies of Deconstruction*

Herlinde Pauer-Studer, ed., *Constructions of Practical Reason: Interviews on Moral and Political Philosophy*

Jean-Luc Marion, *Being Given That: Toward a Phenomenology of Givenness*

Theodor W. Adorno and Max Horkheimer, *Dialectic of Enlightenment*

Ian Balfour, *The Rhetoric of Romantic Prophecy*

Martin Stokhof, *World and Life as One: Ethics and Ontology in Wittgenstein's Early Thought*

Gianni Vattimo, *Nietzsche: An Introduction*

Jacques Derrida, *Negotiations: Interventions and Interviews, 1971–1998*, ed. Elizabeth Rottenberg

Brett Levinson, *The Ends of Literature: The Latin American "Boom" in the Neoliberal Marketplace*

Timothy J. Reiss, *Against Autonomy: Cultural Instruments, Mutualities, and the Fictive Imagination*

Hent de Vries and Samuel Weber, eds., *Religion and Media*

Niklas Luhmann, *Theories of Distinction: Re-Describing the Descriptions of Modernity*, ed. and introd. William Rasch

Johannes Fabian, *Anthropology with an Attitude: Critical Essays*

Michel Henry, *I am the Truth: Toward a Philosophy of Christianity*

Gil Anidjar, *"Our Place in Al-Andalus": Kabbalah, Philosophy, Literature in Arab-Jewish Letters*

Hélène Cixous and Jacques Derrida, *Veils*

F. R. Ankersmit, *Historical Representation*

F. R. Ankersmit, *Political Representation*

Elissa Marder, *Dead Time: Temporal Disorders in the Wake of Modernity (Baudelaire and Flaubert)*

Reinhart Koselleck, *The Practice of Conceptual History: Timing History, Spacing Concepts*

Niklas Luhmann, *The Reality of the Mass Media*

Hubert Damisch, *A Childhood Memory by Piero della Francesca*

Hubert Damisch, *A Theory of /Cloud/: Toward a History of Painting*

Jean-Luc Nancy, *The Speculative Remark: (One of Hegel's bon mots)*

Jean-François Lyotard, *Soundproof Room: Malraux's Anti-Aesthetics*

Jan Patôka, *Plato and Europe*

Hubert Damisch, *Skyline: The Narcissistic City*

Isabel Hoving, *In Praise of New Travelers: Reading Caribbean Migrant Women Writers*

Richard Rand, ed., *Futures: Of Jacques Derrida*

William Rasch, *Niklas Luhmann's Modernity: The Paradoxes of Differentiation*

Jacques Derrida and Anne Dufourmantelle, *Of Hospitality*

Jean-François Lyotard, *The Confession of Augustine*

Kaja Silverman, *World Spectators*

Samuel Weber, *Institution and Interpretation: Expanded Edition*

Jeffrey S. Librett, *The Rhetoric of Cultural Dialogue: Jews and Germans in the Epoch of Emancipation*

Ulrich Baer, *Remnants of Song: Trauma and the Experience of Modernity in Charles Baudelaire and Paul Celan*

Samuel C. Wheeler III, *Deconstruction as Analytic Philosophy*

David S. Ferris, *Silent Urns: Romanticism, Hellenism, Modernity*

Rodolphe Gasché, *Of Minimal Things: Studies on the Notion of Relation*

Sarah Winter, *Freud and the Institution of Psychoanalytic Knowledge*

Samuel Weber, *The Legend of Freud: Expanded Edition*

Aris Fioretos, ed., *The Solid Letter: Readings of Friedrich Hölderlin*

J. Hillis Miller/Manuel Asensi, *Black Holes/J. Hillis Miller; or, Boustrophedonic Reading*

Miryam Sas, *Fault Lines: Cultural Memory and Japanese Surrealism*

Peter Schwenger, *Fantasm and Fiction: On Textual Envisioning*

Didier Maleuvre, *Museum Memories: History, Technology, Art*

Jacques Derrida, *Monolingualism of the Other; or, The Prosthesis of Origin*

Andrew Baruch Wachtel, *Making a Nation, Breaking a Nation: Literature and Cultural Politics in Yugoslavia*

Niklas Luhmann, *Love as Passion: The Codification of Intimacy*

Mieke Bal, ed., *The Practice of Cultural Analysis: Exposing Interdisciplinary Interpretation*

Jacques Derrida and Gianni Vattimo, eds., *Religion*

The authorized representative in the EU for product safety and compliance is:
Mare Nostrum Group
B.V Doelen 72
4831 GR Breda
The Netherlands

www.ingramcontent.com/pod-product-compliance
Lightning Source LLC
Chambersburg PA
CBHW020644230426
43665CB00008B/306